cators

Becoming Multicultural Educators

Geneva Gay

Editor

Becoming Multicultural Educators

Personal Journey Toward
Professional Agency

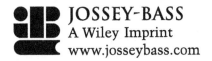
JOSSEY-BASS
A Wiley Imprint
www.josseybass.com

Published by Jossey-Bass
A Wiley Imprint
One Montgomery, Ste. 1200, San Francisco, CA 94104 www.josseybass.com

The poem "We Wear the Mask" is from *Paul Lawrence Dunbar: Selected Poems,*
Paul Lawrence Dunbar, Dover Publications.

Jossey-Bass books and products are available through most bookstores. To contact Jossey-Bass
directly call our Customer Care Department within the U.S. at 800-956-7739, outside the U.S.
at 317-572-3986 or fax 317-572-4002.

Jossey-Bass also publishes its books in a variety of electronic formats. Some content that
appears in print may not be available in electronic books.

Library of Congress Cataloging-in-Publication Data

Becoming multicultural educators : personal journey toward professional
agency / Geneva Gay, editor.—1st ed.
    p. cm. —(The Jossey-Bass education series)
Includes bibliographical references and index.
 ISBN 0-7879-6514-6 (alk. paper)
 1. Multicultural education—United States. 2. Classroom
management—United States. I. Gay, Geneva. II. Series.
 LC1099.3.B43 2003
 370.117—dc21   2002156565

FIRST EDITION
HB Printing 10 9 8 7 6 5 4 3 2

The Jossey-Bass
Education Series

To our children, real and symbolic:
those who are already with us,
others who are yet to come,
and in memory of those who came
but stayed for only a little while.
You deserve the best education imaginable.

Imani	*Melissa*	*Bo-Rong*
Alex	*Caleb Jamal*	*Isaac*
Micai	*Marcus*	*Neftali*
Terron	*Kalyn*	*Shemille*
Arion	*Bo-You*	*Iman*
Kelly	*Mi'Shar*	*Eugene*
Wesley	*Zoe*	*Imani*
Will	*Marvin*	*IMCC Students*

Pinoy Teach Participants

⁓ Contents

⸺ Preface

This is a book about multicultural education. It grew out of our concern that teachers are not being adequately prepared to work effectively with ethnically, racially, culturally, socially, and linguistically diverse students. To help these teachers on the journey ahead, we offer our personal stories in the hope that our successes, missteps, and evolution as multicultural educators will provide insight, affirmation, solace, and hope.

We, the authors of this book, are a diverse racial, cultural, ethnic, and linguistic lot. We are male and female, and of African, European, Italian, Japanese, Filipino, and Taiwanese ancestry. We come from different geographical regions and sociocultural backgrounds. Some of us grew up in the United States, and others have moved here from other countries. By the nature of our current positions, we are middle class and professionals, but this was not always the case. Some of us are intimately familiar with poverty and blue-collar working-class living. We have taught pre-K, elementary, middle, and high school, college, and university; science, English, social studies, special education, ethnic studies, teacher education, English as a Second Language, and multicultural education.

Our diversities are complemented by some worthy commonalities. We are all committed to social justice and equity for ethnically diverse people in schools and society. We work diligently to improve the quality of the educational opportunities, experiences, and outcomes of students from underachieving, marginalized, and underrepresented ethnic groups.

We believe that teachers are pivotal in determining the kind of education these students receive. Consequently, their professional preparation for working with ethnically and culturally diverse students is paramount. An important part of that preparation is becoming critically conscious of one's own knowledge, attitudes, and skills in multicultural education and the process of how these evolve. Facilitating the development of self-consciousness for teachers and helping them learn how to teach their students to do likewise is a major reason that we decided to undertake this writing project.

We are intimately involved in and passionate about what we write about. We believe it, advocate it, live it, and do it. All of us are engaged, in some way or another, in classroom teaching, teacher preparation, and multicultural education. Some of us approach these issues from the disciplinary vantage points of curriculum and instruction, while others do so from training in educational psychology, and educational leadership and policy studies. These diverse disciplinary perspectives are complementary strengths that enrich our efforts to speak comprehensively, deeply, and cogently about what we consider to be fundamental in preparing for multicultural teaching. We see the issues of our concern from personal and professional, insider and outsider, experience and novice—that is, multiple—perspectives.

Our concerns about teachers being adequately prepared to work effectively with ethnically, racially, culturally, socially, and linguistically diverse students are primarily focused on the United States. On occasion, they extend beyond these national boundaries. We are aware that multicultural education is growing in significance in other countries as well. Fortunately, among us are authors from other countries who have brought an international flavor to this project.

In creating and crafting this book, we worked together to address our common goal of using our own stories about how we are progressing toward becoming multicultural educators as means to teach others to do likewise. We, the authors of this book, bring insights gleaned from all of these vantage points to bear on the writing of the individual chapters and the collective project.

⟶ The Authors

Geneva Gay is professor of education at the University of Washington, Seattle, where she teaches graduate courses in general curriculum theory and multicultural education. She is internationally known for her scholarship in multicultural teacher education, curriculum design, and classroom instruction and the intersections of culture, ethnicity, teaching, and learning. Her writings include more than 135 articles and book chapters; she is the coeditor of *Expressively Black: The Cultural Basis of Ethnic Identity* (1987) and the author of *At the Essence of Learning: Multicultural Education* (1994) and *Culturally Responsive Teaching: Theory, Practice, and Research* (2000), which received the 2001 Outstanding Writing Award from the American Association of Colleges for Teacher Education.

John Ambrosio is a doctoral student in multicultural education at the University of Washington, Seattle, and an adjunct instructor in the graduate teacher education program of Lewis and Clark College, Portland, Oregon. Prior to beginning his graduate studies, he was a high school social studies teacher. His research interests are theory analysis, theory synthesis, and theory building in multicultural education and how power, politics, and privilege affect educational equity for ethnically diverse students.

Yukari Takimoto Amos received her Ph.D. in multicultural education from the University of Washington, Seattle. Her master's degree, in the same area, is from Doshisha University in Kyoto, Japan. Prior to beginning graduate studies, she taught at a tutoring school in Singapore and taught English to business employees in Japan. During her doctoral studies, she taught at the Seattle Japanese School in Bellevue, Washington, and taught Japanese language at the University of Washington, Seattle. Her research and teaching interests include the ethnic identity development of Japanese citizens living in other countries, first-language maintenance, bilingual education and English as a Second Language, and comparative multicultural education. She is conducting research on the ethnic and cultural identity of Japanese sojourner adolescents in the United States.

Mei-ying Chen is a doctoral student in multicultural education at the University of Washington, Seattle, and an instructor of beginning and intermediate Chinese for the Asian Languages and Literature Department. She was an elementary teacher for seven years, a secondary English teacher for six years, and a resource teacher for English in her native Taiwan. Her research interests include Taiwanese and Chinese ethnic identity development in Taiwan and other countries, multilingual education, the education of indigenous groups in Taiwan, cross-national comparative multicultural education, and learning about ethnic and cultural diversity in informal settings.

Jeannine E. Dingus, a former high school English teacher, is a doctoral student in curriculum and teacher education at the University of Washington, Seattle. She is particularly interested in the professional socialization of teachers, intergenerational family influences on the career choices of African American teachers, and the recruitment and retention of individuals of color in preservice preparation programs and K–12 classrooms. Her research examines three generations of teachers in the same families and how their perceptions of and commitments to teaching are affected by the ethnic identity, cultural socialization, and professional socialization they receive within their family.

Patricia Espiritu Halagao is an assistant professor of multicultural education and social studies at the University of Hawaii at Manoa. She received her doctorate in these areas from the University of Washington, Seattle. She also has experience as an elementary school teacher. She is the coauthor and executive director of Pinoy Teach, a middle school curriculum on Filipino Americans. In 2000, she received the first Young Pioneer Award from the Filipino American National Historical Society. Her research and teaching interests include designing and implementing ethnically specific curricula for different groups of color, and examining the effects that these innovations have on members of the groups they target, as well as other ethnic groups.

Audra L. Gray is a doctoral student in educational psychology at the University of Washington, Seattle, and an elementary school teacher for the Compton, California, Unified School District. Her research interests include reading development among early African American readers and other students of color, as well as the effects of ethnic literature on reading achievement. She has done some preliminary teaching of the ethnic literature and reading skills development ideas by creating book clubs for middle school African American girls.

Terri L. Hackett received her Ph.D. from the University of Texas at Austin in community college education. Her public school experience was teaching language arts and reading to middle school students. She is currently the assistant director for admissions for the Seattle (Washington) Central Community College. She is particularly interested in determining the survival or persistence strategies of students of color in general and African Americans specifically in community colleges. She also is involved in developing techniques for improving the recruitment, retention, and academic success of community college students of color.

Mary Stone Hanley is an assistant professor of aesthetic education at the University of North Carolina at Chapel Hill, where she teaches courses in using the arts in education and multicultural education. Prior to entering graduate school, she was a playwright and a community activist. Her research and teaching interests include knowledge construction among middle school African American students, the effects of multicultural education on teacher performance and student achievement, and drama as pedagogy. She received her Ph.D. in multicultural education from the University of Washington, Seattle.

Chia-lin Huang is a doctoral student in multicultural education at the University of Washington, Seattle. She is a former secondary school teacher of Mandarin Chinese to indigenous Taiwanese students and English to mainstream Han high school girls in Taiwan. Her research and teaching interests include first-language maintenance among indigenous groups in Taiwan; bilingual, multilingual, and multicultural curriculum development; the effects of multicultural education on student achievement; global perspectives on multicultural education; and multicultural teacher education. She is conducting some research on the responses of students from an indigenous group in Taiwan to curriculum on their own history and culture delivered in their first language.

Carolyn W. Jackson is a doctoral student in multicultural education at the University of Washington, Seattle. She has taught early childhood, elementary, and college students and has been actively involved in the recruitment of students of color into colleges of education. In 1998, she received the Graduate Opportunities Award. While completing her dissertation research, she is also collaborating with a team of educators involved in a National Science Foundation grant, Expanding the Community of Mathematics Learners. Her research and teaching interests include multicultural literacy, women's studies, and sociocultural foundations of education. She is conducting research on the educational achievements, careers, and ethnic identity development of former military dependents.

Kipchoge N. Kirkland is assistant professor of multicultural education and social studies at Indiana University, Bloomington. He received his Ph.D. in multicultural education from the University of Washington, Seattle. He is a former middle school science teacher, an accomplished poet, and a well-established community activist. He is interested in teaching and conducting research on poetry as a pedagogical tool for implementing multicultural education, developing critical cultural consciousness among marginalized students of color, and teaching skills for social justice and cultural transformation. He is conducting research on the educational experiences, coping devices, and cultural efficacy of African American males in predominantly White suburban high schools.

Laura Kay Neuwirth is a former teacher of middle-level special education in Kansas City and Columbia, Missouri. While teaching in Kansas City, she was introduced to Project REACH (Respecting Ethnic and Cultural Heritage), which called to her attention to the importance of students learning about ethnic and cultural differences. This exposure also encouraged her to return to graduate school. She received her master's degree in multicultural education from the University of Washington, Seattle.

S. Purcell Woodard is a doctoral student in educational leadership and policy studies at the University of Washington, Seattle. He has worked in student services in higher education and as a research assistant for the Seattle branch of Education Matters, an independent agency that studies middle school reform and seamless education initiatives throughout the United States. He is interested in researching, writing, and teaching about the intersections among higher education policy, multicultural education, and feminist poststructural theory and the implications of these for promoting social justice in education.

Becoming Multicultural Educators

CHAPTER ONE

Introduction

Planting Seeds to Harvest Fruits

Geneva Gay

We know for certain that teaching in U.S. schools is increasingly a cross-cultural phenomenon, in that teachers are frequently not of the same race, ethnicity, class, and linguistic dominance as their students. This demographic and cultural divide is becoming even more apparent as the numbers of individuals of color in teacher preparation and active classroom teaching dwindle. In our work in K–12 and college classrooms, we repeatedly encounter prospective and in-service teachers who are doubtful, even intimidated and fearful, about the prospect of teaching students from different ethnic, racial, and cultural backgrounds.

These situations caused us to ponder how to help teachers deal with these dilemmas. We begin in this book by envisioning how to talk to teachers about multicultural education, especially those who are beginners. One way to accomplish this goal is to minimize its perceived threat and to counter some of the misconceptions surrounding teaching to and about cultural diversity. We think telling our own stories about our emergence as multicultural educators is a viable means to stimulate these conversations. In doing so, we have chosen to be simultaneously personal, professional, and autobiographical about our own multicultural development.

Within our profession, much is said about the necessity and value of variety in teaching styles or using multiple means to achieve common learning outcomes. This is especially true in multicultural education, given the diversity of learning styles, histories, cultures, and experiences that ethnically different students bring to the classroom. Traditional styles of academic writing and classroom teaching are not amenable to capturing some of the subtle nuances of becoming and being multicultural educators. A poem conveys a level of poignancy and feeling that is impossible in the best crafted descriptive text. Writing in the form of letters allows a kind of intimacy that is beyond the capability of dispassionate analysis. Interactive dialogues invite readers to think along, become more deeply involved with what the author is saying, and unveil their own positions. Furthermore, we try to convey through example to our readers that diverse techniques are needed to capture and convey the essence of multicultural education. We also want the process dimensions of our project to exemplify its substantive messages, one of which is the value of collaboration and cooperation in multicultural teaching and learning.

TEACHER EFFICACY AND EMPOWERMENT

A number of ideas have shaped our thinking about ways to respond to the needs we address and thus determined the structural contours and substantive text of this book. All of them speak to the need for teacher efficacy and empowerment in multicultural education—that is, to be competent in and confident about one's ability to do multicultural teaching. Teacher educators and staff developers must find ways to bridge the developmental divides between the recommendations of multicultural education scholars and the needs of novice practitioners. Making these bridges involves accepting the reality and respectability of multiple levels and approaches to implementing multicultural education.

The need to bridge multicultural theory and practice, age and youth, experienced and initial involvement helped to shape our project on becoming multicultural. It led us to emphasize processes over products, which means we concentrate on our own emerging knowledge, thoughts, beliefs, and skills about multicultural education rather than on specific techniques for how to do multicultural teaching with students. Nevertheless, many instructional strategies are implied in our particular developmental processes that have utility for teachers in general.

Peer Modeling and Teaching

Who can best teach what to whom, and how? As we thought about this question, we grappled with the developmental divide between novices and experts. Logically, the most knowledgeable should be the best teachers. But we know that this is not necessarily true in real life. We explored and then accepted the possibility that individuals who are in the early stages of their career as multicultural educators might be able to talk about what it means and how to do it in ways that resonate better with their peers than do expert leaders. If so, they can be effective teachers for other beginners in the field. Their progression in acquiring multicultural knowledge and teaching skills also may serve as directions and inspiration for others to follow. Early-career multicultural educators have the added advantage of being close to their own K-12 classroom teaching experiences and can infuse theoretical principles with current and authentic practical applications. Preservice and young in-service teachers may identify and work better with them than with individuals who are much further along in their career development.

We have noticed that many multicultural education novices are captivated when the leading scholars in the field write and speak, but rarely do they genuinely engage in dialogue with them. They will not analyze, critique, challenge, or reinterpret what they read and hear from the "experts." Conversely, many of the scholars who spend much of their time engaged in conceptualizing and theorizing about multicultural education have difficulty responding to requests from practitioners for help in translating these general principles into specific classroom practices. We think individuals who are the peers of multicultural novices can broker some of these developmental gaps between theory and practice and different levels of maturation in the field. Consequently, the contributing authors in this book are in the earlier phases of their careers as multicultural educators. We think of ourselves more as peer coaches rather than experts and authorities.

But our stories are not offered as exemplars or as panaceas for how everyone can or should become multicultural. Nor are they methodological in the sense that the emphasis is on how to do multicultural teaching in the classroom. Our focus is on personal preparation for being multicultural educators. It reflects our belief that teachers must be multicultural themselves before they can effectively and authentically teach students to be multicultural. At the heart of this personal becoming is self-knowledge.

Our stories are real examples of how individuals are engaging with the challenge of personal growth as a requisite of multicultural teaching. They illustrate the dynamic, diverse, complex, and developmental nature of the process. None of us would ever think of suggesting that our multicultural development is complete. But we are not disturbed by the fact that we have a lot more learning and growing to do. Rather, these prospects are exhilarating for us. We look forward to the enrichment that our further multicultural pursuits offer.

We hope that our processes of becoming multicultural will entice preservice and novice in-service teachers to join the journey and become more reflective of and critically conscious about their own multicultural beliefs, experiences, and behaviors and to develop personal and professional competence and confidence in multicultural education. For those readers who are responsible for teacher education, we hope our stories will provide them with some ideas, information, and actions for inclusion in the design and implementation of their instructional programs.

Personal and Professional Journeying

Multicultural teaching is both a personal and professional process. We strongly believe that who we are as people determines the personality of our teaching. Who the person is who inhabits the role of teacher shapes how that role is performed.

Some of the best ways to find out about the interactions of person and performance in teaching is from the self-studies and personalized reporting of teachers. These ways of knowing are referred to by various terms, including *reflection, narratives, storied research,* and *autobiography.* As research methodology, content, and pedagogy, they are becoming increasingly popular among educational researchers, theorists, and practitioners. They also fit well with our desire to share how our personal and professional multicultural development is at once discrete and intertwined, individual and collective.

We are persuaded by Sonia Nieto's (2000, p. 353) argument that "*becoming a multicultural teacher . . . means first becoming a multicultural person* [emphasis in original]. Without this transformation of ourselves, any attempts at developing a multicultural perspective [for teaching and learning] will be shallow and superficial." This transformation involves a deep "personal awakening and call to action" (Nieto, 1999, p. xviii), but it is more than that. It is a transformative journey of acquiring more knowledge about ethnic and cultural diversity; confronting our own racism and ethnic biases; learning to see reality from a variety of ethnic and cultural perspectives; challenging inequities in conventional school policies, programs, and practices; working collaboratively with others with similar concerns; and being change agents in and outside of classrooms and schools (Nieto, 1999, 2000). Teachers need to be well into their own multicultural journey before they can prepare the way for and guide students to follow. They also need to realize that there are no absolute guarantees and no one, regardless of how gifted and insightful a guide or teacher they may be, can ever determine the exact course of action for anyone else to take to be effective multicultural educators.

Teacher educators and staff developers can offer guidance, resources, encouragement, support, and models, but how or whether to act on these is always an individual decision. Each of us must take our own journey toward becoming multicultural educators. This journey does not have to be a lonely, isolated one. By engaging in dialogue with ourselves and sharing our stories with other travelers, we can find confirmation, companionship, and community (Newman, 1990). In addition, as Mayher (1990) suggests about becoming teachers in general, "By transacting with these stories of unfolding journeys, we can enrich and enlighten our own parallel, but necessarily individual, roads" (p. xv).

Throughout this book, we offer unfolding multicultural education journeys and invite our readers to learn from what we are doing and then to join the journey and add to the conversation by writing parallel stories about their own multicultural development. For us, these processes translate into growth in knowing, thinking, feeling, and doing about multicultural education, both personally and professionally. A word of caution is due here: Do not expect to find what

Mayher (1990, p. xvi) calls the "surety of adoptable answers" or a catalogue of universally applicable "how-tos" for classroom instruction in this book. That is not the most important function or value of teaching through stories. Rather, it is to model and motivate self-consciousness, self-reflection, and self-critique of our own knowledge, feelings, beliefs, and practices and to offer opportunities for camaraderie in a common cause. The greatest benefits you can expect to receive from stories of our multicultural development are "the excitement and rewards of becoming part of a wider professional community that takes our journey seriously and recognizes the need for mutual respect along the way" (Mayher, 1990, p. xvi).

The Power of Story and Telling Your Own

Another idea that converges around our project is the power of story or narrative as a mechanism for improving teaching preparation and practice. Narratives are valid and viable ways of knowing for teachers and students. According to McEwan and Egan (1995), narrative is "essential to the purpose of communicating who we are, what we do, how we feel, and why we ought to follow some course of action rather than another" (p. xiii). Because the "function of narrative is to make our actions intelligible to ourselves as well as others, narrative discourse is essential to our efforts to understand teaching and learning" (p. xiii). In speaking specifically about the use of stories of culturally diverse students in classroom teaching, Dyson and Genishi (1994) tell us that they have "the potential for empowering unheard voices" (p. 4).

These observations are especially meaningful for us because of the nature of most existing scholarship on multicultural teacher education. Much of quality is written on what should be included in these programs, why, and how. But nothing exists about multicultural teacher education from the insider perspective of people going through the process—that is, individuals telling their own stories as they are lived. Our stories in this book deal with people who are in the process of becoming multicultural educators, told in their own voices.

Multicultural education, like other kinds of teaching, is a moral enterprise that requires deep personal engagement, commitment, advocacy, and agency from those who participate fully and genuinely in the enterprise. Trying to convey the sense and significance of these dimensions of multicultural preparation and classroom practice to teachers through technical knowledge and objectified analyses is extremely difficult, if not impossible. Narratives allow us to visualize these ideas in storied behaviors, as well as reveal and examine the thoughts, feelings, beliefs, and intentions of the agents of the actions (Coles, 1989; McEwan and Egan, 1995). We use metaphors in constructing our narratives to help convey feelings, beliefs, and values and to demonstrate that becoming multicultural is greater than developing pedagogical knowledge and skills; it is a style of living outside as well as inside the classroom.

Too many educational leaders are mystified about finding instructional strategies that will improve the academic achievement of underachieving students of color. In their search for the "best programs and practices" throughout the country, we believe they are overlooking the obvious: the personal experiences of successful individuals. Some researchers are demonstrating that the answer lies within the lives of teachers, and within teachers telling their own stories (Cochran-Smith and Lytle, 1993; Nieto, 1999). Our work is within these traditions. We strongly believe in the viability of autobiography as a research methodology and a rich source of substantive data for multicultural teacher preparation and classroom practice.

bell hooks (1998) explains that autobiographical narratives enable us to look at aspects of our past experiences from different perspectives and to use the knowledge we glean from them as means of self-growth and change in practical ways. These personal stories act as mirrors, opportunities, and invitations to participate in "I-to-I encounters" with others similarly engaged and for them to unveil and tell their stories in their own voices, in their own ways, about becoming multicultural, as we have done (Jackson, 1995). In so doing, they will join the community of other sojourners en route to becoming multicultural educators, and the process of sharing will improve the quality of their efforts. We believe that the essence of being good multicultural educators is more than powerful content or skillful pedagogy; it is how we live our lives as people and as teachers. Our personal narratives serve the dual function of helping us to look inward and outward in becoming multicultural educators.

Importance of Reflection

The final conceptual orientation that helps to contour our project is the importance of reflection in becoming and being good teachers. Developing reflective practitioners is the clarion call of many teacher education programs throughout the United States (Schön, 1983; Valli, 1992; Zeichner and Liston, 1996). Reflection and narrative go hand-in-hand; narratives are the form that give external embodiment to the internal thinking processes that comprise reflection. Being critically conscious and analytically reflective about one's own personal knowledge, beliefs, values, and actions are necessary skills in becoming effective multicultural persons and professionals.

In reflecting on our becoming multicultural educators, we are more concerned about making personal and professional sense of some benchmark events in our development than merely describing them. We explore, wonder, question, and speculate about how these events cause us to know, think, feel, and do differently about issues related to teaching for and about ethnic and cultural diversity. Talking about the insights and perceptions gleaned from these analyses is essential to the reflective process (Richert, 1992). Sometimes this discourse is necessarily internal and individualistic, but it is more imperative for it to be external and communal. That is, teachers need to talk about their reflections with others who are engaged in similar processes. Individuals must have the skills to convey these internal thoughts and feelings in ways that capture their integrity, intensity, and essence and are understandable to others.

Thus, conversation and community are essential to reflective teaching. In this book, we have tried to build both among ourselves and with our readers. Our need to find expressive techniques that were amenable to conveying the nuances and the content of our inner thoughts was as instrumental in our decision to use a variety of writing styles as was our desire to model the multicultural education principle of multiple perspectives and modalities in teaching and learning.

ABOUT THIS BOOK

The chapters that comprise this book are unique, yet they share several commonalities. They are unique in that the various authors' journeys toward becoming multicultural persons and educators are different. Some of them focus on classroom events as students and teachers, some concentrate more on learning experiences that occur in social settings outside the boundaries of any formal educational institutions, and others include both. Some of the authors take readers down memory lanes that go all the way back to the beginning of formal schooling in kindergarten, through elementary and secondary schools, college and even graduate school, and into the early years of their professional lives. Others center their narratives in adulthood as classroom teachers, young parents, and adult children. Some talk about how moving across different geographical regions within national boundaries and the experiences they encountered in doing so affected their knowledge, consciousness, and commitment to multicultural education. Others extend these journeys across international boundaries as they travel back and forth between their home countries and the United States. Yet there is a common thread embedded in these differences: becoming multicultural is a dynamic process of growing, a journeying, a transformation, and a transcendence in both a literal and metaphorical sense.

The writing motifs used to give order and structure to our ideas and convey our messages include interviews, letters, narrative essays, interactive dialogues, and poetry. These choices are deliberate, since we wanted to give legitimacy to the idea that alternative and multiple means of teaching and learning are essential to multicultural education. We agreed to include the same types of information in our chapters so that the conversations across them would have some cohesive and centralizing focus. Therefore, all of the chapters include three types of information: descriptive, reflective analytical, and interpretative. The descriptive provides factual information about the details of transforming experiences that contribute to our multicultural education development. In the reflective and analytical information, we try to make sense of our experiences and reveal their deeper meanings. It is woven throughout the descriptive text. The interpretative information extrapolates broader multicultural education messages that are embedded in our personal stories. They are identified separately as "Principles for Practices" and suggestions for how others can "join the journey" in becoming multicultural educators.

All of the chapters also address several of the major concepts, components, and principles of multicultural education: multiple perspectives, culturally responsive teaching, congruity between school culture and the cultures of different ethnic groups, combating racism, and achieving social justice and educational equity for ethnically diverse groups. By arranging these conversations in this way, our collective efforts converge on multicultural education from somewhat different vantage points and are complementary. Together, they present a more comprehensive profile of teacher preparation for multicultural education than any one chapter could do alone. We try to simultaneously attend to the particular and the general within multicultural information.

In Chapter Two, "We Make the Road by Walking," John Ambrosio traces his journey in becoming a multicultural person and educator through a series of intellectual, political, and sociocultural experiences, reflections, and autobiographical snapshots. He explains how these helped to breach his cultural isolation, challenge his internalized biases and stereotypes, and facilitate his transformation from encapsulation within European and Italian American cultures to an increasing awareness, knowledge, and appreciation of ethnic and cultural diversity. John's story is anchored in the multicultural education components of personal commitment to and engagement in activism to achieve social justice, dignity, and equality for ethnically diverse issues, perspectives, experiences, individuals, and groups; having the moral fortitude and will to act on one's own multicultural values and beliefs; and the reallocation of political and academic knowledge, power, and privilege among ethnically diverse groups.

Carolyn Jackson next shares paths that she has taken that have led to increases in her multicultural personal strength and professional wisdom. She likens the journey to the process of crystallizing and classifying diamonds that involves clarity, carat weight, cut, and color. She chose these images to signify the strength of will, depth of knowledge and purpose, and the continuous personal and professional development that are needed to be a good multicultural educator. These emphases are embedded in the title of Chapter Three, "Crystallizing My Multicultural Education Core." Carolyn's story is centered in the multicultural education components of self-understanding, cultural clarification and ethnic identity development, efficacy and empowerment for ethnically diverse students, and diversity within ethnic groups and cultures.

Chapter Four deals with a series of symbolic conversations that Audra Gray engages in as she encounters experiences that cause her to rethink some of her assumed truths about cultural differences, race relations, and the schooling experiences of diverse ethnic groups. She titles the chapter "Conversations with Transformative Encounters" and explores four events, or encounters, that have been instrumental in initiating or accelerating her multicultural consciousness and competence: reflections on early schooling experiences; situating particular issues of one ethnic group within the general parameters of multicultural education; resolving the tensions between a given discipline or subject area and multicultural education; and the effects of reading a fiction novel about intergenerational relationships among women in a Japanese American family. Her multicultural becoming converges around the components of deconstructing existing realities and multicultural claims of "truth," building community within and among diverse ethnic groups, and using insider ethnic group perspectives and various media of expression in developing multicultural education programs.

Jeannine Dingus begins Chapter Five with an excerpt from Paul Laurence Dunbar's poem, "We Wear the Masks," setting the tone for how she characterizes her multicultural journey and explaining why she titled the chapter "Making and Breaking Ethnic Masks." "Mask" is a metaphor for the negative academic expectations and ethnic stereotypes imposed on students of color by teachers, peers, and sometimes even themselves. Using vignettes that she witnessed personally or participated in, she examines how teachers' assumptions about race and ethnicity affected her own and other students' personal identities and academic experiences and how she created her own masks to insulate herself from these teacher expectations. She also shows how she began to crack these masks and eventually remove them entirely. Jeannine's story exemplifies multicultural education components having to do with historical legacies and past experiences of ethnic group; improving the self-esteem and ethnic identity of students of color; and the interactions among culture, ethnicity, expectations, and achievement in teaching and learning for ethnically diverse students.

Chapter Six, "Steppin' Up and Representin'," by Kipchoge Kirkland, focuses on connections that he makes with himself, his family, cultural community, multicultural education colleagues, and future teachers. By "connections," he means "experiences, learnings, insights, relationships, discourses, reflections, and actions." He uses personal, poetic, and academic narratives to express his concerns, thoughts, convictions, and aspirations for becoming an effective multicultural educator. The most prominent components embedded in Kipchoge's multicultural journey are authentic role models and mentors for ethnically diverse students; school, family, and community partnerships in multicultural education; developing advocacy and agency in multicultural teaching; and using culturally responsive techniques to teach ethnically diverse students to better demonstrate their intellectual, personal, social, and cultural competencies.

In Chapter Seven, "Clearing Pathways for Children to go Forth," S. Purcell Woodard writes an open letter to his son. Although this is addressed specifically to Alex, the messages are applicable to the numerous sons and daughters of today's parents who will be tomorrow's students in multicultural classrooms across the country. He shares a wide range and variety of resistances to ethnic and cultural diversity he has experienced in his journey toward becoming a multicultural educator; how his growing multicultural competencies help him to deal with them; and how he is strengthening his resolve to make life and learning better for ethnically, culturally, racially, and linguistically diverse students. The central multicultural education components addressed in the chapter are developing deep self and social consciousness; building multicultural networks, coalitions and communities; and personal activism for social change and cultural equity.

Chia-lin Huang, the author of Chapter Eight, "Professional Actions Echo Personal Experiences," uses echo as the metaphor for major landmarks in her multicultural education journey. The echoes discussed are reevaluating her relationship with her grandmother; interactions with students from two indigenous minority groups in her native Taiwan; being a student in a foreign country, with its attendant foreign culture and language; and returning to her ancestral cultural roots. These experiences become echoes because what she encounters or learns in one setting or situation is reexperienced in others, either by herself or students she teaches. For Chia-lin, "echoes" are parallelisms in the experiences of different ethnic groups and memories or residues of earlier social, personal, cultural, and academic learnings embedded in subsequent professional understandings and actions. Her story exemplifies the multicultural education components of cross-cultural understanding, teaching the histories and heritages of diverse ethnic groups, and modifying instructional styles to better fit the cultures, background experiences, and perspectives of ethnically diverse students.

Patricia Espiritu Halagao, the author of Chapter Nine, "Unifying Mind and Soul Through Cultural Knowledge and Self-Education," uses a technique called *balagtasan* from Filipino literary traditions to frame and focus her process of multicultural becoming. It is a form of poetic debate where facts and feelings, thinking and doing, and mind and soul battle with each other. In sharing her journey, she highlights important experiences and pivotal individuals who have contributed to her growth as a multicultural person and educator. Some of these are positive, and others are negative. Many of these dilemmas were provoked by prejudices of European American teachers and peers toward Filipino Americans. Patricia's story illustrates four prominent components of multicultural education: positive ethnic identity development; holistic teaching and learning about ethnic and cultural diversity; designing ethnically specific curriculum and instruction; and bringing the cultures, experiences, voices, and contributions of marginalized groups onto the center stage of the educational process.

In Chapter Ten, Mei-ying Chen situates her journey toward becoming a multicultural person and educator in the learning obtained from social interactions with ethnically diverse groups. In "Hanging Out with Ethnic Others," she reflects on multiculturalism in her daily life and the importance of social, experiential learning in the preparation of multicultural educators. She explains how and why her interactions with ethnic others cause some cultural shocks, require some border crossings, and create some confrontations with prejudices and stereotypes. She considers all of these essential to good multicultural teaching and learning. Her early "miseducation" in schools about ethnic and cultural diversity led her to be skeptical about "book knowledge" in this area. To counter these lingering doubts, Mei-ying develops the habit of seeking out opportunities to mingle socially with members of different ethnic groups in their own cultural contexts. She believes these "firsthand, up-close, authentic experiences" are the best multicultural education teachers. The key multicultural education components embedded in her journey are debunking ethnic and cultural myths, prejudices, and stereotypes; locating and listening to authentic voices and experiences of ethnic groups; and combining academic and school knowledge about ethnic and cultural diversity with social and experiential learning.

Mary Stone Hanley employs her prior training and experiences as a playwright to present the process of her becoming a multicultural educator in Chapter Eleven. The play she presents in the chapter, "Footsteps in the Dancing Zone," is a series of life-altering experiences dealing with education about ethnic and cultural diversity, civil rights protests, social and political activism, and confrontations with racism. The cast of players involved in the construction of Mary's multicultural knowledge, commitment, and skills include individuals and events that were major actors in the social and political civil rights movements of the 1960s and 1970s and promoters of educational equity for ethnic diversity in the 1980s and 1990s. Her writing technique provokes multiple layers of simultaneous engagement with her characters, ideas, and experiences. Mary's substantive text exemplifies the multicultural education components of analyzing critical socio-political issues and events of different ethnic groups to combat racism and other forms of oppression.

In Chapter Twelve, Laura Kay Neuwirth explains the transformation of her personal ideology and pedagogical practices as she moves "From Color Blindness to Cultural Vision." She examines the futility of trying to be "color-blind" in teaching students of color—that is, pretending that race and ethnicity are not important variables in education and therefore trying to ignore them and treat all students the same. In so doing, she demonstrates that having strong intentions to "do good" for ethnically diverse students without having corresponding knowledge and skills is insufficient. Laura explains how she abandoned the color-blind philosophy and how this change affected her subsequent choices of curriculum materials, instructional strategies, and personal understandings. The multicultural education components emphasized in her story are acquiring accurate knowledge about the cultures, experiences, and contributions of different ethnic groups; deconstructing prevailing assumptions about teaching ethnically diverse groups; and developing multicultural curriculum and implementing culturally responsive teaching.

In Chapter Thirteen, "Navigating Marginality: Searching for My Own Truth," Yukari Takimoto Amos explains her personal experiences with marginalization and how they contribute to her multicultural education knowledge, convictions, commitment, and skills. Some of this marginality is geographical, since she is an international student who travels back and forth between the United States and Japan. Other margins are symbolized by gender stereotyping, ethnic profiling, linguistic differences, and one's own self-definitions and those imposed by others. Yukari describes how she became conscious of these margins, how they operate, and what she does to cope with and transcend them. She presents a compelling portrait of the tensions and uncertainties associated with being caught between different cultural borders. The multicultural education components exemplified in Yukari's story are cultural style-shifting skills; understanding the variable of immigration within the experience of different ethnic groups; and developing knowledge and skills needed to function in different ethnic, cultural, social, and national settings.

Learning to be a multicultural educator takes place for Terri Hackett, the author of Chapter Fourteen, "Teaching Them Through

Who They Are," in the process of teaching ethnically and racially diverse middle school students. She describes how her general philosophy of teaching and openness to ethnic and cultural diversity made her receptive to teaching students in culturally responsive ways. As she tries to ensure that her teaching behaviors reflect her personal and professional values and beliefs, she learns that she has to be diligent about connecting the knowledge and skills she teaches to the students' experiential frames of reference. Terri also explains some of the challenges she encounters in the process of trying to accomplish these goals and how her understanding of who her students are helped to overcome them. Terri's process of becoming a multicultural educator highlights the components of using novel teaching strategies to make learning interesting and relevant to ethnically diverse students; using the prior social knowledge and lived experiences of diverse students in formal classroom instruction; and being an advocate for diverse students, programs, and practices.

JOINING THE JOURNEY

We believe that success in multicultural teaching is more a journey than a destination. With this in mind, we invite you to join our journey in becoming multicultural people and professionals. Journey with us in two ways: by extrapolating general messages and methods for becoming and being multicultural educators from our particular stories and by adding your personal stories to ours. As the discourse prompted by our collective stories expands, our individual competencies for multicultural teaching will be enriched and enabled even more, and more children will be better served in our schools.

References

Cochran-Smith, M., and Lytle, S. L. *Inside/Outside: Teacher Research and Knowledge.* New York: Teachers College Press, 1993.

Coles, R. *The Call of Stories: Teaching and the Moral Imagination.* Boston: Houghton Mifflin, 1989.

Dyson, A. H., and Genishi, C. "Introduction: The Need for Story." In A. H. Dyson and C. Genishi (eds.), *The Need for Story: Cultural Diversity in Classroom and Community.* Urbana, Ill.: National Council of Teachers of English, 1994.

Foster, M. *Black Teachers on Teaching.* New York: New Press, 1997.

hooks, b. "Writing Autobiography." In S. Smith and J. Watts (eds.), *Women, Autobiography, Theory: A Reader.* Madison: University of Wisconsin Press, 1998.

Jackson, S. "Autobiography: Pivot Points for Engaging Lives in Multicultural Contexts." In J. M. Larkin and C. E. Sleeter (eds.), *Developing Multicultural Teacher Education Curricula.* Albany: State University of New York Press, 1995.

Mayher, J. S. "Foreword." In J. M. Newman (ed.), *Finding Our Way: Teachers Exploring Their Assumptions.* Portsmouth, N.H.: Heinemann, 1990.

McEwan, H., and Egan, K. (eds.). *Narrative in Teaching, Learning, and Research.* New York: Teachers College Press, 1995.

Newman, J. M. "Finding Our Own Way." In J. M. Newman (ed.), *Finding Our Way: Teachers Exploring Their Assumptions.* Portsmouth, N.H.: Heinemann, 1990.

Nieto, S. *The Light in Their Eyes: Creating Multicultural Learning Communities.* New York: Teachers College Press, 1999.

Nieto, S. *Affirming Diversity: The Sociocultural Context of Multicultural Education.* (3rd ed.) White Plains, N.Y.: Longman, 2000.

Richert, A. E. "Voice and Power in Teaching and Learning to Teach." In L. Valli (ed.), *Reflective Teacher Education: Cases and Critiques.* Albany: State University of New York Press, 1992.

Schön, D. A. *The Reflective Practitioner: How Professionals Think in Action.* New York: Basic Books, 1983.

Valli, L. (ed.). *Reflective Teacher Education: Cases and Critiques.* Albany: State University of New York Press, 1992.

Zeichner, K. M., and Liston, D. P. *Reflective Teaching: An Introduction.* Mahwah, N.J.: Erlbaum, 1996.

CHAPTER TWO

We Make the Road by Walking

John Ambrosio

Becoming a multicultural educator results from deliberate study and action over time, and it involves intellectual, psychological, emotional, moral, and pedagogical changes. For me, it has been a process of maceration, the slow softening and transformation of a European American psyche stiffened in the shape of U.S. culture.

In this chapter, presented in the form of an interview conducted by Amy Ambrosio, my wife and colleague, we explore some of the pathways on my journey to multicultural educator. Sometimes these pathways appear in unexpected forms and take unanticipated turns. Throughout them, I challenge prevailing norms and expectations that are contrary to equity and social justice; seek out encounters that broaden my own personal, ethnic, and cultural experiences; and interact with ideas and individuals who stretch my mind and strengthen my resolve to promote educational equality for ethnically diverse students. As you will see, power, politics, and activism are central issues in my process of becoming multicultural. I strongly believe that educators should deal overtly with these issues. If I am to do this well for my students, I have to do it for myself as well.

To become a multicultural educator, we must have firm beliefs about multicultural education and act on them. The actions we take may not be popular or endear us to those in positions of power and privilege, but they must be done. We must be courageous and self-motivated in taking action instead of always waiting for others to tell us what to do. And we can act for change without having a final resolution to all the problems we wish to solve.

Action starts with critical reflection. Michael Parenti (1993), a political scientist, observes, "It is desirable and necessary for human beings to examine the society in which they live, possibly as a step toward making fundamental improvements" (p. 7). Thus, we begin acting as multicultural educators as soon as we start to critically analyze the distributions of power and privilege in schools and the differential effects they have on ethnically, culturally, racially, socially, and linguistically diverse students.

The values and beliefs that are symbolized by my priorities in multicultural personal and professional development are articulated by Maxine Greene (1978), who explains the idea of "emancipatory education" as "enabling individuals to reflect on their own lived lives and the lives they lead in common with one another, not merely as professionals or professionals-to-be, but as human beings participating in a shared reality . . . transformation . . . to the end of overcoming oppressiveness and domination, . . . collective self-reflection . . . [and] attentiveness to one's own history, one's own self-formation" (pp. 54, 100, 103). Furthermore, Greene notes, it is important for educators to change "what they find deficient [and] surpass what they find inhumane . . . not only for the sake of overcoming ignorance and warding off manipulation, but in order to resist the cynicism and powerlessness that silence as they paralyze" (p. 55). Learning how to promote the redistribution of privilege and social justice implied in these comments for ethnically diverse people is at the heart of my multicultural development.

ORIGINS IN ETHNIC IDEOLOGY
AND ISOLATION

AA: Sonia Nieto talks about the idea that becoming a multicultural educator means becoming a multicultural person first. How do you see yourself as becoming a multicultural person? What are some of the early experiences in your life that brought you there?

JA: In the summer of 1965, when I was eight years old, my family moved from a working-class area of northeastern New Jersey to a middle-class suburb about forty miles to the south. I was not conscious of cultural diversity. I grew up encapsulated in a White world, and my awareness of ethnic differences was mostly limited to those among my European American friends and neighbors. Because my parents were uncomfortable with people outside their class and ethnic boundaries, our social life revolved mostly around extended family. These connections and relationships exemplified for me the importance attached to family that Patrick Gallo (1981) describes. He says, "For Italian Americans, the family is the chief source of nourishment and joy, of conflict and struggle. It is in the family that moral values are quietly and silently inculcated—honesty, questioning, obedience, respect for others, manners, courage, cynicism, civic responsibility" (pp. 161–162).

Like many other people, I was exposed to a steady stream of cultural and ethnic stereotypes through television, movies, newspapers, and magazines and from being socialized within the dominant White culture. Although we lived less than an hour's drive from New York City, a global center of cultural diversity, I grew up culturally isolated and completely unaware of the ethnic biases and stereotypes that influenced my thinking and behavior. Richard Alba (1985) provides an explanation that has helped me to understand why my cultural isolation was possible. He suggests that geographical pockets of "intense ethnicity allow individuals to submerge themselves in an ethnic world, reducing their need to accommodate to the larger society. As a result, ethnic communities tend to preserve distinctiveness . . . stand as reminders of a recent ethnic past . . . [and] help to keep ethnicity as a social and personal characteristic in the limelight" (pp. 116–117).

AA: How would you describe your own ethnic identity, and how has it affected your development as a multicultural person?

JA: My ethnic roots on both sides of the family can be traced to Italy. Three of my grandparents passed through Ellis Island, the port of entry into the United States for most immigrants from Europe to the United States during the late nineteenth and early twentieth centuries. My paternal grandparents were poor farmers from a small village in the mountains of central Italy. My maternal grandfather immigrated to the United States as an infant, and my maternal grandmother was one of thirteen children in a first-generation Italian American family.

My parents grew up a block apart in Jersey City, New Jersey, which at that time was a mix of Italian, Irish, and Jewish families.

That's one important piece of my identity, my Italian American ancestry. The other piece is that I grew up in a working-class family one step removed from the values, attitudes, and cultural practices of my immigrant and first-generation grandparents. After finishing high school, my father worked as a butcher and meat manager in a supermarket chain, and my mother held a succession of secretarial jobs after my three siblings and I were old enough to attend school.

Although I was raised in a middle-class European American neighborhood, our family culture was working-class Italian American. Our social life revolved around Catholic holidays and rites of passage (christenings, first communions, confirmations) and extended family gatherings on holidays. Every few weeks, we would drive to my grandparents' house in Jersey City for Sunday dinner. I would help my grandmother, Rosa, make fresh macaroni. We rolled out, cut, and curled the dough on her kitchen table while a large pot of gravy with meatballs and chunks of pork simmered on the stove, filling the room with an unforgettable aroma. On holidays, we sat for hours, eating and drinking at a long table in the basement of my aunt and uncle's house, while I listened to the strange inflections of the Italian dialect reserved for adult conversations. We mixed red wine with our 7-Up and watched *March of the Wooden Soldiers* on television every Easter.

My parents believed they had a responsibility, a duty, to exercise absolute authority over their children. Because of this, there was a conspicuous absence of dialogue between adults and children in our family. Parental relationships consisted mostly of orders from above and passive resistance from below. That was how my parents grew up, and it was unimaginable to them that we should be raised any differently. I responded to this silencing by ignoring and openly defying their authority whenever possible. This behavior absolutely infuriated my parents, especially my father, who would reach for his belt whenever he wanted to teach me a lesson I wouldn't forget.

My parents instilled a strong moral center in all of their children. They worked hard, paid their taxes, and played by the rules. The moral compass they passed on to us continues to be a vital part of my character. There was no higher value in my family than work. It had a special aura, occupying a sacred place in our pantheon of cultural values. It didn't really matter what kind of work you did, as long as you made a decent living from it. For my parents, personal identity and self-worth were derived from family, not a career. They took great pride in having achieved a middle-class lifestyle, successfully providing for their children, and giving us opportunities in life they could not even imagine.

Remembering my personal ethnic history and cultural socialization is an important aspect of my becoming multicultural. It helps me to better understand how I came to be who I am, where I am headed in relating to my own and others' ethnicity, and how I can get to where I want to be as a multicultural person and educator. Gallo (1981, p. 275) suggests, "The study of one's past is part of self-discovery and self-understanding. It is part of greater maturity." This self-study should not be totally idiosyncratic or merely ethnocentric ego-tripping. Instead, Gallo proposes, it needs to be part of a thorough understanding of how the "American pluralistic society has evolved. As such, the study of the past will help to illuminate the present and point the way in the future" (p. 275). Furthermore, knowing my own and my students' cultures can help me create conditions for more effective learning. This is possible because understanding the terrains of a society's or group's culture helps us to relate to others better and to achieve our own purposes (Pai, 1990). My purposes are to improve the quality of the lives and learning of ethnically diverse people.

As a high school student, I spent most of my weekends and summers washing dishes, busing tables, and cooking in a local restaurant. I really enjoyed working, not only because it put money in my pocket, but also because I felt valued and was given adult responsibilities. Work served as a kind of antidote to school, where I rarely felt affirmed or acknowledged. I had a tremendous desire to be known but always felt anonymous, overlooked, and underestimated. Because of this, I did pretty poorly academically and socially.

This pervasive feeling of being underestimated was reinforced one day in economics class when the teacher challenged students to name the chairman of the Federal Reserve system. While he scanned the room with his usual self-assured grin, I quietly responded with the correct answer: Arthur Burns. He quickly turned toward me and demanded: "Who said that?" As I timidly raised my hand, he was seized by a look of perplexed bewilderment. For a fleeting moment, I shined in the glow of his astonishment, my pressing sense of anonymity temporarily lifted. Encounters like this helped crystallize my self-awareness around the realization that I was an intelligent person with a compelling desire to know how things worked. In retrospect, I can see that the seeds of my intellectual curiosity were germinating in high school.

RACIAL PREJUDICES
AND CULTURAL BIASES

AA: What kind of racism or cultural biases do you think you may have held as a consequence of growing up in a mostly all White community?

JA: It's virtually impossible for anyone steeped in U.S. culture not to be affected by racist and ethnic stereotypes, especially concerning African Americans. To some extent, everyone has internalized racist images and beliefs, whether they're conscious of them or not. Except for my paternal grandfather, who had a long list of ethnic prejudices, I don't recall anyone in my extended family ever uttering a blatantly racist remark. That doesn't mean they didn't hold racist views, only that they may have been unwilling to voice them openly. For my parents, the issue of race was really a question of culture. Their litmus test of acceptability was based on a person's willingness to emulate dominant cultural practices—the ways of speaking, interacting, and dressing that my parents considered normal.

As first- and second-generation Italian Americans, my parents expected immigrants to adopt the language and culture of their new country, just as their parents had done. They couldn't understand the desire of some ethnic groups to live in the United States without becoming "American." My father became enraged at the Latino men he worked with because they refused to speak English to each other. It absolutely infuriated him: "Why can't they learn to speak English like everyone else?" The reality, which my father knew, was that they could speak English but chose not to. He saw their choice as a repudiation of everything he and his family had worked to achieve.

Because I grew up in a nearly all-White community and went to public and parochial schools that were much the same, my hidden cultural biases did not become apparent until I began studying political economy in college. That was when my beliefs about why particular ethnic groups, especially people of color, were disproportionately poor were challenged by an emerging understanding of how wealth and poverty are produced in capitalist systems and which groups have historically paid the social cost of other people's affluence.

The stereotypes I grew up with about the work habits and lifestyles of different ethnic groups began to change as I realized how the larger social and political contexts shape economic opportunities and as I became increasingly aware of the long history of racial and economic oppression in the United States. Michael Parenti (1983) once commented that ghettos are not the problem but the solution. What he meant was that ghettos are not a blight on an otherwise benevolent society but an integral part of our economic system, the logical and necessary outcome of the tremendous disparities in wealth produced by capitalism. He also said that policy decisions made by governments are always political and seldom, if ever, neutral. Instead, "They almost always benefit some interests more than others, entailing social costs that are rarely equally distributed. . . . Politics is the process of struggle over conflicting interests carried into the public arena; it may also involve the process of muting and suppressing conflicting interests. Politics involves the activation and mediation of conflict, the setting of public priorities, the choosing of certain values, interests, and goals and the denial of others" (pp. 3–4).

When I apply this thinking to being a multicultural educator, it means that I have to understand the politics involved and stand ready to be political about what I do to advocate for ethnic and cultural diversity. Most certainly, I want to minimize the unequal distribution of educational benefits among students from different ethnic groups and promote the values of cultural pluralism.

AA: Has anyone in your family ever experienced ethnic bias or discrimination?

JA: My father has vivid memories of being the frequent target of ethnic slurs as a child. These were apparent as soon as he stepped beyond the boundaries of the Jersey City neighborhood, inhabited almost exclusively by Italian immigrants, where he grew up. My parents felt the sting of ethnic prejudice when they were denied the right to buy a bungalow in Oceanside, New Jersey, in the early 1960s. They had found a house and obtained a mortgage but were asked to fill out an application in order to purchase the home. One of the questions on the form asked where their parents had been born. He answered the question honestly, and their application was rejected without explanation. They later discovered that no one could buy a home in this area unless they were first admitted to a social club, a device that Polish and Ukrainian Americans used to exclude people from ethnic backgrounds they found undesirable.

AA: How do you think becoming a parent has influenced your development as a multicultural person?

JA: Given my own cultural isolation growing up, I'm very conscious of trying to expose our son, Isaac, to a variety of cross-cultural experiences through books, cultural events, and videos and by explicitly discussing cultural differences. He became conscious of differences in skin color at an early age and has always been very curious about people unlike himself. I see his natural curiosity about other people as an opportunity to discuss issues of physical and cultural differences.

I'm also concerned with trying to limit his exposure to cultural biases and stereotypes embedded in our commercial and media-saturated society. We do not watch television, except for an occasional special on PBS, and do not allow Isaac to view socially and culturally biased media products, especially Disney films. Being a parent has heightened my consciousness of how stereotypes are marketed and transmitted to children and given me an opportunity to learn how to discuss cultural issues in a more direct and uncomplicated way.

ALIENATION IN SCHOOL

AA: You said you weren't a very good student. What happened in high school? Why did you feel you weren't being successful?

JA: My parents made the unfortunate mistake of sending me to a Catholic high school when I reached the ninth grade. They believed it would keep me out of trouble and give me a proper moral education.

Shortly after arriving, I realized it was a closed social world. As an exile from the public school system, I was a permanent outsider. Worse, the school had a military-like culture. Teachers and administrators were given free rein to abuse students verbally and physically for whatever reason they believed warranted such treatment. And many of them did. One day, a lay teacher pinned me up against a locker in a hallway and threatened me with further physical abuse if I ever failed to follow his orders again. My response to this situation was to disengage from school, to withdraw from my classes, both intellectually and physically. I shut down academically; I stopped going to classes and spent an increasing amount of time not in school at all. But by my junior year, it was clear that if something didn't change, I was unlikely to finish high school. Seeing the writing on the wall, my parents reluctantly agreed to send me back to the public school system, but it was too little, too late. There was no way I could regain the lost years of learning I had missed out on.

There are many other ethnically diverse students who experience alienation and displacement in school similar to what I encountered. They don't fit well with conventional education programs, protocols, and practices even though they may be intelligent and place a high value on education. These are some of the students I am most concerned about. They certainly need some nontraditional ways of teaching and learning if they are to access their right to quality education that is personally appropriate for them. Multicultural education can provide these learning opportunities. This is one of the reasons that I am strongly invested in developing the knowledge and skills to advocate for students who have needs and challenges like the ones I had in high school.

The personal fallout from my years in Catholic high school is that I became extremely sensitive to the idea of anyone exercising authority over me and avoided situations where I was susceptible to the capricious use of authority. The other side of this feeling was a strong attraction to democratic and egalitarian forms of social organization.

When I graduated from college, I considered living in a kibbutz in Israel. After months of weighing my alternatives, it finally came down to a choice between joining the Peace Corps or doing an internship at the Institute for Policy Studies in Washington, D.C. I wasn't emotionally ready to make the leap abroad, and so I settled on the second option.

TURNING POINTS

AA: Something must have happened when you went to college. What was the connection between your experience and feelings of powerlessness, of being ruled in an arbitrary and whimsical kind of way, and your discovery of political science? I would also like you to discuss particular teachers you had in college, not only in terms of what they taught but of who they were as people, and whether they may have offered you a model of how to be an adult, of how to be a different kind of person.

JA: My feelings of powerlessness and social isolation as a teenager carried over to my college years and provided the inner tension that made political science so compelling for me.

A course I took in my freshman year, "Politics in the '70s," made my feelings of discontent intellectually coherent by helping me see the social, historical, and political reasons for my alienation from U.S. society. It wasn't just some idiosyncrasy on my part. The course examined and compared different forms of social and economic organization. We read several books from a variety of political perspectives. One of them, *Democracy for the Few*, by Michael Parenti (1983), is a devastating critique of American government and society. This book completely transformed my understanding of U.S. society and helped locate my personal situation and struggles as a working-class Italian American in the social and economic relations of a capitalist society.

Reading Parenti's book was very important, but it wouldn't have been as powerful an experience without the respect our professor, Bill Daly, had for his students. For the first time in my life, I was asked to think critically, to use my knowledge and experience to analyze and explore the validity of opposing ideas and arguments.

Our final project was to write a paper on what we thought was the best form of social organization. I worked very hard. When I got the paper back, there was a typed note attached. It began, "This is a fine job, Mr. Ambrosio. Congratulations," and went on to discuss the strengths and weaknesses of my argument. I had never received that kind of praise from a teacher before. Bill Daly's words lifted my self-confidence and convinced me that I could succeed in college.

The irony, and I'm a bit embarrassed to admit it, is when I reread the paper recently, I was horrified to discover that this twenty-page paper consisted of a single very long paragraph! Although other aspects of my writing were fairly well developed, my technical skills left much to be desired. Despite this, it was my ideas that counted, the quality of my thoughts that was important. Bill could have easily crushed my fragile self-confidence by making an issue out of the organization of the paper. Instead, he chose to focus on what I was saying rather than how I presented it. At the end of the course, I switched my major to political science and became involved with a politically active student organization working on issues such as recruiting on college campuses by the Central Intelligence Agency. I had finally found an intellectual home, a direction, and a community.

The critical element in my college education was the personal relationships I formed with teachers. It was in those moments when my teachers let down their guard, took off their professorial personas, and spoke to me in unritualized ways—even cursed in my presence—that I felt most at ease, most accepted. They were effective teachers largely because they also were able to be human beings: people with feelings who got angry and upset, who could be funny and playful as well as serious and scholarly.

One of the most valuable gifts a teacher can give students is to hold up a mirror, to offer them an important insight into their character. I received such a gift from Joe Walsh, a former Catholic priest turned philosophy professor, who was a personal and intellectual mentor. In a letter of recommendation, he noted that I possessed a strong commitment to my values, while being genuinely open to and tolerant of the views of others. At the time, it didn't make much of an impression on me. But in retrospect, he clearly pointed out a central aspect of my character, something that has been critical to my development as a multicultural educator. My college years were a real breakthrough period when my identity began forming around politics as a way of understanding and living my life.

AA: In what other ways did your disengagement from high school leave you unprepared for college? How did you discover what you had missed?

JA: It became clear, through conversations with friends and in class discussions, that I had missed out on a whole range of learning. The books everyone else seemed to have read were unfamiliar to me. I felt a bit like Rip Van Winkle waking up under a tree and trying to catch up on the missing years. For the first time in my life, I began reading seriously, voraciously, everything I could get my hands on. Reading became a compulsion, an irresistible urge. *Metamorphosis,* by Franz Kafka, helped me explore my emotional and psychic landscapes. I discovered what is now one of my favorite writers, Eduardo Galeano, the Uruguayan author of *Open Veins of Latin America* (1973) and many other remarkable books. It slowly dawned on me that my intellectual interests are wide ranging. I have an insatiable curiosity about everything. Most of all, I wanted to understand how societies function, what makes them tick, and why they are organized in certain ways.

AA: After graduating from college, you worked as a research assistant with Michael Parenti at the Institute for Policy Studies (IPS), a progressive think tank in Washington, D.C. How do you think that experience influenced your development as a multicultural educator?

JA: Working at IPS was an incredible learning experience. There was a constant stream of people giving lectures, seminars, and classes from all over the country and the rest of the world—scholars, writers, artists, politicians, and political activists. IPS wasn't just a home to resident scholars like Michael Parenti. It was also a forum, an international meeting place, a kind of mecca for progressives from every corner of the globe.

Being a research assistant for Michael Parenti on the fourth edition of *Democracy for the Few* (1983), the same book that turned my world upside down in college, was a thrilling experience. Parenti treated me with enormous respect. He introduced me to his social world, befriended me, and eventually asked me to join the collective household in which he lived. We would sit for hours on warm summer nights eating watermelon on the back stoop of the house, talking about politics, relationships, books, or whatever was in the air.

The two and a half years I spent at IPS were critical to the development of my political and cultural awareness. It's where I met Ariel Dorfman, the Chilean writer and political activist who had been living in exile since the U.S.-backed military coup in Chile in 1973. And there was Isabel Letelier, the human rights activist and widow of Orlando Letelier, a former ambassador to the United States and cabinet minister in the Allende government in Chile who was assassinated in Washington, D.C., by agents of Pinochet's secret police.

They were exiled from their country by a murderous regime supported by the U.S. government, yet they had no bitterness or anger and made no recriminations. Instead, they radiated humility, empathy, and dignity. What I remember most are the small gestures of recognition, the moments of kindness, and the warm, open embrace of their smiles. They helped me understand that there are alternatives to the market values and utilitarian relationships that characterize U.S. culture.

These encounters were the starting point of a deeper cultural awareness that allowed me to begin reflecting on my own cultural identity. I was disillusioned with the dominant values of U.S. society—the materialism, the competition for status and power, the elevation of work and money, of having and possessing over life and living. I was looking for something different, trying to figure out how to live in a way consistent with my deepest values and desires. The summer after I left the Institute for Policy Studies in 1983, I took my first trip abroad, a four-week tour of Southern and Western Europe, followed by several trips to Mexico and Central America in subsequent years.

OUTSIDE LOOKING INWARD

AA: Let's talk about your travel outside the United States. You mentioned that after going to Europe, you made several trips to Mexico and Central America. Could you explore how these experiences affected your understanding of cultural differences?

JA: Traveling outside the United States, especially to underdeveloped countries with very different social and cultural traditions, gave me the distance I needed to reflect on how my own identity and consciousness were shaped by U.S. culture.

My trip to Nicaragua in the summer of 1986 had a profound effect on my cultural consciousness. The contra war, the U.S.-sponsored war against the Sandinista government, was raging at the time. Since the defeat of the Somoza regime by the Sandinistas in 1979, I had been closely following events in Nicaragua and was intensely curious about what was going on there. From everything I read and from conversations with friends who had traveled to Nicaragua after the revolution, it appeared that something remarkable was happening— a revolution that was transforming the lives of the poor. I felt compelled to witness the revolution in action.

I signed up for a six-week Spanish-language program in Estelí, a small town a few hours north of the capital, Managua. I was placed with a local family; I ate all my meals with them and spent most of my evenings in their house. Normally, I would have slept there too, but our entire class had to stay in a local hotel because contra soldiers had recently been caught infiltrating the town, which had been chosen as the site for the celebration of the seventh anniversary of the revolution. Because our host families were highly visible and viewed as Sandinista supporters, they became potential targets for violent attacks.

The day we arrived, we met our host families in the courtyard of the school, where we were briefly introduced before setting off. As we walked together in the street outside the school, I struggled with my Spanish: "Yo soy Juan Ambrosio," was about all I could get out. My family was very patient with my limited Spanish, and we gestured to facilitate communication.

We attended classes in the morning and periodically went on school-sponsored field trips to meet with a variety of people: government officials, representatives of mass organizations, human rights groups, opposition political parties, journalists, and even a stop at the

U.S. embassy in Managua. We also visited schools, health clinics, and artist collectives.

I'll never forget the kindness and generosity of the people I met. Despite their relative material poverty and wartime shortages, they were incredibly generous with the little they had. My Nicaraguan family always made sure I had enough to eat, even if they didn't.

One morning, the family matriarch, whose four children and three grandchildren shared three small rooms in her house, asked me what I liked to eat. Without a second thought, I responded that I enjoyed eating fish. She made special trips to the market to buy fish for me, which I later found out was not only very difficult to obtain but extremely expensive. She was getting fresh fish for me when she could barely buy enough rice and beans to feed her family. When I realized how thoughtless I had been, I was deeply ashamed of my ignorance and insensitivity. It's a lesson I've never forgotten.

I was relieved and astonished to discover that the vast majority of Nicaraguans had no enmity toward North Americans. Here I was, a gringo from the United States, from an imperialist power waging an illegal and immoral war against their country, yet I never felt unwanted or unwelcome. The family I was staying with even had a son fighting in the mountains north of Estelí and may have already lost friends and relatives in the war. They explained that the people of a country and the government are two different things and that the latter is generally unrepresentative of the former. Working-class Nicaraguans were much more politically conscious and sophisticated than most well-educated North Americans.

I learned in Nicaragua that I was a North American, not simply an American, that the Americas consist of more than just the United States. I learned to question the unexamined cultural assumptions, the taken-for-granted beliefs, that always place the United States at the top of the international social hierarchy. I came to see this perspective as ethnocentric—as the view of an arrogant imperial power that didn't care to recognize the existence of other people who might also have a legitimate claim to being American. Being in Nicaragua gave me the opportunity, perspective, and space to see the United States in a way that I probably couldn't have done while living within the society. These insider and outsider viewpoints are critical dimensions of multicultural teaching and living in both national and international contexts.

AA: How did it feel to be in a situation in which you were compelled to function in a language you didn't really know?

JA: It was the most painfully frustrating experience of my life. I lived with a family that I desperately wanted to communicate with, whose stories I would have given anything to know. I could communicate on a very rudimentary level but couldn't converse independently with most people in the country. Every conversation required a translator and thus had to be mediated. I was completely dependent on other people to initiate and interpret conversations for me. I've never been in a situation where I've felt so helpless, so unable to function.

I was probably a great disappointment to my Nicaraguan teachers, who despite their gentle and persistent efforts, never observed much progress in my Spanish-language acquisition. I had never learned a second language in school and had little confidence that I could do so at that point in my life. Having gone through this experience, I have some understanding of what it must feel like to be an English as a Second Language student learning a new language while trying to function in an unfamiliar culture.

AA: Let's shift gears here a bit. You spent several years doing graduate work in sociology and political science at the Graduate Center of the City University of New York. What were some of the most important influences in your intellectual development at that time?

JA: The work of Antonio Gramsci, the Italian Marxist political theorist, had a profound effect on my thinking. A collection of Gramsci's writings, *Selections from the Prison Notebooks* (1971), fundamentally changed the way I think about the process of historical development, of social and political change. Gramsci's work also gave me a theoretical framework for understanding the social function of education, of its essential moral and political nature. His writings on education were the intellectual stimulus and entry point for the development of my pedagogy.

The other major influence was Paulo Freire, the Brazilian educator and author of *Pedagogy of the Oppressed* (1970). I was introduced to Freire's ideas during a workshop on popular education techniques. I was intrigued by his approach and drawn to his focus on the relationship between power and pedagogy. Like Gramsci, Freire situated the educational process within a larger sociopolitical and historical context and insisted on the impossibility of neutrality. Education is inherently and inescapably defined by moral and political choices. It is always for something. Rather than seeing students as empty vessels to be filled with the expert knowledge of teachers, Freire argued that students must make their own meanings; they must be producers of knowledge themselves.

AA: How did living and going to graduate school in New York City influence your development as a multicultural person?

JA: Like traveling abroad, living in Brooklyn for more than four years had a major influence on my cultural consciousness. Most of the people living on my block and in the surrounding neighborhood were African American or Afro-Caribbean. For the first time in my life, I was an ethnic and cultural minority. Being on the outside looking in made me acutely aware of the dominant cultural practices in my community.

There was a barbershop nearby that was always filled with men, mostly from Haiti. They used the shop as a sort of social club, a daily gathering place to sit, talk, discuss the news, play card games, and enjoy each other's company. This was a stark contrast to the socially sterile barbershops I went to as a kid.

Another important influence was teaching at Brooklyn College and at City College. Both schools have very diverse student populations, with a significant number, if not a majority, of students of color. The day after the rebellion began in South Central Los Angeles in 1992, I walked into my class at Brooklyn College and raised the issue for discussion. Without realizing it, I had unleashed a firestorm of clashing perceptions between students of color and the mostly working-class European American students in my classes.

The European American students tended to view the rebellion as an irrational explosion of rioting and looting, as a communal act of self-destruction. Students of color saw it as a righteous response to the persistence of racism and economic oppression. In the heat of the debate, African American students revealed their deep-seated anger and resentment toward White power and privilege, and their furious rage at having to endure the daily insults and humiliations of living in a racist society. For a brief moment, the thin veil of civility was lifted, and I saw what social reality looks like from the perspective of people at the receiving end of racial discrimination and oppression.

AA: Were there other experiences while you were living in New York City and going to graduate school that were an important part of your personal development?

JA: In the 1980s, under Presidents Reagan and Bush, the United States was involved in a number of military adventures, including the war in El Salvador and the contra war against the Sandinista government. I expressed my opposition to U.S. imperialism by participating in dozens of demonstrations against military intervention in Central America, getting arrested several times in the process.

As a graduate student, I joined a group of my peers in occupying the main building of the Graduate Center to protest systemwide budget cuts proposed for the City University of New York. For several days, we prevented access to the building while we held strategy meetings, met with students from other campuses, issued a stream of press releases, fielded telephone calls, and held daily speak-outs. Because the takeover was largely unplanned, we had to improvise as we went along. We had to organize ourselves, assign tasks, and figure out how to process collective decisions democratically. The occupation was a powerful lesson in political organization.

I also attended quite a few concerts. One of the most memorable was the annual performance of Sweet Honey in the Rock at Carnegie Hall. I'll never forget how the group got the entire audience thinking, feeling, relating, reacting, and even dancing. The power and beauty of their voices lifted up the crowd and moved it to action physically and spiritually.

AA: What happened in the process of leaving graduate school in New York that shifted your focus to teaching in high school? What underlies that shift?

JA: It all happened quite inadvertently. I was working as an evaluation specialist at the New York City Board of Education when I was asked to join a delegation on a visit to Central Park East Secondary School. It was another one of those epiphanies for me. The school embodied many of the educational principles and practices I valued. It was small and personalized and had an integrated curriculum divided into a two-period school day. Students were assigned teacher-advisers whom they met with daily. Their learning was evaluated through exhibitions and other performance-based assessments. Teachers practiced student-centered pedagogy, were given structured planning time for collaborative teaching, and shared a common educational philosophy. The school itself was run by teachers, parents, and administrative staff, who shared responsibility for making important decisions about every aspect of its operation. I left that day feeling absolutely exuberant, with a renewed faith in the possibilities of public education.

I was also seized by the thought of how different my own life might have been had I attended a school like Central Park East. Perhaps there was some inner compulsion pushing me forward, some desire to fix what had happened to me as a high school student, to return to the past and replay the drama from a different, more powerful position. Whatever the reason, I was convinced that school restructuring was the essential ingredient in creating humanistic and liberatory learning environments. I dreamed of taking a metaphorical sledgehammer to the huge impersonal comprehensive high schools—of breaking them into smaller, more human-sized pieces.

INSIDE OUT

AA: How do you see yourself as a multicultural educator? What is it about your teaching that makes you a multicultural educator?

JA: What makes me a multicultural educator is my commitment to cultural democracy, to creating learning experiences and opportunities that allow students from diverse cultural groups to see themselves in my curriculum, instructional practices, and classroom climate. In effect, this means I have a personal and professional commitment to displacing the Eurocentric curriculum with a broad array of cultural perspectives. I consider myself a multicultural educator because I see students as creators rather than consumers of knowledge, as makers of meaning rather than passive recipients of socially sanctioned truths. My pedagogy uses the personal knowledge and experiences of students to reflect critically on issues presented from a variety of perspectives.

One of my objectives is to radically decenter students, to make the familiar strange and the unfamiliar familiar, to incite students to question what they think they know by challenging their assumptions about education, culture, and society. I invite students to suspend their beliefs and judgments temporarily in order to see what social reality looks like from the perspectives of others. What makes my teaching multicultural is that I value and honor the cultures, knowledge, and experiences of my students and help situate their lives, identities, and struggles within a larger social, political, and economic context. I want my students to become historical actors, to be subjects rather than passive objects of history.

AA: How did you come to the field, to your vision of multicultural education? What got you there?

JA: It began shortly after I had moved to Portland, Oregon, from New York City. This move occurred because I was searching for new career and educational opportunities. One day, while browsing in a bookstore, I discovered a copy of *Rethinking Our Classrooms,* a teaching guide and classroom resource edited by Bill Bigelow and others (1994). It introduced me to the concept and pedagogical practices of multicultural education.

Another contributing factor was the centrality of culture, stressed throughout my teacher education program at Lewis and Clark College in Portland, Oregon. This focus helped solidify my commitment to multicultural education, which seemed like a natural extension of what I had been learning and thinking about for a long time. Like Gramsci and Freire, multicultural educators see culture as a form of social power and authority.

AA: Your interest in multicultural education sort of parallels what you felt was missing in your own education. You talked about it in discussing your yearning to be recognized and valued. Do you think your own experience is generalizable to other students?

JA: I think all people have these needs, although they're expressed in culturally specific ways. For me, it all boils down to the issue of respect, of valuing the knowledge, experiences, opinions, and feelings of students. In effect, this means considering students inherently worthy of being treated with dignity—as responsible, competent, and intelligent adults-in-the-making.

You can't force students to learn. You can only invite them to learn by offering them a compelling reason to want to learn. My goal is to create an inviting and stimulating learning environment by constructing educational opportunities and experiences that meet the needs of all my students, from the mainstream majority and from the ethnically and culturally different groups. I want my students to be visible and active participants in their learning process. As a multicultural educator, I see my role as a friendly guide who, while affirming their ideas and experiences, continuously challenges students to think more deeply.

AA: Tell me a little about your teaching at Lewis and Clark College and where it fits in with your goals of developing yourself as a multicultural educator.

JA: I teach a core class in the graduate teacher education program that focuses on educational inequities related to class, race, gender, and culture. To prepare for the class, I spent many hours researching and reading dozens of books and articles. In the process, I discovered the work of James Banks, Geneva Gay, Sonia Nieto, Carl Grant, Gloria Ladson-Billings, Christine Sleeter, and many others.

The course is a laboratory for developing my practice as a multicultural educator. It's where I strive to translate the principles of multicultural education into instructional practices that inform my theoretical understanding in a feedback loop. The concepts of cultural conflict and culturally responsive teaching are infused throughout my curriculum. Recently, I added a set of readings on Ebonics so we could explore the issue of language as a source of personal identity and cultural power. Whether we are discussing standardized testing, tracking, school knowledge, or other forms of educational inequity, we always circle back to the issue of culture as one of the common connecting threads.

AA: How do you perceive what you do in the classroom as having a broader effect on education?

JA: Multicultural education places a high value on critical thinking, on the personal truth making that enables students to challenge the moral and intellectual authority of the dominant culture. For this reason, it has come under sharp attack by neoconservatives, who fear its challenge to their social authority.

My hope is that my own practice will serve as a model for students, for informing the development of their pedagogy. Given the demographic changes in U.S. society, educators who hope to teach all their students well will need to integrate the principles of multicultural education into their practice. Because of this, I believe that an increasing number of educators will come to see the value of multicultural education for all students, not just those from marginalized social groups.

AA: What education community do you see yourself as a part of now?

JA: Before beginning the Ph.D. program, I worked for two years with a group of teachers from the Portland, Oregon, chapter of Rethinking Schools, the organization that publishes the journal *Rethinking Schools*, developing curricula about sweatshops and the global economy. As a new high school teacher, I found being connected to a community of like-minded educators essential to maintaining a critical stance and developing my instructional practice. Because I'm relatively new to the field of multicultural education, I've just begun connecting to the larger community of researchers and practitioners. Intellectually, I feel a strong affiliation with colleagues who see multicultural education as effective pedagogy and as a form of social action.

AA: Do you have any big messages, any general lessons or thoughts you want to share?

JA: One of the issues that comes up with my students at Lewis and Clark College is the feeling of being overwhelmed by the complexity of becoming a multicultural educator. They worry about having to become familiar with so many different cultures, with such a broad range of knowledge. They are concerned about their ability to function effectively as culturally responsive teachers in increasingly diverse classrooms.

My response is that teaching is learning—a process of slowly integrating knowledge into practice. Expect to make mistakes and learn from them. The most important aspect of teaching is developing the mental habit of reflecting on your instructional practice and of altering your practice according to what you discover about how students learn best. Knowledge of multicultural theory and practice will give you the reflective space, the necessary reservoir of cultural insight, to intelligently address pedagogical issues as they arise in your everyday practice.

In teaching, as in the rest of life, we make the road by walking.

PRINCIPLES FOR PRACTICE

At its core, multicultural teaching is about personal and social transformation, about challenging deeply held assumptions and perspectives that shape our individual and collective identities. Multicultural education focuses on helping students cross multiple borders of difference; it is also vitally concerned with addressing issues of social justice and equity that produce diverse educational experiences, opportunities, and outcomes.

Multicultural teaching demands that we examine the beliefs and values central to our identity, that our internalized habits, rituals, and routines of thought and practice are explicit and ongoing objects of self-reflection. Because multicultural education addresses issues of social justice and the systems of belief that facilitate multiple forms of domination, it can have a profound and destabilizing effect on people. Uncovering and confronting the deep structure of cultural values, attitudes, beliefs, and assumptions is a difficult and prolonged process, but change at this fundamental level is precisely the aim of multicultural education.

As multicultural educators, we must understand that students are situated differently in terms of their knowledge and experience of cultural diversity. Their specific location within the intersecting matrix of race, class, gender, and culture results in a particular set of social blinders that limits perception. We must begin where our ethnically, racially, culturally, and linguistically diverse students are rather than where we would like them to be. We must encourage them to use what they already know to analyze and evaluate truth claims. Thus, a first principle for practice is to *respect and use the experiences students bring to the classroom and accept that multicultural learning begins from a variety of starting points.*

Multicultural education is a social and relational process that relies on sharing ideas, perspectives, and personal experiences. Like critical pedagogy, it challenges the social authority of a single master narrative to name reality, to define and determine the standard for what is true and legitimate knowledge. As multicultural educators, we should encourage and assist students in learning how to talk back to voices of social authority, question the veracity of dominant opinions, and challenge hidden assumptions. Because multicultural education values socially constructed ways of knowing, it is vital that students and teachers feel secure enough to take emotional and intellectual risks in learning, to share their ideas and perceptions. Therefore, the second principle for practice is that *students and teachers should have space to explore and reflect on multicultural ideas free from evaluative constraints and preconceived outcomes.*

Multicultural education requires an open field of inquiry in which differing, and sometimes clashing, perceptions must be given a safe and supportive forum for exploration, where ideas rather than individuals are the object of evaluation and judgment. Because perceptions are constrained by the social location of knowers, a more complete and complex understanding of social reality can be obtained only by employing a multiplicity of lenses. Multicultural educators rely on disciplinary knowledge and diverse ethnic perspectives to decenter dominant social referents and cultural narratives, redefine what counts as knowledge, and reframe the kinds of questions that students and teachers can imagine. It also emphasizes examining significant differences in social experiences through academic learning aimed at uncovering the hidden histories and experiences of marginalized social groups; by placing individual experiences in their social, political, and historical contexts; and by using autobiographical narratives that convey personal experiences and meanings. My own multicultural journey illustrates a third principle for practice: *academic learning about multicultural education can help students make sense of their own emotional, psychosocial, and cultural dilemmas.*

Becoming multicultural is more than a cognitive process of acquiring knowledge about diverse cultures; it also encompasses developing cross-cultural attitudes, values, beliefs, and communicative dispositions. As Lisa Delpit (1995) argues, crossing cultural boundaries requires more than just respectful listening. It means learning how to hear, of suspending judgment while we consider other people's perceptions and understandings on their own terms, of imaginatively entering their social reality. Thus, the fourth principle for practice is to *consider what you learn about ethnic diversity within appropriate cultural contexts.*

Multicultural education produces varying degrees of cultural and psychic disequilibrium. We must anticipate the resistance of some students to addressing issues of cultural democracy and social injustice. Students will occupy a range of positions along a continuum of acceptance and refusal in accordance with the degree to which their core beliefs, knowledge, and experiences are challenged. One of the greatest joys of multicultural teaching is witnessing the heightened sense of freedom that students experience when they gain the personal and intellectual confidence to challenge dominant values, attitudes, and beliefs. The fifth principle for practice is that in breaking through barriers of received truth about ethnic and cultural diversity, we must learn (and teach students) to *develop self-confidence coupled with strong feelings of social responsibility and political efficacy.*

Some people respond to becoming multicultural by feeling guilty about their privileged position, feeling helpless in the face of such enormous injustices. This is a reasonable and understandable reaction to what feels like a Herculean task. My answer to this is: turn your privilege into social action. Nothing is gained by feeling guilty over an accident of birth. What matters is what you do with your privileges (being a teacher is itself a privilege!). A final principle of practice in becoming a multicultural person and educator is to *use our privileges not just for our own benefit but to contribute them to the collective struggle for a more equitable and just society.*

JOINING THE JOURNEY

Our multicultural journey is enriched when we seek out places where we are a minority and experience a disorienting sense of "outsiderness." Visiting or living in countries with different social and cultural traditions is the most powerful way of encountering cultural differences, but there are other ways to place yourself in unfamiliar worlds:

• To develop cross-cultural understanding, take academic classes that focus on the history and culture of different ethnic groups and participate in community-based cultural events. While living in New York City, for example, I attended the annual West Indian Day parade in Brooklyn, a gigantic carnival of fantastic costumes, glittering floats, and pounding rhythmic music. I frequented the Nyorican Poet's Café in the Lower East Side, which featured poetry slams and showcased a culturally diverse array of poetic voices. You might consider engaging in similar activities by identifying places and events where different ethnic groups gather. By participating in these events, you can observe the nuances of cultural diversity exhibited in everyday life.

• Participating in family rituals can facilitate cultural border crossing. I was given such an opportunity when Jewish friends invited me to their Passover seder, which helped me gain a better understanding of Jewish history and identity. When you attend weddings, religious rituals, birthday celebrations, and cultural ceremonies of other ethnic groups, examine the extent to which what you have learned about cultural differences in academic settings is exhibited in lived experiences.

• Record the feelings of cultural dissonance that you experience. Reflect on what you notice, and then ask yourself the following questions: What have I learned about my own culture and myself from the perspective of an outsider? Has the familiar begun to appear strange, and the strange familiar? Why is this so? How can I construct similar experiences with my students, and for what pedagogical purposes?

• Identify issues or behaviors among students, colleagues, friends, and yourself that are contrary to multicultural education. These might be ethnic prejudices, stereotyping, fears, discriminatory behaviors, or other forms of social injustice. Then develop a strategic plan for dispelling these behaviors that includes anticipated oppositions and what you will do to overcome them. In both identifying the problems and creating corrective plans of action, attend to knowledge, values, feelings, and actions related to ethnic and cultural diversity.

References

Alba, R. D. *Italian Americans: Into the Twilight of Ethnicity.* Upper Saddle River, N.J.: Prentice Hall, 1985.

Bigelow, B., and others (eds.). *Rethinking Our Classrooms: Teaching for Equity and Justice.* Milwaukee, Wisc.: Rethinking Schools, 1994.

Delpit, L. *Other People's Children: Cultural Conflict in the Classroom.* New York: New Press, 1995.

Freire, P. *Pedagogy of the Oppressed.* New York: Continuum, 1970.

Galeano, E. *Open Veins of Latin America: Five Centuries of the Pillage of a Continent.* New York: Monthly Review Press, 1973.

Gallo, P. J. *Old Bread New Wine: A Portrait of the Italian-Americans.* Chicago: Nelson-Hall, 1981.

Gramsci, A. *Selections from the Prison Notebooks.* (Quintin Hoare and Geoffrey Nowell Smith, eds. and trans.). New York: International Publishers, 1971.

Greene, M. *Landscapes of Learning.* New York: Teachers College Press, 1978.

Kafka, F. *Metamorphosis.* New York: Vanguard Press, 1947.

Pai, Y. (1990). *Cultural Foundations of Education.* Old Tappan, N.J.: Macmillan, 1990.

Parenti, M. *Democracy for the Few.* (4th ed.) New York: St. Martin's Press, 1983.

CHAPTER THREE

Crystallizing
My Multicultural
Education Core

Carolyn W. Jackson

D evelopments and discoveries in my multicultural
journey are analogous to the crystallizing process and grading system
of diamonds. A diamond's value is determined by its clarity, carat
weight, cut, and color (also known as the 4C's). Combined with the
crystallizing process, these 4C's are metaphorical symbols of the continuous process of growth, understanding, endurance, and change that
are occurring in my personal, professional, and academic multicultural
knowledge, ideologies, and practices. Each of the 4C's is a synergistic
metaphor for my process of becoming multicultural.

In this exploration, I am symbolizing the process of becoming
clearer and stronger in my knowledge of and commitments to multicultural education. It is somewhat like a diamond that can cut through
mirrors, smokescreens, and glass by making positive incisions in negative reflections and encounters. The metaphor of a diamond, the
hardest and strongest of all minerals and gemstones, speaks to the
strength involved in becoming and being a skillful multicultural person and educator. Whereas the diamond is complete at the point of
discovery and its qualities only have to be recognized and assessed, as
a multicultural educator, I am still in the process of becoming. I am

trying to shape my knowledge and skills in the way of diamonds by making them strong, clear, enduring, and luminous.

THE CRYSTALLIZING PROCESS

The core of a good multicultural educator crystallizes (in the sense of becoming clearer and stronger) as new critical perspectives are researched, examined, and incorporated into learning, understanding, and teaching. As I strive for personal and professional development, I am engaging with historical experiences, cultural origins, ideological precedents, and illustrative practices that are illuminating my core. This core is culturally and racially mixed. At its essence, it is Baptist, Black, African American, and woman. Crystallizing is difficult to describe because it is an evolving and experiential process that involves continuous change.

I know of novice and veteran educators who attempt to understand and implement principles and practices of multicultural education by reducing them to recipes, formulas, holidays, heroes, and hypersensitive acts of political correctness. My peers and I regularly discuss how many teacher education students just want us to give them a multicultural education formula so they can do it for a day or two and move on. Yet there are no simplistic formulas that can duplicate or substitute for the transformative aspects of becoming actively and effectively involved in multicultural education. It requires critical understanding of connections among self, schools, home, and culture, and dealing with sociopolitical realities about ethnic and cultural diversity within society and schools (Macedo, 1994; Nieto, 1996). These goals represent what I am aiming for in my multicultural education journey.

If the intense pressures and complicated nature of our sociopolitical lives are understood, then there is no room for simplistic recipes that promote only ethnic holidays and heroes. The diamond metaphor illustrates this point. The core of a diamond consists of pure carbon that is crystallized under a combination of extremely intense pressures and very high temperatures that only nature can create. Despite attempts to reproduce these unique and natural combinations, people have been unsuccessful in capturing the essence and authenticity of a natural diamond when creating replicas (Walker, 1989). Synthetic products do not possess the same radiance and quality that nature produces.

Like the crystallizing process that creates authentic diamonds, there is no way to generate a recipe for becoming a good multicultural educator. It is a complex social, political, academic, personal, cultural, and pedagogical process that is cultivated over time.

MULTICULTURAL CLARITY

An essential part of my multicultural journey is striving for clarity and understanding of myself in relation to my gender, familial, ethnic, cultural, and racial backgrounds. I am examining the roles that these characteristics and contexts play in the private and public spheres of my life.

The clarity of a diamond is influenced by inclusions that can be thought of as internal birthmarks. Inclusions have the potential to interfere with the path of light that travels through a diamond, diminishing its radiance and sparkle and ultimately its value. Inclusions also may contribute to a diamond's illumination and beauty (Gubelin, 1974). Transferring these ideas to my multicultural journey suggests that I must examine the internal and external "birthmarks," or influences that shape my beliefs and behaviors about multicultural issues and ideas. If I do not do this, I will diminish the value of myself and others, and my ability to teach to and about ethnically and culturally diverse groups.

One of my internal birthmarks is my identity as a military dependent. It is a facet of my life that is not readily visible, but this experience has shaped some of my perspectives. The following reflections represent snippets of emerging clarity for me about how being a member of a military family influenced my becoming multicultural.

Stepping Outside My Context

I remember a situation that occurred shortly after my family left the military. I was in middle school and living in a civilian community. I visited my cousin, and we went to a movie. At first, everything seemed normal. My cousin and I had paid our admission to the movies, purchased our snacks, and found seats. As the lights went down and the curtains parted, I placed my snacks in the holder and stood up: I knew that the U.S. flag would appear on the movie screen accompanied by the national anthem, and I was ready. But suddenly I realized that my cousin wasn't standing (in fact, she looked as if she was refusing to stand), and she was looking at me as if I was some alien being. When I took my eyes off my cousin to look at the screen, I realized that the flag had not appeared and that the national anthem was not piping through the speakers. I remember thinking that there were going to be serious repercussions for the person who had omitted the flag and national anthem for the sake of coming attractions. I remained standing and looked for allies who shared in my dismay, but there were none. Finally, my confusion turned to embarrassment, and I sat down.

Had I experienced a cultural collision? When and how had I become such a creature of habit? What other inclusions had military living implanted in my core, and how did these affect my interactions?

Later, of course, I realized that civilian theaters did not practice the patriotic military procedures that were familiar to me. But at the time I went to that movie with my cousin, I had not begun to understand why I had so diligently accepted and followed numerous patriotic military procedures. Nor had I made the distinction between a stationary civilian lifestyle and a highly mobile military lifestyle. As I began to recognize more differences between my experiences and those of others, my questions and observations altered my preconceived ideas.

Other things began to happen as well. During one conversation with my new peers, who were not from military families, I asked a girl named Mary if she was Catholic or Protestant. When she answered, "Episcopalian," I was dumbfounded and for a brief moment, I thought that she was speaking another language or did not understand my question. The simplistic solutions and divisions of Catholic and Protestant military church services had been my template, but they did not necessarily bring immediate clarity for me in the civilian world.

Religious customs, familial ties, relationships, experiences, affiliations, and cultural beliefs are types of inclusions that need to be carefully examined when I think about how and what I understand about my ethnically diverse students and myself. Relying solely on assumptions based on media portrayals and inaccurate sources can only hinder my crystallizing process.

Changing Phases and Places

This process of knowing, thinking, and reflecting began to intensify as I faced interior and exterior struggles in a new nonmilitary environment. It was my first time living in a neighborhood that was middle class as well as racially and ethnically diverse. My father was an officer in the army, and our family had lived in areas on military bases that were predominantly European American and middle class. The schools that I attended were racially and ethnically mixed, but our immediate neighborhoods on various military posts were not. Moreover, we had not lived near our relatives.

As I began to adjust to school in a new environment, I noticed that many of my civilian classmates were surrounded by extended family. I also discovered that many of my classmates had known each other since kindergarten or first grade. My classroom was racially and ethnically diverse, but I was unable to explain why I did not quite fit in with any particular group. When I had moved in the past, I had been able to weave in and out of culturally diverse groups. But now, new questions and new dilemmas began to emerge. Was this happening because of me, my identity, the new civilian environment, or because I was becoming more cognizant of racial and ethnic differences and alliances? In some ways, I had framed relationships through a military-civilian lens. I had not begun to think of race and ethnicity in very complex ways. I wanted to continue to weave in and out of different groups without jeopardizing my African American membership card. But I found that racial and ethnic affiliations began to carry more significant meaning for my classmates and me.

In retrospect, my youthful core was feeling the intense pressures of crystallizing, and I did not realize that this was only the beginning. Now I know that I was probably starting to come of age ethnically, as Gay (1994) explains: "Although some variations exist by ethnic groups and age, the general pattern of ethnic identity development begins with self-ethnic unawareness, denial, or disaffiliation. It then progresses through increasing levels of consciousness, pride, affirmation, and acceptance of the validity and worth of one's own ethnic culture and heritage" (p. 152).

Achieving Clarity as a Multicultural Educator

As a multicultural educator and human being, I strive for clarity in my knowledge, teaching, personal values, and practices. I do this by examining my perceptions of authenticity and self through explorations of perspectives, explanations, and insights gleaned from a wide variety of knowledge sources. I read and explore fiction and nonfiction books by ethnic-specific and cross-cultural writers. For instance, I read books and articles that feature historical activists (Duster, 1970), invisible entertainers (McBride, 1995), medical specialists (Carson, 1990), social and coming-of-age themes (Gaines, 1993; Yep, 1975), and a variety of schooling and familial experiences (McCluskey and Smith, 1999; McCourt, 1996; Qoyawayma, 1964; Soto, 1985; Tan, 1989).

These stories and testimonies demonstrate social and personal acts that have benefited immediate communities and significantly contributed to society. I also seek out nonmainstream media forms, such as independent and international films, documentaries, and news resources (through the World Wide Web) to gain a wider knowledge base about ethnically and culturally diverse perspectives on social issues. Visiting museums and art galleries provides me with emotionally stirring and thought-provoking experiences. I remember visiting a Jacob Lawrence exhibit and staring at the "Legend of John Brown" series of paintings. The story of a White abolitionist who was hanged for leading covert missions that supported freedom for Black slaves unfolded before me. Each painting in the series represented a piece of oral history that Lawrence captured in his artwork. For me, this legend was a stark and vivid reminder that freedom fighters come in many hues.

When attending museums and galleries, I often critique the captions, summations, and historical accounts against what I have read, heard, or experienced. I recall visiting a local historical and cultural museum that featured a "Pacific Voices" exhibit about the historical experiences of Native Americans in the Northwest. I examined the ways in which language was used to describe social tensions, political power, and policies. I viewed countless recollections of indigenous men and women discussing how their customs, teachings, ceremonies, stories, and languages were banned. Although the exhibit represented several generations and was informative, I noticed that manifest destiny, colonialism, racism, and the need to "civilize" were never clearly named. Instead, euphemisms mentioned difficult times with treaty making and the U.S. government. I interpreted some of these watered-down captions as attempts to appeal to a mainstream audience.

I continue to search for resources at events, museums, and galleries that will increase my multicultural knowledge base or point me in an inquisitive direction. I enjoy attending cultural, familial, and community events such as powwows, gospel music extravaganzas, interdenominational events, and ethnic-specific and multicultural dance and theater presentations. During these ceremonies and events, I often wonder what history lies behind the regalia and costumes. What are the performers and producers sharing about their own culture and family legacy that I might be misinterpreting through my own lens? What have they had to endure and survive? How do our experiences overlap and differ? What familial and personal contexts have played pivotal roles in their lives? In my metaphor, these ancestral, historical, and contemporary influences that I inquire about are analogous to the carat weight of diamonds.

MULTICULTURAL MODELS AND MENTORS

Carat weight cannot be omitted from the equation when determining the size and value of a diamond. Similarly, specific persons and experiences that continue to influence my perspectives and practices cannot be excluded from my multicultural journey. I am reminded and inspired by Meltzer (1994), who suggests that we have extraordinary things to learn about history and ourselves from ordinary people and in their own words: "History isn't only the kings and presidents and generals and superstars. If we search the records deep and wide enough we can find evidence of what the anonymous ones have done and continue to do to shape history. They struggle to survive, they take their lives into their own hands, they organize and agitate to make America realize its promise" (p. 69).

There are anonymous ones in my presence, and they form a profound part of my past, present, and future. As I think about carat weight and significant scenarios in my life, my family's move to New Jersey comes immediately to mind. I recall that our temporary civilian environment was becoming more permanent because our parents were not going to reconcile. We now lived close to my mother's family, and I began to develop meaningful relationships with my cousins, grandparents, aunts, and uncles. It was like discovering a part of myself that I had not known was missing. I had known extended family members from visits, telephone calls, and photographs, but to be with them relatively regularly provided keys to my family history and herstory that I had not begun to understand or embrace fully.

For instance, I learned that a series of historical events and policies had provided women in our family with opportunities that had been unavailable to previous generations. During the Korean War, two major telephone companies changed their hiring practices and began to employ African Americans. My mother and two of her sisters were part of a group of women who were hired. The youngest of my aunts obtained her doctorate in nursing when she received funding through President Lyndon Johnson's initiatives in the 1960s to support ethnic minorities in higher education. My grandmother went back to school and received her nursing degree when she was in her fifties. I remember some of their conversations about the racial tensions that existed in their work and school environments because many people made it clear that they did not want "coloreds" in their presence. My multicultural crystallizing began when I contemplated those persons who resisted equal opportunity practices and saw race before anything else.

We also began to reconnect with Miller Memorial Baptist Church in Philadelphia, the church that my mother and her sisters had attended from childhood through adulthood. We did not attend regularly and we were not members, but we went for a variety of special events and celebrations, such as Women's Day and Men's Day. These events were always inspirational to me because they featured men and women who were implementing plans and projects to improve the educational and life experiences of youth and elders in the church and surrounding community.

During our drives to Philadelphia, my mom often showed us her old neighborhoods and told us stories about people and families who lived there during her youth. She also reflected on growing up in the Richard Allen Projects, low-income housing complexes in Philadelphia. Some of her classmates had gone on to become change agents in the community and the nation; others were caught in the violence and the circumstances that accompanied poverty in the city and died too young. Although I did not articulate it at the time, I began to think seriously about issues of access and discrimination and the influence they have had on so many lives.

After church, older church members told us stories about my grandparents and great grandparents, as well as my mother and aunts. The elders of the church described an era when Black ministers worked together for social and political change and to uplift our cultural communities. At the time, ministers as political activists were something new for me to contemplate and hear about firsthand. Later, I came to realize that this was not unusual, at least in the African American historical legacy. Some of the elders felt that things had really changed in regressive directions and that struggle and uplift were becoming increasingly more difficult.

I began to understand how much our family legacy was tied to this church. My great grandfather, Wilkens E. Jones, had been a community leader and pastor of Miller Memorial during its early years. After his death, my Great Uncle John succeeded him and continued to lead the church and assist in the surrounding community. But not all congregational members shared Uncle John's vision and direction for the church; they left Miller Memorial and formed another church in Philadelphia, Jones Memorial (named after my great grandfather). Decades passed before any other of my relatives officially led the church. Then in the mid-1990s, my cousin Wilkens O. Jones was chosen to pastor Miller Memorial into the new millennium.

All of these realizations gradually helped me to begin to crystallize my multicultural core. As long as I can remember, photographs of my Great Grandfather Wilkens and Uncle John hung at the front of the church near the balcony. Now I began to notice them not merely as valued family members but as something greater than themselves, as symbolic of a greater tradition, movement, and context. I began wondering what I could learn about broader issues of ethnic and cultural diversity by developing a better understanding of and appreciation for my forebears. I would eventually come to know that my ministerial relatives and their leadership activities were in line with such legendary luminaries in African American history (although not on such a grand scale) as Richard Allen, Martin Luther King Jr., Jesse Jackson, Barbara C. Harris, and Vashti McKenzie.

My parents had shared African American and family history with me before, but gradually new meanings began to emerge. My father stressed the value of seeing humanness within everyone. He rigorously questioned us about any derogatory remarks that we may have heard or repeated inside or outside our household. I cannot pinpoint one particular moment of discovery, but the following poem highlights several revelations that occurred over time and brought cultural diversity within my personal experiences into sharper focus:

> At first glance, it was a cultural collision
> Previously, countless relocations, and military divisions
> Sibling bonds with loving and playful rivalry
> as we woke up to the sounds of reveille.
> Freezing, stopping, standing, during retreat—
> the lowering of the flag at sunset brought us to our feet.

Now, the salutes and flags were gone.
How much longer would this go on?
The divorce became final,
now a new plan for survival.
A different time, a different place,
a new understanding of my race
towards crystallizing at my own pace.

Wade in the water, a historical scene.
Full immersion, I had never seen.
Down went my brother in the baptism pool.
These were things I didn't learn about in school.
Lessons from congregational members who
knew my folks before I was even a life—
they recognized me as I beheld our struggles and strife.
Was it my ancestors' flair that showed in the contours
of my face, my eyes, my spirit, my hair?
My ancestors, they were calling me for real.
My spirit came alive with more fervor and zeal.
My great grandfather and great uncle smiled at me
for they knew I was beginning to embrace our legacy.

Anxious to learn more—lessons from the pulpit.
Put away childish things or be the culprit.
Have the faith of a child and even the size of a mustard seed.
The lessons reiterated that all humans are really in need
of security, acceptance, justice, and love
Be not misled, put on your armor and don't cower
We fight not against flesh and blood,
but against principalities and powers
of deceit, evil, hatred, indifference, and fear.
Be careful of what goes in your ears.

Parables of judgment and compassion for a saint or a nemesis
Women and men, multiple ethnicities—starting in Genesis
Looking for guidance and my mission
Helped me to get started and take a position
And facets of my core began to glisten
With every hymn, and every word I listened.

New friendships of brothers and sisters of great diversity
From the city, the "burbs", the country, and university
Interactions with family, growing stronger than ever
Lessons from the pulpit extended beyond being clever.

But the questions came—What can I do? How can I help?
It is not enough just to be heart felt.
How can I support children who are often forgotten?
When I am so imperfect and my gifts still to be begotten
I would have to become a new creation
My cultural collision became a connection
Pointing me and my core in a different direction
A spiritual conviction has made a deep incision
In my heart, my soul, my mind and my vision
I'll continue to embrace my crystallizing multicultural core
Even when people tend to ask me why and what for?

This poem echoes some of Freire's thoughts (1970) on the significance of "reading the world" and "reading the word." He means that
"word and world" encompass the dynamic relationships that occur
when culture, language, written text, and personal experiences are
transformed into practices of social justice and political acts linked to
principles of democracy. These reflections on the world and the word
ring true for me as I become more involved in navigating my multicultural place and practices as both a person and an educator.

As I look back on earlier days, I recognize that although I have
embraced extended family ties, I have missed other opportunities with
family. My father was adopted and did not locate his biological father
until the latter part of the 1980s. Shortly afterward, our family was
invited to an eightieth birthday celebration for my newly found grandfather. I was uncertain about how my brothers and I would be received
by our new relatives. Anticipating this experience was somewhat like
venturing into learning about ethnic and cultural groups previously
unexplored. But everything went well with my new relatives. We had a
wonderful time, and I bonded with a cousin, Stephanie, who was a few
years older than me. We were open to learning as much as possible
about each other during the weekend celebration, and we intended to
keep in touch.

At the time, I did not fully appreciate or even understand the
deeper layers of meaning within our celebration. Later, my paternal

grandfather and I corresponded through a few letters. Since his death, I have not maintained steady contact with my paternal side of the family. Writing this chapter and trying to characterize my multicultural crystallizing process has inspired me to establish more meaningful ties with my paternal family members, who are a significant part of me. Becoming multicultural opens new avenues of insight into self and others, as well as developing commitments to act differently in cultivating self-expanding relationships and experiences.

As I reflect on my multicultural emerging, my thoughts blend, extend, and resonate with Freire and Macedo (1994). In particular, I am referring to Freire's recollection of his "first words" and the world of his first reading. He wrote, "In perceiving these [words, texts, and letters] I experienced myself and the more I experienced myself, the more my perceptual capacity increased. I learned to understand things, objects, and signs through using them in relationship to my older brothers and sisters and my parents" (p. 30).

I believe that as we continue to become multicultural, our relationships with family, friends, students, and colleagues lead to a better understanding of our own cultural symbols and codes and to valuing those of ethnically diverse groups. Valuing oral histories, relationships, and familial experiences is part of the self-knowing clarity that strengthens my core and facilitates my becoming multicultural. The knowledge, insights, and challenges I gain from them prepare me to endure the "cuts"—those constructive and negative criticisms, obstacles and opportunities—that are endemic to being a multicultural person and educator. Stated differently, what I learn from my personal past fortifies me to deal better with the broader challenges of multicultural teaching and living in the present and future.

DIAMOND CUTTING AND MULTICULTURAL CRAFTING

The cut of a diamond is carefully calculated and executed by the skill of a master craftsperson or lapidary. Multicultural educators, like lapidaries, must be careful and deliberate in how they contour the experiences of their students. But we do not make these decisions in isolation or alone. We are shaped by our students, colleagues, communities, and personal backgrounds. An uncut diamond is analogous to a rough stone, because its unique prism-like qualities cannot be seen until the cutter releases its sparkle and fire (Gubelin, 1974). Just as master craftspeople must be meticulous yet bold when they are cutting diamonds, multicultural educators have a similar mandate. As teachers, we have the responsibility to release the sparkle and fire of our students, but we should not predetermine their shape by basing our teaching practices on old, ineffective notions, or only on what we believe to be true.

Master craftspeople study diamonds thoroughly before they begin and continue to do so as they proceed through the cutting process. They know the irreparable damage that can be done to a potentially valuable gem if they make mistakes. As teachers, we must think similarly with our ethnically and culturally diverse students. They too are precious gems. We must know them well so that we minimize the risk of damaging them beyond repair with teaching techniques and curriculum materials that are insensitive to their cultural heritages, experiences, and perspectives. As Pang and Barba (1995) suggest, "Schools should be places that excite rather than inhibit learning of culturally diverse students. When children are not allowed to incorporate their prior knowledge with new experiences provided in the classroom, learning is slowed and the child constructs a disjointed view of the world" (p. 341).

The skilled lapidary and multicultural educator are both master craftspeople who must uncover ideal ways of bringing out the life and brilliance of their "gems." How they understand their own roles and perspectives of what and who are valued is just as significant as their intentions, skills, knowledge, values, and actions.

Some of Spindler and Spindler's ideas (1994) about becoming multicultural apply to my own developmental process. They suggest that we need to delve deeper into our own backgrounds and experiences to see how we value or disenfranchise culturally and ethnically diverse groups. Becoming multicultural also requires that we build our critical understanding skills.

This understanding did not make things easier for me when I began to put these theories into practice. When I started teaching a multicultural class to preservice teachers and noneducation undergraduates, I was nervously excited, and my stomach was in knots during the first class meetings. My students would probably never believe that sometimes it was just as difficult for me to initiate discussions on historical untruths, racism, issues of access, discrimination, and privilege as it was for them to accept them. I was the first African American female instructor for many of my students. I felt a tremendous responsibility to represent women and people of color in general, and African Americans in particular. I was teaching at an institution where a campuswide multicultural course requirement had been rejected amid heated debate. I did not welcome the tension that this political climate and my course content yielded, but I believed that multicultural knowledge and skills were necessary for teachers to address because children's lives were at stake.

The first assignment I gave the students was inspired by my reading Hollins (1996). She recommended that preservice teachers construct their own personal histories to make more meaningful connections with the human experiences, prejudices, and discriminations of others. The initial required readings included explanations of ethnic identity development and constructing personal histories with the use of surnames. I also provided my students with a few other articles and book chapters to guide the creation of their own autobiographies (Hajela, 1997; Howard, 1996; Ling, 1995). In addition to researching their surname, I asked them to write about their cultural traditions, exposure to ethnic diversity, and challenges they anticipated in their own classrooms with teaching culturally diverse students.

Most of the students seemed intrigued by their autobiography assignment. A few told me that they were not quite sure what I wanted because they were "just White," but they were willing to work through the uncertainties. At the end of the first day of class, one European American female student approached me and angrily stated words to this effect: "I celebrate Christmas just like everybody else! My parents wanted me to go to this university since birth just like everybody else! And I am White, just like everybody else in this class. I resent you making this autobiography assignment a racist issue." She stormed out of the room, leaving behind the syllabus that I had spent hours preparing. The few lingering students looked shocked, but they did not say anything. Less than a week later, I received notice that she had dropped my class. This student's defensive reaction indicated to me that perhaps her existing assumptions about the universality of her cultural customs and beliefs had become even more ingrained.

It was hard to distance myself from this situation and other resistances like it. I tried not to view every attack or act of opposition as a personal assault, but it was difficult not to, and dealing with them was exhausting. My intentions were to represent the principles and practices of multicultural education appropriately so all my students would embrace them, but at times the resistance was overwhelming.

I struggled with how to achieve balance in multicultural education. I provided my students with an array of readings that represented variety within and among European American, African American, Latino American, Asian American, and Native American groups. I used excerpts and stories from individuals, case studies, and anthologies of multicultural voices. My resources came from social science and education, historical and contemporary analyses, and personal experiences of men and women. In addition, I urged my students to expand their knowledge base by confronting their tendency to overemphasize contributions from athletes and entertainers of color.

Still, some of the students believed that the examples that I used were negative and blaming European Americans for everything. Others questioned the credentials and qualifications of authors and researchers such as Wade Boykin, Sonia Nieto, Valerie Pang, Eugene Garcia, Stacey Lee, Peggy McIntosh, and Ronald Takaki, who write about marginalized people, cultural affirmation, ethnic identity, privilege, deficit theories, social disadvantages, equality, and inequitable practices. Some students revealed in their reflections and class discussions that they had never considered cultures, identities, policies, legacies, economics, and perceptions of entitlement as significant factors that affect the quality of education that students receive. They admitted that their views about the value of multicultural education were being challenged, and they expressed gratitude.

I really was not sure how to address the students who were resisting discussions and reflections related to race, class, gender, and social injustices. I told my students that it was easier to talk about similarities, but we had to come to terms with our assumptions about differences because our actions and reactions were based on our preconceived ideas. I remember coming home and frequently talking to my husband about how I had to keep working to achieve better understanding between my students and me. The reality that these future teachers could some day teach our children, our nieces and nephews, and the children of our friends and peers was sobering. I was convinced that shallow conversation and superficial knowledge of multicultural education were extremely damaging. From extensive discussions, readings, and personal interactions with colleagues, friends, and parents, it was clear to me that cultural blinders and misinformation have serious consequences. I knew that a cultural misunderstanding or deficit assumption from a teacher or school administrator could cause any of our children to encounter life-

altering detours toward a history of expulsions or unwarranted assignments to special education tracks. These detours would ultimately lead
to personal self-doubt and tragic academic underachievement.

Eventually, I learned to find my own self-validation and renewal
from colleagues and mentors who were more than willing to listen,
empathize, and provide advice or encouragement. Key professors
helped me to understand what was happening in my classroom. One
told me that my responsibility as a multicultural educator was to agitate, for our children. She would often say, "Agitate, agitate, and
agitate some more" (G. Webb-Johnson, personal communication, fall
1997). As far as she was concerned, I was fulfilling my responsibility
because some students were trying so hard to focus on anything but
race, privilege, social responsibility, and injustice in education. She
explained that acts of resistance come in many forms, and it was up to
us to continue the struggle to combat them for the sake of all children.

Two other professors whom I greatly admire, Patricia Larke and
Gail Cannilla, shared some of their student resistance stories with me.
Their experiences gave me more defined contours for making sense
of my own multicultural teaching experiences. They helped me realize
that if I chose to move forward, my core would have to get stronger. I
also recognized that I would have to increase my multicultural knowledge base and pedagogical skills. Their support illustrated that
alliances were a vital part of my multicultural strengthening and crystallizing process.

In preparing for future classes, I reviewed themes and patterns that
emerged from some of my resisting students. I shared samples of them
with the entire class without naming the authors. I introduced newspaper articles and modern personal examples of racial hatred and various acts of discrimination. Some of the resources were from my
network of support; others I gathered on my own. Since their academic readings were not "real" enough for some of the students, I
thought it would be best for them to see that life and death instances
of racial discrimination and injustice occurred in contemporary times.
For example, we discussed the murder of twenty-seven-year-old
Vincent Chin. An unemployed auto worker, Richard Ebens, and his
nephew believed that Chin was Japanese and vented their jobless frustrations on him by beating him to death with a baseball bat (Ling,
1995). I brought in an article from the *Chicago Tribune* entitled "The
Crime of Shopping While Black" (Page, 1997), which discussed the unwarranted suspicion that is bestowed on shoppers who are Black or

Brown. This particular story was about three African American youth who won a lawsuit because they were falsely accused of shoplifting. I used articles and information that documented hate crimes and injustices from the Teaching Tolerance Series of the Southern Poverty Law Center. I gave personal examples of discriminating acts that have happened to me and others that I know.

I asked my students about the university's Legacy Scholarships, which provide financial support for students with generations of alumni family members. I wanted to know if they were aware of the history of how their university restricted the rights of White women in addition to students of color who wanted to attend their beloved institution. I asked them if they thought that these historical legacies and policies had any influence on current and future generations of individuals from these backgrounds. I also asked them how people who were legally prohibited because of race from attending this university benefited from a Legacy Scholarship. I wanted them to grapple with their conceptions of preferential treatment.

Many of these encounters and related questions were met with silence (another form of resistance), but some students did try to understand. I was striving to share issues of educational inequity and place them on our collective shoulders, as well as in our hearts, souls, and minds. My intention was to convey the idea that teaching and learning are cultural, social, political, and moral endeavors, not simply academic activities. I repeatedly asked students what they would do to make things more equitable by starting in their classrooms and in their communities. What were they willing to give up or to give? I wanted all of us to strive towards what Howard (1999) called personal consciousness.

COLOR IN DIAMONDS AND MULTICULTURAL EDUCATION

Diamonds are graded by color, and the most valued diamonds are those that are totally colorless. Multicultural education, however, vehemently opposes "decolorizing" and making students raceless. Instead, it advocates recognizing, respecting, valuing, and centering students' race, ethnicity, gender, and culture in teaching and learning.

While discussing colorlessness, I must note an example parallel to society's mainstream views of race. Mainstream society blindly and boldly benefits from the talents and skills of students, entertainers,

artists, athletes, civil servants, laborers ("blue collar"), and professionals ("white collar") of color. But they are often viewed suspiciously
when they step out of these contexts or places. One of the most vivid
examples of this irony involves the growing number of tragic deaths
and injuries of undercover African American police officers by their
uniformed colleagues. Charles and Coleman (1995) documented the
rise in cases of White police officers who see "Black before seeing blue."
They wrote, "Because of what they see as a fatal trend and not isolated
incidents as claimed by police authorities, many Black law enforce-
ment officials have been clamoring for reform of training methods,
closer scrutiny of police culture and investigations by federal authorities" (p. 28).

This problem is not limited to police officials. Others in positions of
power and privilege hold the personhood of people of color hostage
when we are perceived as a threat based on pervasive stereotypes and
racial prejudices. Our human dignity is attacked, and our lives are
often threatened, and sometimes violently and unjustly taken from us.
Frequently, the message from society is that those who are "colorless"
are most valued, while those with "color" have little or no value at all.
Thus, current conversations about "racelessness," shopping while
Black, and racial profiling (or DWB, that is, driving while Black or
Brown) are increasingly prominent in certain circles and in the media.

Highly esteemed "colorlessness" also is advocated by well-meaning
educators who advocate maintaining a color-blind perspective in a
race-conscious society. I have heard many teachers proclaim that they
do not see color. What do they really mean? Does a color-blind perspective propose that we value a person when we perceive his or her
racial or ethnic identity as irrelevant to whom the person is and how
he or she might be perceived in society? What kind of social reality
does this point of view suppose? Does a color-blind perspective
absolve educators from the responsibility of using curriculum
resources that reflect culturally, racially, and ethnically diverse experiences? As I ask these questions, Schofield's Wexler study (1997)
comes to mind. After examining contexts and relationships in an
interracial middle school, with faculty members who embraced a philosophy of color blindness, she concluded that a color-blind perspective "fosters an environment in which aversive racists, who are basically
well intentioned, are prone to act in a discriminatory manner. Further
it makes it unlikely that opportunities inherent in a pluralistic institution will be fully realized and that the challenges facing such an

institution will be dealt with effectively" (p. 267). A multicultural educator acts as a true connoisseur of gemstones who values every gem (student) for its unique beauty, facets, and origins.

During my second year of college, I attended a cultural studies lecture sponsored by an interdenominational organization. I was the only African American in a room that seated approximately two hundred people, and the room was packed. I was engaged with the speaker throughout his lecture and found his words somewhat interesting. The speaker began to talk about research based on eye contact. Suddenly, he (a European American) turned his full body toward me and made gestures in my direction as he said something like, "Blacks don't maintain eye contact when someone is speaking to them." I was stunned. Were his actions (and underlying assumptions) really necessary? When did I give him permission to put me in the spotlight? I wondered, *Do I look away and prove his theory, or do I stare him down before an entire crowd of people?* I really couldn't tell you how long I looked back at him, but eventually, I looked down to avoid his gaze. I wanted him to stop staring at me. I felt so terribly uncomfortable and did not enjoy the unsolicited spotlight.

His research and explanations did not reflect my experiences. My mom always firmly said, "Don't walk away from me when I am talking to you," and "Look at me when I am talking to you." To me, that meant giving her respect and indicating that I was not distracted by anything else. Did this mean that I was not truly African American or Black enough (a question that I wrestled with when my differences were pointed out)? Suddenly, I had trouble believing or accepting everything else that the lecturer had said about several other ethnic and cultural groups. It was easy to accept most of his information until my experience was called into question. For a while afterward, I became critical and skeptical of all research about ethnic and cultural diversity.

In retrospect, this represented a crystallizing experience for me. As I characterize my becoming a multicultural educator, it reminds me to be very careful about how I interpret and relay information about ethnically diverse groups. It is imperative that I examine the contexts and kinds of questions and assumptions that are present in the research literature. For instance, does the researcher already assume a deficit posture when talking about a particular group of students? Does the research study suggest a pervasive or underlying theme of blaming the victim? Does the study value input from the group being studied, or are observations merely interpreted without the group's contribution? Are learning styles dogmatically and emphatically portrayed with no context? Who in the study is expected to do most of the accommodating, and why? As I traverse the multicultural path, I recognize that it is important to continue to develop my own criteria and refine my grading scale for research and resources that I select to represent culturally diverse groups.

As an aspiring multicultural educator and scholar, I wonder in what ways I might be graded by my students and colleagues (of color and European American) because of my hue and all that it symbolizes. What kinds of questions and acts of resistance might my students display because I am an African American woman introducing them to multicultural education and engaging them with racism and social justice? Are the encounters of African American males different from mine? How do these challenges compare with males and females from other ethnic groups? How can I successfully convey the power and beauty of understanding and honoring the racial, ethnic, cultural, and social diversity among people? Asking these kinds of questions is as important in becoming and being multicultural as how they are answered.

PRINCIPLES FOR PRACTICE

Multicultural educators should begin their processes of becoming by critically examining their own identities, personal practices, cultural biases, instructional materials, and interpretations of the value of multicultural education. Four other principles can be extracted from the discussion in this chapter.

The first principle is that *multicultural transformation begins in many places, such as communities, classrooms, schools, and especially within ourselves and in the ways we choose to value and approach our students.* As we strive to become multicultural, it is imperative to understand the tremendous influence of our behavior on our students. Media and other societal influences also can be perpetuated or critiqued within our classrooms. There are transformative opportunities in how we respond to and interact with students, as well as how we present instructional materials. Other multicultural transformations may range from classroom climate to total school climate; political correctness to personal consciousness; self-ethnic unawareness to self-knowing; classroom action to social action; and supplementary single-subject multicultural education to full infusion of culturally relevant materials in all subjects. As we become more confident in our understanding of and commitment to multicultural education, we will be able to create larger connections across disciplines and beyond the classroom. Multicultural educators should not attempt to transform alone. Feedback from an array of sources and a variety of people is essential to this evolving process.

The sparkle of multicultural educators will diminish quickly if we do not cultivate ways to access networks of support. In doing this, we should look to the progenitors of the field and foster mentoring relationships among researchers, scholars, teacher educators, and students. We need to create alternatives to solely rewarding individual accolades. The second principle is that *by practicing collaboration in our personal and professional multicultural development and critical reflection, we learn to investigate our own cultural assumptions and frames of reference.* Technology may be able to assist with these needed collaborations through e-mail, chatrooms, videoconferencing, and multicultural Web sites. Cooperative learning is not simply a learning style for students; it is an avenue for growth and strength for teachers as well. When practiced appropriately, it leads to clearer understandings of social issues, histories, attitudes, and values. It also facilitates the inclusion of culturally affirming materials and multiple perspectives into our learning and teaching.

For clarity, we need to remind ourselves constantly why we are committed to the principles and practices of multicultural education. Practicing multicultural education in any environment is intellectually rigorous and personally demanding. Thus, the third principle is that *cultivating a commitment to multicultural education blends personal development with professional development, and extends beyond existing instructional materials, knowledge, and techniques.* This is true for multicultural educators as well as the students whom we teach and mentor. Because there is much opposition to and misconceptions about multicultural education, leaders in the field must be committed to understanding its authentic research, philosophies, and practices thoroughly. The commitment involves modeling for students, colleagues, family, and friends how to gain more resources and information about academic, political, and social injustices in schools and in society. The influence that this knowledge has on our personal and professional development is profound.

The fourth principle is that as multicultural educators, *we must abandon the use of simplistic recipes for learning and monolithic representations of people based on their cultural backgrounds, physical appearances, and intellectual abilities.* In addition to considering intergroup diversity, we should be concentrating on intragroup diversity. Diversity within groups can be identified when we critically examine our own and others' inclusions. For nonmainstream students in particular, generational influences, home and host country affiliations, geographical history, socioeconomic status, and exposure to mainstream values, languages, and mores are significant factors that contribute to the sociocultural adjustments that they make in schools and society. Authenticity also alludes to a balance of strength, tenacity, and humility as multicultural educators learn from their own mistakes, miseducation, and reeducation. Cultivating transformation, collaboration, commitment, and authenticity are challenging but worthy tasks. The long-term rewards outweigh the consequences of not using culturally affirming approaches in educating present and future generations of ethnically diverse students.

JOINING THE JOURNEY

The journey toward developing multicultural education competence starts in many places and develops in many different ways. Here are a few suggestions:

• Develop criteria for the instructional materials that you will use in your classroom. Determine how you will identify authentic and inauthentic representations of culturally diverse people, what resources you will use to justify your selection, and how you will incorporate multicultural education in all subjects. Locate research and contact persons in the field of multicultural education who can assist you with critiquing your criteria and selection process.

• Based on research, explain your understanding of differences between political correctness and personal consciousness. Look for examples of each in multicultural instructional materials and multimedia resources. Keep a portfolio of your observations and interpretations. Describe how you might use your observations and responses with teachers, administrators, and students.

• Design ways for students and teachers to examine and appreciate their own cultural and ethnic backgrounds. Create a journal or portfolio that lists examples of meaningful activities that can lead to cultural awareness. Select five of the activities to perform, and find purposeful and creative ways to introduce your activity and findings to colleagues, students, family, and friends. These might include demonstrations for teachers, peer briefings and exchanges, and presentations at professional conferences.

• Consider how you might create a network of support for multicultural educators. How would you ensure that your network includes an array of ethnically diverse men and women with varied experiences in their communities and in the teaching arena? Initiate and arrange a gathering of supporters. Create an agenda and vision for how to address major multicultural concerns and goals for this group. In planning the agenda, be sure to include information and activities that focus on multicultural knowledge, beliefs, feelings, and actions in personal living and classroom teaching.

• Collect some student and teacher case studies and critical incidents on a variety of multicultural issues, such as examples of racism, ethnic group affiliations, cultural border crossing, effects of culturally responsive teaching, and successful cross-cultural and interethnic group interactions. Interpret the contexts and your response from at least three perspectives that are different from your own. Make every effort to abandon deficit theories in your explanations, responses, and potential solutions. Ask a group of novice and veteran multicultural educators to create a collective forum to discuss some of the case studies. Videotape your session, and review it with the entire group.

References

Carson, B. *Gifted Hands: The Ben Carson Story.* Grand Rapids, Mich.: Zondervan Publishing House, 1990.

Charles, N., and Coleman, C. "Black and Undercover: White Officers See Black Before Seeing Blue." *Emerge,* 1995, 6, 24–30.

Duster, A. M. (ed.). *Crusade for Justice: The Autobiography of Ida B. Wells.* Chicago: University of Chicago Press, 1970.

Freire, P. *Pedagogy of the Oppressed.* New York: Continuum, 1970.

Gaines, E. *A Lesson Before Dying.* New York: Vintage Books, 1993.

Gay, G. "Coming of Age Ethnically: Teaching Young Adolescents of Color." *Theory into Practice,* 1994, *33,* 149–155.

Gubelin, E. "The Origin of Gemstones." In E. A. Heiniger and J. Heiniger (eds.), *The Great Book of Jewels.* Boston: New York Graphic Society, 1974.

Hajela, D. "Getting in Touch with Being White: It May Be a Myth That All European Immigrants Eagerly Assimilated." *Houston Chronicle,* Mar. 16, 1997, p. 40A.

Hollins, E. R. *Culture in School Learning: Revealing the Deep Meaning.* Mahwah, N.J.: Erlbaum, 1996.

Howard, G. R. "Whites in Multicultural Education: Rethinking Our Role." In J. A. Banks (ed.), *Multicultural Education, Transformative Knowledge and Action: Historical and Contemporary Perspectives.* New York: Teachers College Press, 1996.

Howard, G. R. *We Can't Teach What We Don't Know: White Teachers, Multiracial Schools.* New York: Teachers College Press, 1999.

Kunz, G. *The Curious Lore of Precious Stones.* New York: Dover, 1971.

Ling, A. "Footholds on an Icy Slope: One Chinese-American Story." In C. A. Grant (ed.), *Educating for Diversity: An Anthology of Multicultural Voices.* Needham Heights, Mass.: Allyn & Bacon, 1995.

Macedo, D. *Literacies of Power: What Americans Are Not Allowed to Know.* Boulder, Colo.: Westview Press, 1994.

McBride, B. *Molly Spotted Elk: A Penobscot in Paris.* Norman: University of Oklahoma Press, 1995.

McCluskey, A. T., and Smith, E. M. (eds.). *Mary McLeod Bethune: Building a Better World: Essays and Selected Documents.* Bloomington: Indiana University Press, 1999.

McCourt, F. *Angela's Ashes: A Memoir.* New York: Scribner, 1996.

Meltzer, M. *Non-Fiction for the Classroom: Milton Meltzer on Writing, History, and Social Responsibility.* New York: Teachers College Press, 1994.

Nieto, S. *Affirming Diversity: The Sociopolitical Context of Multicultural Education.* (2nd ed.) White Plains, N.Y.: Longman, 1996.

Page, C. "Crime of 'Shopping While Black.'" *Chicago Tribune,* Oct. 19, 1997, p. 25.

Pang, V., and Barba, R. "The Power of Culture: Building Culturally Affirming Instruction." In C. A. Grant (ed.), *Educating for Diversity: An Anthology of Multicultural Voices.* Needham Heights, Mass.: Allyn & Bacon, 1995.

Qoyawayma, P. *No Turning Back.* Albuquerque: University of New Mexico Press, 1964.

Schofield, J. W. "Causes and Consequences of the Colorblind Perspective." In J. A. Banks and C.A.M. Banks (eds.), *Multicultural Education: Issues and Perspectives.* (3rd ed.) Needham Heights, Mass.: Allyn & Bacon, 1997.

Soto, G. *Living up the Street: Narrative Collections.* New York: Bantam Books, 1985.

Spindler, G., and Spindler, L. (1994). "What Is Cultural Therapy?" In G. Spindler and L. Spindler (Eds.), Pathways to *Cultural Awareness: Cultural Therapy with Teachers and Students.* Thousand Oaks, Calif.: Corwin, 1994.

Tan, A. *The Joy Luck Club.* New York: Putnam, 1989.

Walker, B. *The Book of Sacred Stones: Fact and Fallacy in the Crystal World.* New York: HarperCollins, 1989.

Yep, L. *Dragonwings.* New York: HarperCollins, 1975.

CHAPTER FOUR

Conversations with Transformative Encounters

Audra L. Gray

M y personal and professional journey toward becoming a multicultural educator involves a series of encounters that prompt ongoing conversations with others and myself. These encounters are interactions I have with others, my engaging with something I have read or seen, and my dealing with personal tensions and inquiries. An encounter is a "meeting" or connection between you and someone or something where an exchange takes place. It is an occurrence that results in thought, feeling, reflection, and action.

Encounters drive our daily interactions with new ideas and information, which lead to new meaning. Saxe (1991) suggests that "over time with repeated encounters, false starts, and efforts to come to terms with problems encountered over and over again . . . we transform what we already think we know into new thought domains" (p. 140). Many of my multicultural encounters are reoccurring and spiraling; they are previous provocations that resurface through persistent questions left unanswered. Each new encounter or revisiting of older ones sparks internal conversations around key issues and concerns that arise for me along my journey to be a good multicultural educator and person.

Having conversations with myself and others helps me to make sense of my worlds and engage in the reflective process. I engage in self-talk to help work through complex ideas, pose additional questions, and monitor and evaluate what I have come to understand and how I have come to understand it. The literal conversations I have with others serve the same purpose. In this sense, I am constantly engaging in conversations that inform me about my beliefs and my own thinking about how we interact with the world and with each other.

Four encounters in particular have triggered conversations that have helped to further my thinking about myself as a multicultural person and how I view multicultural teaching and learning.

SCHOOL DAZE

One of the first transformative encounters in my becoming a multicultural educator was a telephone call from one of my former grade school teachers, Ms. Butler, which prompted me to deconstruct my earlier school experiences. Over the years, we had stayed in touch (typically by mail) while I was away at school, and when I came home, I always visited her. Her call was a surprise more by the form of contact than anything else.

Our conversation started out as they always did. We asked about one another's families, and Ms. Butler asked about school. She listened and commented on how proud she was of my accomplishments. We shared a few laughs, and she filled me in on some of my fellow classmates who also kept in touch with her. Ms. Butler had become an administrator in a school with a lot of ethnically diverse students, so I asked her how that was going and if she missed classroom teaching. She responded by saying that what she missed most was interacting with students in ways other than as the primary disciplinarian. As a teacher, Ms. Butler had had a reputation among students for being tough. She had a distinctive way of calling the names of students caught misbehaving in a stern and forceful way that nevertheless seemed loving and caring to me—somewhat like a mother might call to her children to keep them from doing something they had no business doing.

That evening, Ms. Butler began telling me about a recent meeting she had with parents. Several parents were upset and concerned that their children always seemed to be in trouble or complained about the school. Many of the children felt they were always isolated from situations, the only ones being punished, and were not given a chance to explain themselves. Ms. Butler was obviously frustrated by these circumstances.

Although I was concerned for her obvious pain, my mind raced ahead and began to focus on the students. I recalled research and writings by Nieto (1994), Donaldson (1994), and Steele (1997) about the negative effects of racism and marginality on the social adjustment in school and academic performance of students of color. Karen Donaldson's explanation especially came to mind: "If students of color do not feel safe, academically challenged, or included in the curriculum, they will not produce at their most efficient or creative capacity. With the burden of racism, many students of color tune out, burn out, act out, or drop out of school . . . it damages the self-esteem of students, as well as influences their educational motivation and feelings of belonging" (1994, p. 4).

The majority of the parents at the meeting with Ms. Butler were African American. Many of them were not satisfied with the responses given to their concerns, and they became agitated. Ms. Butler, who is European American, explained that she became increasingly frustrated as the conversation grew more accusatory. The parents brought up numerous incidents of their children coming home with stories of Ms. Butler's being mean and yelling at them in the halls. She assured the parents that her disciplinary actions were the same for all students. Nevertheless, the parents remained convinced that their children were not lying or exaggerating. No one's explanation was able to satisfy the other's concerns. Some of the parents suggested that the entire school, including Ms. Butler, was racist. Ms. Butler told me that she explained over and over that she was not a racist. "I am not a racist!" she repeatedly told me. The meeting ended without any resolution or comfort.

When Ms. Butler paused to signal that she was waiting for a response from me, I started out saying, "Well, you're not a racist, as if it's something I even need to state." I went on to say that I doubted if the parents truly felt that she personally was one either. But then I said, "On second thought, perhaps they do, especially if this is the first time you all are meeting under the escalation of these circumstances." I added that it sounded as if the meeting was emotionally charged from the outset, and those frustrations had to be resolved.

I ended by expressing my concern that neither side in the controversy heard what the other was saying, which was unfortunate because the concerns of both sides appeared to be legitimate and had some truth to them. Given that fact, my question to her (and other teachers as well) is, How do we proceed to build trust and credibility with the parents of ethnically diverse students?

This conversation with Ms. Butler unleashed (and continues to provoke) memories of other conversations I have had with myself and others about my earlier school experiences, particularly the junior and senior high school years. At the start of those years, my mother, sister, and I moved from our predominantly African American middle-class neighborhood in the Los Angeles metropolitan area to a predominantly European American dairy farm community approximately forty-five minutes from the city. Our new neighborhood had only two other African American families and one Latino family, and our school was approximately 10 percent Black and Latino with an even smaller number of other U.S. students of color (such as Samoan and Filipino). There was a single teacher of color, an African American male who taught computer science as an elective. The only other persons of color present were a few Latinas who worked in the cafeteria. Even as a seventh grader, I was aware of the lack of racial and ethnic diversity at my school and wondered about it, but I didn't dwell on it.

I was energetic and talkative in class and active on campus, and I built strong relationships with my teachers. While growing up (and even now), I gravitated toward older women who could offer answers to my questions that could not be found in textbooks. To find the answers to life's questions, I have engaged in conversations with older women in particular, peers from diverse backgrounds, my teachers and mentors. I don't know if this inclination stems from my socialization in African American culture, which gives high priority to oral discourse (Gay and Baber, 1987; Kochman, 1981); my investments in being a learner; or my individual personality traits. The following comments by Nell Noddings (1991) resonate with the oral discourse features of my learning style:

> Schools should become places in which teachers and students live together, talk to each other, reason together, take delight in each other's company. Like good parents, teachers should be concerned first and foremost with the kind of people their charges are becoming. My guess is that when schools focus on what really matters in life, the cognitive ends we are now striving toward in such painful and artificial ways will be met as natural culminations of the means we have wisely chosen [p. 169].

A few weeks into the eighth grade, my math teacher and the principal (two European American men) told me that since I was doing so well, I was being moved to Algebra I. I was welcomed by the teacher and told that I could sit anywhere. I immediately looked in the direction of the only other African American in the class and, pointing to the seat behind her, said, "I'll sit there." I often wonder why I made this apparently instinctive choice and whether it was a significant cultural signal. I also wonder what I would have done and how it would have affected me emotionally and otherwise if the teacher had vetoed my choice of seat.

The demographics of race and ethnicity play a prominent role in my reflective analyses of my middle and high school educational experiences. This is probably so because of the close relationship between these characteristics and school achievement as measured by grade point averages, class placements, attendance records, disciplinary referrals, and subsequent college matriculation (U.S. Department of Education, 2000). These certainly were present in my high school. The tracking system placed three African American students (two others and me) out of a graduating class of six hundred in honors or advanced placement classes across the core subject areas. Four of our classmates self-identified as Filipino, Chinese American, Indian, and Peruvian; everyone else was European American.

The high school I attended blended students from four or five junior high schools in the area. It included about 15 percent African American and Latino and 15 percent Asian/Pacific Islanders. Although the ethnic composition of the student population in the district's schools was increasing, the teachers did not mirror this change. I do not recall any of the core subject areas, except for language classes, being taught by teachers of color. I now know that the ethnic and racial representations in my high school are quite similar to teacher and student distributions nationwide.

The curriculum in my classes was fairly traditional, with no real attempt to incorporate multiple perspectives of knowledge or nonmainstream cultural information in any subject area. For example, my English classes included almost exclusively the Western European literary canon. Literature by authors of color was introduced by individual students or relegated to supplemental reading lists. Examples like this kept me aware of the few ethnically diverse students in my classes. Surely it wasn't a matter of scarcity since I saw quite a few others around school. As these issues at my school moved into the forefront of my internal and external conversations, they evoked questions of educational inequity and disproportionality.

The apparent glass ceiling for so many caused me great tension, particularly in relating to other African American students. My African American friends accused me of "acting white," but unlike the students in the studies conducted by Fordham and Ogbu (1986) and Fordham (1996), I did not sacrifice my African American friends or my academic achievement. Nor was I asked to do so by my peers (Hemmings, 1996). If anything, I became more intrigued by the source and meaning behind their accusation, and my peers and I talked openly about this prevailing tension. I eventually came to realize that the critique of me had less to do with my own inner psychological struggle, the validity of my ethnic affiliation, the desirability of academic achievement or lack thereof by my African American peers, or their lashing out at me personally. It was more of a response to the circumstances, stratification, and over- and underrepresentations that the educational (and social) system had created for and between us. I was a jock, so my school activities connected me to the school culture. My close friends were my classmates and teammates, who represented a mixture of students of color and European Americans. My primary social network, however, consisted of predominantly African Americans in school and the community.

There was a huge academic gap between the majority of African American students and myself in high school, although I stayed connected socially. At the center of that tension was my friendship with another African American, Shauna; both of us were categorized as successful students.

Over the years, Shauna and I have talked about various personal and systemic issues related to how we experienced junior and senior high school:

- Realizing that we were placed in an academic track beginning in junior high school that became a predetermined distinction and impenetrable barrier once we reached high school

- Never really seeing ourselves reflected in the curriculum in any subject area

- Recalling the racial tension, fights, and even riots, often along racial lines, that seemed to escalate each year and resulted in mostly the Latino and African American males being stigmatized

- Our fond memories of the guidance and support we received from most of the teachers, coaches, counselors, and administrators

- Our frustration that so many of our African American peers appeared to be resisting that support
- Why there were so few African and Latino American students in honors, advanced placement, and college preparatory classes
- Our feelings that many of our peers (again mostly males) did not maximize their potential and that no one recognized their genius

All of these remembrances were triggered by the telephone conversation with Ms. Butler. I didn't know how to articulate why her story prompted the thoughts it did for me or how to connect my own thinking about my schooling to the broader issues of multicultural education. I wonder if she is aware of the position I was in as an African American student and the various ways I had to adjust to and negotiate my surroundings. Despite our being very close, I do not think that Ms. Butler is even aware of the many times I defended her to my African American peers when they called her mean or said she was always picking on students of color. Now I am beginning to wonder if Ms. Butler was as kind and caring as I thought she was. Maybe she treated me differently from other African American students, or that was what I wanted to believe, while other students saw reality.

Ms. Butler and I have never engaged each other in conversation about the differences in the educational experiences of students of color; how traditional schooling makes little attempt to be relevant for these students; how students of color are consistently asked to change and fit into a certain mold at the expense of leaving aspects of their ethnicity, culture, and experiences behind; how these dynamics are subtly and blatantly conveyed; how students resist and become resilient, or concede to pressures for conformity and become alienated from self; or how even the most successful students struggle to make sense of these dilemmas. These issues are deserving of serious external dialogue (as they are in my internal conversations) in our processes of becoming and being multicultural people and educators.

I AM NOT NAMED!

Working through an ongoing tension I have between my home discipline of educational psychology and whether it is adequately serving multicultural needs in my professional development is another encounter for me. I feel a pressing need to rethink some of the key principles of educational psychology using a multicultural education framework, particularly as they relate to improving the educational experiences of students of color. This encounter is centered on questions about what kinds of thinking and analytical processes we should undergo, questions we should raise, and actions we should take when we realize that our disciplinary or professional training is not a one-to-one fit with principles of multicultural education. For instance, what if we come to multicultural education from a background in history? Recent analyses of history textbooks show that historical understanding is still taught as definitive fact instead of variations in opinions, experiences, and perspectives (Wade, 1993; Cruz, 1994; Romanowski, 1996). Using a multicultural education framework in research and teaching will cause us to question traditional conventions of what is included in the subject matter we teach and the very nature of how we view knowledge.

A multicultural education framework for thinking about history may move you to view it as a collection of personal stories and accounts of individuals who are the "victors" and are empowered to tell their versions of events. This may cause you to raise additional questions: Whose stories are not being told, and why? Where are the equal representations of ethnically diverse people who make up historical events? What events were simultaneously going on in other nations that may or may not have had an impact on the growth of the United States? Answers to the last question would help us to understand that our own history did not occur in a vacuum. For example, creating a time line of concurrent historical events that show intersecting information that is typically taught separately in U.S. and world history classes would require the use of alternative historical texts such as *Before the Mayflower* (Bennett, 1993), *A Different Mirror: A History of Multicultural America* (Takaki, 1993), *Crossing Boundaries: Comparative History of Black People in the Diaspora* (Hine and McLeod, 1999), and *Behind the Trail of Broken Treaties: An Indian Declaration of Independence* (Deloria, 1974). It is consistent with Banks's description (1996) of transformative academic knowledge as one of "the major types of knowledge [that] can help teachers and curriculum specialists to identify perspectives and content needed to make the curriculum multicultural" (p. 8).

Another question I frequently wonder about is how different ethnic groups respond to what is often thought of as common cultural conceptual, symbolic, and iconic representations of the United States. For example, do the flag, the Pledge of Allegiance, and "The Star-Spangled Banner" evoke different responses among African, Native, Asian, Latino, and European Americans? What do immigrants from different countries think of these national symbols? How do factors of age, education, time, and location within and across ethnic groups affect reactions to them? Questions like these represent intellectual and experiential encounters that provoke internal and external conversations for me. They help me to become critically conscious about multicultural issues within multiple contexts. These dialogues and self-consciousness are key benchmarks in my becoming multicultural and ones that I will teach to my students.

These kinds of questions and insights about historical understanding are similar to the ones I am encountering in educational psychology. There are some critical disjunctures between its views of teaching and learning and those of multicultural education. Both make powerful conceptual claims about how we learn best, interact with the world, and relate to each other. For example, contemporary educational psychology claims that the thoughts and behaviors of individuals cannot be separated from their social and historical contexts. Through our interpersonal interactions, we make meaning of our worlds, selves, and others. Therefore, "individual thinking is [not] separate from the kinds of activities in which people engage and the kinds of institutions in which they are a part" (Rogoff and Chavajay 1995, p. 866). Individuals shape their environments as much as the environments shape them.

These claims are a way to begin understanding how learning occurs and new knowledge is created. However, some questions persist for me when I try to take the general claims of educational psychology and apply them to multicultural populations and issues. What is it that I mean by examining how students learn? How am I situating learning itself? Am I interested in achievement, the transfer of learning, and problem solving? How do the ethnic, racial, cultural, and social identities of individuals affect these learning processes? In other words, what does the idea of sociohistorical contexts within educational psychology mean in relation to teaching ethnic and cultural diversity (Portes, 1996)? I believe that learning is as general a process as it is highly specialized. I am consistently asking myself, "What are those conditions that make teaching and learning simultaneously general and unique?"

A central premise of multicultural education is that thoughts, beliefs, and behaviors cannot be removed from their cultural context.

According to Gay (2000), "Culture refers to a dynamic system of social values, cognitive codes, behavioral standards, worldviews, and beliefs used to give order and meaning to our own lives as well as the lives of others" (p. 29). In this sense, human thought and behavior can be understood only by how we are culturally socialized. As I work through multicultural and educational psychology frameworks to understand the processes of teaching and learning better, initially it seems as if they are saying the same thing. If this is true, why do I feel a persistent tension? Now I understand that the tension I am having within educational psychology stems from trying to tease out the subtle differences between it and multicultural education. The sociohistorical contexts I deal with in educational psychology refer to how people interact with each other when working in a particular activity-setting or problem-solving situation, such as learning to read or master a science skill. Within any activity setting involving diverse individuals, several different social and cultural systems of communication and interaction may be operating simultaneously. Is the culture of ethnic groups explicitly named in a sociohistorical analysis of educational issues?

To personalize these issues, I often modify the last question to read, "Am I named?" Are the generalities and specificities of my being taken into account at all times? Here "I" represents myself and is symbolic of the various identities of different ethnic groups. If I were to identify myself, it might be as an African American female, who was raised Baptist in a middle-class Black neighborhood on the West Coast, and whose parents are both from the rural South. These multiple identities of my belonging and affiliation are implicated in the naming of myself. To know me and how I think, feel, and do requires understanding the combination of these social and personal identities, as well as what they mean culturally and historically. What does it mean to have grown up African American in the rural South during the 1940s (my grandmother's generation), the 1950s (my parents' generation), and the 1980s and 1990s (my generation)?

The direct lived experiences of my grandparents and parents are not mine, yet my experiences carry some of the nuances of theirs as well. They may be embodied tacitly in my beliefs, values, and behaviors as well as nested in common proverbial sayings like, "Don't be a fly in the buttermilk," "What goes around comes around," and "If you lay down with dogs, you will get fleas." For me, all of this means that we as teachers cannot genuinely know our students if we do not know something about their near and distant social, cultural, ethnic, and experiential histories. If "we (ethnically diverse people) are not named" in the subjects and curricula taught in schools, then what professional obligations do educators have to break this cycle of exclusion? Once inclusion occurs, how does it benefit students from different ethnic groups?

I suspect this need to resolve inconsistencies among the orientations of my discipline and multicultural education is not idiosyncratic; it probably is a concern of others as well. It certainly is a significant transforming encounter that is at the center of my multicultural education development.

A BRIDGE BETWEEN US

My third transformative encounter involves personal discoveries made while reading *A Bridge Between Us* (Shigekuni, 1995), a fictional account of four generations of Japanese American women who live together in the same household. The connections among the great grandmother (Reiko), grandmother (Rio), mother (Tomoe), and daughter (Nomi) are revealed through how they uphold family and tradition, particularly the maternal lineage; the secrets and silences that are designed to protect the young generation from burdens of the past but fail to do so; and the love that is shared though often veiled. A bridge is used as a metaphor throughout the novel for the different pairs of unique mother-daughter relationships among the four women, as well as their relationship to the lived and sometimes imagined past.

Reading this novel had a profound effect on me and my multicultural education development. In this book, I found parallels to my own family reflected in the story of the Hito family. I was in a position similar to Nomi (the granddaughter), whom everybody is trying to protect by not openly sharing their generational pasts with her (especially the troublesome and highly intimate ones). This protective posture was evident in the tensions and unspoken details of past and ongoing pains that were kept from Nomi and her older sister. Nomi shares a special, although sometimes perverse, kinship with her grandmother, Rio, that is different from the relationship Rio shares with her own mother (Reiko) and daughter-in-law, Tomoe. It is Rio who finally begins to realize that another generation of women in the Hito family has been plagued by the silences and ills of the past.

As I read, I often drifted into thinking about my own female family relationships across generations and how the bridges between them might read. While I did think about parallels to my own life's story, I fought against the tendency to displace the particulars of the Hito family in the configuration of my own "her" story. Viewing the story from within my own cultural and familial context allowed me to engage with it on an intimate level. However, had I read it only from an African American cultural perspective, I would have missed a lot of what the story revealed about this fictional family and the author's overall naming of the Japanese American female experience. I consciously grappled with these tensions in my responses to the novel.

The story evoked a lot of empathy, which I welcomed, but I did not want to appropriate the Hito family's realities and make them mine. This caveat did not come automatically; it resulted from conversing with myself and responding to the story. We hear a lot about having dialogues with culturally different others as part of multicultural teaching and learning. It is also important to have dialogues with self. *A Bridge Between Us* prompted me to do both.

Long after my reading the book, the story stays with me. I keep thinking about and trying to understand why these women and their dilemmas seemed so familiar. Why did these characters spark such emotions and personal meaning? What were the common threads? Why did their "unfamiliar become so familiar" (another mandate of multicultural education) to me? I have only begun to reach some tentative answers to these questions. Perhaps it was the commonality and complexity of the mother-daughter relationships that included sacrifice, coupled with tormenting memories and agony of past decisions, that created omnipresent personal skeletons. Perhaps it was the overall pervasiveness of silences and secrets around the lived past that were meant to free the next generation from the burden of knowing the truth. But by not engaging in candid conversations about the ills of the past, history was bound to repeat itself. As Rio said about Nomi, "She no longer needs me—I realize it now—she has become me, and I feel for the first time truly afraid" (Shigekuni, 1995, p. 109). Perhaps the intense connection I felt with *A Bridge Between Us* is in the familiar way that cultures, traditions, families, and mother-daughter relationships are affected by oppression, subjugation, and grief. It is a challenging combination because the grief often becomes mourning for one's own self, past, present, and future.

This novel evoked and symbolized an even greater race memory for me. It triggered memories of how U.S. society fails to deal with past and present atrocities committed toward people of color. How frequently do we still hear African Americans being told to "forget slavery and move on," or the government's finding it problematic and impossible to offer a simple apology for the horror of slavery suffered by people of African ancestry? Maybe the failure to reveal these horrors openly is the reason that rampant acts of racism toward African Americans continue to be committed. History may indeed be continuing to reinvent itself. There are some powerful implications here for what I must do in combating the silences that surround oppression as a multicultural person and educator.

Finding elements of my own lived experiences in the women in *A Bridge Between Us* made their lives more personal and powerful. Reading the story and my own encounter with it were a microcosmic parallel of my entire process of becoming multicultural. It has the same elements of knowing, feeling, reflecting, and acting. The power of my conversations makes me wonder about the effects that encountering ethnic literature will have for my students. If literature can have this kind of profound effect, what will actual ethnic individuals and groups and their cultural experiences do for us? It's exhilarating to ponder the possibilities. Empathy, new knowledge, personal reflection, kindredness, and cross-cultural community building are only a few of them; many more are likely, such as those Mei-ying Chen shares in Chapter Ten in this book. I know that engagement with many kinds of literature and lived experiences from different ethnic groups will be major elements in my continuing process of becoming a multicultural person and educator.

YOUNG, GIFTED, AND BLACK

The final conversation with a transformative encounter that I share is centered around a question that I am deeply engaged with at this point in my journey: Can I simultaneously advocate for the diversity of ethnic groups within multicultural education and for my own particular ethnic constituency? I have to ask myself if, in fact, these two stances are inherently contradictory. What are the messages I have received regarding my ability to do so? Where have I begun to find different perspectives and possible answers to my initial question?

I have encountered arguments that ethnic group–based affiliations are divisive and contradictory to multicultural education. This belief argues that we should not separate ourselves along ethnic lines because it maintains boundaries and biases among us. When we talk about intergroup relations, a common tendency is to call into question the role of ethnically and culturally based student or professional organizations such as Black Student Unions, La Raza, and Filipino Heritage Clubs on college campuses. This specific question was raised in a graduate studies class that I was taking. We were talking about the fact that on my undergraduate campus, there was a Black premedical society. The question was asked about why such a single-focused ethnic group organization was necessary. Someone wondered, "Can't we all just form one premedical society so we can benefit from one another? Don't we all need to learn the same professional knowledge?" These comments are not far removed from questions about why we need ethnic-specific curricula, instruction, or schools. They sound very familiar to the "Why can't we all just get along?" perspective in the larger society.

Although I agree with some of the underlying sentiments of these reactions, the continued assumption that such associations and group-based affiliations are in opposition to an all-inclusive viewpoint is disturbing to me. The questions that I seek answers to are, "Why are these assumptions still held?" and "Why does one assume that particular and general identities and affiliations are mutually exclusive?" Both arguments have some legitimacy, but we should avoid placing them in opposition to one another. Perhaps there are larger ideological understandings and beliefs that explain our tendency to perpetuate this assumed incompatibility.

I am struggling to find answers because I do not disagree with the "Can't we all just get along?" viewpoint. I can see what kinds of sentiments and frustrations are being expressed in that question. But if I were to accept this line of thinking unquestionably, I might miss some important issues and insights about how professional knowledge cannot be removed from personal dimensions. Using the premedical society as an example, one can argue that a lot factors into being a successful doctor beyond professional knowledge. For instance, physicians of color will continue to be confronted with race-based challenges and resistances. They may be ethnically isolated because there are no other physicians of their particular ethnicity in their specialization or workplace. Their formal programs of study (as was the case with my degree) may not filter medical knowledge and treatments through ethnically, racially, and culturally diverse contexts. Ethnic-specific organizations may fill this void. These professional absences and reactions have serious ramifications for one's personal and professional well-being, especially if you accept the importance of connection, community, and culture for individual wellness. Many doctors of color have to network nationally to accumulate a sizable mass of physicians from their own ethnic groups. Teachers have to do the same thing because there often are so few of us in the local settings in which we live and work. P. L. Dawson, author of *Forged by the Knife* (1999), provides a poignant analysis of how ethnicity, isolation, and gender affect the professional development of six Black female surgeons.

I am beginning to believe that we need to rethink the notion that there is a universal human experience. This is not to say that we are not bound by our humanness and our biological relationship to one another. However, the particulars of human experiences differ from one person and group to the next. Racial, ethnic, and gender affiliations are some major causes of differences within the human experience that should not be ignored in teaching and learning. I think the particular and the general in dealing with multicultural groups and issues can (and must) coexist. Some of the thoughts of Maxine Greene (1978) helped me to arrive at this conclusion:

> Each of us belongs to many social groups and plays a variety of social roles; our involvements affect the ways we use "the stock of knowledge at hand" to make sense of the social scene. The stock of knowledge, the disciplines, the schemata made available to us not only give our culture its identity, they enable us to participate in a common meaning structure, to inhabit a common world. Even as we do so, however, we maintain our individual perspectives; we make personal interpretations of what is shared. Each of our undertakings, therefore, each of our projects remains distinctive; each vantage point is unique, despite all the association and communication essential to communal life [p. 126].

In another explanation, Greene (1993) declares that dialogue across differences is essential to achieving freedom, equality, justice, caring, love, and trust. We need to strive for "as much intersubjective agreement as possible, 'the desire to extend the reference of 'us' as far as we can.' But, as we do so, we have to remain aware of the distinctive members of the plurality, appearing before one another with their own perspectives on the common, their own stories entering the culture's story, altering it as it moves through time" (p. 194).

These ideas are clear to me when I apply them to my personal interactions and conversations, but they are less so when I relate them to my professional activities. Wherever I go and whatever I do, I always take my African Americanness (both its tangible and intangible forms) with me. Frequently, I am not interacting with only African Americans. I am fairly successful in relating to people from different ethnic groups, and we can engage satisfactorily with substantive issues that are transcendent of any particular group. In thinking about this, I ask myself, "Why is this habit that is so common and easily accomplished in personal and social relations so problematic in the professional arena?"

I have sought out a number of other conversations within multicultural education and ethnic-specific scholarship to gain some perspectives on these issues. This course of action seems reasonable since people more experienced in dealing with these dilemmas may have some thoughts and strategies to offer that are more insightful than my own. Turning to elders is consistent with how I launch and anchor my process of multicultural becoming. I have gained further assistance in understanding the false dichotomy between the particularity and universality of ethnic groups' experiences from Afrocentric theorists Molefi Asante and Asa Hilliard and from playwright Lorraine Hansberry.

I have learned from Asante that teaching students from different ethnic groups about their histories, cultures, and heritages is a good thing to do. He explains that "the true 'centric' curriculum seeks for the African, Asian, and Hispanic child the same kind of experience that is provided for the [Anglo] child" (Asante, 1991–1992, p. 29). This statement suggests to me that all children have the right to see themselves in what and how we teach. It is important because our center has everything to do with our lived experiences, how we situate ourselves in the world, and how we engage in relationships with others. Teaching and learning about our own ethnic particulars and our common human experiences across ethnicity are not mutually exclusive. Hilliard (1991–1992) helped me to know this when he wrote, "I do not believe that it is necessary to choose between uniqueness and commonality. . . . Human minds and human systems are powerful and flexible enough to handle both" (p. 13).

In fact, our particularity and our generality are reciprocally related; we cannot fully know and appreciate one without the other. Nor can we ever separate what we do from who we are. We carry our culture, our ethnicity, our race, and our socialization with us in all our engagements. Although we may not be conscious of these influences, they are always there, so we can never assume that our behavior is abstracted from our identities. As I am becoming more multicultural, these understandings and the importance of my owning myself and teaching my students to do so are getting clearer.

Along with Molefi Asante and Asa Hilliard, I am indebted to Lorraine Hansberry for these illuminations. In responding to an interviewer's comments that her play, *A Raisin in the Sun* (1958), could be about any family instead of being specific to African Americans, she replied,

> I'd always been under the impression that Negroes are people. . . . I believe that one of the most sound ideas in dramatic writing is that in order to create the universal, you must pay very great attention to the specific. Universality, I think, emerges from truthful identity of what is. . . . I think people, to the extent we accept them and believe them as who they're supposed to be, to that extent they can become everybody [Nemiroff, 1969, pp. 113–114].

I understand this to mean that we should not ignore, lose, or pretend to divorce our personal selves from the professional work we do. How we do multicultural education is shaped significantly by who we are ethnically, culturally, and racially. I can now move forward with greater clarity of mind and devotion of heart knowing that I can (and should) help myself as I help others.

I can simultaneously promote my unique African Americanness and multicultural education, which is inclusive of many ethnic and cultural groups. By doing this, I can learn and teach my students to engage with different peoples and experiences without compromising my own or others' cultural and ethnic integrity. I can be African American in the midst and mix of multicultural, multiracial, and multiethnic environments, interactions, and conversations. Therefore, I will follow (as others should about their respective ethnicities) the counsel and model of Melanie Carter (2001) about promoting my own ethnically and culturally grounded perspectives in my teaching of everybody's children in mainstream contexts. She says this is important for three reasons:

> First, it is personally important [that as] an African American woman I . . . locate my experiences in the dominant narrative. Insisting upon authentic inclusion challenges the validity of a narrative that does not give space and/or voice to people of color. Second, it is collectively important. . . . Sharing our personal stories is a strategy to identify common experiences. While we are not necessarily seeking personal validation or corroboration, there is a need to refute the universality of the dominant narrative. Our collective stories are self-affirming and are substantive testament to the inadequacy of a supposedly all-encompassing narrative. Third, truth telling is a counterhegemonic strategy. It troubles taken for granted assumptions and long-held notions that protect and sustain the status quo [p. 154].

PRINCIPLES FOR PRACTICE

The first principle for practice in becoming a multicultural person and educator that can be extrapolated from my own narrative is that *ethnic-specific literature is a viable source of knowledge about and experience with ethnic and cultural diversity.* Ethnic-specific literature refers to fictional or nonfictional writings about people of color in the United States where the author is a member of the same ethnic group that the story represents (Hansen-Kréning and Mizokawa, 1997). Fictional texts cannot replace factual information that we gain from nonfictional texts, interaction with others, and personal stories. However, as Harris (1997, p. 5) suggests, "Reoccurring themes, topics, and motifs in a group's literature can offer insights into aspects of the culture that seem to have a particular significance to members of that group." Ethnic-specific literature provides different ways to view a similar phenomenon within a particular ethnic group and across groups. It also can speak to ethnic and cultural diversity beyond the composition of our immediate environments or experiences.

A second principle for practice is that *critical discourse about ethnically and culturally diverse issues, challenges, and opportunities is essential to the multicultural education agenda.* It is not enough to get factual information or to receive it passively; rather, one needs to analyze it, critique it, reflect on it, and act on it. It also is imperative that we bring in experiences and stories from various ethnic, cultural, social, and gendered backgrounds. When we do this, we are able to have conversations about mainstream educational domains using a multicultural framework against the backdrop of the realities of our social world. Even within a monolithic group, various ethnic and cultural perspectives should be included in how we view and evaluate information and knowledge.

Related to the second principle for practice is a third one, which calls *for analyzing and reflecting on personal experience with ethnic cultural diversity as a means of multicultural education teaching and learning.* Our personal and professional dimensions of self are inseparably connected with one another. Multicultural teaching has everything to do with living a multicultural existence. Therefore, critically engaging our own assumptions about race, class, and gender must occur.

A fourth principle for practice is the *need to restructure disciplinary premises, content, and methodologies to make them more reflective of and responsive to multicultural education.* Many conventional subjects and disciplines taught in schools still do not include the culture, contributions, experiences, and perspectives of ethnically diverse groups. To compensate for this, we must learn how to weave multicultural education into all subject areas. Because this process is not customarily or automatically done, it requires conscious thought and deliberate actions from a new breed of educators.

A final principle for practice embedded in the transformative conversations in this chapter is to *translate multicultural principles to personal and professional domains of being.* Similar to the third principle, it suggests that you should make yourself your own subject of multicultural education. Hold yourself accountable for the same kinds of processes you expect of your students around issues of multicultural education. Another aspect of linking the personal and professional domains is the need to internalize what you learn about multicultural education and to live according to it.

JOINING THE JOURNEY

The principles for practice imply some general strategies that can be used in developing programs and actions for becoming multicultural education:

• Develop a list of ten ethnic literature essentials, and read them all. These should be novels for youth and adults and children's picture books from different ethnic groups that deal with being ethnic and cultural. This seemingly easy task can be difficult. Begin by trying to identify literature by specific ethnic groups. As you read each book, keep a log in which you respond to the books' authors, characters, and situations. Include the feelings, thoughts, questions, memories, and concerns that were provoked in you by the readings.

• Create a multicultural reading club for you and your students. Focus on ethnic-specific children's and young adult literature. If possible, work in groups of no more than five students. Be certain to include books across several different ethnic groups and various books within a particular ethnic group. Here are some suggested criteria for choosing K–12 ethnic-specific literature (Bishop, 1990, 1997; Harris, 1990, 1997; Hansen-Kréning and Mizokawa, 1997):

Contains ethnic portrayals and identities in the narrative text and visual representations that are clearly identifiable

Includes an engaging story line and authentic illustrations

Is acceptable to or endorsed by the ethnic group being portrayed

Evokes responses that can be explored through discussion, critical analysis, and reflection

Avoids ethnic stereotyping and type casting

Reveals shared cultural values in a contemporary setting

Provides alternative ethnic perspectives on U.S. historical developments

Displays different perspectives and experiences within ethnic groups for telling the same or similar stories

Represents diverse literary devices and genres, such as biography, autobiography, essays, poetry, and letters

Does not celebrate one ethnic group at the expense of another

• Have students do reciprocal peer teaching about the books they read by predicting outcomes, generating questions, summarizing details, and clarifying cultural nuances embedded in the development of plots, characters, and relationships. This may require you to prompt young students with questions like these:

> "Is there anything about the characters, their relationships, and story that is familiar or new to you?"
>
> "Can you identify or empathize with the topic, characters, and narrative content?"
>
> "Are there any social justice and equality issues raised in the books that parallel real life that you feel need to be corrected? What are you willing to do to make these changes?"

Have students compare characteristics of various books within the same ethnic group and then across different ethnic groups and compare their reactions to them. Offer models for your students to follow by answering these questions from your own experiences.

• Recall situations and events from your prior schooling experiences in which key issues of multicultural education were either facilitated or ignored. Consider, for example, how your teachers encouraged or discouraged students to embrace their own and others' ethnic identities and cultural differences. Conduct some observations in classrooms or interview students to see if they are having similar encounters to yours. Plan some instructional strategies to change the negative encounters into more positive multicultural ones.

• Do a self-study (or with a partner) to name, describe, and analyze the nature and effects of your own transformative encounters in becoming multicultural, both as a person and an educator. Begin by thinking of major multicultural discoveries that were turning points in your recognition of and engagement with ethnic and cultural diversity. Write, audiotape, or videorecord your responses to them. Examine the list you have generated to discern patterns and trends. Then choose one and construct a conversation around it. Name the encounter, briefly describe it, and explore your thoughts, feelings, and actions about it. Do these conversations with several other encounters. Then read them all together and assign your own logical ordering to them (placing them in some preferred relational order, for example). Share some of the conversations with your multicultural encounters as models for your students to emulate, and invite them to join the dialogues.

References

Asante, M. K. "Afrocentric Curriculum." *Educational Leadership,* 1991–1992, *49*(4), 29–31.

Banks, J. A. "The Canon Debate, Knowledge Construction, and Multicultural Education." In J. A. Banks (ed.), *Multicultural Education, Transformative Knowledge, and Action: Historical and Contemporary Perspectives.* New York: Teachers College Press, 1996.

Bennett, L., Jr. *Before the Mayflower: A History of Black America.* (6th ed.) New York: Penguin Books, 1993.

Bishop, R. S. "Walk Tall in the World: African American Literature for Today's Children." *Journal of Negro Education,* 1990, *59,* 556–565.

Bishop, R. S. "Selecting Literature for a Multicultural Curriculum." In V. J. Harris (ed.), *Using Multiethnic Literature in the K-8 Classroom.* Norwood, Mass.: Christopher-Gordon, 1997.

Carter, M. "Race, Jacks, and Jump Rope: Theorizing School Through Personal Narratives." In R. O. Mabokela and A. L. Green (eds.), *Sisters of the Academy: Emergent Black Women Scholars in Higher Education.* Sterling, Va.: Stylus, 2001.

Cruz, B. "Stereotypes of Latin Americans Perpetuated in Secondary School Textbooks." *Latino Student Journal,* 1994, *7,* 51–67.

Dawson, P. L. *Forged by the Knife: The Experience of Surgical Residency from the Perspective of a Woman of Color.* Seattle, Wash.: Open Hand Publishing, 1999.

Deloria, V., Jr. *Behind the Trail of Broken Treaties: An Indian Declaration of Independence.* New York: Delacorte Press, 1974.

Donaldson, K.B.M. *Through Students' Eyes: Combating Racism in United States Schools.* New York: Praeger, 1994.

Fordham, S. *Blacked Out: Dilemmas of Race, Identity, and Success at Capital High.* Chicago: University of Chicago Press, 1996.

Fordham, S., and Ogbu, J. U. "Black Students' School Success: Coping with the 'Burden of Acting White.'" *Urban Review,* 1986, *18,* 176–206.

Gay, G. *Culturally Responsive Teaching: Theory, Research, and Practice.* New York: Teachers College Press, 2000.

Gay, G., and Baber, W. L. (eds.). *Expressively Black: The Cultural Basis of Ethnic Identity.* New York: Praeger, 1987.

Greene, M. *Landscapes of Learning.* New York: Teachers College Press, 1978.

Greene, M. "The Passion of Pluralism: Multiculturalism and the Expanding Community." In T. Perry and J. W. Fraser (eds.), *Freedom's Plow: Teaching in the Multicultural Classroom.* New York: Routledge, 1993.

Hansberry, L. *A Raisin in the Sun.* New York: Random House, 1958.

Hansen-Kréning, N., and Mizokawa, D. T. "Exploring Ethnic-Specific Literature: A Unity of Parents, Families, and Educators." *Journal of Adolescent and Adult Literacy,* 1997, *41,* 96–106.

Harris, V. J. "African American Children's Literature: The First One Hundred Years." *Journal of Negro Education,* 1990, *59,* 540–555.

Harris, V. J. (ed.). *Using Multiethnic Literature in the K-8 Classroom.* Norwood, Mass.: Christopher-Gordon, 1997.

Hemmings, A. "Conflicting Images? Being Black and a Model High School Student." *Anthropology and Education Quarterly,* 1996, *27,* 20–50.

Hilliard, A. G. "Why We Must Pluralize the Curriculum." *Educational Leadership,* 1991–1992, *49*(4), 12–16.

Hine, D. C., and McLeod, J. (eds.). *Crossing Boundaries: Comparative History of Black People in Diaspora.* Bloomington: Indiana University Press, 1999.

Kochman, T. *Black and White Styles in Conflict.* Chicago: University of Chicago Press, 1981.

Nemiroff, R. *To Be Young, Gifted, and Black: Lorraine Hansberry in Her Own Words.* Upper Saddle River, N.J.: Prentice Hall, 1969.

Nieto, S. "Lessons from Students on Creating a Chance to Dream." *Harvard Educational Review,* 1994, *64,* 392–426.

Noddings, N. "Stories in Dialogue: Caring and Interpersonal Reasoning." In C. Witherell and N. Noddings (eds.), *Stories Lives Tell: Narrative and Dialogue in Education.* New York: Teachers College Press, 1991.

Portes, P. R. "Ethnicity and Culture in Educational Psychology." In D. C. Berliner and R. C. Calfee (eds.), *Handbook of Educational Psychology.* Old Tappan, N.J.: Macmillan, 1996.

Rogoff, B., and Chavajay, P. "What's Become of Research on the Cultural Basis of Cognitive Development." *American Psychologist,* 1995, *50,* 859–877.

Romanowski, M. H. "Problems of Bias in History Textbooks." *Social Education,* 1996, *60,* 170–173.

Saxe, G. B. *Cultural and Cognitive Development: Studies in Mathematical Understanding.* Mahwah, N.J.: Erlbaum, 1991.

Shigekuni, J. *A Bridge Between Us.* New York: Anchor Books, 1995.

Steele, C. M. "A Threat in the Air: How Stereotypes Shape Intellectual Identity and Performance." *American Psychologist,* 1997, *52,* 613–629.

Takaki, R. *A Different Mirror: A History of Multicultural America.* New York: Little, Brown, 1993.

U.S. Department of Education. *Digest of Education Statistics.* Washington, D.C.: U.S. Government Printing Office, 2000.

Wade, R. C. "Content Analysis of Social Studies Textbooks: A Review of Ten Years of Research." *Theory and Research in Social Education,* 1993, *21,* 232–256.

CHAPTER FIVE

Making and Breaking Ethnic Masks

Jeannine E. Dingus

> *We wear the mask that grins and lies,*
> *It hides our cheeks and shades our eyes,–*
> *This debt we pay to human guile:*
> *With torn and bleeding hearts we smile,*
> *And mouth with myriad subtleties.*
>
> *–Paul Laurence Dunbar*

Ten years after first reading these lines from Paul Laurence Dunbar's stirring poem, "We Wear the Mask" (1997), I react much the same way I did when I first encountered them. As I slowly read each stanza of the poem, I block the rest of the world out as I reflect on the times when I too have donned "the mask." The haunting lyrics move me, touch my soul, and shake my dungeon while a flood of memories rushes over me. Dunbar wrote this lyric poem and others to express his feelings of anger associated with being discriminated against as a Black poet; the hurt of being limited by perceptions of what and where a Black bard could write; the pressure to write and perform in roles so different from one's true self; the coping devices African Americans frequently have to employ in the United States; and the frustration of being powerless to change the system that relegated him to this status. Within each line of Dunbar's poem, I recognize elements of my process of becoming a multicultural person and educator.

As a child, I attended predominantly White Catholic schools where I was among the very few African American students. Although I performed well academically, my successes more often than not occurred within the confines of preordained roles for myself and the few other African American students: the unassuming bookworm who never questioned the inner workings of the school, the streetwise troublemaker, the shuckin' and jivin' class clown, the athlete, and the special education candidate. There were as well some high-achieving and accommodating model minorities (Japanese and Chinese American students). I liken such roles to a mask—a grinning, lying, misinterpreted facade, unrealistic images and expectations imposed on students of color.

The process of masking is one of ascribing perceived negative or constraining features or characteristics to someone, or in this case, people of color, by the privileged others (that is, people of power in mainstream society). As a result, what one sees is what one gets: a superficial rendering of people's complexities and a failure to see their depth. The way I am using it, *masking* has some similarities to negative teacher expectations toward ethnically diverse students, ethnic stereotyping, and racism in education (see, for example, Good and Brophy, 1994; Oakes, 1985; Oakes and Lipton, 1999; McLean Donaldson, 1996; McCarthy and Crichlow, 1993).

In this chapter, I explore the several masks that were imposed on me and other students as we went through school, how I eventually came to unveil these masks, and how these processes are critical elements in my becoming a multicultural educator. These are presented as prompts for further reflection and discussion. I ask you to join me in these analytical dialogues so that we may become more critically conscious of the influences teachers have on the academic experiences and ethnic identity of students from different racial and cultural backgrounds. Invitations to participate in these dialogues are extended by a series of questions that follow each masking or unmasking scenario.

PREMASKING: THE JOURNEY BEGINS

Kindergarten was a transitional period for me, as it is for most other five-year-olds. For two years prior, Community Day Care Center (CDCC) was my school. Surrounded by urban housing projects,

CDCC was conveniently located close to my home on the bus route my friends and I would later call the "Ghetto Express." Started in the 1960s, the center was housed in a converted Victorian mansion, tucked away on a quiet traffic-restricted street. I felt secure there, and my mother felt comfortable with the school as well. She had various levels of accountability checks on it since she knew an employee who worked at the center, members of the board of directors, and friends whose children had graduated from the center. These connections were multilayered; she had established them through networks at her job, community, and church.

My comfort level was also evident in the friendships I made at the school. I liked the other children and never got into any quarrels or disagreements. Looking back at the pictures from my small graduation ceremony, I realize that all of us little girls were replicas of our mothers with Afro puffs, slick press-and-curls, and bell-bottomed pants. The little boys in their varying shades of brown sported Afros in heights ranging from Shaft to the Jackson 5. We had good times, and although I do not recall the specifics of our daily activities, I do remember feeling very happy at the CDCC with my friends, teachers, and Nate, the cook. But even as I now reflect on these experiences, I do not recognize the existence of any masks and wonder why. Is it possible that my early educational experiences stripped away the necessity to engage in masking? If that is the case, what caused this nonveiling? The answers to these questions probably lie within explanations such as those offered by Spindler (1997), Pai and Adler (1997), and Noddings (1992) about the positive effects of cultural affirmation, community, and caring on the identity and achievement of students.

The prospect of graduating from nursery school to kindergarten excited me. The idea of attending the same school as my sister and two older cousins made me feel that I was finally moving up from baby status to that of big kid. Graduation day was just the beginning. My family rolled out more than ten deep in our usual style—loud and proud. Southern migrants, my parents had forged a network of blood kin and extended family consisting of in-laws, co-workers, and church family, a common African American cultural practice (Stack, 1974, 1996). We all considered ourselves family and did not distinguish between blood and fictive kin. The children were the core of the family. The educational and extracurricular activities of the children were full-fledged family events that everyone attended and contributed in some way to make the occasions special. Even a nursery school graduation became a major occasion for celebration. Under my cap and gown, I wore a dress sewn by my Aunt Norma. My fashion-conscious older cousin combed my perpetually out-of-place bangs. My parents, aunts, and uncles flashed pictures of me with the same cameras, film, and flashes they would spend the better part of their adult lives producing on the Kodak assembly lines. In the midst of those events, we seem to be wide open, free, relaxed and natural just being ourselves. There was no place or reason for hiding ourselves, or "puttin' on airs," as my home folks might say. My early years, wrapped in the snug embrace of my family and community, still anchor my personal and professional being.

QUESTIONS FOR REFLECTION. Do my early educational experiences and cultural traditions prompt memories of critical incidents or events in your own lives? What made you feel safe among your family and care-givers? Did these feelings automatically transfer from one phase of your schooling to the next?

BEGINNING OF MASKING

My transition from nursery school to kindergarten proved difficult and puzzling. Very early on, I felt out of place, always two steps behind my classmates, with no hope of catching up. Although I could not describe how, the environment felt strange, even cold. In retrospect, I realize such feelings began at the school threshold and filtered down into my basement classroom.

Located near the university, the quiet, shady tree-lined street with meticulously manicured lawns and flower-trimmed sidewalks lead directly to brightly colored center-hall colonials. The neighborhood could have passed easily for the set of *Leave It to Beaver*, the popular 1950s television portrayal of the ideal family. In my mind, it seemed just that perfect. Because of the proximity to the university, the student population of my school was the most eclectic ethnic mix in the city. My sister and I were among the few African American students who were bused in from across the river, presumably to round out the racial mix. Because I was too young to ride the bus, my father took us to school in the mornings. When he left, I felt as if my security blanket went with him.

The "walkers," as the children from the surrounding neighborhood were called, lived in a world totally removed from my own. From the first morning that we lined up outside in the cool autumn air, I kept waiting for that same cozy feeling I had at the CDCC to resurface. It never did. Parents or classroom moms maintained order outside the school as students piled off the buses and lined up by grade. I noticed immediately how these moms knew some of the children by name. It bothered me that I was never referred to by my name, and I realized soon that "Sweetheart" and "Honey" were generic substitutes for it. The atmosphere at the CDCC had been very different. All adults made a point of calling us by our names. I missed being playfully addressed as "Lil' Mama" and began to attribute this difference to race.

I hated my new school. To my dismay, I was surrounded by White kids. There was one other Black boy in my afternoon section, but he seemed oblivious to my presence. When he did notice me, he teased me because of the large gap in my front teeth. It did not help my situation that the other children knew each other and came to school with established friendships. I remember coming home complaining that I did not even have an in-class boyfriend. In my mind, little Black boys were the only candidates for the role. Eventually, my parents switched me to the morning class, but the situation was worse. I was now the only Black child in the whole class. As in the afternoon class, these students too had established friendships, and I was excluded from these circles. I attributed my social status to the fact that I was Black. Invisibility, isolation, dislocation, and the need to cope in a strange place began to weigh heavy on me. What is a child to do? Some real possibilities are to fight, run away, or hide, but when these are not physically possible, then what? You find other ways of self-protection.

I soon learned that there were differences among the White faces of my classmates. A few of them were from European countries and spoke other languages. Jillian, for example, was from Ireland, and her heavy brogue tickled me. Jillian's mother was among the many moms who frequented the classroom. Every craft, project, or daily routine was shaped by the presence of the mothers of my classmates. Initially, I did not understand how or why the mothers were there all the time. My mother was at work, which was where I thought all mothers were. My cultural realities were not a part of the influences that shaped the details and dynamics of my classroom activities.

QUESTIONS FOR REFLECTION. Can being unnamed be a form of invisibility? I believe so. Can invisibility be a type of mask? And of whose making? Will I create my own masks to counter those that others construct for me? How do I know if, when, and how this masking begins? Do teachers create masks for themselves, or are they given masks by others? What is the multicultural message in this? What do you think?

A MASK OF MY OWN MAKING

Although I eventually made friends, I still felt out of place. It seemed as if being from a foreign land made some children special. They could speak other languages, tell stories of their travels abroad, dress in traditional clothing, and share ethnic foods. Jillian did an Irish dance, and other children brought in various cultural artifacts. Not wanting to be outdone, I asked my mother for something special that represented our culture, something that distinguished me as the "other." She gave me a small birch canoe, a souvenir from the family's yearly picnic at Niagara Falls. Ashamed at how unglamorous and "uncultural" my offering was, I left the canoe at home. I did not understand what the canoe symbolized: the rides on my Granddaddy Go-Go's shoulders, picnics of fried chicken and homemade pound cake, the mist of the falls in our faces, and the coming together of family from North and South. I didn't realize then that the canoe symbolized how my family members had made it out of the Jim Crow South to raise their own families up North. In other words, I didn't know my own cultural history and legacy.

As my year in kindergarten progressed, my desire to be something other than the only African American child in the class grew. If I was going to be Black, I reasoned, I would create a special kind of Blackness. Influenced by my uncle's Puerto Rican neighbors, I made myself into a "Black Puerto Rican." I started by creating my own version of Spanish, which was more like incoherent babbling. But I didn't have enough courage to be a Black Puerto Rican in school and so I flashed my new identity at home or on car rides with my family. My mother understood exactly what was happening. She realized that being in such a different environment left me without an anchor. I was trying to create a personality that mirrored my classmates' languages and cultures that made them special. In my mind, being Black in that situation made me a total outsider.

Making sense of this experience is an important step in my multicultural journey. I often wonder if other African Americans and members of other ethnic groups of color face similar dilemmas, especially those learning in school populations like mine. And I wonder what my teachers could have done to circumvent the need for me to create a mask of false identity. Reflecting back on this experience, I think that my teacher could have assisted in the transition by assigning a classroom mother to work closely with smaller groups of students, making them feel comfortable and getting them acclimated to the school environment. Although classroom mothers were present, their assistance was arbitrary.

In your own opinion, what else could my teacher have done? What will you do if or when you have a student like me as a five or six year old or English language learners (ELL) to make them an integral part of your classroom? These are reasonable speculations to ponder because positive ethnic identity development is one of the essential goals of multicultural education.

I often laugh now when I recall my father's reaction to my newfound "Black Puerto Rican" identity. After asking me a question and getting a response in my constructed language, he looked to my mother as the interpreter. The conversation went something like this:

"What is she talkin' about?" Dad would ask flustered.

"Oh, she thinks she is a Black Puerto Rican," my mom would add in my defense.

"Where the hell did she get that idea?"

"From school, where most of the kids are international. And from Jimmy's neighbors. They're from Puerto Rico."

"Well, how long is she going to speak like this?"

"It's just a phase. She'll grow out of it."

My mother was right. I did grow out of my Black Puerto Rican identity. Although it took me years to understand why I created the identity, my mother understood all along. Some masks serve useful purposes even though the causes that prompt their need are detrimental.

Outside school, being Black meant a great deal to me, although I couldn't necessarily articulate it then. As a child of the 1970s, I was surrounded by burgeoning expressions of African and African American overt ethnic identity and cultural consciousness in my community. I remember watching the Mighty Liberators, an all-Black marching band, strut proudly in their red, black, and green uniforms. I never played with anyone except Black children because there were no families of other ethnicities living in my neighborhood. And despite the fact that my family was fifth-generation Presbyterian, an overwhelmingly White denomination, we attended an all-Black Presbyterian church around the corner from our home.

QUESTIONS FOR REFLECTION. I have often heard European Americans say they "don't have a culture." Why might someone say that? Why might someone be ashamed of his or her ethnic identity and cultural heritage? What should teachers do to prevent or counteract this self-shame among ethnically diverse students in their classrooms?

CRACKS IN THE MASKS

As early as elementary school, I sensed that the African Americans in class received different treatment, even within our ranks. Often, the differences were quite subtle, but the effects were always important. These messages were reinforced with the selection of certain students for classroom activities or participation in school functions. When our class was selected to sing at the First Friday masses, the tambourines and drums always ended up in the hands of African American students. We were being ethnically type-cast. We found that amusing and ironic and laughed about it. The negative effects of these differential treatments were similar to those found by Karen McLean Donaldson (1996) in her study of racism in U.S. education through the eyes of affected students.

My fourth-grade class had six African American students, the largest number of any other class I had been in up to that point. I believe this mass posed a problem for my teacher, Mrs. Ellensworth, who always seemed intent on keeping us apart. For example, after returning our science tests, she announced that only those scoring ninety or above would be eligible to participate in an experiment on sedimentary rocks. I was among the eligible group; my friends were not.

For the first time, I began to realize that my academic abilities separated me from the children with whom I felt most comfortable with socially. I was pulled in two directions, as if being intelligent automatically made it difficult to maintain friendships with kids I knew from the neighborhood, kids whose mothers worked with mine, and kids whose parents came from the same rural Georgia home town as my mom. I felt extremely uncomfortable. One day my good friend Curtis pulled me aside and in his fourth-grade wisdom broke it to me: "Girl, don't feel bad. You go over there and do that experiment. Don't you know you are representin' us?" Curtis's words have stayed with me throughout the years. They relate strongly to my feelings about surviving in school for students of color and how multicultural education can facilitate this process.

Because I performed well academically, I received better treatment in school than some of the other African American students. I felt a tremendous amount of guilt about it. But as I think about it now, I don't believe my feelings of guilt related to acting White, as Fordham and Ogbu (1986) and Ogbu (1992) have explained. Black students, as their research is often interpreted to mean, equate academic success with "acting White." Yet this explanation is oversimplified and does not take into account the complexities of why and how ethnically diverse students have to negotiate multiple demands made on their commitments, loyalties, relationships, and skills as they move in and out of different cultural settings. Certainly, my feelings extended far beyond a Black-White dichotomy.

My feelings of guilt centered on the fact that I took honors classes and was able to escape the preordained masking of low academic expectations, negative judgments, and invisibility, but my ethnic peers were not so fortunate. It bothered me greatly that my peers, many of whom I believed were actually smarter than I was, did not receive the same attention from teachers to help them learn, attend conferences, serve as class representatives, and deliver speeches at eighth-grade graduation. The academic neglect they suffered constituted a devastating mask.

I felt torn between my culture's collective group orientation and the competitive individualistic nature of the school environment. I clearly got the message that group dynamics did not account for individual academic success, and school achievement sometimes came at the expense of social relationships. My affiliation with other African American students and the small number of Latinos I attended school with enabled me to survive and remain true to myself. Beyond the level of friendships, these group connections provided an emotional outlet in a school environment that differed significantly from my world outside school. I am still mystified about how I was able to accomplish this compromise. Continuing to work at solving the mystery is a major thread in my becoming multicultural. No student should have to sacrifice cultural heritage, ethnic identity, and social networks in order to obtain an education. They should be able to develop skills in all of these at the same time. Some teachers recognize this need, such as those in the research of Michelle Foster (1991, 1995,

1997), Gloria Ladson-Billings (1994), and Gay (2000), and are responding positively to it.

My social group connections affirmed me culturally and buffered me from the ethnic isolation and separation occurring in the classroom. Lunchtime romps on the playground singing choruses of "Hambone" (a traditional song and dance routine performed by Black children) helped us to widen the cracks in the masks others imposed on us and create masks of our own. Our European American classmates stared in amazement and amusement at our singing and dancing. Song and dance meant much more to us than mere entertainment. The ability to sing together gave us survival, power, and perseverance; we were singing our souls out loud, in a school environment that barely recognized our ethnic identity and culture. We evoked and applied our ancestral legacies of looking as if we were doing one thing while in fact doing something quite different (Pasteur and Toldson, 1982).

QUESTIONS FOR REFLECTION. What activities or events in school made you feel ignored, marginalized, important, recognized, and powerful in your surroundings? What types of curriculum and learning activities can you provide for your ethnically diverse students for them to experience feelings of cultural and personal empowerment?

UNVEILING THE MASKS

My fifth-grade teacher made my academic-social tensions even stronger. A favorite among the African American students, Mrs. Marshall was considered a good teacher. She was warm, always open to hugs, and gave memorable class parties. To be in Mrs. Marshall's class was considered a privilege. Yet even Mrs. Marshall, with her good intentions, engaged in masking African American students. I learned this the hard way.

One day I was bending down to pick up a pencil when she came over to my desk in a huff and proceeded to pull me up in my chair by the root of my ponytail. Maybe she thought I wasn't paying attention. Out of instinct and pain, I swatted her arm and told her to let go of my hair. She insisted on conferencing in the hallway. I was frightened. Would she call my mother? Would she take me to the principal's office, where I would be suspended? Never before in my life had I hit an adult. She had always treated me as if I was special.

In the hallway, Mrs. Marshall explained why she felt justified in pulling my hair: "I expect more out of you because you are my best colored student. I don't want to lose you." What did she mean "lose me"? (I wasn't planning on going anywhere.) Many of my Black friends had always suspected that teachers treated us slightly different, but I never imagined hearing it from a teacher, especially Mrs. Marshall. Perhaps she thought of herself as a savior or that in some small way she was helping the "colored" folks by making distinctions among us. As I stood there listening to her lecture, my feelings ranged from anger and confusion to betrayal. How could she do this to me? Did she only see me as "colored"? How could she think so little of the other Black students? Although I did not have a full understanding of what she meant, I resented her for pulling my hair and for her words. I cried for myself and for the other Black children because she misled us into thinking that she really cared about us. She never apologized to me.

Much masking and unmasking were operating in this situation. The masks had prevented Mrs. Marshall from genuinely seeing me and the other African American students—all of our beauty, capabilities, and potentialities. Among these masks were negative expectations, false illusions, good intentions, and racial prejudices. This realization stripped away another mask that revealed an ugly truth. Clearly, Mrs. Marshall didn't expect much from us. What we thought of as "nice," in retrospect, was patronizing control. I knew enough about race at that time to know how uncomfortable I was at being addressed as "colored." In my mind, her comments demonstrated that she was caught in a time warp. "Colored" was what I associated with segregated fountains and images of Bull Connor's dogs unleashed on Black children in the 1960s. I did not talk about the incident for a long time because I did not want to be in a situation of my word against hers.

Now I wonder if, by being silent, I was engaging in complicity with Mrs. Marshall and helping to mask myself. I also wonder how many African, Asian, Native, and Latino American children are still facing variations of this kind of ethnic and racial prejudice from their teachers. Becoming multicultural helps me understand the horror and injustices of these kinds of experiences and the long-range negative effects they can have on children's academic performance and psychological well-being. A truly multicultural person would never treat a child in this way. Instead, respecting and honoring the cultural, racial, and ethnic diversity of children in the classroom is paramount.

QUESTIONS FOR REFLECTION. What other masks are operating in this situation? How else might Mrs. Marshall have expressed her concerns? What other factors may have influenced my decision to remain quiet about Mrs. Marshall's actions, and other students like me with their teachers? What would you advise these students to do?

MASKING AMONG CHILDREN

I often look at my eight-year-old stepson and wonder how he will fare over the course of his schooling. How will he be masked, and will he know how to unveil them? Jackson is intelligent with a quick wit, a good command of numbers, and the uncanny ability to tell a good story. When he started first grade, he was one of two African American boys in the first grade. Because he has always been educated in school environments that are overwhelmingly European American, Jackson does not know anything about any other classroom demographic. He is used to being either the only one or among a select few African American children. Although he never directly expresses displeasure with the classroom demographics, his comments do reveal some cognizance of race-based differences.

Early on in the school year, Jackson was placed in the second highest reading group. As the semester progressed, however, he was reassigned to the lowest-level ability group because of some reading difficulties. Two things bothered him most about the move: leaving the group where his friends were and being placed in the group with Darnel. In the upper-level reading group, Jackson sat with his classroom buddy, Michael. When the move occurred, Jackson would speak of Michael in glowing terms as if Michael were the measure of smartness. Jackson could tell you all about Michael's high grades, how Michael read all the Harry Potter books by himself, and how Michael is moving up to the gifted classes. It was as if Jackson idolized and placed Michael on a pedestal because his academic achievement was well known and heralded by the teacher and after-school-program helpers.

I wondered if Jackson associated academic achievement with little White boys like Michael and the others in the upper-level reading group, because this perception—a mask—can set the course of his academic future. I was even more disturbed by Jackson's thoughts on his new reading group, which he solely associated with Darnel. When asked, Jackson described Darnel as never listening to the teacher, having a "smart mouth" that got him into trouble, teasing the other kids, assigned to a seat placed away from all the other children, and, overall, being the "bad Black boy." I cringed. Somewhere along the way, Jackson had come to believe the negative perceptions of Darnel and used him to signify the lower-level reading group. His shame at being placed with the group was based not on ability but on the presence of Darnel. With Darnel as the bad Black boy, Jackson placed himself in the position of the "good Black boy" who frequents the homes of his classmates, attends their parties, and buddies around with them on the playground. With both masks in place, Jackson is acceptable in the eyes of his friends, and Darnel is increasingly distanced and marginalized.

I am repeatedly amazed at how these and other acts of marginalization begin so early in children's lives. But I know that racial prejudices show no immunity to age; even the very young are strongly affected by them. I wonder if things might have been different if there were more students of color from a variety of ethnic groups in Jackson's classroom and school. And I wondered where Jackson had learned this prejudice and discrimination. Surely it was not self-taught.

QUESTIONS FOR REFLECTION. How might Jackson's perceptions of Darnel been shaped by classroom factors, such as seating arrangements, reading group selection, and teacher attitudes and expectations? In what ways does the established dichotomy between the two African American males affect Jackson and Darnel, their classmates, the teacher's instruction, and learning? What should we as teachers do to eliminate these kind of masking behaviors?

MUSCLES WITHOUT MINDS

Another masking situation that remains with me happened when I was in high school. It involved Jamal, a tall, muscular, athletically gifted sixteen-year-old junior. His world revolved around football and track. These abilities determined the expectations our teachers held for Jamal and created a mask for him that read, "Much brute strength but little intellectual ability." Most of the other African American students, including myself, knew that Jamal was very intelligent and had a real knack with numbers and an uncanny ability to assess situations. Yet he was never pushed to improve his academic performance. Jamal did the minimal that was expected of him and was asked to do no more.

In retrospect, I often wonder why he was not placed in honors classes where the work was more challenging. I also realize that most of our teachers probably were unaware of his intellect or saw him only as the school's saving grace on the football field. I believe these teachers played an integral part in creating a mask for Jamal that covered up and ignored his potential in the classroom. In some ways, the athlete mask allowed him to hold on to a piece of himself, which very few people were allowed to see. Jamal eventually accepted the mask and used it as a measure of his worth. He too focused exclusively on athletics, letting his schoolwork slide. His choice ultimately left him without football and without a high school diploma. Jamal is not the only one caught in this trap, whether in athletics or some other distortion of their capabilities. Many students of color continue to be undertaught in schools.

QUESTIONS FOR REFLECTION. In what ways was Jamal placed at a disadvantage by his teachers' perceptions? Think about your own interactions with students from different ethnic groups. How do your perceptions shape your interactions with students and define their educational opportunities? How are perceptions, interactions, and masking connected to being a multicultural educator?

TURNING THE MASKS INSIDE OUT

In high school, my understanding of how academic learning could coexist with my race and culture deepened. The pressure to maintain honors-level grades was intense. My teachers sent home weekly and quarterly progress reports that detailed the rise and fall of my grades. The pressure to perform also resonated with my classmates, who openly lamented over how hard they studied. To counter these forces, I developed a silent, cool mask under which I hid my insecurities and fear and acted as if the testing, studying, and high expectations did not concern me. I participated in class, offering answers and opinions, but I never disclosed my grades to my classmates. I needed others to believe that I belonged in the honors classes; most of all, I needed to convince myself that I was just as smart as, if not more so than, the other students. I needed my mask for survival.

The mask of coolness tempered the competitive edge with a practicality that allowed me to remain calm and not succumb to the pressures. In many ways, my motivations and maneuvers were reminiscent of those exhibited by the Black females Signithia Fordham (1996) studied and wrote about in *Blacked Out* and the students who participated in Stacey Lee's study (1996) of the "model minority" stereotype among Asian Americans. Our teachers were oblivious to what was going on and did not attend to our signals for help. Multicultural teachers would understand these dynamics, their needs and consequences, and would intervene to unveil and change them.

At the same time I was engaging in academic camouflage, I began a personal crusade to read all of the literary works of African Americans that I could get my hands on. From the time I read Maya Angelou's autobiography, *I Know Why the Caged Bird Sings* (1970), I developed a deep love and appreciation for African American literature. Reading these works expanded my knowledge of the world beyond the realms of the prescriptive Eurocentric curriculum of school. My reading gave me a deeper understanding of who I was as a young Black woman, affirmation I had never received in school. Maya Angelou, Alice Walker, Richard Wright, Claude Brown, and Ralph Ellison were among the writers whose lives and characters allowed me to see how Blacks could overcome adversity, attain their goals, and maintain a semblance of sanity in a racist and oppressive society. Through African American literature, I realized that I was not alone in my feelings of isolation, fear, and guilt. For the first time, I was reading authors and events I was able to identify with. I laughed and cried, struggled and celebrated, grieved and hoped, recalled the past and planned the future along with the characters I met in these books.

As my reading list expanded, worlds of knowledge opened for me. The autobiographies and biographies of famous and unheralded African Americans took me to corners of U.S. and world history that I never knew existed. I began to question why apartheid, racism, oppression, power, and privilege were not discussed in class. If we were learning about liberation theology, why weren't we taught such principles within the context of the work of Catholic nuns in Central America? I realized that our lessons were very removed from the real world. This bothered me, and I began to question the underlying purposes of my schoolwork. With this shift in my unmasking process, I began to target more broad-based social and educational premises and practices related to ethnic and cultural diversity, along with my own personal ones.

I began to understand the importance of learning on my own as I realized how much I missed out by relying solely on school-based knowledge. In my textbooks, enslaved Africans were still depicted in the cotton fields, along with Native Americans bearing gifts to the European settlers. Latinos appeared only in the section on California, and Asian Americans showed up to work on the western railroads. In my English classes, Richard Wright's *Black Boy* (1969) offered the only ethnic dimension to a White male-dominated reading list. Our teacher's treatment of *Black Boy* left me yearning for invisibility, especially when my classmate whispered to me, "Is it true all Black folk sit on the porch and eat watermelon?" (I grabbed him by the tie and punched him. He never asked such a question again.) These pedagogical mishaps furthered my resolve to read on my own. I had the ability to shape my own intellectual course, completely unmask myself, and lift the shroud of invisibility that surrounds the historical and cultural legacies of other ethnic groups in school curricula.

Through my love of African American literature, my confidence in bridging the two worlds of school and home grew. So too did my anger and resentment toward the curricular choices of my teachers. The more I read, the angrier I became, because in excluding my ethnic group's cultural heritage, teachers denied me a piece of myself. I saw the beauty, strength, and intelligence in my culture, so why couldn't my teachers and schoolmates see these attributes too? I realized that school would not automatically uplift or even recognize my culture. At times, I felt as if publicly acknowledging my Blackness was taboo. But I began to build the bridge between home and school on my own and with my friends, who were experiencing similar periods of growth.

As we looked around at how African American students at the other area Catholic high schools celebrated Black History Month, my friend Tracey and I set out on a similar mission. Through much political red tape, including petitions and a plea to the school's board of directors, we managed to plan a book display and assembly celebrating Black History Month. On our own, Tracey and I scripted out the entire assembly, which included portrayals of Rosa Parks's stance, Dr. Martin Luther King Jr.'s writing his famous "Letter from the Birmingham Jail," a guest speaker, and a gospel choir in which the school's Black and Latino students sang. I remember how good it felt to celebrate who we were. For many of the African American and Latino students, the assembly was our only chance to shine; it was an opportunity to shed our invisibility, if only for a day. We defined ourselves on our own terms that day and did not worry about what the

White kids would say. The assembly allowed us to shed our masks and be our cultural selves.

QUESTIONS FOR REFLECTION. What forms of sociopolitical action might students in your school initiate to combat racism and other social injustices? What role do you as a teacher have in helping students develop and shape activities that reflect their ethnic diversity? How might such activities affect the classroom performance and behavior of students?

TEACHING WITHOUT MASKING

These childhood experiences are salient and quite relevant when considering the secondary teacher I became and the professor I aspire to be. The process of introspection can be a powerful tool for effective teaching. At times in my own career, questioning myself about my interactions with students and peers has caused me to change some of my teaching practices. After a day of teaching and coordinating after-school programs, I would often rethink how I approached different situations. Sometimes when I returned to school the next day, I would apologize to my students for an unintentional but nonetheless powerful insult or insensitivity I had imposed on them. A teacher cannot be above apologizing for something said or done. In my efforts to motivate students, I was tough on them. Sometimes my attempts would come across as harsh, intractable, and uncaring. When I apologized, I tried to get them to understand why I pushed so hard and that the underlying reasons were sincere.

Throughout my first few months of teaching, students constantly accused me of being from the "burbs." I can recall one young man passionately stating, "You just drive in here from the burbs to get your money." The comments hurt on several levels. I was not from the suburbs; I lived in the same urban neighborhood many of my students were bused in from. I too had known adversity and the stigma associated with our "hood." Was I that far removed from where I lived? What was it about me that gave these students the impression I was there only for a paycheck?

I also realized that the suburbs represented to most of my students a perfect world of green lawns and White folks—a place from which both their Black and White teachers looked down on their gritty urban realities with disdain. I could not blame them for viewing me as such either. I entered the classroom with my expensive private school education totally unprepared for the fine balancing act of teaching students in a tumultuous social and educational school environment. My teacher education training never addressed real-life issues of students missing school because they had to contribute to the household income, students who provided child care for their siblings or their own children, or kids who had never been encouraged or taught how to succeed in school. These students had seen their share of uncommitted teachers come and, in the case of my school, stay.

I questioned if I relied too heavily on our shared racial identity and cultural background. I wondered, in my initial interactions with them, if I expected students to bond with and follow my guidance instantly because I was Black, female, young. and from the hood. The first week teaching, my administrative assignment was hall duty. One day I noticed a tall, slender, young Black woman lingering in the halls after the bell rang. When I asked her for a pass in what I thought was a kind tone, she responded, "Hell no, I don't have a pass, bitch." I can laugh now, but at that moment, I was hot! Had I been at home, I most likely would have retaliated with a few choice words of my own, but I remained in professional mode. I simply took her name and reported her to the school administration. I later learned that Tasha had no idea I was a new teacher.

Tasha and I eventually established a good relationship. She would often come and visit me at my parents' home, just around the corner from her home. I helped Tasha and her younger cousin with their prom shopping and shared laughs and pictures of my own high school experiences with them. I vividly remember my first interaction with her because it taught me a valuable lesson in dealing with my students: respect is earned, not given. I also learned that if I were to avoid masking my students, as had been done to me, I have to mix and mingle with them in a variety of teaching-learning settings, be up front about my teaching intentions, admit my mistakes, and continue my own cultural learning and reflections on my instructional practices. I had to ensure that I didn't become convinced of my infallibility. Tasha and the other young African American students were not impressed by my presence among them. I had to take the time to learn about them, foster worthwhile interactions, and demonstrate my professional and personal commitment to them.

In her first reaction to me, Tasha was speaking through a mask. She was being hostile and defensive in an environment that did not allow her many other alternatives. Her attitude of attacking before she was attacked functioned as a means of self-protection. Given what I would come to know about this school, her masking strategy is not surprising. What can teachers do to prevent and diffuse defensive masks such as Tasha's? In hindsight, many possibilities come to mind. They are a consequence of my process of becoming multicultural.

Tasha and some other young women at school inspired me to start a girls' step team in my second year of teaching. Based on West and South African dance traditions, stepping became a popular form of dance, artistic expression, solidarity, and tradition among African American sororities and fraternities beginning in the 1960s and 1970s. The team began with a core group of girls and rapidly expanded by word of mouth. I enjoyed the camaraderie, sisterhood, and self-confidence that planning and choreographing the step show provided.

Shortly after we began practicing, I learned that another group of girls had formed their own team because they thought I would not let them participate on "my team." The situation caused me to consider whether I was elitist in my approaches to working with students. Did I seek to create "mini-me's" as opposed to allowing students the freedom to be themselves? Was my vision of good students consistent with their goals and dreams? How could I balance out my wishes for their lives with their own desires? Could I be a useful role model for them without masking students in my own image?

QUESTIONS FOR REFLECTION. What factors cause you to recognize potential in a student? In your interactions with students, how do you demonstrate your goals for their intellectual, social, cultural, and personal growth? At times, do your goals clash with theirs? How do you resolve these conflicts? Do you routinely think about your own thinking and teaching? How do these reflections affect your personal and professional actions? Can you recognize culture in your own and your students' attitudes and behaviors? When you do, how do you feel about what you see?

MY JOURNEY CONTINUES

The process of writing this chapter has prompted a great deal of introspection and reflection on my part. Long-distance conversations and e-mails with my mother assisted in bringing these memories to life once again. An appearance of a classmate on a television court show also brought back humorous memories of elementary school experiences.

As my multicultural journey unfolds, I always seem to gravitate back to how I "made it over." How did I survive, persist, and achieve academically? With the divergent worlds of my school and home community, how did I negotiate my way through? In addition to my family's support, I would be remiss not to mention the support mechanisms of community-based cultural organizations, especially my church, which provided me and other African American children with a solid foundation of learning, warmth, and affirmation. To this day, the bulk of my knowledge of Black history stems from the lessons my Sunday school teachers imparted. Beyond that, the young people had an active role in the congregation from ushering, singing, playing our instruments, and serving as lay readers. We delivered the messages on Children's Day. When hip-hop became our music of choice, our Sunday school teachers encouraged us to write raps on biblical characters to perform in church. And there was never a shortage of role models. If we expressed an interest in a particular profession, a church member stepped up to mentor us. A young man who mentioned his interest in becoming a minister was taken under the pastor's guidance and taught how to craft and deliver sermons. These individuals did not wear masks and demonstrated to us that we did not have to either, at least in supportive, caring, and culturally affirming environments.

As my friends and I grew older, the church members continued to support us by finding us summer jobs, writing letters of recommendation, and attending our school functions when our parents could not. I still marvel at the incredible acts of love, kindness, support, and generosity from the congregation. Recently, I learned that one family had purchased an airline ticket so that I could come home at Christmas from my freshman year at college. The unyielding presence of these adults filtered into my school performance in so many ways and continue to contour my conceptions of being a multicultural educator.

Knowing that a collective other than my biological family believed in my abilities to succeed as a person enabled me to begin the process of unmasking in school. I developed competence and confidence I did not acquire in school. My church role models, in their words and deeds, demonstrated how I could achieve and remain true to my cultural self. With their assistance, I began to bring the worlds of my school and my home closer together. As the gap closed, I felt more at ease being myself, free of the constraints of the masks so often imposed on African Americans and other people of color by mainstream society and schools.

From these acts of community, caring, compassion, and cultural affirmation, I gained what Jaime Escalante describes as the "roots" and "wings" he intended to accomplish for his inner-city Latino students in East Los Angeles (Escalante and Dirmann, 1990): knowledge of my cultural heritage, validation of my personal worth, confidence in my intellectual abilities, and the volition to succeed in school. These are fitting goals for every multicultural educator to accomplish for ethnically diverse students. They certainly are the mandate and mission I claim for myself.

PRINCIPLES FOR PRACTICE

Several general implications for developing knowledge, attitudes, and skills needed to be effective multicultural educators can be derived from the specific experiences described in this chapter. Four of these are suggested for consideration for inclusion in crafting your own journeys toward competence in multicultural education.

The first principle is to examine *how teachers and the school environment contribute to the isolation, invisibility, and marginalization of students of color.* After-school activities can be a starting point from which to analyze these issues. First, think about what happens in your school when the last bell of the day rings. What sounds fill the halls? Are children excited about their after-school activities? What activities do the students participate in? Who are the teachers, coaches, and administrators who work with students? Second, think of the students who stay after school for such activities. How many students of color from which ethnic groups are involved in what activities? Do students participate in the decision making about these activities? When students form their own ethnic groups or clubs, how can they contribute to the development of their cultural and ethnic identities and the improvement of the overall racially, ethnically, and culturally diverse climate of the school? What proposals would you suggest to modify current school practices so that they are more multicultural and equitable for ethnically diverse students?

Individual educators, as well as school systems, must assume responsibility for making multicultural education an integral part of the schooling experiences of all students. They can do this by demonstrating genuine caring and advocating for ethnically diverse students. In my own teaching, I made time at least three days a week for students who needed assistance with writing or for those who wanted to talk about a particular book. These hours proved invaluable for the students and for me. While assisting students, I found out things about them I would not otherwise have known. The one-on-one atmosphere allowed those who were not comfortable in the classroom to feel at ease asking questions, get the help they needed, or just debrief their day's experiences.

My relationships with the students enabled me to serve as their advocate and intermediary if they were in trouble. You can do similar and other things to get to know students better, help them negotiate educational processes, or master what is called the cultural and social capital of schools. The results are beneficial for both students and teachers. The second principle is that *one teacher makes a lot of difference in the lives of children.*

In teacher-student interactions, teachers must be mindful of the messages these relationships convey. What do your overall interactions with students reveal about you? More specifically, what do your interactions with ethnically diverse students reveal about your process of becoming multicultural? Sometimes in attempts to be more multicultural, teachers and students try color-blind approaches to dealing with ethnic and racial differences. Tantamount to masking, these approaches render students of color as vague entities, with prescribed attributes or, even worse, totally invisible. The third principle is that this process of masking can stifle the fact that *teachers need to reflect on and critically analyze their perceptions of students of color and how these affect their relationships, instructional actions, and overall educational quality.*

The case of Mrs. Marshall in this chapter provides an example of the negative consequences of these attitudes and behaviors. In her efforts to be sympathetic, she failed to realize that sympathy impeded the expectations and limited the standards set for students. Multicultural educators must strive for empathy as opposed to debilitating sympathy, an emotional response that can lead to pity and disempowerment. This empathy should be accompanied by expectations for high levels of performance and teaching techniques to facilitate their achievement.

Ethnically diverse students who are uncertain about or ashamed of their ethnic identity spend a lot of their intellectual and emotional efforts hiding from or disguising it. This takes time, energy, and attention away from academic performance. Furthermore, their interpersonal relationships are not as good as they could be because they are not based on realities. Sometimes teachers are faced with similar dilemmas about themselves. Nor do they necessarily understand what is going on with students or self. They may try to help these students to perform better in school by focusing totally on academics. The results are not encouraging because the problems reside in the students' ethnic self-concepts. The final principle is that *becoming and being multicultural educators should include understanding processes of ethnic identity development, how they affect teaching and learning, and acquiring strategies to improve the quality of these for both students and teachers.*

JOINING THE JOURNEY

I hope my exploration of the events and reactions that were catalysts for my developing skills in multicultural education motivate you to begin your own multicultural journey. If you have already begun, I hope they encourage you to continue with the process. If you need some other ideas for how to start or renew your multicultural education development, here are four suggestions to consider:

• Get to know your own ethnic self by writing a letter to yourself about your understanding of and feelings about your ethnic identity. You don't have to share this letter with anyone else, so be candid and specific. Try to answer questions like these: What are the most salient features of my ethnic identity? How do I feel about these: proud, ashamed, confused, ambivalent, or something else, and why? Under what circumstances is my ethnic identity most evident? When do I feel others are ignoring, dishonoring, and validating my ethnic identity? When my ethnic identity is under attack, what do I do to protect it?

• If you are already in classrooms, find out how your ethnically diverse students are relating to each other. Observe their friendship networks, or ask them to answer a series of questions or conduct a multicultural sociometric survey. Who are their best friends? Whom do they prefer to play or socialize with in and out of school? When they have work to do, who are their preferred partners? Whom do they prefer to be like (other students in the class)? Who are considered the leaders in class? Ask the students to provide reasons for their choices. Then analyze their choices and reasons to see if you can discern anything about how they are being influenced by their own and others' ethnicity. Think about ways you can use these insights in your classroom teaching.

• Take advantage of the opportunities provided in the mass media that are a part of our daily lives to facilitate your multicultural learning about how ethnic images are made and masked. They are also good places to start learning how to deconstruct and reform these processes. Over a concentrated period of time (two weeks, perhaps), focus on specific ethnic groups (African Americans, Vietnamese Americans, Native Americans, Mexican Americans) and examine how they are portrayed in newspaper stories, television prime-time programs, and magazine, television, and billboard advertising. Use the information you collect to name the ethnic masks that are created, and develop profiles of them. Then develop "reverse-image masks that are the direct opposite of those in the mass media. These media analyses provide practice in problem solving on ethnic issues like prejudice, stereotyping, and discrimination. They can be done in partnership with students. Videos such as *Ethnic Notions* (Biggs, 1987) and *Still Killing Us Softly* (Lazarus, 1987) can help orient you to this activity, and visualize its possibility by seeing how others have dealt with similar tasks.

• Challenge yourself to improve your multicultural teaching and classroom interactions with ethnically diverse students. Start by videotaping your teaching and interactions, and examine the tapes for how you relate to students from different ethnic groups in the act of teaching. Look for the kinds of invitations you offer different students to participate in instruction, the frequency of these opportunities, who gets what kind of feedback, who is ignored, how you react to students with different ability levels, and how different students respond to your patterns of interactions. At first, you may find it difficult to discern any differences in your behavior. If this is the case, it may be helpful to work initially with a colleague or a multicultural consultant in analyzing these tapes. You may be surprised with what is revealed. After you get better at analyzing the tapes, describe what you feel about what you see, and develop an action plan for improving your classroom interactions based on these revelations.

References

Angelou, M. *I Know Why the Caged Bird Sings.* New York: Random House, 1970.

Biggs, M. (producer and director). *Ethnic Notions.* San Francisco: California Newsreel, 1987. Videotape.

Dunbar, P. L. "We Wear the Mask." In G. Mott (ed.), *Paul Laurence Dunbar: Selected Poems.* Mineola, N.Y.: Dover, 1997.

Escalante, J., and Dirmann, J. "The Jaime Escalante Math Program." *Journal of Negro Education,* 1990, *59,* 407–423.

Fordham, S. *Blacked Out: Dilemmas of Race, Identity, and Success at Capital High.* Chicago: University of Chicago Press, 1996.

Fordham, S., and Ogbu, J. U. "Black Students' School Success: Coping with the 'Burden of Acting White.'" *Urban Review,* 1986, *18,* 176–206.

Foster, M. "Just Got to Find a Way: Case Studies of the Lives and Practice of Exemplary Black High School Teachers." In M. Foster (ed.), *Readings on Equal Education,* Vol. 11: *Qualitative Investigations into Schools and Schooling.* New York: AMS Press, 1991.

Foster, M. "African American Teachers and Culturally Relevant Pedagogy." In J. A. Banks and C.A.M. Banks (eds.), *Handbook of Research on Multicultural Education.* Old Tappan, N.J.: Macmillan, 1995.

Foster, M. *Black Teachers on Teaching.* New York: New Press, 1997.

Gay, G. *Culturally Responsive Teaching: Theory, Research, & Practice.* New York: Teachers College Press, 2000.

Good, T. L., and Brophy, J. E. *Looking in Classrooms.* (6th ed.) New York: HarperCollins, 1994.

Ladson-Billings, G. *The Dreamkeepers: Successful Teachers of African American Children.* San Francisco: Jossey-Bass, 1994.

Lazarus, M. (producer and director). *Still Killing Us Softly.* Cambridge, Mass.: Cambridge Documentary Films, 1987. Videotape.

Lee, S. J. *Unraveling the "Model Minority" Stereotype: Listening to Asian American Youth.* New York: Teachers College Press, 1996.

McCarthy, C., and Crichlow, W. (eds.). *Race, Identity, and Representation in Education.* New York: Routledge, 1993.

McLean Donaldson, K. B. *Through Students' Eyes: Combating Racism in United States Schools.* New York: Praeger, 1996.

Noddings, N. *The Challenge to Care in Schools: An Alternative Approach to Education.* New York: Teachers College Press, 1992.

Oakes, J. *Keeping Tracks: How Schools Structure Inequity.* New Haven, Conn.: Yale University Press, 1985.

Oakes, J., and Lipton, M. *Teaching to Change the World.* New York: McGraw-Hill, 1999.

Ogbu, J. "Adaptation to Minority Status and Impact on School Success." *Theory into Practice,* 1992, *31,* 287–295.

Pai, Y., and Adler, S. A. *Cultural Foundations of Education.* (2nd ed.) Upper Saddle River, N.J.: Merrill, 1997.

Pasteur, A. B., and Toldson, I. L. *Roots of Soul: The Psychology of Black Expressiveness.* New York: Anchor Press, 1982.

Spindler, G. D. (ed.). *Education and Cultural Process: Anthropological Approaches.* (3rd ed.) Prospect Heights, Ill.: Waveland, 1997.

Stack, C. B. *All Our Kin: Strategies for Survival in a Black Community.* New York: HarperCollins, 1974.

Stack, C. B. *Call to Home: African Americans Reclaim the Rural South.* New York: Basic Books, 1996.

Wright, R. *Black Boy: A Record of Childhood and Youth.* New York: HarperCollins, 1945.

CHAPTER SIX

Steppin' Up
and Representin'

Kipchoge N. Kirkland

Multicultural growth occurs in many places, spaces, and ways. My own development began in the hearts, spirits, and hands of my family—not because of anything exceptional or extraordinary, but simply in the way my parents and other family members introduced me and my brother to the learning, related joys, expectations, and obligations that come with living in an ethnically and culturally pluralistic world. Although these were not the only sources of my multicultural becoming, they were the foundations of other things I have learned along the way. Other contributions have come from what I have learned in classrooms as a student and a teacher, observations and experiences with ethnically diverse people in a variety of social and cultural settings, and interactions with people in the communities of which I am a member: my own ethnic group, my friendship network, and my professional peers.

All of these influences individually and collectively have taught me a fundamental message that underlies my beliefs about being an effective multicultural educator and is reflected in my behaviors: the idea that we are morally obligated to promote human dignity, educational equity, and social justice in teaching and interacting with students from different ethnic groups. I agree with Edmund Gordon (1999) that "once the issue of human diversity is permitted to enter the calculus of human affairs [and it must], the question of social justice becomes critical" and that "concern for social justice is a necessary condition for education" (p. xiii). These are recurrent themes in my multicultural education development, as they should be hallmarks of our classroom teaching.

FAMILY FOUNDATIONS

Some of the early beginnings of my journey toward becoming a multicultural educator are illuminated in the following poem entitled "Family Time," which gives credit to my first multicultural models and mentors, my parents:

FAMILY TIME

You took the time to teach us to read . . . with daily instructions of
    Proverbs
and through children's books you helped us to get through the mail.
You took the time to teach us the power of poetry in children's
    rhymes,
that were right on time . . .
teaching us 'bout "Lias! Lias! Bless de Lawd, don' you know de day's
    er broad?" from Dunbar's classic "In the morning", (a poem you
    remembered from a Black teacher who you said knew how to
    tell it).
You took the time to teach us, especially my brother, to learn our ABCs
    in more than just a song.
I can remember him crying and singing while you were constantly
    telling him to "Say it and stop singing!" (as you masked your light-
    hearted joy with a stern look of love and concentration)
You took the time to teach us the power of travel through first hand
    experience,
exploring distant countries, languages, histories and cultures, though
    never losing sight of our own.
You taught us the power of the African Spirit through giving us names
    from the continent . . . Kipchoge Neftali and Hasaan Amiri . . . so
    that we would never forget our distant heritage.

You took the time to teach us that family was an extended collective
    expanding from the west of Sacramento to the east of Youngstown,
sprinkled with authentic homegrown tones in the southern moans of
    Oklahoma, Mississippi, and Georgia.
You took the time to teach us that in all the many places and spaces
    we've been . . .
ain't nothing like a good friend we have in each other . . .
which is why I cried when I thought I was going to lose my brother
    behind
the ignorance of my young racial, cultural, and Kirkland identity.
You took the time to teach us to reflect and connect with the spirit of
    learning . . .
telling us to never stop asking questions,
keep reading,
and most importantly, never forget where we came from.
And when it is all said and done,
don't let our work be in vain
and leave something for the next generation to claim!

These teachings, experiences, ancestral roots, family explorations,
loyalties, learnings, and lovings that I learned from my family as a
small child still anchor, nourish, and guide me. My parents' lives and
legacies are constant reminders of the kinds of responsibilities I have
to fulfill as I try to guide my own family while touching the lives of
students. They taught me that without conscious spiritual, cultural,
and personal connection with those who give me strength in my daily
life, there are limited possibilities for me to make meaningful connections with others. The meanings of their lessons are similar to the inspi-
rations that Joyce King (1999) gained from her "community family":

> The neighborhood where I grew up was very much like an African
> village: the people who lived there were related by family ties, social
> bonds, and survival struggles over several generations. . . . For gener-
> ations they had followed the harvests doing the work that made it pos-
> sible for them to survive and for me to be educated and to become a
> sociologist, teacher, educator, and researcher [p. 102].

Her words reflect connections to the ones I have experienced and serve
as powerful examples of lessons learned from collective experience
and struggle.

THE BEGINNING OF MY MULTICULTURAL ME

My mother taught me important components of multicultural teaching, learning, and living, and the need to maintain close connections with other African Americans. These lessons have been useful in guiding my life's work, responsibility, and sense of joy in the process of becoming a committed multicultural person, scholar, and teacher. The lessons that I can distinctly remember stem from her demands for my brother and me to read the Bible. Her instruction was for us to read a different story or passage daily. During dinner, we had to discuss what we read and find ways to apply it to our lives. She was very concerned about the development of our minds, but more important, she wanted to be sure that our souls would be made whole. My mother and father were persistent in teaching us in the ways of the "truth and the life." Their concern for souls was crystallized for me on a particular day my brother and I chose not to fulfill our daily responsibility of reading.

My brother and I have always been close. Growing up with him was and continues to be a lot of fun. Together, we created a world of ideas that allowed us to explore the joys that came from being with each other and from engaging in the "dozens" (a verbal technique that involves talking negatively about other kids, their games, and sometimes their homes and family members). On the day of our spiritual revelation, we had lost track of time and forgot to read before our parents came home. It was during dinnertime that the soul-stirring incident happened.

Dinner was wonderful. My mother had prepared a spread of fried chicken, white rice, green beans, and some good sun tea. Time with the family was good too. Pops asked us about how the day went, and we both chimed in like champs, "It was cool!" We all had smiles to go around. My brother and I were thinking, *Please, let's hurry up and finish so they don't remember to ask us about what we read.* But then Ma asked us, just as we were about to clear the table, "What did y'all read today?" My mind was racing, and my heart was setting the pace. Hasaan, the risk taker, took it with ease. He began describing in detail and with the conviction and skill of a young griot in the making. I was both nervous and amazed to see how far he developed his story. He had me thinking that perhaps this storytelling thing would work for me too. But something wasn't quite right. I could sense the mood change. My mother asked softly, and with a hint of the ominous, "Didn't you read that yesterday?" Hasaan was caught! "Ah, yeah," he replied. "I thought I told y'all to read something new every day," Ma responded, looking at him as if he had lost his mind. Pops jumped in like a flash of black lightning, scolded my brother, and told him to "get upstairs!" Their tone struck fear in the both of us. I quickly confessed that I had not read either. I was spared for not lying, but my brother was not so lucky. I tried to run out of the house as quickly as possible because I did not want to be around any kind of disciplinary action being dealt out by my father. My parents' lessons, disappointment, and concern for our souls on that day served as a constant reminder that we must continue to be diligent in our daily devotion and not forget our daily responsibilities.

My folks taught us many lessons about spirituality and justice, several of which came from biblical parables, stories, hymns, and proverbs. The ones that I remember, and find myself still turning to, come from Proverbs. For example, my father would always quote Proverbs 1:8–9: "My son hear the instruction of your father, and do not forsake your mother; For they will be a graceful ornament on your head, and chains about your neck"—in other words, "pay attention to what I and your mama got to say, and everythang will be everythang." Pops would often pair these biblical proverbs with African American traditional cultural parables that were much clearer and more concise. He often said, "I brought you in this world and I'll take you out!" We knew he was saying something serious to us, but we never imagined it was a threat of physical harm. Now, I think it was a signal to let us know that we had crossed the acceptable limits for testing his authority. Other times he would tell us, "A hard head makes a soft behind." These phrases were instructive directions that helped us to maintain our focus on wisdom that would come through studying and taking heed of my parents' advice.

Another story that has affected me is one my mother often told Hasaan and me about two brothers, Jacob and Esau. The younger brother, Jacob, with the help of his mother, stole Esau's birthright, a deceptive act that forced both brothers into exile. Jacob received his father's blessings and lived better than Esau did. Jacob ran away in fear that Esau would retaliate and kill him because of his misdeeds. But over time, Esau forgives Jacob and reconciles with him. This story has been a difficult one for me to understand because of the value that I place on family, brotherhood, sisterhood, truth, justice, equity, and cultural responsibility. Jacob's corrupt behavior called these ideals into question. Stories such as this one have helped me to raise questions about contemporary schools and communities where inequities exist in educational practices, funding, resources, and teaching quality for ethnically and culturally diverse groups. Why do we continue to deny massive numbers of students their birthrights to quality education, equality, justice, and freedom? How can these inequities be corrected? These questions form the ethical and pedagogical core of my becoming a multicultural educator.

My struggle with the story of Jacob and Esau and others like it has helped me to become a stronger, more vocal, and critically conscious advocate for students of color. I have included in the charge to myself bringing about social change for people of color and other groups who encounter oppressive and marginalizing circumstances that deny their inalienable rights. I strongly believe, along with Sleeter (1996), that in the process of becoming and being multicultural educators, we must actively engage in social change by embodying the principles of justice and equality in our personal and professional behaviors. This social action dimension of multicultural education is demonstrated in Gay's suggestions (1994) that "all children should be taught that they have the responsibility to claim and honor these prerogatives as their human and civic birthrights and to actively resist all actions that might compromise or constrain the same rights of anyone else" (p. 101).

The guidance that I gained from reading the Bible and listening to my folks' spiritual guidance has been tremendous. As I developed physically, intellectually, and spiritually, my curiosity increased as well. This growth led me to be creative with my reading habits, and I began to include other areas for exploration. I became captivated by stories about science, animals, microbes, chemical experiments, and the numerous cultural creations of various indigenous groups that we encountered in our travel.

I enjoyed animated characters that raised morality issues and was especially captivated by Aesop's fables. These short stories served as reminders of the need to develop a good and healthy life that allows one to reflect on day-to-day interactions with others. They also provided opportunities for me to visit Greece, Rome, and Egypt in my imagination and see the ancient ruins. These places were great for a kid expanding his imagination. I would imagine myself sharing stories in the Colosseum in Rome with many people. Then I would imagine them returning to their homes and discussing my latest creations. My imagination worked well for me. By being able to visualize the Greek ruins, I was able to make Aesop's fables come to life in my head.

I also was fascinated with my mother's romance novels, and they later became a personal bond between us. Together, we read these books and discussed the plots and characters. She taught me about being a good, loving, and caring man as she challenged many of the male characters in the books. I can remember her often telling me that "he ain't right" as she informed me how the man was "supposed to act." Her lessons were intimate and endearing, humorous and informative as she explained her connections with my father.

One of my mother's favorite phrases was, "It takes two to tango." She used it to demonstrate that relationships are dynamic connections among individuals. Ma pushed, prodded, and loved me to think, question, reflect, and check myself. She was always there to talk about anything and everything. The values and lessons she taught me opened up avenues for me to begin to explore my ethnic, cultural, and gender identity and my interactions with others beyond the family circle. My mother constantly reminded me that relationships with women were to be valued, respected, fun, and always open for discussion and exploration. She was developing in me a sense of gender equity and ethical responsibility.

Ma's instructions have had a tremendous impact on my life. Her influences are embedded in my daily effort to become a better multicultural person, teacher, and scholar. They are a constant reminder never to forget my ethnic and cultural roots. She prepared me to resist the racial prejudices that I might face. Her life was an example for me to follow. Her lessons of culture, consciousness, connections, love, and persistence are key motivators that pushed me to seek holistic life experiences, joy in reading, love of learning, and building communities and networks with others who share my passions of social justice and quality education for ethnically diverse groups. I thank her for initiating my journey in becoming multicultural.

Ma died from breast cancer when I was seventeen, but she is still with me. I often see images of her through different words and creative ideas, and in the physical and spiritual presence of individuals who touch my life. I sense that it is her way of keeping watch over me.

My father equally stressed the significance of reading, studying, and maintaining a spiritual foundation. His teachings instilled in my brother and me the power of exploration and risk taking. During our years growing up and while he was in the U.S. Air Force, Pops took us places we had known nothing about and never hesitated to explore the histories, cultures, traditions, and geographies of these countries. He was excited about traveling the world and being able to see first-hand some of the places we had heard or read about.

My father often purchased books about the traditional culture of the people whom we encountered. In England, we collected museum guidebooks after we visited. In other places, he bought us picture books, photographic essays about the lives of past political figures of the country, and other materials that discussed different aspects of the cultural or military history of particular countries. While we were in Turkey, we experienced the "Whirling Dervishes" during their cele-bration of the solar system. This Turkish tradition was amazing. It was fascinating to see so many people gathered to watch Turkish men, young and old, twirling around in circles for hours to rhythmically captivating songs and music. We had this experience because of my father's curiosity and desire to learn about different people, cultures, events, and experiences.

Pops's interest in military history took us to Pearl Harbor in Hawaii, Okuma Falls in Okinawa, Japan, and different sites in the Philippines. We boarded military fighting vessels, saw massive can-nons and old and new nuclear weapons, and visited war memorials. I remember feeling a strong sense of confusion, anger, and disbelief when we visited a place in Okinawa called "suicide cliff." It marked the area where Japanese students committed suicide as a result of not wanting to be taken prisoner by U.S. soldiers who were invading Okinawa during World War II. Each of these opportunities allowed me to see for myself the extent of U.S. military power, as well as the powerful destruction caused by war. Through these experiences, I developed deep questions about the circumstances and effects of war and the importance of freedom. This questioning (or what might be called critical reflection) has become a habit that I find myself engag-ing in at any circumstance that even hints of oppression, imperialism, containment, assaults on human dignity, and restraints on freedom, whether intellectual, cultural, social, personal, or national. In so doing, am I engaging in the process of becoming multicultural? I think so.

I believe my father wanted my brother and me to develop healthy perspectives about other people's cultures and histories as well as our own. His commitment to our cultural growth was demonstrated through his support of the arts, too. He took us to plays, museums, castles, ruins, art galleries, gospel extravaganzas, and numerous other cultural events that exposed us to the diversity of the world. He also made sure that we were able to make connections with U.S. urban life in New York City; Youngstown, Ohio; Oakland, California; and San Francisco.

My father's worldview has taught me a great deal about independence, cultural sensitivity, and respect for diversity. It continues to sustain me as I search for opportunities to learn about the world around me on my own and with my family. During my sophomore year in college, for example, I went to Alaska with my roommate to work in a fisheries cannery for three months. I went on my own without the comfort of home and worked sixteen-hour days with a majority of people whom I did not know. This was my first opportunity to develop and express my own sense of independence and to apply some of the other lessons my Ma and Pops had taught me.

My parents' lives, lessons, and struggles provided me with many more opportunities for success. They taught me the value of freedom, diversity, spirituality, and creativity. In the process of becoming a multicultural educator, I am seeking to have a similar impact on the lives of students in ways that honor my folks's expressions of life. Their teachings have moved me deeper into the field of education with a committed passion for knowledge and wisdom. This passion brings many personal and collective challenges to my family. For example, my father, aware of my pursuit, often asks me, "When you gon' get a job?" seemingly concerned that I will be in school for the rest of my life. I assure him that in due time, all this education is going to work for me, my family, and our community in ways we have yet to imagine.

ETHNIC CONNECTIONS

Although my journey in becoming a multicultural person and educator begins with my parents, it extends into the collective experience of African Americans. My people's journeys have affected me in profound ways that have caused me to express my soul's creativity. In this section, I invite you to witness the inflection of a cultural tone that helps me to express my Blackness, which is the underpinning of my multicultural education commitment. Contrary to what some believe, the two commitments are not contradictory or mutually exclusive.

In fact, they are complementary and enrich each other. I do not have to leave behind or forsake my Blackness in order to promote multicultural education. Gay (1987) says that

> Black culture is a lifestyle that emphasizes the artistry and aesthetics of being; emotionalism over rationality; the poetry of being over the mechanics of doing; the quality of interpersonal relations over accolades of positional status; mean processes over end products; and spontaneity and improvisation over structured and preplanned action. There is a propensity among Afro-Americans to react holistically to environmental stimuli by using, in concert, affective, intellectual, and kinetic response mechanisms. Afro-Americans are also inclined to incorporate music, movement, art, aesthetic, poetry, oratory, and spirituality into their everyday activities [p. 4].

Gay's points are well taken. Through the following poetic statement, I say back to Gay what I think African Americans and others, especially teachers, need to know about our cultural expressiveness:

EXPRESSIVE BLACKNESS
"Mine eyes have seen the glory . . . "
through our ways of being we have gleamed like sun beams,
powerfully brilliant.
"Amazing grace how sweet the sound"
of sistas' and brothas' hearts and minds
working in tandem
to connect with the essence of the
African-American Spirit!
Hip Hop has taken its place of importance
but not over the prominence
of our people's souls!
"We have come . . . A zoom zoom zoom before I step!"
to the crossroads and we are moving towards the horizon
singin', dancin, proclaimin'
Hallelujahs and Word ups and Right Ons!
as we speak our Ancestors into existence.
We are cultural blends of racialized pasts
touching future elements of greatness . . .
We are active factions of Blackness in action
moving collectively through time.

We teach our babies, heal our sistas, fill our brothas and
Thank our Fathers and Mothers
for giving us life to breathe.
We be expressions
of our brothas' verbal fluidity
Of our Nanas' spiritual orality
Of our Sistas' Black creativity
Of our Poppys' cultural sensitivities
to our Ancestors' struggles for us to be . . .
"You go on wit yo' bad self!"
demonstrate your cultural wealth
"cuz we sho' nuff be right!"
as we stand as a unified light
to illuminate the world with our
Expressive Blackness!

In hearing my poem, I feel the energy of my people rush through me. Being Black and becoming multicultural are live. I hope you can feel the dynamism of this poem about my view of cultural expressiveness and the joy I feel sharing it. Its motivation, creation, and content signify the value of telling your own story in your own way that helps others take a glimpse, get a taste, or perhaps catch a bolt of cultural lightning as you demonstrate your vibrant ethnic heritage. We African Americans and other groups of color must continue to declare that we do not come from pathological, exotic, or exalted cultures that have been noted in the distortions of some research studies. It is imperative that we explore different facets of our cultures to understand the complexity, depth, and possibilities of our separate and collective existence.

From one of my many intellectual mentors, I have learned the importance of critically analyzing the historical, contemporary, collective, and personal cultural stories of different ethnic groups and individuals. In discussing the ethnic identity of African Americans, he says, "When we walk through this world with an understanding of our history, we are able to maintain an intellectual arsenal that not only affirms us as individuals but also allows our collective community to better defend and produce a healthy, inclusive vision for generations to come" (Rochon, 2000, p. 303). His words are instructive for African Americans and other ethnic groups that want to maintain their authentic cultural experiences and challenge how they are represented by others in our schools, communities, and society. This is a major mission of multicultural teaching and learning.

As I become more multicultural, I am learning to step up and represent my sense of cultural family and ethnic kinship and make connections with the larger cultural community. I collaborate with African American, Filipino American, and European American poets. We create and participate in a celebration of words, thoughts, music, ideas, and experiences as we engage our audiences in a verbal journey. Many of our topics discuss the difficulties of being who we are in a color-conscious society. Other topics demonstrate our delight, anger, pain, and hope for future generations of folks who will be in our space. In this community, I try to share my feelings, knowledge, and beliefs about what it means to be in the multicultural education movement and why it is important to celebrate the contributions that different ethnic groups make to U.S. society and the rest of the human family. This seems almost too obvious to be worth declaration. But there are still too many people who question whether groups of color have (and do) made significant contributions in all aspects of life, or just do not know what they are. Combating this skepticism and ignorance are high priorities in my own multicultural teaching. I want all people to know and value their own legacies as well as those of other ethnic groups.

PERSONAL COMMITMENTS

In this space, I'ma bring da noise in this flavorful connection that leads you in a direction of deeper thought and reflection on the selections that we each must bring. These words are mine, but they come at a time that is a synergy of those that have gone on before me and have instilled in me the will to "keep keepin' on." My progenitors have taught me that in my efforts to "resist the resistance" against our existence and future persistence, I and we must learn to reflect on the past, connect with the present, and create for the future. In other words, I must "step up to the plate and represent," or as John Ambrosio says in Chapter Two of this book, you have to "make the road by walking." Experiencing my own and observing some of the efforts of others preparing to do this provoked some mental images and messages that rendered themselves in poetic form:

MINDS IN ACTION

Witness minds in action
Visual demonstrations
Exploded in colorful contemplation
Of folks daring to be different.

Witness minds in action
And feel their connected presence
Fulfilling the ethnic essence
Of cultural groups we seek to honor.
"My how time flies"
as we engage in the surprise
of application
through our pedagogical fascination
for multicultural education.

Witness minds in action
Active factions
Of human souls letting go,
Gently holding onto
Particular dispositions
For a general recognition
Of the massive work being done
To liberate our minds.

Yes!
Witness minds in action
That put together thoughts and emotions
In hopes to create a multiethnic commotion
That WILL bring about a positive notion
Of Change!

Peace.

I wrote this poem as a response to a series of pedagogical performances that were created by college students enrolled in an introductory course in multicultural education. The diversity of creative talents, ideas, and perspectives of the students illuminated major principles of multicultural education. It was fascinating and encouraging to see each of them working on their cultural analyses of the ethnic groups they chose to explore and begin to bring to life through research, theory, practice, and the arts. They were talking with each other and working diligently to create presentations that were inviting, exciting, and enlightening. Each group developed a community personality that was interesting and unique. The different forms their personalities took provided our class with great energy and variety. These unique characteristics were evident in the groups' work habits. Some groups delegated tasks and had their members work separately and then come together at the end. Some groups had a few main people doing most of the talking while working simultaneously on creating posters, coloring patterns, and assembling material. Others worked collectively throughout the entire process. I became intimately engaged with this class of women and men who began to experience and realize the uplifting possibilities of working through a variety of teaching applications based in multicultural education theory and practice. I witnessed their minds in action, and their growth resonated with my own.

Their actions inspired me to create a poem that allowed me to reflect on their work and my own thinking about being multicultural. Through my poetry, I could demonstrate my joy, amazement, and interest in a personal and passionate way to affirm students who were working diligently to illustrate some of the principles of multicultural education. Their beaming smiles, laughter, and quests for more information about the ideas raised by Geneva Gay, James Banks, Val Pang, Christine Bennett, Sonia Nieto, Carl Grant, Christine Sleeter, Gloria Ladson-Billings, Young Pai, Joel Spring, and other multicultural educators were but a few of the positive responses to the impact of this introductory course on their own thoughts and behaviors, and the possibilities of learning that could happen for others.

I chose to represent my observations and understandings of the students' minds in action because their becoming gave me an opportunity to reflect on my own. This venture, this journey, this mission, this mandate to be multicultural educators, is simultaneously individual and communal, personal and professional, academic and ethical. My poetic reflections and affirmation of students let me know that I am moving in the right direction. I want to engage with students and struggle along with them, sharing the celebrations of their successes and the pains of their failures. At the same time, I want to take a step back and let them represent themselves in the process of learning. When I am in sync with the dynamics that are taking place in class, my poetic presence seems to take over and flow. My mind is in action and moving toward a transformation of the academic into the spiritual. Truly an education that is multicultural is spirit filled. Giving voice to it in poetic form is my expressive style of representing. Others might choose oratory, song, dance, visual art, and essay.

PROFESSIONAL COMMITMENTS

Good multicultural teaching honors our diverse cultural and ethnic experiences, contributions, and identities. It is a source of great energy and creativity that can reveal the talents and aspirations in all of us. It is captured best in Gay's views (2000) of culturally responsive teachers—those who embody the spirit and essence of multicultural education. She explains:

> Culturally responsive teachers have unequivocal faith in the human dignity and intellectual capabilities of their students. They view learning as having intellectual, academic, personal, social, ethical, and political dimensions, all of which are developed in concert with one another. . . . [They] validate, facilitate, liberate and empower ethnically diverse students by simultaneously cultivating their cultural integrity, individual abilities, and academic success [pp. 43–44].

I am learning to collaborate with my students, colleagues, mentors, and family members in ways that help me know where we are and where we have come from, and to imagine where we will go. I created a poem that serves as a metaphorical challenge to and affirmation of those who have helped me to gain a better understanding of what it means to engage in multicultural teaching, living, and learning:

SPIRIT OF TEACHING

Like conductors
We perform with a stunning magnificence
Exploding and directing with the tempo
Of minds roaring with the sound of
Creativity.

We glide like dancers
Energetically bounding across cultural boundaries
While gracefully pirouetting in the honor
Of their powerful place of prominence
And possibilities for change.
We hear the echoes of our souls responding back
In the mouths, the eyes, and the expressions of spirits
Freed to think freely, give back creatively, and to question critically,
While specifically attending to the need for growth.

Like diamonds
We glisten, sparkle, and illuminate
Any presence with a luminescent essence
That was created in pressure and pleasure
through generations of compressed thoughts
from the souls of Black coal.
We are four pointed, multifaceted, touched on all sides
By different elements, rendering us
Unbreakable, impeccable, strong and present,
And shimmering in the sunlight of minds radiating!

We are a gentle breeze of ancient eastern thoughts
Naked and exposed revealing our inner most feelings
About becoming one with ourselves for ourselves
In support of each other.

We are the calm in the storm
Of little hands that spread imagination
In blues, "lellows," and pinks!
Across walls, dresses, lil' gator t-shirts, Pokemon shorts,
And bright colorful faces.

Like the struggle for freedom,
We have connected with other folks' younguns, us included,
And colluded to engage in the performance
Of the political and the spiritual.
Through our expressiveness we illuminate the possibilities
Of becoming multicultural
And we have blended with the spirit!

We are
Freedom.
We are
Raw.
We are
On a journey.
We are
Art in motion.
We are
Living poetry.
We are
Sounds of thought.
We are
A kaleidoscope of colors.
We are
The Spirit of Teaching!

This poem addresses the need to develop specific processes that allow us to express our most intimate, active, political, creative, and cultural ideas about teaching diverse students. I hope that as you expand your own and your students' hearts and minds about ethnic and cultural diversity, you will establish kindred connections with others. By working together, we can begin to realize the power, passion, and transformative potential of teaching, acquire a better sense of ourselves as educators, and build more effective multicultural communities among us and our students.

ASPIRING MULTICULTURAL EDUCATORS

Through the process of becoming a multicultural educator, I have often found myself alone. Being solitary has been an important opportunity to clarify my beliefs, sharpen my focus, and reflect about multicultural education. It allows me to examine my connections with the spirit of teaching that I have been seeking to develop and instill in others who also want to touch the lives of ethnically and culturally diverse students. Actively promoting equity, justice, freedom, democracy, and appreciation of ethnic and cultural diversity through multicultural education is a critical need since socioeconomic and educational disparities among ethnic groups continue to exist. This struggle has to be waged by multicultural educators and others as well.

As we become more effective in serving the needs of ethnically diverse students, we should periodically regenerate our energy for social, intellectual, and cultural change and reflect on the quality of our efforts in daily personal and professional behaviors. This is what I am learning to do. The process helps me sharpen my focus, enhance my understanding, and improve my teaching skills. Although I may be the only one in the particular place where I function who is engaged in the multicultural efforts I endorse, I know that others in other places are doing similar things. This is encouraging to me, and I realize that I have to be diligent in making connections with them and participating in the national network of multicultural educators.

I want others to join me in stepping up and representing all that our ethnically diverse students are capable of accomplishing. I want us to follow the advice of multicultural specialists like Nieto (1996), Banks and Banks (1995, 2001), Bennett (1999), and Gay (2000) to understand the experiences and perspectives they bring to educational settings and be responsive to the cultures of different groups in designing curriculum, learning activities, classroom climates, instructional materials and techniques, and assessment procedures. I also have learned a lot about how to do this from high school students and their diverse expressions of self. By using these students' words, ideas, and experiences, all of us can acquire a deeper understanding of the content and contexts of learning activities that work best for them.

Becoming a multicultural person and educator is an amazing and wonderful journey. It has the potential to transform our very being as we become involved in reforming our teaching, schools, communities, and society. Becoming multicultural is a liberating process that is helping me to understand the importance of knowing where I have come from, who I am, and who I will be. In an effort to affirm everyone who is genuinely committed to this transformative process, I wrote a poem that is a charge for everyone to step up and represent the power of multicultural education in their teaching and personal lives:

REPRESENTING YOU!

You are sensational, inspirational, and a generation of exploded
    creativity
A diversity of songs wrapped and twisted and tangled
On the deep rooted rhythms of Ancient heart beats

That speak fluid languages of Freedom, Power, and Intellectual
    genius!
Your creative flows of dance demand our fullest attention
As you take us through dimensions of laughter, sorrow, and pain
Only to exclaim in the resonating exchange of
Que Viva La Raza!
Que Viva Mi Gente!
Yes, those wonderful proclamations of life made right
In the excited light of a sista's mind being turned on
Touched by distant cultural stories that seep into us like
African Spirituals of Freedom and Resistance
Mystically transforming us
Into improvised syncopations that burst into
Little boy laughter and little girl giggles
As they laugh in the face of supremacy's ignorance and impotence.
Yes, you are amazing
A colorful array of blended images that radiate
A tremendous brilliance of jubilation
That simmers in reflective contemplation
About your Lola's windsong and Poppy's hand prints
Across your cheeks and neck
As they whisper secrets of love into your ear
With the moisture of a magical language that converts
English into a colorful pasticcio of Irish, Ibo, Tagalog, Hindi,
Ojibwe, Mandarin, Korean, Southern European, and
A Spray of ebonics that sends sonic shock waves
Of love passed through the ages into your young souls.
Captivating your energy,
Catapulting you into tomorrow's galaxy of diversity's wonderful
    complexity
From simply being you and me.
Connected to a collective effort to redefine the essence of unity.
Yes, you are a tremendous presence of beat boxing guaguancos
Folded into poetry in motion
Forcing a commotion of raw rapid fire flows
Of mouths and minds that speak a spiritual code
That shouts out to the world
That "You have always had the right to be here!"
So "Step up and represent"
You artists

You leaders
You singers
You dancers
You creators
You innovators
You prophetic thinkers
You aspiring teachers
And take the time as we create a design
That illuminates our individual perspectives
In the spirit of the collective
And propels us all through time
With the hope for the future of our children in mind!

Peace.

PRINCIPLES FOR PRACTICE

The act of creating poetry can be a liberating process. It gives the poet the freedom to express deep emotions and thoughts about particular issues. When I write poetry, I find myself thinking through several aspects of being. By this, I mean that I try to convey the essence of a problem from different angles and make intellectual, emotional, and experiential connections with audiences. *Using alternative means for students and teachers to express themselves* is a key principle for practice that can be derived from how I explain my process of becoming a multicultural person and educator. My expressive modality is poetry, but there are many others: song, dance, drama, dialogue, prose, painting, and rhetoric. Other individuals en route toward being multicultural educators should use their personally preferred expressive styles. Opportunities also should be provided for using them to capture and convey their knowledge, insights, feelings, reflections, and commitments to multicultural education.

Educators have as much right to explore their creative skills as students have to claim their rights and possibilities to grow and learn. They should unleash their creative thoughts to think deeper, question often, and reflect more frequently about ethnically diverse cultures, heritages, histories, and experiences throughout the learning process. This act of crafting one's rawest emotions and thoughts into pedagogy as an art form is truly a revolutionary act. It allows us to be more comprehensive in our growth and development—that is, to link thinking with feeling, knowledge with action, self with others, and aspirations with realities. More important, it shows students that teachers are expressive, affective, and creative individuals and that they can be too. Thus, *learning how to use artistic and creative pedagogy to teach ethnic and cultural diversity* is another principle for practice in becoming multicultural educators.

The process of becoming multicultural requires a great deal of study and a commitment to reflecting on what is learned. This principle is implied in my parents' teaching my brother and me to develop and maintain critical reading habits. As a result of these habits, I continue to seek greater insight into diverse cultural groups within the United States and elsewhere to connect what and how I learn personally to curriculum development and culturally responsive pedagogy for use with students. It is imperative that we constantly question our assumptions and ideas about diverse cultures, ethnic identities, languages, and lived experiences in the contexts of teaching, learning, and living in pluralistic settings.

Diligence in constructing new ideas, deconstructing old ones, and collaborating with others to engage in transformative action on issues of educational equity and social justice for ethnically diverse students helps us to build and maintain the intellectual and ethical arsenal that children need to function well in diverse societies. Developing skills embedded in this principle will equip students to combat the ethnic ignorance that exists in our schools and society, and create communities that genuinely support diversity in practice as well as in principle. The more we read, discuss, critique, and act on cultural information, the better we are able to create pathways for diverse students to become academically, socially, culturally, and personally successful. Critical reflections and culturally responsive actions are essential to being good multicultural educators.

A fourth principle for practice is to be *playful, have fun, and enjoy what you do* in the process of becoming and being multicultural. Playfulness should not obscure profundity. I believe that if teachers do not have fun with what they are teaching, they may prevent students from developing their excitement about learning. Think of the joy you have when your mind is actively engaged with something you like. It feels wonderful to make the personal connection to the problems you have encountered. And it feels great when you and your students witness minds in action as you embrace and own issues, ideas, and actions. Having fun during multicultural teaching and learning can be energizing, transcendent, and transformative.

Multicultural learning also helps us to think and act creatively. Students who have been reserved in their feelings, thoughts, and actions become much more fluidly and frequently expressive when they are liberated from the constraints of conventional educational practices. Some of these students create multicultural performances, dramatic dialogues, art displays, critical discourse, and imaginative teaching behaviors. They realize that this learning process does not have to be stifled and stiff; it can be vibrant, electrifying, and inviting. As you pursue your journey toward becoming multicultural, be creative with your questions about other cultures and ethnic groups that are unfamiliar to you. Dig deep into the stories that you hear, and determine how to connect them to your life. Try new ideas, experiences, ways of learning, and relationships with diverse ethnic and cultural groups in your community. Learn to work, struggle, share, and laugh with them. Finally, recognize that your playfulness is not the same as being trite, disrespectful, or uncommitted. It means you are actively engaged in the process of transforming the lives of students and their schooling experiences, and you know that profound substances can be conveyed in playful wrappings. The principle for practice that derives from these suggestions is to *use multiple techniques that are holistically engaging to learn about and teach multicultural education and enrapture one's total ethnic being by cultivating the mind, body, soul, emotions, actions, ethics, and aesthetics simultaneously.*

Becoming multicultural educators and people is an intensive process that I have come to embrace, be frustrated by, enjoy, and love. It is a journey into self as you explore the experiences of yourself and others to create better learning experiences for students. For those of us who choose this path, we can expect to face some opposition from mainstream people and positions who fear the revolutionary changes that multicultural education can produce. We have to struggle to validate our perspectives, research, pedagogies, and lives in schools, universities, careers, and even our own communities. Our efforts to develop instructional strategies and learning climates that are culturally inclusive are not to be taken in vain. It is equally fulfilling and encouraging to know that we do not have to work alone—that other kindred spirits are achieving educational equity and excellence for ethnically diverse students. Thus, *developing networks, collaborations, and partnerships with others with commitments similar to yours and learning how to persevere in the face of opposition* are important principles for practice in multicultural education.

Multicultural education messages and ideals are not always overt and explicit. Sometimes they are subtle, implied, and indirect. Nor are they always rational and cognitive. Many powerful ideas about ethnic and cultural diversity are conveyed through or embodied in emotional, ethical, and affective expressions. This is so because *multicultural education is a holistic endeavor that engages knowing, thinking, feeling, valuing, caring, and doing, simultaneously.* Alternative sources of information should be used that have the ability to capture and convey these nuances of ethnic and cultural diversity. Therefore, another principle is that *personal narratives, oral histories, proverbs, and parables, as well as more conventional content sources, are powerful conduits of multicultural messages.*

A final important principle for both students and teachers is to *remember where you come from.* Personal stories are important sources of information about ethnic and cultural diversity. They can provide some insights into multicultural issues that are not possible from other knowledge bases. Teachers should not hesitate to share their experiential encounters with ethnic, racial, and cultural differences as they invite students to do so as well. Our histories, heritages, and ethnic identities are always with us wherever we are and in whatever we do, including teaching and learning. Personal stories should be integral parts of multicultural curriculum and instruction, along with other forms of knowledge. We should acknowledge and support ethnically diverse groups, identities, and experiences in the classroom as a means of helping students become more psychologically healthy and academically successful.

JOINING THE JOURNEY

Becoming multicultural is an active and interactive process. You have to do more than passively receive or memorize factual information about ethnic and cultural diversity. You have to immerse yourself in and engage with a wide variety of multicultural encounters and experiences where you are learning, thinking, feeling, reflecting, and acting. I hope you have gleaned some ideas from this chapter that will be helpful in stimulating or affirming your own journey toward becoming good multicultural individuals and educators. If you are stymied about how to get the process started, here are a few suggestions:

• After reading, discussing, and interacting with some of the basic principles of multicultural education, respond to them in free verse.

Include in these poetic renditions your thoughts, feelings, and insights about how these principles affect you personally and your teaching possibilities. Then share these poems with others in your teacher education classes or schools where you teach. Afterward, have these others express their emotional reactions to all of the poems and then conduct performances (using nonverbal motions, sounds, and actions) to demonstrate the impact of the lessons learned from them. You can use similar activities with students and include other forms of creative expression. Active participatory learning and converting ideas from one form to another help to deepen multicultural education understanding.

• Working with your students, collect or create photographs, drawings, and symbols that represent encounters and experiences of ethnically diverse peoples in the United States. Make these into posters and place the images throughout the classroom. Identify the principles of multicultural education that these images illustrate. Ask students to explain why the images convey the messages they do. An extension of this project could involve each of you creating several scenarios from the images that ask questions about the personal, ethnic, and cultural histories of the people and situations portrayed.

• Prior to and during a discussion, activity, or event focused on issues about ethnic identity and cultural diversity, make a list of questions that you want to think about, have answered, or were prompted by the experience. Share your questions with some colleagues or students, and ask them to develop a list of ten questions about your questions. Use this composite list to interview teachers, students, and members of ethnic communities to determine their understanding of and reaction to ethnic identity, cultural consciousness, and cultural diversity. Posing questions can be a powerful medium for learning.

• Develop a series of scenarios that challenge you and your students to rethink the impact of social action that is expressed in multicultural education research and practice. These might include deconstructing stereotypes, creating multicultural curriculum, and matching different teaching and learning styles within various subject areas such as reading, math, social studies, and science. Analyze these to determine how they exemplify principles of multicultural education. Declare which of these principles and actions are most promising and problematic for you in doing multicultural education. Then develop some strategies for how you can advance the promises and solve the problems.

• Use criteria for studying ethnicity and cultures that you can find in some writings of multicultural education scholars (such as those introduced in this chapter) to profile your own cultural and ethnic identity. Include descriptions of artifacts, ideas, values, beliefs, and behaviors and how you learned these. Describe how you feel about your culture and ethnicity and how people outside your ethnic group think about and relate to them. Also, examine how your culture and ethnicity affect your personal relationships and professional interactions with people from different ethnic groups of color.

References

Banks, J. A., and Banks, C.A.M. (eds.). *Handbook of Research on Multicultural Education*. Old Tappan, N.J.: Macmillan, 1995.

Banks, J. A., and Banks, C.A.M. (eds.). *Multicultural Education: Issues and Perspectives*. (4th ed.) Needham Heights, Mass.: Allyn & Bacon, 2001.

Bennett, C. I. *Comprehensive Multicultural Education: Theory and Practice*. (4th ed.). Needham Heights, Mass.: Allyn & Bacon, 1999.

Gay, G. "Expressive Ethos of Afro-American Culture." In G. Gay and W. L. Baber (eds.), *Expressively Black: The Cultural Basis of Ethnic Identity*. New York: Praeger, 1987.

Gay, G. *At the Essence of Learning: Multicultural Education*. West Lafayette, Ind.: Kappa Delta Pi, 1994.

Gay, G. *Culturally Responsive Teaching: Theory, Research, & Practice*. New York: Teachers College Press, 2000.

Gay, G., and Baber, W. L. (eds.). *Expressively Black: The Cultural Basis of Ethnic Identity*. New York: Praeger, 1987.

Gordon, E. W. *Education and Justice: A View from the Back of the Bus*. New York: Teachers College Press, 1999.

King, J. E. "In Search of a Method for Liberating Education and Research: The Half (That) Has Not Been Told." In C. A. Grant (ed.), *Multicultural Research: A Reflective Engagement with Race, Class, Gender, and Sexual Orientation*. Philadelphia: Falmer, 1999.

Nieto, S. *Affirming Diversity: The Sociopolitical Context of Multicultural Education*. (2nd ed.) White Plains, N.Y.: Longman, 1996.

Rochon, R. S. "Black Success or White Emulation: Who Shall Sit at the Table to Create Effective Solutions That Empower African American Children?" In L. Jones (ed.), *Brothers of the Academy: Up and Coming Black Scholars Earning Our Way in Higher Education*. Sterling, Va.: Stylus, 2000.

Sleeter, C. E. *Multicultural Education as Social Activism.* Albany: State
University of New York Press, 1996.

CHAPTER SEVEN

Clearing Pathways for Children to Go Forth

S. Purcell Woodard

L etters and poems are powerful means for communicating complex ideas and revealing deep feelings and beliefs. This is one of the reasons that I chose these motifs to share some of my developmental experiences in becoming a multicultural educator. Another reason is the monumental risk that ethnically diverse children face when they are placed in the care of educators and others who do not honor their human dignity or fully develop their intellectual potentials. This resistance must be resisted completely and unequivocally.

Using a correspondence format, Bob Teague (1968) wrote *Letters to a Black Boy,* his twenty-two-month-old son. He followed this initial effort twenty years later with *The Flip Side of Soul: Letters to My Son* (Teague, 1989). Teague's intent was to alert his son in particular, and children in general, to the facts and effects of living in a racist society. He was prompted to act by his belief that "if you can pick up some idea of what reality is like early, before it intrudes unannounced, you may not be caught off guard—unprepared and undone—as often as most men [and women] are" (Teague, 1968, p. 1).

Teague teaches these lessons to his son by sharing his own experiences with the forces of dehumanization, marginalization, and denial and the perpetual need to struggle against them. I follow his example by sharing my journey toward becoming a multicultural person and educator with my own son, Alex. Here, I focus on one theme that I think is imperative to the process and that will be especially relevant to Alex and his teachers, as it has been (and continues to be) for me: the need to resist resistance. As Teague (1989) warned his son, Adam, because opposition to rightness, justice, freedom, goodness, and human dignity for African Americans was so prevalent, "With whatever resources I could harness, I had to keep fighting back" (p. 17). I extend Teague's argument to other ethnically diverse people as well and to educators who want to implement multicultural education. Some forms of resistance to some of these efforts are a certainty, and so must be ways and means to counteract the resistance. This is the intent of the following correspondences with my son, Alex.

Dear Alexander Kamal, a.k.a. Lotus,

I write this letter specifically for your eyes, but it also is useful for your mother, future siblings, me, and even your generational peers. You were still in your mama's womb the first time I purposefully wrote to you. We had just come from our prenatal visit with the midwives. The first ultrasound was performed that morning. After our appointment, I had to go back to work, and later attend a graduate seminar. Near the end of that day, I wrote you a poem that I entitled, "For a sun":

> I can hardly keep my eyes open.
> I'm completely and utterly drained.
> Trying to sit still has brought to my attention just
> How excited I am about you, our first child.
> My excitement, to date, has only barely been contained.
> You see, I saw you today for the first time; but,
> Trust that I've loved you long before you showed on film.
> Sure it's a computer-generated image.
> Yet, you look just like me.
> I'm able to prescribe an attitude to your first portrait.
> Better yet, a personality.
> I write these thoughts in hopes of one day sharing
> With you my overwhelming experience of meeting you.
> I floated throughout the building showing off your picture
> To anyone who would stop and look.

From the dean, all the way across to people
I haven't shared so much as a word with in the two years
We've been here.
Little Lotus, I may never be able to explain to you
How I feel right now, in this specific way.
Just know that the plan is to demonstrate
How I feel about you everyday.

Lotus, you may one day hear people say that we mature in a constant, upward trajectory and our life's experiences reflect this "natural" progression. You will not find any claims to such a fluid time line in the telling of my personal route toward becoming multicultural. Indeed, some experiences pushed my knowledge, thoughts, and abilities forward. Others knocked them sideways. There are even powerful, positive experiences that had the opposite or little effect on me. Within this letter, I will share only the experiences that I feel had a meaningful impact on my continuing course of development.

One such experience involves a step I took to move closer to reaching my goal of inspiring your generation to become leaders, not statistics. I wrote an inspirational poem during my first year as a college academic adviser. It was included in a cultural magazine that was devoted to expanding awareness and respect for diversity. The poem reflects an early stage of my journey toward becoming a multicultural educator. Although I wrote it years before your birth, it traces the thought process behind choosing your name. Kamal means "lotus" in Hindi and loosely translates to "perfect" in Arabic. The poem is aptly entitled, "The Lotus Flower":

The line between success and failure is thin.
Smaller yet if you're African American.
Even smaller if you're male.
So easy is it to falter.
So hard it is to thrive.
Life can at times be like the murky depths of a pond.
So strive to be the lotus flower.
It sprouts from the muck
To open its divine petals
Outward to the sky.
Just as the lotus,
You too can overcome obstacles [Woodard, 1996, p. 19].

My method for writing about my process of becoming multicultural is to talk about encounters with resistance, or "the murky depths of a pond." Specifically, I write about resisting resistance in a letter format that is open and fluid. Its messages require that you be a reflective critical thinker and doer. This writing genre challenges you to examine and extend my interpretations by judging their utility against your own knowledge and experiences. It also demands that you share what you learned from my story with others.

RECOGNIZING ENEMIES AND OPPOSITION

Lotus, you should know that resistance is the purposeful and unintended strategies used in our daily lives to maintain our personal definition of a given situation when faced with conflicting information that challenges our understandings or interpretations. Resistance is not always negative or external. This conception conjures up two distinct, but not mutually exclusive, images. The first is an image of someone bracing against the onslaught of external forces. The second image shows the same person having internal dialogues about personal privileges and vulnerabilities. According to Archibald and Crnkovich (1995), developing consciousness and participating in dialogues are ways of being that entail how we see others and ourselves existing in the material world, critique personal historical and cultural biases, and avoid presuming that what we take for granted is universally accepted truth.

The resistances that I address may be different from the ones you will face. The strategies used in my generation to resist resistance will undoubtedly leave spaces for new resistances to emerge that perpetuate inequities, injustices, and exploitations of certain ethnic groups. This entrenched cycle of oppression and resistance will be shaped differently as children like you make it necessary to use multiple and imaginative means to define self and other. In many ways, you are a reflection of me, and in other ways you are not. Your eyes, smile, nose, and ears are like mine. But your hair is thin and fine, not thick and coarse like mine. Your skin tone is many shades lighter than mine as well. To see you is to behold a living example of the margin that I confront in so many of my thoughts and actions—two worlds colliding into one. To know you is to understand how beautiful and complex that margin can be. Yet I know that the world in which you will live may resist and even deny your beauty simply because you do not fit neatly into conventional racial, ethnic, and cultural categories. How do I resist these resistances in ways that model strategies for you to do the same? Potential responses to these questions took poetic form:

> Temporary clairvoyance.
> Where the world view of the
> Dominant culture and the
> Oppressed culture
> Collide
> Rests
> A seldom acknowledged
> Connection called the
> Margin.
> It is here that you will
> Find me
> For my inner-tension
> Both begins and
> Ends in this region.

Lotus, the key to identifying and resisting resistance lies at the core of this poem's definition of "the margin." The inner tension noted corresponds to my journey toward becoming a multicultural person and educator. It is critical for you to understand that "the dominant culture and the oppressed culture" constitute shifting identities that reveal power relationships grounded in class, culture, race, gender, ethnicity, and sexuality. Other insights about different forms of resistance can be derived from examining others' reactions to families like ours. For example, Teague (1968) wrote about a fictional meeting of the minds between the Black and White cultures. In this encounter, European American culture is prepared to spend money on programs that will eradicate the miserable conditions within the African American community. Their offer begins with "an unmistakable sign of good faith. We are prepared to pass a Civil Rights Act giving [Blacks] the right to marry [Whites], if both parties in the marriage submit first to a painless sterilization process to prevent any children" (p. 196).

Multicultural kinships have existed throughout time, but many people will question my ability to teach you how best to navigate the relationships you will encounter. After all, I am Black and your mother is White. You are neither and both. Based on our different ethnicities and cultures, how can we possibly relate to you beyond the bonds of paternalism? Sharing my journey not as your parent but as one who is developing personal and professional skills to make the world a more accepting place for your racial, ethnic, and cultural diversity is one response to this question.

Resisting resistance is a legacy of our ancestors that I, and eventually you, must carry on. At the turn of the twentieth century, a brilliant African American philosopher named W.E.B. Du Bois (1989; 1903) examined why some Whites believed the humanity of Blacks is a tertium quid. He wrote, "[This is] something that is undefined but connected in some way to two things which are known or definite" (p. 235). The connection I make from his words to you is that you are linked to two knowns within the United States—one Black, the other White. In this pairing, one group is centered and privileged, while the other is marginalized and powerless. Your mom and dad represent these two realities. Lotus, you are the undefined connection between us—not one of us, yet both of us. Your racial and cultural duality will cause you to struggle to find a place among the interpersonal politics of your own country.

Near the end of the twentieth century, Senna (1998) in her novel, *Caucasia,* described individuals like you and her as the "canary in the coal mines" (p. 335). Before technological advances, canaries were used to determine the quality of air in mining shafts. If the air became toxic, the canaries felt the poisonous shift long before the miners did and fled, thereby signaling the danger to the humans. Senna's analogy suggests that by examining the historical experiences of people of multiple ancestry, the cultural and racial air in the United States can be gauged. I extend Senna's argument to you to better understand the conditional willingness of both African Americans and European Americans to embrace you as their own as long as your physical appearance and personality traits do not remind them too much of what they despise or distrust about each other.

These two ways of seeing the world book-end the twentieth century and serve as a diagnostic projection of the pulse of the United States regarding multicultural tolerance in this new century. Lotus, you are a child of the new millennium. Remember, though, that you are the offspring of parents from the old. We are not apologetic for bringing you into this world. You need to know that the world is going to trouble you and be troubled by you. Concealing you within the protective cocoon of our love is not a wise course of action to prepare you for this reality. Helping you learn how to reflect and act critically on your experiences is a much better strategy.

RESISTING SEDUCTION

This letter is one way to model the critical reflection process that I plan to teach you and others of your generation. It fits well with my process of becoming a multicultural educator since some levels of your existence represent what I am working to achieve. Lotus, I am committed to helping people think and act beyond concerns for immediate personal costs and benefits, and interacting with the world in more transformative ways, and in both schools and society at large. I want you to understand that resistance for you and your generational peers will come in many complex, subtle, and sophisticated forms. Some will even be enticing. You will have to be very astute to recognize and resist them. My goal is to prepare you to do so. To facilitate this process, I will share specific resistances I have encountered in my life. I begin with a poem:

Why don't you share your voice?
My voice?
Don't ask me about voice until you
Better understand silence.
You presume that
Silence equals absence.
And that's hard to refute.
But, you're blind to the steps that render me mute.
Because what is absence?
Absence is structured into classroom etiquette.
I get three minutes to state my claim.
But, let's problematize this time frame.
I get three minutes to
Bring folks up to speed on a non-traditional
Way to be.
This, of course, presumes that my colleagues and
Students will even believe me.
In that three minutes, I need to
Advance the history of my thoughts,
Find room to expand and
Extend my thinking,
As well as address mis-quotes that are lingering.

And we wonder what it means to lack voice?
In some cases it's my only choice!
Forgive my, so called, uncivilized manners.
Folks stare at me with hidden (dis)content.
But only in the privacy of the classroom environment.
To acknowledge me elsewhere would require sincere
Investment in my intellectual and personal advancement.
Look, there's no room for you in our ideology.
Wait, do you mean value system?
No, our apology. We mean there's no room for you
In our merit system.
We all have access to the material.
You know you are lacking.
Value your education and
You will do what it takes to get up to speed.
Sorry for the smile; we can't contain our greed.
You see, we know that we are better than you.
So we suppose it's an unfair request.
We'll help you help yourself to the
Muck at the bottom of the well.
But save a little for the rest who think like you.
You see, as we help you, we all validate the
Informational (which is to say cultural)
Capital system necessary to perpetuate
Your meager existence.
Resistance is not futile—it's a prerequisite.
You want our understanding of voice?
Voice is our choice of tactics used to sidetrack you
In your quest to connect with those like us.
Please, we realize that liberation is a must.
We hate our powerful position.
We hate that our chosen lifestyles have
Created this "unforeseen" division.
There's that smile again.

This poem cites ten forms of resistance that I continue to encounter along my journey toward becoming multicultural: (1) being misunderstood (so I'm told) when I take unpopular stances on issues in social and academic discourses; (2) not being recognized and acknowledged by classmates and professors "out of the university context"—I become simply an uncontextualized, "invisible" African American male; (3) not being publicly supported by peers when I challenge racial, gender, and culturally insensitive comments that demean the dignity of the diverse—in critiquing the culprits' comments, I am accused of destroying intergroup unity and harmony; and (4) not being permitted to raise my voice in discussions because such displays of emotional and passionate responses are considered inappropriate for academic study and settings. The dubious assumption is that my American classmates and instructors will genuinely engage the ideas, feelings, beliefs, experiences, and analyses of me and other students of color in the first place.

I group these first four resistances together because they represent attacks on individual personhood. Their effect is to render my colleagues and me void of individual uniqueness, cultural legitimacy, and intellectual rigor. If I am discouraged from expressing myself from my own vantage points, then how will others even know who I really am? Also, how do we build trust with those who are different from us if conflict is avoided? Resisting these resistances requires that we take ownership of our private thoughts and (in)actions and strive to share and examine them publicly. I implore you to refuse the security found in being a member of the faceless, voiceless, and motionless masses.

Before beginning my journey toward becoming a multicultural person and educator, I had fallen prey to the seduction of facelessness, racelessness, and culturelessness. I vividly recall the day students of color picketed on the front lawn of my university president's house, demanding the establishment of an ethnic studies program. I was on his patio at an invitation-only formal party celebrating the contributions of undergraduate student representatives such as myself. I did not participate in the protest and was completely blind to the issues that prompted it. Yet I was considered to be an official student representative at campus-sponsored events. Lotus, remember that I said that unless a person purposefully chooses to fight injustices, he or she can rationalize most inequities away. I suspect that now you see I am speaking from lived experience.

Other resistances in the poem include (5) being put on the spot and expected to provide counterpoints to conservative views; (6) having to find intellectual allies from multiple backgrounds and worldviews to validate my own personal experiences; and (7) being considered one of a few "safe and acceptable others" with some mainstream power and influence. Whereas the first set of resistances was primarily about our rights as individuals, this set is more about our responsibilities as members of communities and other larger entities. In order to resist them, we must willingly make ourselves accountable for the welfare of others. This, however, does not mean that you always have to present the dissenting opinions and perspectives. Sometimes it is enough to assist others in recognizing the fallacies of their own ideas and making their own corrections. Another way of saying the same thing is that sometimes the best antidotes to oppression come from the oppressors, not the oppressed.

The final set of resistances noted in the poem is equally troubling: (8) being isolated academically, professionally, and personally because you are the only one of color in a meeting, class, or social gathering; (9) being expected to accept ignorance and good intentions as a justifiable explanation for degrading racial, ethnic, and cultural remarks; and (10) having the fluidity and importance of my concerns constrained by the dictates of the clock. Typical expressions of these last resistances are restricting ethnic and racial diversity issues to superficial treatment, assigning them to the last agenda items of discussion, and including them in discourse only if people of color are present and advocate for them.

PERSISTENCE MUST PREVAIL

Dear Lotus, as I pursue my goal of being a social justice and antioppression educator, I am learning that resisting must be explicit and deal with specifics. Analyses of opposition to multicultural education must focus on particular encounters and actions instead of loosely defined general observations and principles. In applying this idea to myself, I need to acknowledge that I make mistakes. Facing your own fallibility is a necessary strategy in resisting resistance. I almost made an irreparable mistake along my multicultural journey in relation to this point. A few weeks into the first term of my doctoral program, I was ready to pack up our belongings and head back home. If not for the emotional, spiritual, and intellectual support from your "Auntie" Jeannine Dingus and "Uncle" Kipchoge, this letter to you might look very different. Their involvement in my life is an additional key to resisting resistance. You cannot (or at least should not) journey alone toward becoming multicultural and combating oppositions. Building support systems and establishing networks are imperative.

When I say I was ready to pack us up and go home, I do not mean this literally. As a California State University predoctoral scholar and doctoral incentive–forgivable loan participant (both affirmative action programs), I had institutional investment and financial support to help me complete my graduate studies. Thus, "packing up and leaving" refers to a form of personal resistance I call "intellectual withdrawal." Let me explain what I mean through example. Very early in the doctoral program, I felt the added pressure and isolation of being the only African American man in classes. A case in point was my sociology of education course. The reading assignments were not what disturbed and disenfranchised me the most. It was the in-class discussions that frustrated and silenced me.

One day, the class was examining whether being African American and a model high school student were contradictory. The majority of my classmates accepted, with some reservations, that these identities were polar opposites. In her work, Hemmings (1996) identifies the peer culture of Black students as the culprit in their academic failures. C. Wright Mills (1975), a well-known European American sociologist, identifies these as "personal troubles" (having to do with the abilities and attributes of the individual), not "structural issues" (problems rooted within larger institutions or the economy). I argued vehemently that structural explanations could better account for the disparities in the achievement of African American students. My pleas fell on sympathetic but deaf ears, since I did not have specific examples of research or theories to challenge Hemmings's findings. I asked my colleagues to explain how I could be in our class if the research was accurate. Achieving students like me were considered by my peers as the exception to the established rule of poor academic performance among African Americans. The resistances in this conclusion included denial of my intellect and isolating me from my ethnic group.

Lotus, my mistake was participating in intellectual withdrawal. I resolved to disengage from class discussion for the remainder of the term. I was certainly not going to be anyone's token voice of difference. Here is where Jeannine and Choge showed me the error in my logic. They reminded me that although graduate school was my personal choice, my pending successes were bigger than I was. To collude deliberately in my own alienation was to sacrifice my goal of advocating for those students most often left behind in our public schools, the truly disenfranchised. Your "Uncle" Choge said best what was required of me: "You need to calm that mess down and tighten up. We've got work to do."

The "mess" was peers' refusing to take my contributions to discussions and my decision to disengage intellectually seriously. In order to "tighten up," I had to resist my resistance and reengage in classroom discourse. With some initial apprehension, I did just that. I asked the professor if I could share some thoughts on the current week's reading assignments on the social dynamics of gender differences in classrooms. Six structural forms of bias were analyzed during the discussion: linguistic bias, stereotyping, invisibility, imbalance, unreality, and fragmentation (Sadker, Sadker, and Long, 1997). I encouraged my peers to reflect on why structural issues were considered to impede the successes of European American females, but the academic problems of African American students were attributed to personal troubles. I asked my colleagues, as current and future educators, what the life chances of Black females were in all of this. The silence that befell the room was respectful contemplation. At the beginning of the next class session, a fellow student (an older European American) informed me that the question I had posed helped him think through some tensions he had, but could not articulate, with the literature on African American students and our different responses to it. Lotus, one specific resisting resistance message in this collection of memories is that timing is sometimes everything.

A related resistance involves e-mail discussions. The implications of this medium for helping or hindering a journey toward becoming multicultural are mixed. Another of my class experiences illustrates this point. In one of my educational policy classes, we examined the growth of public charter schools throughout the United States. Some of my colleagues felt that charter schools widened the achievement gap between the haves and have-nots. In their view, only upper-middle-class, stay-at-home moms were politically and culturally savvy enough to navigate the institutional red tape involved in establishing a charter school. I argued that charter schools can meet the educational needs of students of color and poverty better because they have more site-based autonomy and innovative curricula. My viewpoint was more provocative and controversial than I anticipated. Instead of talking to me in person or in the open forum of our class discussion, a fellow doctoral student made his comments over e-mail. In our multiple electronic exchanges, I pointed out that this technology excluded some critical information. Playful and serious vocal tones and different levels of commitment and passion about issues were not transmitted through one-dimensional characters on a screen.

I suspected multiple layers of resistance were occurring in this situation. The one that was most insidious was not the difference of opinion on the charter school issue itself, but the refusal of my peers to engage me in face-to-face dialogue. Putting a computer in the midst of our conversation was a way to edit or control the content of exchanges before any sharing took place. The resistance here was creating illusions of interacting but actually avoiding any genuine dialogue with ethnically diverse students, peers, and professors. Unfortunately, this is a common occurrence in predominantly White institutions. Resisting resistance requires teasing out layers of opposition so that you can respond appropriately to them.

CHOOSING PLATFORMS FOR ACTION

Lotus, be aware that I purposefully limit this discussion of internal and external resistances to academic-related issues. The reason is I put my faith in the potential of public schools and my concern for the life chances of ethnically diverse children placed in the care of educators who are unprepared to help them reach their full genius. Lotus, you may become one of these kids. This frightens me and causes me to accelerate my understanding of the role that personal and cultural knowledge plays in generating certain forms of resistance and resisting resistance. What if your teachers have not begun their journey toward becoming multicultural? How will their personal, unexamined resistances affect the way they interact with students like you? How will they influence your personal well-being and your academic future?

James A. Banks (1996) describes personal and cultural knowledge as concepts, explanations, and interpretations generated from our experiences within our homes and communities. These perspectives, insights, and assumptions help us evaluate future experiences we will encounter in schools and other institutions. Successfully resisting resistance from others hinges on whether we have begun to grapple with our own personal forms of resistance. I have come to realize that a major factor that is affecting my ability to counter oppositions to multicultural education is that I am a heterosexual male living in a society founded on the oppressive principle of male dominance, which continues to condone these beliefs and behaviors. My process of becoming a multicultural person and educator entails descending into a metaphoric gorge of experiences so as to examine the privileges afforded me by my sexuality and gender. I have had to ask myself hard questions about what I believe to be true, just, and right with respect to gender, racial, ethnic, cultural, and social class differences. Traversing this rugged, and sometimes painful, valley of memories and analyzing the intricate landscapes of recollections have allowed me to practice what Spivak (1990) calls systematically unlearning one's privilege while simultaneously not viewing the process as a loss.

I have always enjoyed reading newspapers. I vividly recall an article describing how African American men rarely graduated from the California State University system. Many years later, when I graduated from that system with a bachelor's degree, I had the phrase, "And they said it couldn't be done," inscribed on the inside cover of my graduation announcements. Ironically, many of the people who received the announcements thought that the "they" was a slight to them. Few realized that I was deliberately connecting my personal success to a larger social issue to show that African American men, with the proper support, could graduate from the California State University system. In making this political statement, I risked alienating those who supported me. To this end, I am reminded of some prophetic advice shared years after this event by a student in a college class I was teaching. He said, "The decisions you face aren't as important as what you do after choosing your option." Because of progress I am making in my multicultural journey, I can now question why analyses of educational disparities of African Americans often focus on males. Any edition of the *Journal of Blacks in Higher Education* confirms that the enrollment and graduation rates of Black women are as dismal as they are for Black men. Lotus, in learning how to resist resistance, a key lesson you must internalize is always to look for alternative funds of knowledge and thorough interpretations of issues.

Surface understandings are themselves resistances. A colleague describes surface understandings as practical but potentially misguided attempts "to manage complexity, boundaries that became rigid and dogmatic through habit and convenient forgetfulness of why they were created." Gaining a deeper understanding (which is to say, resisting this resistance) is hard work. A key strategy is to accept that no issue can ever be fully analyzed by consulting a single source of information. You need to ask many questions and use multiple and varied knowledge sources. Better yet, you should always explore why certain questions never get asked. Through interrogatives like this, you will gain a deeper understanding of ethnic and cultural differences, social justice, and educational equity for diverse groups in society and students in schools.

KEEP GOING FORWARD

Lotus, there is little to be gained from brooding over "would haves" and "should haves." In learning to resist resistance, you should consider making my student's counsel your mantra. If you do not adopt a form of his way of thinking, you stand to be plagued by the memories of when you remained silent when you wanted to speak up, or when you failed to respond to an injustice in a way that you wish you had. The potential guilt derived from this thinking can hinder you from identifying and resisting future resistances. Another excerpt from my journey toward becoming multicultural illustrates this point.

The year was 1995, and it was early September, about two weeks before my first graduate class. Your mother and I were en route from California to North Carolina for a short vacation. I had preregistered for a course on counseling ethnic minorities and purchased the required books, and I anticipated using part of the in-flight time to read ahead. I wanted to make a strong impression since I was conditionally admitted to the graduate school (my undergraduate grade point average was calculated as a mere 2.5 for my last ninety units of credit). Because the cross-country flight was not as long as one might think, I brought my smallest textbook along: *Assertive Black, Puzzled White* by Donald Cheek (1976). While the plane was taxiing on the runway I scanned the book's Foreword. I speculated that the author of the textbook and the professor of my class were the same person. The connection of the author to my graduate program was confirmed by the biographical information on the book jacket. How had I missed the signs indicating that this person was a local author and an African American?

That my first graduate professor was African American was significant; even more so was that it had never occurred to me that he could be Black. I tried to recall all of my African American teachers. My second-grade teacher, Mrs. Sanders, is my first and last example. A series of questions consumed my thoughts for the remainder of the flight. How had I gone through my entire academic career with such a limited exposure to African American teachers? How many other students, Black and non-Black, have done the same?

Two intertwined forms of resistance are deeply embedded within these recollections. The first is that I had unknowingly come to believe that African Americans did not teach in universities. The second was my not knowing that people of color write college textbooks. Experience at the university I was attending had shown that if a class dealt with racial and ethnic diversity, the odds were good that it was not going to be taught by a European American. I didn't make this connection to my particular class even though it focused on racial issues in education.

Lotus, the decision I faced was what to do about my own knowledge, attitudes, and expectations that were shaped by former educational experiences. On the first day of class, Dr. Cheek asked the students what we knew about him. The other students shared a number of flattering anecdotes. I was silent because I was contemplating whether to share the revelations I made on the plane. After all, I didn't know any of these people, and what I had to share would push the unspoken limits of acceptable self-disclosure.

Therein lies a key to resisting resistance: sharing what you really think and feel for fear of rejection is a resistance. It takes strength and courage to break this norm of apprehension—a silence forged in the face of possible rejection, unpopularity, or unconformity. I did share my story. I was unapologetic as I explained why having an African American professor was important to me. I explained what I had already learned about myself because of him. Most of the European American students did not understand my point, although some claimed they did. The only other student of color in the class, a Filipino American woman, showed in her eyes that for very similar reasons in her own life, she understood my story.

Taking that initial risk led to additional genuine dialogues with my professor about my aspirations to join the professoriat. The outcome of these interactions is that Doc Cheek (as you will come to know him, Lotus) became my first formal academic mentor of color along my journey toward becoming a multicultural educator. Throughout my life, I have had many informal mentors who have shared valuable insights with me on a social and impromptu basis. I do not wish to downplay their assistance; I am grateful for all of the help I have received. My point is that the guidance I was receiving in these informal relationships pales in comparison to the formal training that Doc extended to me.

Our connection did not come quite so simplistically, though. Doc Cheek explained that his role in my life (indeed, all of his students' lives) was analogous to that of a sports trainer. As he saw it, we were all preparing for the 100-yard dash. His goal was to push us to run the 120-yard dash. As a former Olympic alternate and current senior Olympian, all of Doc's metaphors contained references to athletics. The transferable resisting resistance strategy in his imagery is to set your goals but equip yourself with the necessary tools to achieve beyond them. Resistance lies within the complacency derived from setting and reaching a terminal goal. For me, Lotus, this theme also underscores why becoming a multicultural person and educator is an ongoing process.

You also should know that I learned through conversations with my European American peers that they believed Doc Cheek was easier on the students of color. Your "Tita" Carina (my Filipina American colleague mentioned earlier) and I carried the burden of proof in debunking this insult. Translating their gripes into Doc's sports analogy, some of the European American students felt that Doc was preparing the two of us to run an 80-yard dash instead of the 100-yard dash like them. These particular students could not see that Doc was actually pushing us all to run 120-yard dashes. Much resistance was embedded in their assumptions, and equally as much resisting resistance was displayed by Doc Cheek's refusal to be derailed or distracted from his goals by these students' misconceptions.

SHIFTING PARADIGMS FOR THINKING AND ACTING

Lotus, I hope you will not face this specific resistance in your professional or personal life—that efforts to help you be your best are interpreted by some as preferential treatment. But I must tell you that unequal educational standards and learning opportunities for ethnically diverse groups are some of the most pervasive resistance of all. Nevertheless, resisting it is not as complicated as many people think. It requires that you believe, and show through your actions, that advocacy for a specific group of people does not diminish your concern (or ability to advocate) for the welfare of other groups. Such a disposition requires a purposeful shift in mind-set from either-or to both-and thinking. Do not brush lightly over the historical and contemporary tensions associated with shifting to both-and thinking, a newer way of seeing the world. For example, as a first-generation graduate student and former college adviser, I am specifically vested in students who are from educationally disadvantaged, low-income, first-generation college and underrepresented groups. This commitment does not mean that I do not concern myself with advocacy issues relative to nonpoor European American males.

Along my journey of becoming multicultural, I have begun asking a new question: How do we accomplish social justice when the way of life promoted by the dominant worldview is so interconnected to oppression that it doesn't even serve well the elite, heterosexual European American males for whom it was initially designed? An attack on either-or thinking is at the root of this complicated question. It is insufficient to claim that a person is either part of the solution or part of the problem. Understanding that individuals can simultaneously be oppressors and oppressed, mainstream and marginal can uncover new pathways for resisting resistances, as well as bring previously unknown resistances to the surface.

I did not have a formal mentor until I was an adult. This need not (and should not) be the case for you and your peers. Good mentors are individuals who are willing to help you face your resistances when you would rather not. They help you learn how to resist the resistances of others by sharing their own experiences and techniques. A transferable lesson to your life about the importance of mentors is conveyed in a poem I wrote for a group of high school students in a summer program. I cofacilitated discussions about diversity and respect for this group, whose members were from underrepresented ethnic groups, first-generation college goers, low income, and conditionally admitted to the university. As we prepared to embark on our discussions, I shared these thoughts:

> Folks tell me that you can't do this.
> This type of discussion is too deep.
> Too hard. Too much.
> Don't upset the kids.
> Please. You're already upset. I can read the
> Body language around this room.
> The next step is to help you put words
> To those emotions.

Spoken language is key.
It is a tool of oppression.
It is also a tool of liberation.
I study voice.
Sometimes that means the lack thereof.
Would it help you to know that I never really thought
About these issues until after I finished college?
Diversity what? Injustice? Say who?
Man, I'm just trying to get through.
That you begin to think about these issues is critical.
I look in your eyes and wonder,
Will you begin tonight?
Nightfall is appropriate imagery.
We start in the darkness of our resistances.
This is not a negative thing.
Refusing to uncloak your resistances is, though.
You need to step out. Take a risk.
True, you'll never get hit by a speeding train
Of thought if you stay inside.
You'll also never see the shared world.
Don't hesitate to say what's in your head.
More importantly, don't forget to quiet down and
Listen with your heart.
Remember, folks tell me that you can't do this.
Don't upset the kids.
Please. I can look around the room and see that
You're already upset.

The resisting resistance lesson of this poem is that students are capable of having deep conversations about complex social and educational injustices, even if they currently lack the language to do so. Mentors and teachers carry the responsibility of teaching students the skills they need to speak their thoughts, feelings, and experiences. Sometimes this requires expressive genres other than writing essays or academic discourse. Lotus, some people who tell you that you can't do this or that will claim that they are protecting you. In many cases, it is well-intentioned educators who are championing this claim. In response to these behaviors, I appeal to Young's idea (1990) that people suffer oppressions and injustices because of the everyday practices of well-intentioned people. Resisting the resistance to shelter others is a criterion for understanding the shared world among us. Sharing our stories about our privileges, vulnerabilities, oppressions, and coping abilities is another way to counteract resistance to the missions of multicultural education.

LOOK, LISTEN, LEARN, AND MOVE FORWARD

Hear me correctly, Lotus: reading and face-to-face interactions build off each another. Both are needed. Much of what I learned as a practicing college adviser directly challenged what I thought I already knew from my own personal experiences with racial oppression and injustice, or from studying the issues at the graduate school level. The major lessons my students taught me are stressed in this last poem:

> Let's identify your first problem.
> For as sure as you desire to understand me,
> You are but spinning your wheels.
> Fruitless in your efforts.
> You still seek to understand on your own terms.
> Yet, if I have long ceased to subscribe to your
> Definitions, what happens to your comprehension?
> Therein lies the mental block retarding our chances of
> Achieving a collective social and political bloc.
> Any attempt to understand me will take a mutual
> Revolutionary act of love on both our parts.
> Oral-historically, you have not shown yourself
> Capable of such a leap of faith.
> Your trust-fall must entail the assassination of that
> Which you have come to know as you and Other.
> Violence—be it epistemic or physical—
> Has come to form your, you presume my, world view.
> It's a major tenet within your old, out-of-touch world order.
> That love could be aligned with death
> Paralyzes your ability to see beyond the shadows
> You partially control.
> You will, therefore, never understand me.
> It has taken me a long time
> But now I understand.
> You will never allow me to define me.

This is not a matter of semantics.
For now I realize that by defining myself
I also necessarily re-define you.
The power to name is also the power to un-name.
Your existence is controlled by the very
Static nature you assign me.
If that changes, you change.
And we wonder why they say change is bad?
You are they.
I sit among you learning of
Or shall I say from, the same folks as you.
However, I am slow to learn that it is I
Who should be teaching.
Truth-tellers lay tracks for truth-followers to find.
Some of us are simply slower to see the signs.
Rest (un)assured that I now know my mission.
I understand the power of definition.
I do not wish to shackle you
As your ancestors may or may not have done to mine.
I want to show you that uncertainty,
The opposite of static, is not something to fear.
Invest yourself in releasing your
Stronghold on definition.
Learn of yourself as others
Like me, define ourselves.

The other poems I have shared with you in these letters were accompanied by introductions establishing the contexts for their text, or outroductions guiding you to lines that I wanted you to focus on. I opt out of that pattern here. This time I want you to reflect alone on the concepts presented in the stanzas. By doing so, I hope you will create meanings that extend well beyond those I might have given you. This is the essence of mentoring relationships: take what you are given, and turn it into something greater. Believe in yourself and in your interpretations. This is the final suggestion I will offer you at this time for learning how to resist resistance.

In closing, you should know that many of my friends and colleagues will be shocked to learn that I am sharing myself with you this way. I am usually not this open about revealing my personal feelings and thoughts. But I believe that sharing our vulnerabilities and strengths, successes and failures, hopes and doubts is a necessary part of preparing students to engage effectively to accomplish social justice and educational equity for the many ethnically diverse people in the United States. I want to leave you a legacy of knowledge, values, and strategies that will serve you well in this struggle. The risk of a little personal discomfort or embarrassment is a small price to pay for ensuring that you are well prepared to construct and live in a more caring, compassionate, and culturally inclusive society. I strongly encourage you to practice the self-reflection, cultural consciousness, and social activism processes I have tried to model throughout these letters.

Dearest Lotus, before concluding this letter, I need to leave you with one last insight. It is a thought that came to me in the middle of the night. You were sleeping in your crib, and your mama had finally dozed off having just finished with your second "midnight feeding" of the evening. I had a lot on my mind, as (you will learn) I often do. Upon finishing this poem, I entitled it "Poetic Epiphany." I sincerely hope that its message encourages you to start or continue with your own personal expressions of thoughts, beliefs, values, and actions about equity, diversity, and social justice. If there is a specific resisting resistance message in it, it is to speak and act when and in whatever way the call of the cause for justice (for yourself and others) commands:

> Sometimes in the middle of the night
> The sensations inside me tell me it is time
> To write so I must move from my bed to the
> Pad of paper down the hall.
> It is not that I cannot sleep.
> It's more that sleep is not needed at this moment.
> For months now I have tried to reclaim the poetry
> That flows through my blood.
> Poetry flows through my veins as it does yours.
> However, we have been systematically trained
> To ignore this inner-voice that yells out to us
> When no one else can hear it.
> It is poetic. Don't let deaf fools tell you otherwise.
> We spend our time trying to be an individual to some
> Extent. We'll change our names, our esthetics, and our
> Circles of friends.
> It's ironic that the one thing that truly separates us is

Personal poetry which comes from inside.
Prose that is so free-verse, so avant-garde,
That those labels do no justice to describe them, only harm.
It doesn't fit because there's nothing like it.
You see, the real free-verse does not necessarily rhyme,
Does not necessarily fit a catchy tempo, and
Does not necessarily end in a coherent statement.
All that is required for it to be my voice, my poetry,
Is that you cannot be me. Or rather, I cannot be you.
So the next time that voice is yelling, be it morning, day, or
Late-late night. Sit up and listen.
Better yet, write what it is saying.
And when it is saying it.
Let your soul be the judge of its poetic validity.

Peace, love, and much respect.

S. Purcell Woodard (Steve)—Your Poppy

PRINCIPLES FOR PRACTICE

Dear reader, I am pleased and honored that you have taken the time to read my letters to my son, Alexander Kamal, and your future student. Although you may never actually teach my child, there is a Lotus in each of your classes every semester, every year. I have explained how my family and I are situated in the midst of the need to resist resistances to the principles and practices of multicultural education so that we can better prepare the way for my child and all other children to go forth into more successful educational futures. I hope that you also have learned something that is useful for your own ownership and advocacy of multicultural education. By learning about ourselves, we are better prepared to shepherd our students through their own processes of becoming multicultural people and citizens. My aim here is to suggest some other principles for practice that may further aid in pursuing these goals. I begin in poetic voice:

You need to know that when I flow
My investment in an "us" takes my
All and leaves very little left.
This theft is so total, so silent,
That you often miss the metaphorical violence

Because the quarrel is on the inside of my being.
But seeing as I continue to strive to create space,
I ultimately seek to end our fruitless chase
That usually leaves neither one of us facing the sunlight.
To come at us right, we must avoid
The easy way out, the instinctual flight,
And stay and struggle through our disconnect.
In effect, I must open myself, and you (too) in turn,
If we are ever to learn how to co-exist and thrive.
So please, I challenge you, me, and us,
Don't miss this genuine gesture to address
Tensions, rather than let them fester.
True dialogue is rooted in sincere acts of
Commitment, a love that only we can co-invent,
A relationship earned through the terms of
Critical endearment and grounded in group fulfillment.

Every time I share this poem, it feels incomplete. I get to the final stanza, and several new ones scream out to be added. I read some lines and feel driven to replace certain words and phrases, or change the punctuation to render a different pause or intonation in the reading of it. My first principle for practice is connected to these reactions: *becoming multicultural is a continuous and challenging, necessary and rewarding journey.* Stated differently, we do not simply arrive at a final destination and say to ourselves, "Now I am multicultural." In becoming and being multicultural people and educators, we must be willing to encounter new information that runs counter to what we think we already know. Remember that resistance is the purposeful and unintended strategies used in our daily lives to maintain our personal definition of a given situation when faced with conflicting information that draws into question our understanding or interpretations.

The most damaging forms of resistance will also be among the most covert. This is my second principle for practice. We recognize, and at times even anticipate, overt forms of resistance. For example, if a student uses a derogatory racial term, we have a general idea of how to address that insensitivity. This is because such resistance challenges our core values. It is within our subtle core values (personal privileges and vulnerabilities) that the most damaging forms of resistance hide and thrive. An example of a covert resistance came to me as I was reflecting on how to talk with students about the antiaffirmative action movement (as with Proposition 209 in California and Initiative 200 in Washington). I concluded that when European American men claim they do not get jobs and promotions because a person of color or European American woman was hired to meet an unspoken quota, they are disparaging the abilities of people of color and females. Their presumptions of privilege, a covert resistance, make them afraid to question if they themselves are chosen, not because they are the most qualified but because they solidify White, heterosexual, elite, male power.

This way of looking at issues rarely gets raised in an open and genuine fashion. Resistance to ethnic and cultural diversity keeps us from getting to a deep level of analysis of inequities and exploitations. Upon hearing this claim, I suspect that many European American males will loudly profess, "I'm not afraid of any such thing!" This hunch relates to my third principle for multicultural practice: *awareness of forms of resistance is not enough; we must learn, teach, and apply deliberate strategies for resisting resistance.* One way to accomplish this in the classroom is by practicing culturally responsive teaching. But you have to be well on your own way to becoming multicultural educators before you can do this kind of teaching. The more you know about your own privileges and vulnerabilities, the better equipped you are to recognize those within your students. What is mostly required is that you take a risk and begin the first steps of introspection and reflection.

The final principle for practice I offer here is that *as you grow, you must reach higher in your understanding and dig deeper into yourself, even if there is discomfort in this growth.* Becoming multicultural persons and educators requires patience and diligence, along with knowledge, values, and skills. Intellectual allies are an intricate part of the ongoing process. This network of colleagues can help you maintain focus as you push yourself and your students, and are pushed by them. Ultimately, our task as teachers is to create classroom environments and learning opportunities where the responsibility of raising sensitive ethnic, racial, cultural, social, and power issues rests with the group as a whole, not just with any one teacher or student.

JOINING THE JOURNEY

Sometimes it is difficult getting started on a journey, and I realize that what you imagine as this massive undertaking called being a multicultural educator may be threatening. To counteract these possibilities ("resisting this resistance," if you will), I have a few suggestions:

• Prepare a multicultural survival kit for your children, your students, or yourself. Within this kit, place artifacts, texts, ideas, and other relevant objects that are important to learning about ethnic and cultural diversity. These items can be tangible or philosophical, even both. The purpose of the kit is to help the user detect the many forms of resistance to multicultural education. It also should provide strategies for overcoming or counteracting resistance. Describe each item, why it was selected, and how it contributes toward resisting resistance.

• Choose one of your textbooks to conduct a biographical sketch of the author. Research other books or articles that have been written by this individual and what his or her philosophical position is on ethnic and cultural diversity. Also, note who is mentioned in the Acknowledgments section of the book. Research what books or articles these "acknowledged" individuals have produced. How do the authors' identities and positions affect how they write about their topics? Do they engage in any specific kinds of resisting resistance? If so, what are these? How do you respond to your findings? Determine if your responses are resistances or resistances to resistance.

• Becoming multicultural encompasses, but is larger than, promoting diversity, respect, and social justice. It means having the courage to address thoughtfully and critically the question, Does one have to identify with or benefit from a cause in order to support it? What multicultural causes do you support? What kinds of opposition have you encountered because of these? How did you respond to this resistance? Choose a partner to practice this exercise. Both of you prepare a separate list of the various causes that you each support. Discuss the features of the causes that led you to support them. Identify any benefits you gain from supporting each cause, trade-offs you had to make, and commonalities you find between your own and your partner's lists.

• Choose a class or set of family situations as the focus of analysis to determine how subtle resistances to ethnic and cultural diversity are expressed. Look for evidence in silences, body gestures, and language behaviors. Be specific in identifying and describing the resistance signals, when they occur, and for what kinds of triggers or prompts. Then develop some strategies for unveiling these resistances and counteracting them. You can work individually or with a small group of peers to complete this task. You can use it with your students as well.

References

Archibald, L., and Crnkovich, M. "Intimate Outsiders: Feminist Research in a Cross-Cultural Environment." In S. Burt and L. Code (eds.), *Changing Methods: Feminist Transforming Practice.* Ontario: Broadview Press, 1995.

Banks, J. A. "The Canon Debate, Knowledge Construction, and Multicultural Education." In J. A. Banks (ed.), *Multicultural Education, Transformative Knowledge, and Action: Historical and Contemporary Perspectives.* New York: Teachers College Press, 1996.

Cheek, D. K. *Assertive Black, Puzzled White: A Black Perspective on Assertive Behavior.* San Luis Obispo, Calif.: Impact Publishers, 1976.

Du Bois, W.E.B. *The Souls of Black Folk.* New York: Penguin Books, 1989. (Originally published 1903.)

Hemmings, A. "Conflicting Images? Being Black and a Model High School Student." *Anthropology and Education Quarterly,* 1996, *27,* 20–50.

Mills, C. W. *The Sociological Imagination.* New York: Oxford University Press, 1975.

Sadker, M., Sadker, D., and Long, L. "Gender and Educational Equality." In J. A. Banks and C. M. Banks (eds.), *Multicultural Education: Issues and Perspectives.* (3rd ed.) Needham Heights, Mass.: Allyn & Bacon, 1997.

Senna, D. *Caucasia.* New York: Riverhead Books, 1998.

Spivak, G. C. *The Post-Colonial Critic: Interviews, Strategies, Dialogues.* New York: Routledge, 1990.

Teague, R. L. *Letters to a Black Boy.* New York: Walker, 1968.

Teague, R. L. *The Flip Side of Soul: Letters to My Son.* New York: Morrow, 1989.

Woodard, S. P. "The Lotus Flower." *Cultures,* 1996, *3,* 18–19.

Young, I. M. *Justice and the Politics of Difference.* Princeton, N.J.: Princeton University Press, 1990.

CHAPTER EIGHT

Professional Actions Echo Personal Experiences

Chia-lin Huang

———〰〰〰———

When I think about my process and progress in becoming a multicultural educator, the idea of teachers being learners and learners being teachers, and their lives and efforts being closely intertwined, keeps coming to mind. I think of all the things I learned from my students when I was a classroom teacher and from other significant ones in my personal and professional lives. What I learned from students became a critical part of my subsequent teaching. It caused me to teach differently and, I hope, better. I also think about how the personal lessons I have learned about ethnic and cultural diversity resonate in my professional values, beliefs, and behaviors. More and more, I am realizing that in preparing for and interacting with students from different ethnic groups and cultural backgrounds, the quality of what I learn is a direct reflection of what I give to the task. In other words, I get back for myself what I give out to others.

These thoughts are sprinkled with memories of specific events and individuals at different times in my life. They are with me as I learn more formal knowledge and skills about multicultural teaching. They respond to me as I look within myself for concrete examples to make general principles of multicultural education more meaningful to particular ethnic groups, teaching demands, and environmental contexts. Filtering these concepts, ideas, and theories through my personal experiences enhances the meaning of both. I am deliberate in my efforts to make theory and practice reflect each other, to "see" and "hear" my personal experiences in my professional behaviors. These echoes are hallmarks of my multicultural becoming.

When I say that professional actions echo personal experiences, I am suggesting that I am who I am now and will be in the future in large part because of my past experiences and encounters. I am both a consumer and a creator of the echoes of my multicultural becoming. In using this theme to craft my journey toward being a multicultural educator, I will share several echoes that I hear repeatedly along the way.

ECHOES OF CULTURAL ORIGINS

"Nainai [Grandma in Mandarin], do you remember who I am?" Sitting at your bedside, I look at your pale face and try to get some reaction from you. You are eighty-eight years old now. Nainai, Soung-Ming Lu Huang, you are my historical echo. I look at you, and I hear memories of my own childhood, and maybe even some of your childhood too. The memories are fresh in my mind. Do you remember how you taught me as a youngster to be a caring, responsible adult and to be a teacher when it came my time to help others learn about our culture, language, and heritage? You can no longer vocalize your verification of my memories because a debilitating disease has robbed you of the capacity of speech. But I hope somewhere deep within you, memories of those childhood teachings are as clear as they are for me.

Although I know you can't respond to me, I persist with invitations and questions to cajole you into conversation. I want to hear you echoing again in your own voice. So I persist, asking you, "Who am I?" "Do you remember my name?" "Do you know I just came back from the United States?" "Do you feel comfortable?" "Would you like to hear about some of the cultural and ethnic differences I have encountered in the United States?" "Do you remember when . . . ?" To try to entice to you speak aloud, I ask these questions in your native dialect, Sichuan, instead of Mandarin. I smile at a bit of irony here. Remember all the times that you tried to get me to speak your language when I was a child? Having learned it as an adult, I hear now that which I couldn't hear as a child; I now value that which I once found embarrassing. When did I begin to recognize you echoing in me and was enriched by this realization? What I wouldn't give if you could witness this change in me. I think you would be proud and pleased.

Every time I return to Taiwan, I go to the nursing center daily or every other day to visit with you, Nainai. Most of the time, I just watch your face and marvel at what it symbolizes for me. It is very different from the one I see looking out from the photo album that sits on my desk in the United States. You look so tiny and pale now. I comb your gray hair. It is cut very short, unlike the curly fashion you once loved so much, and it is not stylish at all. I am familiar with the feel of your hair because I have combed it many times before. I also massage your arms and legs. Your body becomes very rigid, and it is difficult to make your legs stretch out. The many wrinkles in your face are fascinating, and I try to joke about them saying, "Nainai, why do you have so many rivers on your face?"

Watching my Nainai and listening to myself, I hear many things she used to say coming out. How strange it is that I hear all of these sentences in the Sichuan dialect. I seem to hear her voice as these thoughts come into my mind. Suddenly, I realize that my Sichuan cannot be separated from my grandmother's voice. It gives homage to my own heritage. What a wondrous, uplifting sound and acknowledgment this is! So I repeat after "her" again and again:

> The echo is coming from my memories gradually,
> Which are mixed with the present songs I am singing,
> And they become the melodies of my life.

In these memories, I hear unconditional love; my childhood; strength, caring, and pride; my cultural and ethnic center; even the stereotypes of others that I learned from her. As I try to make sense of them with respect to their influence on my becoming a multicultural educator and person, I also hear echoes of statements made by scholars about the permanence and pervasiveness of early cultural socialization on our attitudes, values, and behaviors. One of these statements is made by Christine Bennett (1986): "Where we happen to be born, and when, largely determines the culture we acquire. The family, the neighborhood, the region, and the nation can make a difference. Initially, we have little control over the language we learn to speak, the concepts and stereotypes we acquire, the religion we accept, the gestures and expressions that amuse or reassure us, or the behavior that offends or pleases us" (p. 8). Another helpful scholarly echo comes from Harriet McAdoo (1993). In analyzing the strength of diversity found in ethnic families, she explains that "when we examine ourselves, we find that who we are and who we can become depend in great part upon who we started out to be" (p. 3).

As Nainai sank further into the grasp of an incurable disease, I had to face the prospect of losing her entirely. She was my link to my past. What is going to happen now that she is no longer alive? I wonder how her physical, intellectual, cultural, and emotional absence will affect my present and my future. Will her cultural socialization diminish over time, or will it echo deep within me forever? Her death is too recent for me even to begin to know the answers to these questions. But ensuring that Nainai's cultural gifts to me prevail (and preserving my students' echoes of their own cultural heritages) is paramount in my becoming a multicultural educator and person.

TEACHING THE UNKNOWN

Scared! Anxious! Uncertain! Wondering how soon I would fail! These feelings and thoughts occupied my mind, heart, and action when I approached my first teaching assignment among ethnic minority students. I understood the source of the fear and doubts but didn't dare display it. After all, I was a teacher, an authority, a professional. How would a fearful teacher command respect from her students? Undoubtedly, some of my anxiety came from being a new teacher, but it was more than that. I don't think the level of my anxiety would have been as high if I were going to be teaching students from my own ethnic, social class, cultural, and linguistic background. I empathize with mainstream college of education students in the United States who express anxiety about the prospect of teaching in classrooms with predominantly students of color. I hear echoes of my own anxieties in their uncertainties. I wonder if this situation is common to teachers from any majority group anticipating working with students who are ethnic, racial, and linguistic minorities. I also wonder about the sources and effects of these anxieties and how they are obviated by becoming multicultural.

Before stepping onto the Stella Maris High School campus, I had had only two Taiwanese indigenous friends; now I was going to teach hundreds of Taiwanese indigenous students. I had good intentions but no real knowledge about or preparation for teaching them. They looked and sounded different from me; some spoke Mandarin with an unusual dialect. Most of these students and their parents before them had little chance of going to college without some special kind of educational intervention. The indigenous groups of which my students were members were discriminated against and marginalized by the mainstream Han Taiwanese. I, on the contrary, was privileged, had been taught to value education, and took going to college as a given. I also looked and talked like most of the other people in Taiwan since I am a member of the ethnic and linguistic majority. I wondered, "What am I doing here? How am I going to teach these strangers?"

When I was a part-time teacher in Taipei, all of my students were girls from middle-class families in a Catholic private school. Living in a modern city, they and I had some similar experiences. In teaching them, I felt that I was hanging out with a bunch of "sixteen-year-old younger me's." I was a bit nervous about teaching them but nothing even close to my anxiety about teaching the indigenous students. Is this similar to how some European Americans feel about teaching African, Asian, Latino, and Native Americans? As I learn more about their concerns, I gain greater insights into my own.

I knew very little about the backgrounds and cultures of at least one-third of the indigenous students at Stella Maris High School. Hi-pong, my church brother (the leader of my religious youth group), introduced me to this ethnic group. He expressed confidence in my ability and told me that I had nothing to worry about. He believed I had the personality and character to be a competent teacher for these students. "Yeah right," I thought. I, of course, wouldn't tell anyone about my doubts and feelings of anxiety. As an intelligent college-educated person, how could I admit to these limitations? After all, I proclaimed that teachers should know and respect the cultures of indigenous groups. The words sounded great, but I didn't have the necessary knowledge and actions to go with them.

I gritted my teeth, swallowed my nervousness and uncertainties, and forged ahead into this challenge, hoping all along that wanting to do good would serve me well. In hindsight, I resent my teacher preparation program for putting me in this position. Why didn't I learn about the cultures, lives, and experiences of the ten indigenous ethnic groups in Taiwan? They are not new arrivals, and their presence is not a secret. Nor is it that they haven't made significant contributions to the development of my country, or that they are unworthy people who do not deserve respect and the best educational opportunities possible. I, and other teachers like me, couldn't do justice to their education rights and needs without having some knowledge about their ethnicity, culture, heritage, and background experiences and how these affect their school learning. My thoughts here are in agreement with Young Pai's beliefs (1990) that if teachers are "to work effectively with culturally different children, we must know about their cultural backgrounds and their historical heritages. In addition, we must also be sensitive to the degree of conflict these children may be experiencing in relating to the cultures of the mainstream society and their own community" (p. 210).

My feelings of inadequacy and the resentment they generated echo the position taken by Gary Howard (1999) in his book appropriately titled, *We Can't Teach What We Don't Know*. He is talking about people, not content knowledge. Much attention is now being given to the importance of teachers' having high-level content mastery of the subjects they teach. Why aren't similar emphases attached to being knowledgeable about the ethnically diverse students we teach? Howard's comments described my situation: "Too often we place White teachers in multicultural settings and expect them to behave in ways that are not consistent with their own life experiences, socialization patterns, worldviews, and levels of racial identity development. . . . Too often we expect White teachers to be what they have not learned to be, namely multiculturally competent people" (p. 4). Although he is speaking specifically about situations in the United States, his observations apply to Taiwan as well when "Han majority" is substituted for "Whites" and "racial identity" is replaced with "ethnicity."

I hear even stronger echoes of my situation as a new teacher of indigenous students in Little Soldier's laments (1983) about culturally uninformed individuals trying to teach Native American students:

> Few teachers would dare to introduce a subject without having a background and some measure of command of the topic. How ludicrous it would be to attempt to conduct a Spanish lesson, or perhaps to teach Pythagorean theory in Geometry, lacking understanding of these areas. Yet teachers often plunge headlong into a study of "Indians" without the necessary knowledge and understanding of Native Americans *past* and *present* [p. 51].

I didn't exactly plunge into teaching indigenous Taiwanese students, but I did go willingly and with ignorance. This is something I will avoid doing in the future now that developing a knowledge base about ethnically and culturally diverse groups is a central part of my process of becoming multicultural. I also am working on developing multicultural teaching skills along with my knowledge base. I have come to know that just as you can't teach what you don't know, knowledge alone is no guarantee of effective teaching.

As I think further about teaching across ethnic and cultural groups, as good multicultural educators must do, I know that I will have to be very conscious of how my own culture affects my classroom behaviors. I need to know how to monitor myself to make sure that I don't allow my cultural values and assumptions to unduly interfere with or disdain students who do not share my own ethnic and cultural heritages. Thinking about this need calls to mind a statement—an echo—made by Lisa Delpit (1995) about teaching other people's children:

> We all carry worlds in our heads, and those worlds are decidedly different. We educators set out to teach, but how can we reach the worlds of others when we don't even know they exist? Indeed, many of us don't even realize that our own worlds exist only in our heads in the cultural institutions we have built to support them. It is as if we are in the middle of a great computer-generated virtual reality game, but the realities displayed in various participants' minds are entirely different terrains [p. xiv].

This is a mighty challenge, and I know I must be culturally conscious and respectful of my students and myself. Certainly, my teacher preparation program should have provided some training in multicultural education, but I am coming to realize that I can't be totally absolved of responsibility for my own learning. I have to do some things for myself. This realization is one of the reasons that I chose to do graduate studies in multicultural education in the United States.

Teaching at Stella Maris High was challenging. The same lessons that I gave to classes in the private girls' school in Taipei, which had gone well, did not work at all for the indigenous students. The jokes I thought were smart and funny did not make them laugh, the activities I designed to motivate participation were not interesting to them, and other strategies that were supposed to develop student concentration were useless. I was frustrated and almost felt angry at the students' behaviors. I could not figure out any way to resolve the problems. Since I have been involved in studying multicultural education, I have some explanations for what was going on—ideas such as cultural incompatibility in diverse classrooms; the interaction among culture, education, and ethnicity; and contextual influences on teaching and learning.

Had I known about these at the time I was teaching at Stella Maris, I would not have assumed that instructional techniques used in one setting with a particular ethnic or social group would be equally as effective in other environments and with different ethnic groups. Multicultural education has taught me that this is not a good thing to do if I want to offer all of my ethnically, culturally, and linguistically diverse students the best opportunities to maximize their academic achievement. These messages are conveyed powerfully for me through Pai's ideas (1990) that

> every aspect of education and schooling is influenced by culture. Our goals, how we teach, what we teach, how we relate to children and each other are rooted in the norms of our culture. Our society's predominant worldview and cultural norms are so deeply ingrained in how we educate children that we very seldom think about the possibility that there may be different equally legitimate and effective approaches to teaching and learning. . . . The lack of this wonderment about alternative ways often results in unequal education and social injustice [p. 229].

I am not quite sure how, but I survived my first months at Stella Maris with the Ami students, an ethnic minority group, without doing any permanent damage to them or myself. By summer, things were improving. I was not quite as anxious, and the students were responding positively to me. I had many curious visitors coming to my office during breaks between classes. My tiny office vibrated with their conversations and laughter. Despite much effort on my part, I can't pinpoint what I did to cause these indigenous students to trust me and welcome me into their circle of friendship. I am glad it happened because I learned so much from them. By simply sharing themselves, they began to help me fill some of the voids about the cultural knowledge of ethnically diverse groups that had been a part of my teacher education.

One day, a tall, handsome indigenous male student came into my office, took a guitar from the corner of the room, and loudly said, "Teacher Hi-pong, lend me this guitar!" Without any explanation, he began to play a song and introduced himself as A-fu as he tuned the guitar. He then sang a beautiful song entitled, "Hello, Teacher Chia-lin," as a tribute to me. When the song ended, I said, "Wow! That's so cool, A-Fu!" He smiled and began to play another song softly. "Hey, I can sing this one," I said. So I sang along with this beautiful Ami tenor. When we finished, A-fu turned and asked, "Which one would you like to sing next?" I let him make the decision.

We continued to sing songs in front of all the students who had gathered to listen as they waited for their bus home. Some of A-Fu's female classmates and younger students gradually joined us to form an impromptu choir of beautiful voices from different indigenous groups. Looking at these neatly uniformed girls and boys, and singing along with the music, my worries and nervousness faded away. Music became a common cross-cultural meeting ground for us. I remembered then how much I had enjoyed the music performances of indigenous groups in social settings although I had not known much of the culture. Then I had not felt uncomfortable at all. I had been caught up in the exuberance of the performers. The music of my students had somewhat of a similar effect on me.

Beyond this personal experience I began to wonder about the potential of music as a tool for teaching others about ethnic and cultural diversity and developing better relationships among diverse groups. I continue to think about these possibilities. If I were a musician, I would probably be able to develop my thoughts more quickly and more fully. Yet I strongly believe that music is a powerful medium for multicultural teaching. There are so many common issues across ethnic groups—echoes, if you will—that are embedded in and conveyed through music. Furthermore, music has the ability to evoke the feeling dimensions of learning about ethnic diversity in a way that other content sources cannot do. Since feelings and emotions, along with knowledge, values, beliefs, and skills, are essential to high-quality multicultural education, I intend to continue to explore ethnic music as I proceed with my multicultural becoming.

When I left Stella Maris High School after a couple of years, the lessons I learned there from the indigenous students remained with me. They were not "good students" or "indigenous elites" according to mainstream societal standards. But do we as teachers know them well enough to find better ways to learn from them and teach them? Do we hear their silent voices and songs beyond our limited experiences that may help us create more appropriate learning circumstances for them? I do not think so. These memories and the questions they evoke continue to reverberate in my mind as I study and learn more about being a multicultural educator. Answering them is one of my major personal and professional goals.

Being able to teach students well from different ethnic and cultural backgrounds depends on the extent to which I and other multicultural educators accomplish these goals. This is true regardless of the setting, students, or subjects we teach.

HUNTERS WITHOUT HUNTING FIELDS

"Teacher Chia-lin." Chieng-hwa raised his hand quickly and looked at me with a sparkle in his big black eyes.

"Yes," I responded, pleased that he was showing some interest in participating in class.

"We eat flying mice," he said, smiling shyly but with excitement.

"Wow, really? What do they taste like?" I asked him with a little bit of surprise. I wasn't sure if I were being teased or informed, but I decided to play along to see where Chieng-hwa was going with this announcement. I knew that some of my indigenous students and their families practiced their traditional lifestyles and customs, but I was surprised to know that eating flying mice was one of them. I tried to constrain the distasteful thought (for me) of eating mice, because I did not want to be disparaging about the culture and traditions (including eating habits) of other ethnic groups. This was not as easy as it sounds. I instinctively knew that I needed to listen carefully to what was being shared with me and not judge the students' cultural practices against my own.

In the class that provoked the mention of eating flying mice, we were discussing traditional Ami cuisine. Chieng-hwa is a member of the Hualien Amis ethnic group. The conversation about eating flying mice continued as follows:

"It's very yummy!" Chieng-hwa said.

"That's great! Where did you eat it? Did your parents buy flying mice from the market?" I asked.

"No! My dad hunted them in Meiloon City Park," he answered with a proud smile on his face. "He is very good at hunting because my grandfather was a hunter." Instead of screaming out statements like, "What? Doesn't your dad know it's illegal to hunt in national and public parks? Isn't he afraid of being caught by the police and arrested?"

I asked some other questions: "That sounds cool to me! What kind of equipment does your father use to catch the flying mice?"

All of the boys excitedly started to discuss different hunting weapons and techniques. After the energetic discussion, I reorganized my question about the legality of this practice and proposed it to the students: "I've heard there are laws forbidding people from hunting in the national and public parks. Is this true?" Chieng-hwa was aware of this law. He explained that because it was illegal to hunt in the parks, his dad could go there only at a particular time of the day. These hunters know when the police come around, so it is not a problem for him. Chieng-hwa wanted to know, "Why can't we hunt there, Teacher Chia-lin? It's fun! My father told me that they used to have a huge place to hunt rabbits, birds, and flying mice. My granddad was a great hunter too. Why are we not able to hunt our food in our park, but have to buy it from the market?"

Chieng-hwa's questions are not easy to answer. They become even more difficult the more deeply I become involved in multicultural education and learn about the competing values, cultures, and rights of different ethnic groups. These include indigenous versus mainstream laws and regulations, property ownership, and tradition versus modernity.

Why can't Chieng-hwa and his father hunt in their traditional places? I keep asking this question myself. The law forbidding hunting affects not just Amis' eating habits; it also changes their identity. I don't know if Chieng-hwa will still be proud of his father when an insensitive teacher or someone else tells him that his father "commits a crime" by hunting in the city park. Will Chieng-hwa continue the family tradition and become a hunter too? If so, what and where will his hunting field be? Will he have to become a "criminal" to practice his culture on land that once belonged to his people? Will he, and other ethnic minorities, fare any better in schools when their cultural heritages are excluded from the curriculum, or they are denied the right to learn in ways that are compatible with their cultural backgrounds? Where is the justice and fairness in these practices that are imposed on ethnic minorities by mainstream cultures? Becoming multicultural is causing me to be more critical and questioning about social and educational policies that I might have taken for granted otherwise. Although I can't yet answer many of the questions I ask or resolve the contradictions I see, I think being critical is a necessary step in becoming a social justice change agent. This is something I certainly want to do for myself as a multicultural person and teach my students to do as a multicultural educator.

I have encountered other situations that echo Chieng-hwa's dilemma. The struggle of Native Americans to maintain sovereignty over their reservation lands, preserve traditional fishing locations and rights, and get the U.S. government to honor treaty provisions raises similar issues. So does the plight of Australian aborigines who are fighting for the return of lands stolen from them and the right to have access to their sacred places on lands claimed by others or the government. These are not merely debates over land rights and uses; they are about the survival of ethnic groups and cultural lifestyles. Nor are they completely removed from schools. These issues are important to children too, and they should be a part of their formal education.

As a multicultural educator, I feel obligated to empower my students with the knowledge and skills needed to fight social, cultural, and ethnic injustices. In doing this, I realize I need to be mindful of Christine Sleeter's advice (1991) that education for empowerment means "taking seriously the strengths, experiences, strategies, and goals members of oppressed groups have . . . helping them to analyze and understand the social structure that oppresses them and to act in ways that will enable them to reach their own goals successfully . . . teaching students how to advocate effectively for themselves . . . [and] developing the insights and skills to work collectively for social justice" (p. 6). In other words, I need to resist the temptation to do everything for my indigenous students, to "save" them, or to make all their decisions for them. This would be creating a paternalistic dependency, not developing their own autonomy and self-empowerment. Instead, I need to teach them how to do for themselves as students in schools and as citizens of the societies in which they live. Sleeter's advice is an echo that I must carry with me always and listen to it carefully as I proceed in being a multicultural educator.

SHIFTING LINGUISTIC COMPETENCE

Before coming to study in the United States, I thought my English-language skills were quite good. I had learned pronunciation in the study of Standard American English. It never crossed my mind that I spoke English with an accent. This was not the case when I was in Taiwan, since others speaking English sounded similar to me. I soon learned a big multicultural lesson about language diversity as well as other forms of cultural differences. This is the idea of situational or contextual abilities; that is, skills in one place, setting, and situation do not necessarily transfer to others. In Taiwan, I was complimented on my English skills, but these were called into question soon after my arrival as a college student in the United States. The questionable aspects of my English dealt with my dialogue, body language, ways of asking and answering questions, and identity. Reading in the language wasn't too troublesome. Problems occurred when I had to engage verbally with native speakers. I became frustrated and began to doubt my abilities. The more frustrated and doubtful I became, the more my English skills suffered.

A short conversation with an American woman one afternoon illustrates this cycle of diminished skills. The more I tried to convey my thoughts to her, the more she kept saying she didn't understand. When she finally understood what I said, she expressed relief and shock, saying: "Oh! Sorry I didn't get it, probably because of your pronunciation!" Her reactions and comments made me virtually speechless. It seemed to me that I had suddenly lost my language abilities and as a result, lost the ability to express my thoughts—even to think at all. Surely this must be an example of what multicultural scholars mean by ethnically diverse students' being silenced and made voiceless. They often use these ideas more metaphorically, but it was a literal occurrence for me. For a while, I became almost mute intellectually because people in my learning environment kept saying they could not understand me when I spoke; therefore, I talked less and less.

In this situation, the echoes were from multicultural theory to my personal experiences. I felt what being silenced meant; what it is like to have ideas, opinions, and feelings to convey but not be able to because of language barriers—to be linguistically marginalized. These actions and reactions also brought back to memory something written by Dell Hymes (1985):

> Our sense of well-being and moral worth may depend on communications of which utterances that are less than grammatical, less than complete, are essential means. We seek out and avoid persons and places, sense acceptance or rejection, in ways that may depend upon the interpretation put upon speech, as welcome or not, as sincere or not, as honoring or dishonoring of self [p. xxxii].

In coming to the United States, I expected to learn new teaching methods to use with indigenous students. I knew that I might have a few language problems studying in a very different culture and linguistic setting, but I never imagined how big these problems would be. I was overwhelmed by an unpredicted frustration and feeling of being lost when sitting among professors and classmates who lectured, discussed, argued, and joked about topics we were studying in their speedy American English. Gradually, I called on my courage and cautiously followed the advice and example of more experienced students. I also reviewed my notebook for studying abroad and its suggestions for joining in discussions and expressing my opinions. I wanted to avoid being seen as a "silent Asian female without any opinions." In my mind I knew what I was supposed to do and how, but actually doing it was something else. I felt like a fool even though I was supposed to be intellectually capable. I felt powerless because I couldn't clearly express the complicated ideas and thoughts that were in my head. I felt angry, too, at the circumstances of my dilemma and other people who were involved in them.

Some of my professors were very attentive to American students who spoke eloquently but showed impatient attitudes when I spoke. I pondered silently, *Don't you realize how hard I have to work to avoid drowning in the dilemma of taking notes and understanding the lectures? Do you even care?* Often I wanted to scream out my frustrations, but I did not. As these frustrations increased and the level of my confidence in my English skills declined, I retreated more and more into a small circle of relationships. I hung out with mostly Chinese-speaking friends rather than getting involved in American society or American social life. This was a harsh reality for me because I had prided myself on my ability to relate easily to different ethnic and cultural groups. What was happening to me? This question provoked both memories and speculative echoes of another kind.

One set of echoes about linguistic diversity was memories of the indigenous students I taught in Taiwan. They struggled to learn and communicate in Mandarin Chinese while many members of the dominant Han ethnic group considered them inferior culturally and linguistically. The other echoes came from my developing knowledge of linguistic minorities in the United States who are taught in English. Their linguistic dilemmas, and the effects on their academic performance, are similar to mine. I now know personally what it means when scholars argue that linguistic ability can obstruct or facilitate intellectual expressions and how functioning in one aspect of learning can affect others. When my English language skills were doubted by my teachers and fellow students, I began to doubt them as well. The doubts quickly produced diminishing skills in other academic and social arenas as well. My self-confidence, grades, and relationships suffered. Other linguistically different students in various majority cultures probably are affected in the same way.

These situations are important challenges and opportunities for multicultural educators. Learning how to engage in and facilitate discourse among students with varying degrees of English skills is something I am trying to do. I also want to apply similar attitudes and skills to teaching linguistically diverse students in my home country of Taiwan who have varying skills in speaking Mandarin, the language of power and privilege. This involves developing learning environments in which students feel comfortable, safe, and supported in using dominant society language skills in school and as a complement to their indigenous languages. I am also practicing patience and learning how to listen to different English accents and dialects.

ECHOING EACH OTHER

After one and a half years studying for my master's degree in the United States, I returned to visit my family in Taiwan and to collect data for a research project. The project involved observing an indigenous music and cultural class (IMCC) for members of the aboriginal tribal groups and interviewing teachers and some of the students. The IMCC is part of the new multicultural educational policies in Taiwan that allow indigenous cultures and home languages to be taught in some regions. The students in the IMCC come from small cities and mountain villages and are members of the Ami ethnic group. Their lives and experiences I heard about and observed are applied echoes of the theoretical ideas that I am learning in my university classes. They remind me of the importance of pushing myself to be a multicultural person and educator and to apply the knowledge I am learning to my classroom teaching. One of these students was Lai-lai. She shared experiences with me about her schooling that echoed some of my own about learning in culturally different environments.

When I first met Lai-lai, I was having some serious doubts about my own learning experiences in the United States. I was wondering if I had made the right decision about developing my professional career by studying abroad because of the cultural confusions I was experiencing and the self-doubts that resulted. I arrived for my observation of the IMCC with all of this emotional baggage. While I was there, I heard clear and melodious echoes of these feelings coming back to me. They came from Lai-lai. She had a strong indigenous identity and cultural pride. She told me in an interview that she wanted to be a cultural worker, attend the newly established College of Indigenous Studies at National Dong Hwa University (Hualien province), and major in nutrition because many indigenous children have malnutrition problems. She showed no hesitancy or doubts about her ability to accomplish these goals. Her sense of confidence reminded me of myself a few years earlier when I had felt as certain about and committed to my plans to attend college and then teach in settings populated by people from my own ethnic group. For both of us, our respective comfort and confidence about our plans had something to do with the fact that we expected them to unfold in the midst of a critical cultural and ethnic mass to which we belonged. In other words, we thought we would be working with people familiar to us.

Lai-lai's clarity of purpose and certainty about self did not prevail as her learning contexts changed. In classes other than the IMCC when Han students were the majority, she was the outsider and her competence was suspect. She told me about a situation in which one of her Han classmates asked, "Why do you always have a strange accent when you speak Mandarin?" In reacting to the question, Lai-lai said, "I don't do it on purpose. There is no way to change my accent now because I have grown up in the Ami tribe for more than fifteen years." This simple but poignant statement echoes the more scholarly ideas of Ina Corinne Brown (1972) on the same issue, a message that I am incorporating into my multicultural being:

> No custom, belief, or behavior can be understood out of its social or cultural context. That is, any item of behavior, any tradition or pattern, can be evaluated correctly only in the light of its meaning to the people who practice it, its relation to other elements of the culture, and the part it plays in the adaptation of the people to their environment or to one another. No custom is "odd" to the people who practice it [p. 41].

Lai-lai was angry about and frustrated by comments about her language and culture made by the Han students. They made her and other indigenous students reluctant to speak out in classes because they were afraid of being laughed at by the way they thought and spoke. These dilemmas bring to mind Claude Steele's research (1997) on how stereotypes and prejudices against ethnic groups can derail the academic achievement of individual members.

All of those experiences sounded very similar to mine. I had been experiencing the same kinds of situations in the United States. Although the messages were less vocal, they were equally effective. People seemed impatient with my accented English and hard pressed to understand my thoughts or consider them worthy. The more difficulties they had, the less competent I felt. Yet before arriving in the United States, I had no doubts about my intellectual abilities and my worth as a human being. My culture and ethnic group validated me, as Lai-lai's did for her. But these foundations were shaken when we had to perform in school settings where we were not a part of the majority privileged group. What caused the changes? Did Lai-lai and I become less capable as our learning contexts changed? Or were these merely mismatches between the contexts and our competencies? As I think and learn more about dilemmas like these, the importance of multicultural education principles such as teaching style-shifting skills, modeling, and teaching to the sociocultural contexts of students becomes increasingly clear and imperative.

We as teachers need to know how minority-status students are disadvantaged in majority settings and use instructional techniques to prevent this from happening. Experiencing this myself made me more aware of its possibilities and put me on the alert to avoid discriminating against my students. Experience really is a powerful teacher.

Persevering to learn as a cultural, ethnic, and linguistic minority among the majority is a courageous act. As I become more knowledgeable about multicultural education, I am learning more about the nature of these demands and why some students rise to the challenge and others do not. I use my own personal experiences as a point of departure for examining these issues and imagining ways to intervene as a teacher in order to minimize the obstacles of differences that ethnically and culturally diverse students face. As with Lai-lai, my experiences in these areas echo other students' realities, and my resolutions of problems may be useful precedents for them to follow. Therefore, the challenges and benefits of teachers and students echoing each other suggest that reciprocity is important to being a good multicultural educator. One cannot be adequately developed in isolation from the other. In my process of becoming multicultural, the echoes I hear are bridges that link these different aspects of development together.

RETURNING TO MY CULTURAL ROOTS

This part of my multicultural journey is both literal and figurative. It involves a trip from Taipei to Hong Kong to Chengdu in the Sichuan province of China, a physically exhausting but tremendously exciting journey. I was going to visit the town where my Nainai was born, grew up, and got married during the Sino-Japanese War. Since moving to Taiwan in 1948, none of my family members has visited this place, which is known as the "State of Heaven." My visit was a symbolic and real return to my roots, the place where the values, memories, and influences transmitted to us through Nainai began.

It sounds odd that you can have memories of a place that you have never been to, but this is exactly what happened to me. These memories were vivid in the way that we ate Chengdu-style food cooked by Nainai, listened to the Sichuan dialect she spoke at home, and heard the stories she shared about her childhood, culture, heritage, and experiences during family gatherings. Grandmother's hometown in reality became all of ours in mentality.

Sichuan represents my traditional ancestral culture. I have this impression because of the memories Nainai shared with me about her harsh grandfather who refused to allow her to attend elementary school to keep her from sending letters to boys. She told me about the popular plaza of Chengdu where a little girl could find her favorite desserts. Her descriptions were so vivid that I could almost taste these treats. All of Nainai's happy and miserable memories are like photographs in a family album; they are always there but won't make you feel anything until you open them to the specific pages. I was very excited anticipating and preparing for the trip to Chengdu because I could now examine the stories I heard from Nainai at family reunions and dinners and on boring afternoons before taking a nap.

My dad and some of my friends who had worked in China cautioned me that Chengdu might be a rather "backward" area, and I might be shocked by what I found. I wasn't. Although not as modern as Shanghai, Chengdu is not backward at all. But I was stunned when I first stepped on the land of Nainai's hometown. I felt that I was surrounded by elder family members when everybody spoke the Sichuan dialect, which, as a child, I assumed was only spoken at home for me. It was a cultural shock greater than anything else I have ever experienced. There I was, in a place I do not know but soon realized I knew a great deal about, thanks to my grandmother's recollections. I was talking to people whom I did not know, but somehow have understood for a long time through my most intimate family.

This experience had a deep emotional effect on me. It was a physical connection to the roots of my heritage and an emotional contact with my Chinese cultural background. It helped me to feel more deeply a cultural conflict happening to a young wife leaving her hometown for a totally strange place with her husband and children fifty years ago. When I heard the peddlers and customers talking in a shoe shop, I recalled how, as a child, I laughed at grandmother's Sichuan dialect because she mispronounced *xiezi* (referring to shoes) as *hizi*, which means "child" in Mandarin. It surprised me to see the sausages hanging on the verandas of people's houses in exactly the same way as my family did twenty years ago. I don't remember whether grandmother was angry or embarrassed when my sister and I corrected her Mandarin. I now realized that she had been undergoing the experiences of being an immigrant in Taiwan and had tried to assimilate into a new environment while continuing to maintain her own cultural heritage. Both of these realizations reminded me of my own situation of living in and coping with the United States.

Unlike her granddaughter, who has the resources to reflect on her thinking and action as a self-conscious human being, Nainai (like many other women) was trying her best to make her own and her family's lives better under difficult social, cultural, and political circumstances. She may not have been an ideal teacher from a strictly multicultural perspective, but her influences and the cultural lessons she taught were powerful. One of the greatest lessons she taught me was how culture is practiced in daily life and the magnificent history conveyed through maintaining cultural heritages from one generation to the next.

Near the end of my visit to Chengdu, some local friends shared their impressions of me. They said that I seemed to be a person living fifty years ago because of my Sichuan dialect, some particular ways of using the language, and understanding of this "State of Heaven." I had clearly brought some cultural shock to them as they did to me. Our lives as human beings are full of dynamic interactions when we encounter each other. Not only did I receive echoes of the past from the people in Nainai's hometown, but they also heard some echoes of the future from me. They represented cultural stability, and I symbolized cultural change, although I continue to carry some of the original sources. Through the processes of giving and receiving, learning and teaching, and talking and listening, both of us simultaneously experienced the old and the new. These echoes helped me to understand better the meaning and importance of the multicultural education ideas that ethnic groups need to know their cultural histories; change does not obviate our cultural core; and the importance of learning from the oral histories of cultural elders.

When I see, hear, and feel the "State of Heaven," the sense of kindredness with the people living there, and the history that is talking to me, I know these are echoes from Nainai. The cultural heritages she has been giving me build the melody of my song of life. They play a big part in making me who I am as a multicultural person and educator. When I saw Nainai again after my visit to Chengdu, I said to her, "Thank you so much for bringing all the cultural gifts to me. I want you to know that I will sing my own song by collecting all the beautiful echoes you and others contribute to my life. Please pray for your beloved granddaughter who wants to become a vehicle for empowering and aspiring others to know their cultural heritages as you have done for me. This will be one of the major motivations and characterizations of my being a multicultural person and educator. Thank you, my dearest Nainai, for initiating and anchoring this journey for me."

The realization of just how much my grandmother's influence is a part of me, even when we are separated by many years and thousands of miles, is insightful for becoming a multicultural educator. The essence of it is that I am always present in what I do as an educator. However hard I may try, I cannot separate myself from my teaching. The same is true for students; their personhood and school performance are closely interrelated. In recognizing these inseparable connections, I hear Ricardo Garcia (1982) explaining:

> All classroom activities and factors ... operate on assumptions which are embedded in cultural values, attitudes, and beliefs.... What students learn and what teachers teach are ultimately filtered and strained through their cultural sieves. Understanding the ethnic-culture factor [in education] creates the consciousness necessary to perceive that transmitting culture and socializing students are inherent in classroom teaching and learning [p. 6].

Being conscious of and understanding this interplay among my own and my students' culture, ethnicity, and education in the classroom are fundamental aspects of my process of becoming a multicultural educator.

PRINCIPLES FOR PRACTICE

All personal stories have embedded within them general principles for understanding and acting on the issues that they address. This is also the case with the critical events in my becoming a multicultural person and educator that I shared in this chapter. I hope they prompted you to find parallels in your own development. But if the specifics of my stories do not trigger any progress in your personal development, then maybe some of the general principles that can be extracted from them will.

Teachers frequently face dilemmas about what to know and how to teach about ethnic and cultural diversity. They are surrounded by a lot of different sources about, and kinds of, multicultural information, but they do not necessarily know where to find the best, how to decide what is accurate, and how to select from that which is most appropriate for students. These dilemmas may persist for a long time, but they become more manageable as our knowledge increases. How we go about building our knowledge foundations of multicultural education depends largely on what our goals are. However, we should not overlook the principle that the *personal stories, historical backgrounds, and family legacies of different ethnic individuals are powerful sources of cultural knowledge for multicultural teaching.*

Ethnic individuals and groups within pluralistic societies are engaged in a dynamic interplay of cultural continuity and cultural change, prompted by the fact that diverse peoples living in close proximity to each other participate in perpetual exchanges. They learn many things from cultural others, as well as from members of their own ethnic groups. Therefore, the second principle is that *in developing the knowledge and skills needed for multicultural teaching, we should study the processes of cultural assimilation, cultural borrowing, and cultural maintenance among different ethnic groups.*

For many of us, our ethnicity and culture may not be easily recognizable. This is especially true if we are members of the racial majority within our respective communities and countries. Those who are members of racial minorities are more readily recognizable, and their cultural characteristics are more easily assumed. Among both minority and majority ethnic groups, internal differences are often overlooked, and commonalties are assumed to exist when in fact they do not. These misunderstandings can cause us to underserve or miseducate students from these ethnic groups. Consequently, the third principle is that *in developing our multicultural knowledge and skills, we should understand the overt and subtle manifestations of culture and ethnicity, as well as variations within both majority and minority ethnic groups.*

Too frequently, we assume that when ethnic individuals move from one place to another (such as immigrants coming to the United States), over time they forget all of their affiliations with and memories of their places of origin. This may not be the case. These memories may be kept alive and transmitted from generation to generation through family members and other significant others in ethnic communities. They also influence how people think and behave in social interactions, interpersonal relations, and learning situations. Thus, the fourth principle is that *knowledge about the ancestral memories and historical places of different ethnic groups is an important part of being an effective multicultural educator.*

Who shall teach us what we need to know about ethnic and cultural diversity, and where shall we learn it best? The answer to this question is both simple and profound. The simple answer is we should be taught to be good multicultural educators in our teacher education programs. The more profound response is that we are taught to be multicultural by many different people, in many different ways, and in many different places. Paramount among them are ourselves and our students. The final principle is that *we learn a great deal as we teach and from whom we teach. In this sense, then, ethnically diverse students are some of the most powerful multicultural teachers.* But they should never be placed in the position of being the only such teachers.

JOINING THE JOURNEY

How is your own process of becoming a multicultural educator coming along? Did you get some affirmation and some motivation from reading this chapter to press on with your journey? I hope so. But if you haven't yet begun the journey, or need some stimulation to keep it moving, here are a few things you might consider doing:

• Observe or interview some elder members of your family to determine how they symbolize and transmit cultural traits. You may need to do this over a period of time and across a variety of events. Look for things that are more subtle and intangible (such as values and beliefs) instead of the very obvious ones, like artifacts, customs, and traditions. Focusing on subtleties is important because these are considered the more powerful and persistent dimensions of culture. Also, try to determine the times and circumstances when the teaching and the expressive manifestations of these cultural elements are most prominent for the elders as well as yourself. What did you learn from this experience that was new to you, and how did you feel about these discoveries? If you are already teaching, have your students do this oral history exercise as well, and compare the results within and across ethnic groups.

• Do an Internet search for innovative multicultural programs in K–12 schools. Find out the details of these programs, such as when and why they began; their curriculum and instruction components; and their effects on students' academic, personal, social, and cultural achievement. Determine how and the extent to which these programs deal with some of the issues raised in this chapter, such as linguistic diversity, learning from elders, students as cultural teachers, immigration, ethnic discrimination, and cultural affirmation. What principles or elements of these programs can be applied to your local school situations?

• Spend some time observing in local public school or college classrooms. Focus on how the teachers interact with and relate to students from different ethnic groups. Do the teachers interact in different but comparable ways with ethnically diverse students? What seem to be the teachers' cultural assumptions underlying their interactional patterns? Also, observe how students from different ethnic groups relate to each other. What do the teachers do to facilitate or discourage these interactions? Include specific evidence that supports your claims. Think of some ways that these teachers can improve their personal and instructional relationships with ethnically diverse students.

• Place yourself in an academic or social learning situation where you are a minority. This might be taking a course in a language of which you are not a native speaker or an ethnic studies course, or attending an ethnic cultural event or church service. While in this setting, immerse yourself in the midst of the dominant ethnic group, and do a self-study of your own reactions. Include analyses of your level of knowledge, feelings of comfort and confidence, sense of acceptance (or rejection), and how you coped with these dislocations. What did you learn from this self-study that you could transfer to teaching ethnically diverse students in predominantly majority school settings?

References

Bennett, C. I. *Comprehensive Multicultural Education: Theory and Practice.* Needham Heights, Mass.: Allyn & Bacon, 1986.

Brown, I. C. "Man and Culture." In R. Shinn (ed.), *Culture and School: Socio-Cultural Significances.* San Francisco: Intext, 1972.

Delpit, L. *Other People's Children: Cultural Conflict in the Classroom.* New York: New Press, 1995.

Garcia, R. L. *Teaching in a Pluralistic Society: Concepts, Models, Strategies.* New York: HarperCollins, 1982.

Howard, G. R. *We Can't Teach What We Don't Know: White Teachers, Multiracial Schools.* New York: Teachers College Press, 1999.

Hymes, D. "Introduction." In C. B, Cazden, V. P. John, and D. Hymes (eds.), *Functions of Language in the Classroom.* Prospect Heights, Ill.: Waveland, 1985.

Little Soldier, L. "Help Children Soar with the Eagles!" *Momentum,* 1983, *14*(1), 51–52.

McAdoo, H. P. "Ethnic Families: Strengths That Are Found in Diversity." In H. P. McAdoo (ed.), *Family Ethnicity: Strength in Diversity.* Thousand Oaks, Calif.: Sage, 1993.

Pai, Y. *Cultural Foundations of Education.* New York: Merrill, 1990.

Sleeter, C. E. "Introduction: Multicultural Education and Empowerment." In C. E. Sleeter (ed.), *Empowerment Through Multicultural Education.* Albany: State University of New York Press, 1991.

Steele, C. M. "A Threat in the Air: How Stereotypes Shape Intellectual Identity and Performance." *American Psychologist,* 1997, *52,* 613–629.

CHAPTER NINE

Unifying Mind and Soul Through Cultural Knowledge and Self-Education

Patricia Espiritu Halagao

Several months ago, I came across references to a traditional poetic form of debate used in the Philippines. Like a duel of words, it is a verbal exchange between two opposing viewpoints that employs rhyme, reason, and passion. In the nineteenth century, Francisco Baltazar, popularly called Balagtas, refined this style of poetry into a political tool of expression (Macansantos and Macansantos, 2000). Baltazar's influence resulted in the naming of this poetic form of debate *balagtasan*.

I have been engaging in *balagtasan* throughout my process of becoming a multicultural person and educator, although I did not have the name for the process until recently. As a person of color living in a White world, the *balagtasan* raging inside me is between my mind and soul. I considered them to be dichotomous; I thought the mind was concrete, rationale, and practical and the soul abstract, emotional, and passionate. In my K–12 schooling experience, my mind was taught to process information. I was a passive recipient of information, or as Freire (1988) explained, the "banking" approach to learning. My mind was limited to the knowledge and traditions others provided; later, my soul became the source of infinite possibilities and inspired change.

As I grew older, my soul began to resist accepting a single form of knowledge as truth, especially when it was counterintuitive. My experiences demonstrate that the mind can be colonialized, but the soul cannot be bridled or bought quite as easily.

In this chapter, I take you on a journey through some of the ongoing dialogues I have had within myself and with others as I strive to become a multicultural educator. Like many other educators who care about issues of diversity and equity, my road to personal resolution and revelation has been challenging, marked by struggles to express my ethnic and cultural identity in education. Much introspection and internal debate between my mind and soul have finally led me to valuing my ethnic identity as a Filipina American, finding my voice and presence in curriculum content, using my ethnic and cultural identity in teaching, and realizing my contribution to the field of multicultural education. This chapter is organized around these four junctures that have dominated my experience as a student, teacher, and researcher of color. The real challenge for educators of color is to infuse their sense of ethnic identity, knowledge of ethnic background, and community activism into multicultural curriculum development and classroom instruction.

AN INVITATION TO ENGAGE

I use *balagtasan* to help me construct my story about becoming multicultural because it embodies a native style of writing, synthesizing, and symbolizing my experience as a student and educator of color in a White society. As I journey through my *balagtasans,* I invite you to engage in your own. Here is the beginning of mine:

> Are your mind and soul in contradiction?
> Splitting you into two—causing tension
> The mind reasoning this, the soul feeling that
> Opposing thoughts and emotions that lead you into confusion
> Muddling, addling, and clouding your vision.

Throughout this narrative, *balagtasan* will document the process of my mind as it reaches resolution and my soul as it undergoes revelation. I find a distinction between the two types of progression. *Merriam-Webster's Collegiate Dictionary* defines *resolution* as "the act of solving or finding an answer" and *revelation* as "the act of opening up to view or an enlightenment." As I see it, reaching resolution implies making decisions based on thought and reason, whereas undergoing revelation is engaging in a natural process of psychoemotional discovery.

In my *balagtasans* interspersed throughout this chapter, you will always hear from the protagonist first, which is my mind, *isip* in Tagalog, or the dominant and established order. It is the main way of thinking, the mainstream. My soul, or *kaluluwa* in Tagalog, is the antagonist to *isip*. It opposes the forces of the mainstream. Although my soul's response directly follows my mind's in true *balagtasan* form, the process of revelation was never immediate in my life. Throughout most of my life and education, I accepted what I was taught, even though I knew something was missing or did not feel right. Not until years later did my soul emerge and counter my mind. My openness to continuing self-examination has allowed the soul to be unearthed, produce harmony with the mind, and lead to freedom in expressing my ethnic identity and culture in education.

PRISONER IN MY OWN FORT

"Go back to where you came from!" "I don't accept church bulletins from Flips." "Can you breathe through your flat nose?" These early and repeated discriminatory taunts made me hate being Filipino. I wanted to be White because I foolishly thought I would then be spared ridicule and shame. When I couldn't be White, I built walls around myself to protect me from the cruelties of a racist society. I became a prisoner in my own fort. As a result, I internalized self-hatred and developed low self-esteem and self-perception (Gay, 1978). I have come to realize that a large part of becoming a multicultural educator involves examining my own life experiences and dismantling the barriers that have kept me apart from the rest of the world.

Now as an adult, I do not internalize self-reproach but realize the blame should fall on society. Society made me hate being Filipino because nothing in school and society affirmed or valued my existence. Although I came from an extremely loving and supportive Filipino family, ate Filipino foods, and practiced the usual Filipino cultural traditions, I wanted to be like the Partridge family or to have blonde hair and blue eyes like Marsha in the *Brady Bunch*. I was convinced that not being Filipino far outweighed being Filipino. In retrospect, I was in psychological captivity (Banks, 1997), or the preencounter stage (Cross, 1971; Gay, 1985) of my ethnic identity during most of my childhood years. Gay (1978) describes an individual in the preencounter stage as having little or no exploration of his or her ethnicity. This lack of ethnic consciousness often leads to self-rejection or self-denial.

I was "colonialized." I wanted to be something I could not be. In his portrait of the colonizer and the colonialized, Memmi (1967) states, "The first attempt of the colonized is to change his condition by changing his skin . . . to become equal to that splendid model and to resemble him to the point of disappearing in him" (p. 120). Here is one of my earliest inner dialogues over dissatisfaction with my physical appearance:

ISIP (MIND)

Tall nose, tall nose
My mom tells me so
For beauty I'm taught in books
Is nothing like my looks.
Flat nose, pug nose
Pinch it on the bridge just so
Pray to God, make a wish
And a change will bring happiness.
Light skin, fair skin
The world tells me so
For beauty in the media shows
White over brown, blond over brunette
The European standard of beauty is set.
Brown girl, dark girl
Wash away the dirt
Pray to God, make a wish
Turn my skin into a whitened cream
Achieve the complexion of my dream.

Defeating these notions of self-denial and conformity institutionalized by society was the first step in my process of becoming multicultural. Only later in life did I judge beauty by my own standards, and I responded to my colonialized mind in this way:

KALULUWA (SOUL)
Beauty is God's gift to me
Look in the mirror, what do I see?
Petite nose, dark hair, skin of *kayumangi*
What must be done is to define my own beauty
For God would never create anyone so ugly.

Instead of detesting myself, I should have despised the circumstances I was in. Does society realize how difficult it makes it for children of color to become complete persons? I don't think so. I was willing to change the color of my skin and even to sell my soul, though it would leave a painful, gaping hole inside me. Now I am repulsed whenever I think of wishing to be something I could never be.

Fortunately, when I was eleven, my family moved from Gross Pointe, Michigan, to Stockton, California. It was in this midsize agricultural town in the Central Valley that my healing began. I knew at a very young age that someplace else had to be better. Little did I know that my early encounters in the Midwest planted the seeds for me in the field of multicultural education.

WHERE AM I?

Once I asked a Filipina American student at a Catholic school, "Why do you think you never learned about yourself in school, especially when Filipinos make up 85 percent of the student population?" She replied, "I suppose it's because Filipinos haven't done anything important." She had implicitly assumed that Filipinos were unimportant because the school curriculum did not include her or the accomplishments of our people. Her response starkly confirms what ethnic studies and multicultural education scholars have been advocating: students must see themselves in curriculum in order to be fully functioning individuals (Grant, 1977). An absence, distortion, or biased presentation of one's ethnic self and peoples in curriculum leads to devastating personal, social, and academic effects (Pang, 1990; Swartz, 1992; Woodson, 1933). Because most content in conventional curriculum designs is Eurocentric, most students of color have the extra burden of working across irrelevant instructional materials. These efforts ultimately detract students of color from focusing on learning and academic achievement (Gay, 1977).

When I consider my K–12 education, I never remember seeing or learning about myself. When you don't see yourself in the picture, the experience can be disturbing and produce what Adrienne Rich (1986, p. 199) describes as "a moment of psychic disequilibrium, as if you looked into a mirror and saw nothing." I was invisible. *Unremarkable, unchallenged,* and *colorless* describe the first five years of my formal education. I recall minor instances of spelling words, dissecting sentences, handwriting, and timed math tests. The environment encouraged little questioning or exploration about anything, and particularly about my culture and ethnicity. Facts about the experiences and contributions of European Americans were given, and we were taught to believe they were the only truth.

European American scholars like Franklin Bobbitt (1918) and W. W. Charters (1923) would have been proud to see their theories still holding more than three-quarters of a century after they were first articulated. They advocated a scientific approach to education that molded students into predefined entities. I was a product of Bobbitt, whereby "meeting the standards" was more important than learning and self-fulfillment. My goal to earn the best grade, the most correct answers, the fastest time came at the expense of being put on a path of true intellectual, emotional, social, and artistic growth. I was never made to feel that my outside experiences were relevant to my educational development. Like many other students of color, I left my ethnic and cultural background on the front steps of the school (Gay, 1977).

When my family moved to Stockton, the shackles of Midwest conservatism were finally broken. Transferring into a more ethnically diverse environment moved me along my path of multicultural journeying. I was filled with anticipation of better things to come, even if the reality of living in a diverse community did not necessarily lead to diverse learning. Although a significant minority presence was evident in Stockton, it was not felt in the classrooms. I never had a teacher of color throughout the twelve years of my schooling, and the curriculum content was Eurocentric. In the seventh grade, I remember being required to write a letter about the Boston Tea Party from the perspective of a White woman colonist. The following year, I was an early White pioneer on the Oregon Trail evading Indians and settling the land. My entire social studies education was built on being people I never could be.

My high school curriculum was equally meaningless. English courses consisted of analyzing the works of dead White male authors. I memorized and regurgitated facts in my government and history courses that did not include my ethnic group's history and culture. Subconsciously, I learned that American history was not my history. The curriculum hardly even reached Banks's first stage of ethnic content integration—the "contributions approach" where teachers "focused on heroes, holidays, and cultural elements" (1997, p. 26). I did not even realize what I was missing.

These were my assimilation years, when I felt that my ethnic group's culture was absorbed into the main cultural body. Fitting into the image of the "All-American girl" overshadowed being Filipino. I resisted joining the Asian Club because I was not interested in my ethnic culture. I was in a stage of what Tse (1998) would call ethnic ambivalence, when issues of ethnic identity and awareness were nonexistent, at least not consciously. Although I had a 4.0 grade point average and was homecoming queen, yearbook editor, and varsity tennis player, I always wondered why I had to try so hard to fit into a racially defined mold. By conventional standards, I was a successful student. But in retrospect, I ask myself whether I was all that successful when I was denied learning about my culture and ethnic heritage. My issues even differed from the adolescent teens in *The Breakfast Club* (1984). Most of the characters in the movie felt alienated because they did not belong to the popular crowd; my subtle feelings of exclusion, in contrast, were based on race and culture.

My dilemmas suggest the importance of recognizing that while on the surface everything may appear all right for students of color, particularly Asian Pacific American students, in actuality it may not be. In this next *balagtasan*, I share a constant dialogue I had within myself over what it meant to belong, being a successful student, and eventually staying true to myself:

ISIP (MIND)
You belong in this world
American-brown girl
As long as you play the game
Make the grade,
Do as you're told, imitate
Don't bring shame.
You can be class valedictorian

American-brown girl
Homecoming queen, yearbook editor, and more
Stay ahead
Anything is possible in this world
It is said.
But be forewarned
American-brown girl
To be college bound
Remain inside the box
Don't venture out
Follow the formula of success
And you'll be the perfect student all-around.

As I became older, my soul started to grow stronger, and it began to help foster self-definition and determination. It responded to the mind by questioning:

KALULUWA (SOUL)

How can I belong in a world
that denies my inner core?
Conformity, compromise,
Disregarding what's come before.
Belonging and being successful means
defining my own identity
Resisting tags not native to me
Letting go of imported dreams
Nothing is what it seems.

I reinvented myself when I went to Occidental College in Los Angeles. I signed up to live in Bell-Young, an experimental multicultural dorm. I thought *multicultural* was the same as *international* and presumed I would be living with students from countries around the world. I soon learned that Bell-Young inhabitants represented a microcosm of what was considered an ideal multicultural society: 25 percent African American, 25 percent European American, 25 percent Asian American, and 25 percent Latino American students. Still, we fell short of this ideal because we did not have any Native American students represented in the dorm. Nonetheless, we lived and discussed issues of diversity and multiculturalism. My resident advisers (RA) were Jewish American, African American, Mexican American, and East

Indian American. We were called the DREAM (Dedicated to the Recognition, Education, and Acceptance of Multiculturalism) Team.

Living in Bell-Young had an important impact on me in a number of ways. This was the first time in my life that being different was valued and respected. (Why, I wondered, did it have to take this long?) I became earnestly interested in learning more about my ethnic background and history. Throughout my life, mentors of color like my RAs and my African Latino counselor played an important role in helping me find connection and community with my own ethnic group on campus. With their support, I formed Occidental's first Filipino Culture Club. Our club was a small, passionate group that organized an event called Filipino Night to teach the academic community about Philippine foods and folk dancing. Because our knowledge of our culture was limited to discrete elements, our endeavors stopped at the stage of celebrating "foods, festivals, and folk dancing." It was difficult to move beyond this stage in my multicultural journeying because I did not know any better.

My college education did not reflect my extracurricular activities. I found that learning about myself in the classroom meant learning nothing about being Filipino American, or Asian Pacific American for that matter. The Asian Studies Department covered Chinese and Japanese history, and the American Studies Department offered only one Asian American studies course. The individual social, cultural, and historical differences among Asians were not addressed. I began to wonder whether I was Asian or Filipino. Being lumped together under the "Asian" umbrella did not sit well with me. Although we came from the same geographical regions, our different historical experiences set us apart. For instance, China and Japan were historically considered imperialist nations, while the Philippines was colonialized by the West. In fact, I always felt that the vestiges of Spanish colonization caused me to relate more to Mexican Americans as opposed to my East Asian American counterparts.

Instead of associating with being Asian or having anything to do with European American history and culture, I concentrated on learning about my Filipino roots and history. This was the beginning of my "separation" years, where "individuals emphasize their ethnic culture and withdraw from contact with the dominant group" (Phinney, Lochner, and Murphy 1990, p. 60). I was constantly having conscious confrontations with my ethnicity. I was internally focused on my ethnic group's cultural experiences, values, perspectives, and contributions. This is what Cross (1971, 1991) and Gay (1985, 1987, 1994) call the encounter stage of ethnic identity development.

My determination to learn about my Philippine heritage led me to study abroad at the University of the Philippines, Diliman, during my junior year in college. I was completely immersed in Philippine society: I lived in a women's dorm and took classes in Philippine government, art and society, history, sex and culture, language, and dance. Living and studying in the Philippines was an eye-opening experience. For the first time in my life, the curriculum was about me. It was an odd but comforting feeling sitting in a room full of Filipinos. But as much as I looked like everyone else, my mannerisms, accent, and attitude still distinguished me from my fellow Filipino classmates. It was then that I realized I was truly a Filipino American and not what I considered "Filipino Filipino," a Filipino person born and raised in the Philippines.

Although I returned to Occidental College with a heightened sense of ethnic knowledge, consciousness, and pride, I was bitter. Why did I have to leave the United States to learn about my people's history? A pivotal turning point in my multicultural journey came when I realized I had the right to learn about my own people in the United States in school. Where was my history and culture as a Filipino American in the school curriculum? These questions burned inside me and highlighted the importance I give to teaching about the histories and cultures of ethnically diverse students' countries of origin and within the United States.

SETTLING IN THE TRENCHES

The realities of finding a job after college pushed my previous concerns about self and ethnic identity to the back seat. I joined Teach for America, a national teaching corps that recruits college undergraduates to teach in underresourced schools. I was inspired to teach because I wanted to confront an educational system that excluded children as I had been. What I did not get out of education strengthened my resolve to be an educator, but it gravely limited my capacity to think outside my formal schooling experience.

I taught first-grade sheltered English for a couple years to Southeast Asian and Latino students in a predominantly African American elementary school in Oakland, California. My goal was to impart a sense of ethnic pride in my students as I tried to improve the English language skills of those who were not native speakers. We squeezed in the usual Black History Month, Cinco de Mayo, and Lunar New Year with fanfare and food in between the required mainstream curriculum. We read folktales and made arts and crafts from Africa, Mexico, and Cambodia. Culture was explored out in the world rather than in the homes and communities of my students. These were my first and only attempts at "doing multicultural education" in my classroom. Because I lacked the resources and theory to do it any differently, I reinforced Banks's "contributions" and "additive" approaches, where "ethnic content is merely added to the curriculum without changing its Eurocentric structure" (1997, p. 26).

I now recognize that the contributions and ethnic additive approaches to multicultural education were detrimental to the perceptions of my students of color of themselves and their relationship with others. When I focused primarily on native dances, religious fiestas, and homeland delicacies, I implanted surreal and romanticized impressions of themselves in their minds. These portrayals may have resulted in students' viewing their history and culture as shallow and insubstantial in comparison to those of Europe. In addition, presenting each ethnic group separately and in isolation from one another encouraged ethnocentrism. Bennett (1986) stressed that a crucial aspect of multicultural education is learning about self in conjunction with learning about commonalities with others. I noticed ethnic cliques forming in class and became troubled when I started hearing a group of Cambodian female students declare, "Only Cambodians are allowed to use a certain set of coloring markers." My aim to foster ethnic pride had backfired.

I thus entered into one of my most discouraging periods in the pursuit of becoming a multicultural educator. Banks (1994) outlined four characteristics a teacher must have to be effective in a multicultural society: foundational social science and pedagogical knowledge of culturally diverse groups, clarified cultural identification, positive intergroup and racial attitudes, and cultural pedagogical skills. I met one of the criteria (positive racial attitudes) but fell short of meeting the other three. I did not have deep historical and cultural content knowledge of the ethnic groups represented in class. Takaki (1987) agrees that teachers need a sound knowledge base of the history and culture of ethnic groups to integrate ethnic content into the school curriculum successfully. More notably, I had no ethnic content knowledge about myself. If I had yet to find myself in education, how was I going to help others find themselves?

Second, I did not know how to bring my cultural background and experiences into the classroom to elicit discussion on issues of racism and discrimination. One moment in class reverberates in my mind. During Black History Month, after reciting a Langston Hughes poem, "Black Is Beautiful," I pointed to my skin and said, "See, brown is beautiful, too." One of my Latina students, Nancy, piped up, "No, Ms. Espiritu, you're White." Too stunned to take the time to discuss her comment with the class, I immediately replied, "No, I'm not White; I'm Brown," and proceeded to dismiss the students to recess.

I missed a number of teachable moments like this because I was too flustered to respond to my students' innocent comments and inquiries about race and ethnicity. Paley (1989) contends that open and honest discussion of race and ethnicity in the classroom sends powerful and positive messages to children that being different is valued. If I could relive the moment, I would simply ask Nancy why she thought I was White and discuss her response with the class. I also would provide the students with some basic information about who are White, Brown, Yellow, Red, and Black while giving them the more formal names used to identify these groups. Then I would ask the students to identify the groups to which they belong. This would have been a decent beginning lesson in multicultural education.

Reflecting more on Nancy's observation and comment, I wondered if she equated teachers as being White because they were in positions of power. Or perhaps she categorized people as either Black or White, and because my skin color was not Black like that of the African American students at the school, she presumed I was White. I suspect it may be a little of both, but I will never know because I did not question and listen.

Nothing in my teacher education program prepared or even allowed me to talk about race, ethnicity, and culture in the classroom. Through this severe oversight, I learned that my students' and my own ethnic backgrounds were irrelevant in teaching and learning. But my experiences with Nancy and my own as an elementary and secondary school student of color showed me otherwise. The ethnic identities, cultural backgrounds, and experiences of students and teachers do have a place in the classroom. As a teacher, I have a special responsibility to the students, particularly to those of color, to help them figure out the world around them.

When I was growing up, it would have been powerful to have a teacher who saw the world through my eyes. These experiences generated a *balagtasan* in which my mind doubts the value of bringing my ethnic and cultural identity into the classroom:

ISIP (MIND)

I've had my fill of ethnicity
Been to the Philippines and back
Studied government, art, history
Experienced the culture and society.
I've had enough of ethnicity
I'm over the phase of searching for identity
Wasted moments cultivating my soul
When I need to be practical, rational and fill my expected role.
Leave ethnicity behind
It won't help me earn a living
Find a job of professional kind
Nine to five, on the go
Got no time to be Filipino.

My soul counters these doubts with expressions about the importance of the continuing search for and celebration of our ethnic and cultural selves:

KALULUWA (SOUL)

It's never over
Feeding the soul of constant hunger
The search continues as
a circle of infinity
a steady river flow
an endless journey
into the depths of unknown
Fear not the darkness
Complacency is the real enemy
And not your destiny.

ADDING COLOR TO THE IVORY TOWER

It did not take me long to realize it was senseless to leave my ethnic identity and cultural background at the school door as a teacher. I took steps to rediscover my ethnic being and soul when I returned to graduate school at the University of Washington. I pursued a master's degree and later a doctorate in curriculum and instruction with an emphasis in social studies and multicultural education. Under the tutelage of renowned scholars, I learned the fundamentals of multicultural curriculum design and pedagogy through courses such as "Teaching the Minority Student," "Learning Variables of Minority Children," "Democracy and Discussion," and "Teaching Black Students and Culture." I sat in class eagerly absorbing all the material presented.

As much as I was excited to learn how to teach students of color, I still felt uneasy. Although the course titles referred to issues of diversity and democracy, I still felt absent from the readings and discourse as an Asian Pacific American, and more specifically as a Filipino American student. Most of the research and pedagogy focused on African Americans. It was then that I realized that my contribution to the field of multicultural education must involve my unique perspective as a Filipino American; I have a responsibility to give voice to my ethnic and cultural community. I thereby made a conscious effort to question whether what I was learning in class applied to me and to the Filipino American student experience.

Around the same time, I enrolled in my first Filipino American history and culture course to satisfy my quest for knowledge about my ethnic heritage and identity. I still find it unconscionable that it took me seventeen years of my education to finally learn about myself in the U.S. school system. It was extremely empowering to learn about the contributions of my people to U.S. history, especially the accomplishments of my own relatives. When I conducted an oral history project, I learned that my great granduncle, Macario Bautista, immigrated to the United States in 1912. He was the first Filipino doctor in the Central Valley of California and president of the Filipino Agricultural Labor Association, which led the asparagus strikes in the 1930s for fair wages and decent working conditions. His existence validated my roots as an American and explained the revolutionary spirit surging through my blood. I was proud to be Filipino American.

History came alive for me in our Filipino American history course when I heard a third-generation American-born Filipino playwright and community activist, Timoteo (Tim) Cordova, lecture about the Philippine Revolution. Like sponges soaking up knowledge, my classmates and I listened attentively as he rapped down the "unabridged" version of the Philippine Revolution and its heroes. He told us, "Every revolution has three stages: consciousness, propaganda, and armed struggle. Our Filipino heroes José Rizal, Andres Bonifacio, and Emilio Aguinaldo represent the three stages of any revolution." He questioned, "Did you know the Americans chose José Rizal to be our national hero because he wanted reform and not independence? He was a palatable choice." The students surprisingly responded, "No." Cordova continued to question: "Who knows the first president of the United States?" The class answered in unison, "George Washington." He then asked, "Who knows the first president of the Philippines?" Dead silence. Timoteo prodded, "How come you know the first president of the United States but you don't know the first president of the Philippines?" Why not? I thought, stunned by the barrage of questions.

Within forty minutes, Cordova managed to turn my world upside down, and more quickly than any amount of time spent in the Philippines. He challenged what I had learned, or, rather not learned, in the past about Philippine history. Not learning about my ethnic history from my family or school made me presume that Filipinos willingly accepted Christianity, the Spanish, and U.S. colonialism. Before, I had never considered Filipino people as active resistors to oppression. More important, Cordova took a universal concept like revolution and connected it to me. I was proud of my people and finally felt a part of history.

Meeting Timoteo Cordova opened up an entirely new world to me. My education moved from the confines of academia out into the Filipino American community. I quickly learned that Seattle was the center of the Filipino American movement. It was the birthplace of the nation's first nonprofit Filipino American youth agency, Filipino Youth Activities, and the national headquarters of the Filipino American National Historical Society and the nationally acclaimed Filipino American arts ensemble, Sining KilUSAn.

I became deeply involved in Sining KilUSAn as the associate producer for Timoteo's main stage musical about the Philippine Revolution, *Heart of the Son*. I finally found a sense of community in the passionate individuals who were committed to educating and uplifting the Filipino American community through art. At the same time, I was exposed to a new art form. Under Timoteo's vision and tutelage, Sining KilUSAn created and performed an art form that fused the best of Philippine and American culture. His merging of music, dance, and attitude showed me that Filipino Americans could be innovators instead of imitators of art. More important, Timoteo's work symbolized the beautiful blend between our homeland Filipino culture and the newer Filipino American culture.

I wanted to apply this same passion and spirit to the field of education, particularly the curricular needs of Filipino American youth. Filipino Americans comprise the largest Asian American ethnic group in Seattle, Washington, and the second largest Asian American ethnic group in the United States, numbering 1.85 million. They also have a long historical and colonial legacy with the United States, yet we remain invisible to the mainstream.

When the time came to decide whether to write a master's thesis, conduct a master's project, or take a written exam, I chose a project without hesitation because I desired to put theory into practice. I was eager to convey the ethnic content knowledge I gathered from my Filipino American history and culture course, and my passion from Sining KilUSAn, to young people because no child should have to wait until college to learn about self. I came up with the topic for my project during a panel presentation by Filipino American activists on the need to develop collaborations between community and academia when educating about and to our community. I realized that Tim and I should create a Filipino history and culture curriculum for youth. In our collaboration, I represented academia, and he represented our cultural community.

Next, I considered how we would implement the curriculum in classrooms. I knew from experience that teachers are overwhelmed by the barrage of curricula presented to them every day and often make the excuse that they are too busy to implement multicultural education in their classes. In order to set this curriculum apart from all the others, I developed the idea of creating a resource bank of committed college students passionate about their ethnic heritage and interested in teaching the curriculum to youth. Circumventing my previous concerns, teachers were able to sit back and learn about the history of an ethnic group and experience how to teach a multicultural curriculum. Pinoy Teach was born.

THE GROWTH OF ME AND PINOY TEACH

We called the curriculum Pinoy Teach because we wanted to be up front that Timoteo and I, as Filipino Americans, conceptualized, wrote, and taught the curriculum. *Pinoy* refers to Filipinos or Filipino Americans. Since its inception in 1996, Pinoy Teach has become institutionalized at the University of Washington College of Education. It is a two-quarter multicultural curriculum and teacher education course designed to instruct college students of diverse backgrounds to teach a multicultural social studies curriculum to seventh-grade students in mainstream classrooms. To date, over eighty-five college students, fifteen hundred seventh-grade students, and ten middle schools have participated in Pinoy Teach.

Pinoy Teach transformed as I changed. A large part of my multicultural journeying is how I applied my academic course work and life experiences to curriculum practice. Like most other graduate students, many times I sat in multicultural education classes agreeing intellectually with the theories, but then wondered how to make them work. Overwhelmed, I could not even begin to fathom how multicultural education played out in the classroom. How do I teach in a manner that I never experienced myself? For example, I understood Banks's four approaches (1997) to integrating ethnic content into curriculum, but I did not know how to reach what he would consider the highest approaches to content integration: transformation and social action. The challenge in this segment of my multicultural journeying was learning how to carry out the theory of multicultural education.

In retrospect, how I implemented the theory was a process that involved my growth as a person of color. I find parallels between the stages of my ethnic identity development and how I integrated ethnic content into the curriculum. As much as I would have liked to advance directly to the transformative and social action approaches, I moved through the approaches like stairs on a stepladder. When I lacked content knowledge about my ethnic heritage and downplayed my ethnic identity, my teaching about history and culture took the superficial contributions approach. As I became increasingly centered on my ethnic heritage and identity, Pinoy Teach took on more of an ethnic studies and additive approach.

When I became more at peace with my ethnic identity, I did not feel so compelled to proclaim my history and culture as loudly to the world. I realized that Philippine and Filipino American history need to be viewed within the context of world and American history instead of in isolation from other group histories. Pinoy Teach reached the transformative approach to integrating ethnic content when the focal point was no longer the Philippine and Filipino American perspectives, but universal concepts that connect all people together. Finally, my involvement in community service activities showed me the importance of pursuing a social action approach to teaching.

Developing a transformative and social action multicultural curriculum was not easy. Early drafts of Pinoy Teach reflected a traditional approach to the teaching of history that stressed facts, dates, events, and heroes. At this point, Pinoy Teach was another ethnic studies curriculum merely added to the mainstream curriculum.

The consequences of this approach became evident when we piloted Pinoy Teach with a seventh-grade class in a Catholic school composed mainly of Filipino Americans. I had assumed the Filipino American students would have a natural interest in the subject matter because it was about them. I was dead wrong. The curriculum made the Filipino American students feel uncomfortable. Although I was initially surprised at the reaction, it all made sense. Never before had Filipino American students been placed at the center of study. Instead of embracing the curriculum, they shied away from it like it was a glaring light. Although its intentions and substance were positive, the students resisted being at the center of attention.

The linear focus on a single ethnic group's history did not engage the Filipino American or the non–Filipino American students. In fact, this approach placed the spotlight on the Filipino American students and alienated the non–Filipino students. When evaluating Pinoy Teach, Timoteo and I faced the dilemma of most curriculum developers: Should we stick to what we had, or should we change it and start over again? Change collided with the pillars of tradition. Timoteo wanted to start anew; I wanted to salvage the curriculum. He thought the curriculum should focus on concepts and critical thinking, whereas I had trouble thinking outside the boundaries of a traditional history curriculum. One pivotal evening, Timoteo and I had an explosive *balagtasan* over the meaning of history and the direction of Pinoy Teach. It was as if I represented the mind and Tim represented the soul. Here is how our *balagtasan* went:

ISIP (MIND)

History is about dead people and dates
A string of facts to be memorized
Accepted as truth
Nothing to contemplate
Cut and dry
History doesn't deviate
from a path linear and straight.

The soul responded with emphasis on personalizing and connecting the curriculum to the individual students:

KALULUWA (SOUL)

There's more to history than dead White men
It's about people's lives
Who am I?
What is my origin?
Bring history to life
Personalize.
There's more to history than meets the eye,
It's about multiple connections
Between you and me
Past and present
Universal links and relations
Conceptualize.
There's more to history than what we've been taught
It's about critical thinking
Listen and look for the other side
Who decides what is truth?
Put together the pieces to the puzzle
Exercise your mind.

Into the long hours of the night, Timoteo and I struggled over how to create a curriculum that taught ethnic content and exploration along with fostering common citizenship. In the end, we needed to listen to both the mind and the soul to find the answers. We decided that dead people, dates, and events were important but should not be the focal point of the curriculum. Rather, the curriculum needed to be reconceptualized to emphasize universal concepts and critical thinking skills. We took a new path for Pinoy Teach, which henceforth would focus on the following main concepts: diversity, civilization, multiculturalism, perspective, revolution, imperialism, immigration, racism and discrimination, and ethnic identity. In each case, Philippine and Filipino American history and culture were to be used only as examples or vehicles to understand these concepts and foster critical thinking skills.

Taking Pinoy Teach to an entirely new level required that I critically engage my previous conceptions of history. I had viewed history linearly as a string of unconnected dates, dead people, and events, and through the eyes of White males. Therefore, I had taught history this way. It seemed simpler to view people's histories separately, but this presented an unrealistic perspective of history. I started to let go of my singular focus on self and extend my arms to others. But it was a little bit more difficult to cleanse myself from a Eurocentric perspective of history. A couple of events spurred the process. In one of my multicultural education courses, I remember watching *How the West Was Won*, a movie about westward expansion through the eyes of Native Americans. Encountering the other side of the story was astounding and eye opening.

Working with Timoteo Cordova also helped me to eliminate my Eurocentric perspective. We had long discussions on rewriting Philippine history from the perspective of the noncolonialized Filipino. Like most other countries with colonial pasts, our history has been presented from the standpoint of the oppressor or Filipino "colonialized" person. For example, if you thumb through most Philippine history books, you get a sense that history begins when Spain "discovered" the Philippines. Filipinos also were considered "savage and uncivilized" before the Spanish conquest. In Pinoy Teach, we confront these colonial presumptions. For example, students debated a historical event seen through the eyes of a native Filipino chieftain, Lapu Lapu, and a Western explorer, Ferdinand Magellan. The purpose of this lesson was to teach the concept of multiple perspectives to any world event. We had students analyze the concept of civilization and participate in an activity that showed that the Philippines was an ancient civilization that had flourished long before the Spanish conquest in 1565.

As always, the focus of each lesson was not on Philippine or Filipino American history, but understanding the universal concepts that connect all human experiences. What resulted was a curriculum that was relevant to all students. By focusing on general concepts, Pinoy Teach tries to make all students feel a part of the history lesson, instead of emphasizing Filipino Americans exclusively. In the end, it is difficult to discern whether my experiences with the development of Pinoy Teach thrust me into a more secure sense of ethnic identity, or perhaps it was the other way around. Either way, I felt a deeper sense of ethnic stability, globalism, and pan-humanism that manifested in the way I designed and taught multicultural curriculum.

The final piece of Pinoy Teach was our commitment to spread the curriculum into the community. Of course, an important prerequisite to doing this is to establish links to the community first, whether it is to schools or community agencies. After taking the Filipino American history and culture course during my first year in graduate school, I had felt an incredible urge to share everything I learned in class, but I had no formal vehicle to spread the knowledge. As many of our college students have expressed, it was not enough for them to learn about their Filipino history and culture. Learning about self becomes more meaningful when we can take action with knowledge. For many, including myself, this meant educating friends and family.

Pinoy Teach offers an opportunity for college students to take what they learned about themselves and teach it to others in a substantial way. It also provides my students and me a formal way to have an impact on youth and classroom teachers alike in the area of multicultural education. It is empowering to make a difference in the lives of people and help them expand their knowledge and perspective of our multicultural society.

PRINCIPLES FOR PRACTICE

Many of the lessons I have learned in my journey to becoming a multicultural educator can be used to help others begin and craft their own journeys as well. The first and foremost principle is that *it is important to find your sense of ethnic and cultural self before you can open yourself to others and honor their ethnicities.* I needed to find my ethnic being and identity in the different facets and roles of my life. I needed to feel grounded and secure about my Filipino American identity. It is not uncommon for people of color who grow up in predominantly White environments to spend a significant part of their adult life searching for and then celebrating their ethnic heritage and identity. Multicultural educators need to understand these processes and examine how they compare across (as well as within) ethnic groups. Understanding and expressing self and others is a central theme in multicultural teaching and learning.

The next step was for me to merge my personal and professional sense of ethnic and cultural identity with education. I capitalized on my Filipino American identity in teaching, multicultural curriculum development, and research. If you look at the scholarly lives of most multicultural education leaders, my life has followed a similar path. For example, James Banks's and Geneva Gay's multicultural advocacy emerged from their initial research and personal experiences as African Americans; Sonia Nieto's from her Puerto Rican roots; Valerie Ooka Pang's from her Japanese American background and Asian American/Pacific Islanders connections; and Cornell Pewewardy's multicultural commitments are deeply grounded in his Native American identity and heritage. We must acknowledge that our particular experiences with our ethnic backgrounds and histories shape our unique outlook and contributions to the field of multicultural education. Thus, a second principle for multicultural practice is *the importance of studying particular personal ethnic stories along with the collective ethnic group histories and experiences.*

Finding my voice and self in multicultural teaching and learning has involved letting go of the past. By this, I mean separating myself from the negative elements of what I have been taught. This was not an easy task, but it is necessary. Being exposed to Filipino American history helped me to think outside the traditional academic conventions and unleash my soul as I explored my own ethnic culture and multicultural education. From these experiences, I learned it is important that we take risks and interact with different kinds of people. This does not mean we always have to look outside our own ethnic group for differences. But whether inside or outside our ethnic group, we need to analyze them and be receptive to the new information these analyses will produce. These kinds of learning experiences symbolize the principle for practice of *deconstructing conventional teaching from the perspectives of ethnic and cultural diversity.*

Conflict and tension at a personal level are part of becoming and being a multicultural educator, and they take many different forms. In my case, the tension and conflict were between my mind and soul and freely expressing my ethnic and cultural identity. For others, internal conflict may be over being a White educator advocating for issues regarding students of color, gender, class, or immigrant status. Or there may be conflict over how to be an advocate for all ethnically diverse students and groups without losing integrity with your own ethnic group. Other tensions may arise around how to promote multicultural change without causing controversy and how to cultivate ethnic diversity and unity, educational equity and excellence simultaneously. The point is not to squash or eliminate conflict from your mind, but to bring it out in the open, confront it, critique it, and work to resolve it. Another principle in the process of becoming a multicultural person and professional is that *conflict should be viewed as a productive mechanism for growth.*

If you look closely at the early *balagtasans* in this chapter, you will notice that my mind seems to dominate the soul. But as my life progresses and my ethnic perceptions shift, my soul grows stronger and its responses become longer and more confident. In a true *balagtasan,* one distinct winner emerges, but I have altered the format to accommodate my realization that mind and soul need to complement each other to survive. This final short balagtasan ends not in contrast but in harmony and complementarity. It shows the peace that occurs when the mind and soul are in sync:

ISIP AT KALULUWA (MIND AND SOUL)

It all makes sense to me now
I feel at peace
It is all so natural
I have come full circle with my mind and my soul

These revelations and resolutions suggest another important general principle for multicultural practice: *the process of becoming multicultural encompasses both facts and feelings, knowledge and thinking, reflection and action, individual and collective efforts, and internal and external changes.*

Finally, inner peace and harmony allow people to respond calmly to others who challenge the philosophy and implementation of multicultural education. I never expected it would be easy to be a part of the field of multicultural education. I am still learning that the path to practicing our ideals is as much a process of self-discovery as it is helping other people learn how to understand and do multicultural education. An incredible burden was lifted from my shoulders when I, as an instructor, realized that I could not teach every White preservice teacher education student to be as passionate about multicultural education as I am. Giving up the notion of a fixed destination to our journey allowed me to sympathize with my teacher education students and their uncertainties about multicultural education, as well as to understand that my role is to guide their process of revelation and resolution instead of forcing acceptance. By modeling my own process of infusing ethnic identity and content, as well as community activism, into multicultural curriculum development and implementation, I am best able to facilitate other educators' journeys in finding and emphasizing their ethnic being in education. The principle for practice that derives from these insights is *unifying our personal and professional multicultural agendas, or making the personal professional and personalizing the professional.*

JOINING THE JOURNEY

Have you begun your multicultural education journey as a person and a professional educator? If not, do you know how to get started? If your answer to these questions is no, here are some suggestions that might be useful:

• Because it is often said that we teach the way we learned, write down five statements that describe your K–12 education. Now imagine and write down what students from different ethnic and cultural backgrounds would say. Ask some students to do this too. Then do a three-way comparison of your self-description, your projections about the students, and the students' responses and look for similarities and differences. Explain what accounts for the results of the comparisons.

• Identify some tension points or hot buttons for you in multicultural education: issues, events, values, proposals, principles, or claims that are disturbing. Explain or express why these are problematic for you in a creative manner (poetry, *balagtasan,* or short story, for example). Suggest some techniques for resolving these tensions. Collect information from your students or colleagues in other ethnic groups through observations and interviews about their multicultural hot buttons. Compare these with yours and the reasons for similarities and differences.

• Take a reflective trip down your ethnic identity memory lane. Make three stops along the way. First, recall and describe a time or phase in your life when (1) you were not consciously aware of your ethnic and cultural identity, (2) you were made to feel negative about or disaffiliated from your ethnicity, and (3) you were consciously aware of and actively promoting your ethnic identity. Second, as you reflect on these times, make some assessments about how they affected the quality of your being as a person, student, or teacher. Third, if you had the chance to revisit these times and rewrite their scripts, what changes would you make?

• Choose a sample curriculum from a subject that you are planning to teach or are currently teaching. Find your ethnic self within these materials. That is, analyze them to see how well the culture, contributions, perspectives, and experiences of your own ethnic group are included. In conducting these analyses, look at the narrative text, visual illustrations, language usage, and related activity suggestions. If your evaluations are unfavorable, rewrite the materials to make them more ethnically accurate and responsive. Then select a curriculum sample from another subject area, and do the same kind of analyses and modifications for an ethnic group different from your own.

• Develop a reading list of references on the cultures, heritages, and experiences of different ethnic groups. Include one book each for ten different ethnic groups of color within the United States. The books should be contemporary, nonfiction, and written by male and female members of their ethnic groups. As you read these books, keep a record of what you learned that you had not known and can be taught to students, assumptions and beliefs you had about the ethnic groups that are challenged by the new information, the emotional reactions these readings provoked in you, and some strategies for how you will incorporate some of the new knowledge in your teaching.

References

Banks, J. A. *Introduction to Multicultural Education.* (2nd ed.) Needham Heights, Mass.: Allyn & Bacon, 1994.

Banks, J. A. *Teaching Strategies for Ethnic Studies.* (6th ed.) Needham Heights, Mass.: Allyn & Bacon, 1997.

Bennett, C. I. *Comprehensive Multicultural Education.* Needham Heights, Mass.: Allyn & Bacon, 1986.

Bobbitt, F. *The Curriculum.* Boston: Houghton Mifflin, 1918.

Charters, W. W. *Curriculum Construction.* New York: Macmillan, 1923.

Cross, Jr., W. E. "The Negro to Black Conversion Experience." *Black World,* 1971, *20,* 13–27.

Cross, Jr., W. E. *Shades of Black: Diversity in African American Identity.* Philadelphia: Temple University Press, 1991.

Freire, P. *Pedagogy of the Oppressed.* New York: Continuum, 1988.

Gay, G. "Curriculum Design for Multicultural Education." In C. A. Grant (ed.), *Multicultural Education: Commitments, Issues, and Applications.* Washington, D.C.: Association for Supervision and Curriculum Development, 1977.

Gay, G. "Ethnic Identity in Early Adolescence: Some Implications for Instructional Reform." *Educational Leadership,* 1978, *35,* 649–655.

Gay, G. "Implications of Selected Models of Ethnic Identity Development for Educators." *Journal of Negro Education,* 1985, *54,* 43–55.

Gay, G. "Ethnic Identity Development and Black Expressiveness." In G. Gay and W. L. Baber (eds.), *Expressively Black: The Cultural Basis of Ethnic Identity.* New York: Praeger, 1987.

Gay, G. "Coming of Age Ethnically: Teaching Young Adolescents of Color." *Theory Into Practice,* 1994, *33,* 149–155.

Grant, C. A. (ed.). *Multicultural Education: Commitments, Issues, and Applications.* Washington D.C.: Association for Supervision and Curriculum Development, 1977.

Macansantos, F. C., and Macansantos, P. S. *Philippine Literature in the Spanish Colonial Period.* Manila: National Commission for Culture and the Arts, Aug. 15, 2000. [http://www.ncca.gov.ph/phil._culture/arts/literary/_Spanish.htm#].

Memmi, A. *The Colonizer and the Colonized.* Boston: Beacon Press, 1967.

Paley, V. *White Teacher.* Cambridge, Mass.: Harvard University Press, 1989.

Pang, V. O. "Asian Pacific American Studies: A Diverse and Complex Population." *Educational Forum,* 1990, *55,* 49–66.

Phinney, J. S., Lochner, B. T., and Murphy, R. "Ethnic Identity Development and Psychological Adjustment in Adolescence." In A. R. Stiffman and L. E. Davis (eds.), *Ethnic Issues in Adolescent Mental Health.* Thousand Oaks, Calif.: Sage, 1990.

Rich, A. *Blood, Bread, and Poetry: Selected Prose, 1979–1985.* New York: Norton, 1986.

Swartz, E. "From a Compensatory to a Scholarly Foundation." In C. A. Grant (Ed.), *Research and Multicultural Education.* Bristol, Pa.: Falmer Press, 1992.

Takaki, R. (ed.). *From Different Shores: Perspectives on Race and Ethnicity in America.* New York: Oxford University Press, 1987.

Tse, L. "Seeing Themselves Through Borrowed Eyes." *Multicultural Review,*
    1998, *7*(3), 28–32.
Woodson, C. G. *The Mis-Education of the Negro.* Washington, D.C.:
    Associated Publishers, 1933.

CHAPTER TEN

Hanging Out with Ethnic Others

Mei-ying Chen

Growing up in a dominant Minnan (the largest ethnic group) village in Taiwan, I saw some White Americans living next to my friends, and I knew about a few China Mainlanders at school or in my village, but I didn't have any real friendship with any of them. I have to confess that I probably carried a lot of stereotypes about other ethnic groups in Taiwan—for instance, that the Hakka were stingy and diligent, Americans were rich, and all White people were Americans.

I was stigmatized for being a Minnan and of lower-class status. Entering the Pingtung Teachers College broadened my interaction with Mainlanders, Native Taiwanese, Hakka, and Minnan. It provided me the opportunity to learn about the diversity of Taiwan in the 1980s, when most Taiwanese held myths, fears, and phobias about their own and other ethnic groups. Later, in Taipei, I met people from around the world, and they shared with me information about their cultures and comments on places where they had traveled.

The practical knowledge and skills acquired from different societies and interacting with various ethnic groups is great preparation for being a good multicultural educator. I share this belief with many multicultural scholars who suggest that the dominant groups create myths as tools to exploit the nondominant groups, and most often these myths are far different from diverse people's realities. They are consistent with the Chinese saying, "*Jin xin shu bu ru wu shu*" ("believing in books completely is not as good as having no books"). Chinese culture also values "reading hundreds of books, and traveling hundreds of thousands miles" (*Du wanquan shu, xing wanli lu*). These ideas demonstrate that words on paper and messages transmitted through media do not always do justice to ethnic and cultural diversity. Personal multicultural experiences are needed to complement and correct these perceptions. Socializing with different ethnic groups helps me to understand various cultures and mind-sets better, to become more open-minded, and to appreciate national, cultural, and individual diversity.

In this chapter, I present some of my journeys in crossing cultural borders and hanging out with ethnic others as a critical part of my becoming a multicultural person and educator. These are presented in the form of correspondence to my family and friends. I hope that these stories will inspire you to think of parallel experiences and their effects on your own multicultural emergence.

Dear Sister:

Remember what happened in Shandemen, Pingtung? I shared the episode with you while I was studying at Pingtung Teachers College. You might have forgotten because your life has changed so much since then. It might be good to help you recollect the circumstances of the accident.

I had complained about the suspicions and biases of my classmates at teachers' college regarding my Paiwan aboriginal friends. Some of them believed that Native Taiwanese were headhunters, as the myth created about Wu Feng in the elementary school textbooks suggested. I invited them to join me in a visit to the Cultural Garden of Taiwanese Aborigines, which was supposed to open soon. My aboriginal friends had access to the garden, and they offered to provide transportation for us to go see it. A male classmate expressed doubts about the wisdom of this experience and presumed that riding with aborigines would endanger us. What did he know about the aborigines? Why did he assume that we would be in danger by merely being in their presence or visiting one of their institutions?

None of my classmates had developed friendships with any aborigines even though there were many at my college. It is really too bad that people avoid interacting with ethnic groups different from themselves, because these can be enriching experiences. For example, after mingling with Native Taiwanese, I recognized that their cultures value community and sharing more so than the Han Chinese do. When I visited my Paiwan friends in Shandemen, Pingtung, they always took me to their friends' homes. I was invited to join meals and participate in their activities. The whole community is like an extended family. I recall that there were always some unexpected guests. These people felt at home. One thing I wish I could have done is engage with them more, especially participating in their singing and dancing. They created their own music and lyrics extemporaneously. All men, women, children, and elders sang harmoniously. It was so beautiful, relaxing, and freeing. I wish I could be like them. I love singing like they do. I don't know why I never felt completely involved with their singing. Is it possible that Han Chinese are educated to be more reserved? We certainly don't sing freely like Native Taiwanese. For instance, our family and relatives never sang or danced after meals even though we frequently had hour-long conversations at the dining table.

My experiences with the aborigines have been so wonderful. Sala, whom I met at the University of Washington, invited me to lunch with him and his Minnan wife at their home after giving me driving lessons. I was quite surprised, but I feel comfortable and safe being with aborigines because they mean what they say. I often wonder what Han Chinese mean because they know how to wear masks and put "appropriate" words on different occasions. I am not trying to generalize to every individual Han Chinese or aborigine; there are always exceptions and individual differences.

I realize that there are unkind people in every society, and we have to be aware and know how to protect ourselves in case anything unpleasant happens. Despite this fact, it is wrong to impose stereotypes on those whom we do not know. My classmates made such mistakes in regard to aboriginal groups because they believed the myth created by the national government, which attempts to control the people through education. Sometimes this makes me feel anxious about becoming a multicultural educator because I am afraid that I might unconsciously pass some of these same misperceptions on to my students. Then I think that being a little afraid is a good thing; maybe it will help me be more conscious and more effective in avoiding these kinds of problems.

Sister, it is unfortunate that we grew up in an ethnically isolated Minnan community—what James Banks (1997b) describes as being socialized into and living in ethnic and cultural enclaves. We felt safe because all of the villagers, except one China Mainlander, were Minnan. We assumed our culture and ethnic group were the only valid ones. This isolation caused us to be insecure when we were with other ethnic groups without our even being beware that they were more discriminated against than the Minnan were. I believe that if we had grown up in an ethnically mixed neighborhood or school, we would have gained a better understanding of the Hakka and aboriginal groups.

The event at the Aboriginal Cultural Garden made me connect with some of the aboriginal students who were older than me, especially one painting major two years ahead of me. I didn't know his name until he had a painting exhibition with one of his professors at Pingtung Teachers College. His paintings were about Native Taiwanese and their lives. His images and techniques were powerful and energetic, and they easily conveyed his passion for his own people and anger about the discrimination they received from the Han Chinese.

My aboriginal friend may not know that China Mainlanders exploited Minnans and Hakkas. For example, you and I were punished in elementary school for speaking our first language (Minnan). Those who could speak standard Mandarin had privilege and were labeled intelligent. Remember Zhang Suanqi, my classmate in the first and second grades? His mother taught in our elementary school. He was the only monolingual student in my class, but he always got privileges. Wasn't that unfair? We might be the luckiest group among all non-Mandarin speakers. Although we are discriminated against by Mandarin speakers, we are the largest group, and there are always other Minnan speakers available to us. Therefore, I can't understand why Minnan speakers carry stereotypes against the Hakkas and aborigines. This confusion is stronger after living in the United States. It is similar to some Asian Americans who despise African Americans, or Chinese Americans who are prejudiced toward Vietnamese Americans.

Stereotypes about the Hakkas might have developed because they came to Taiwan after the Minnans and had to farm on lands less fertile than the Minnans'. Their lives were harsh, and they had to manage their resources carefully. China Mainlanders were perceived as extravagant because they exploited the other groups. Later, we found out that many of them actually lived poorly and faced many problems that we didn't have. For instance, their fathers were usually away from home to serve in the military, and they lacked male role models. Knowledge does help to break down stereotypes.

I have been thinking about what causes interethnic misunderstandings and what we can do to prevent them. Do multiethnic neighborhoods and classrooms increase interethnic understanding? I have met many foreign students in Taiwan and the United States who grew up in multiethnic environments and classrooms. They have a strong multicultural awareness and are relatively open-minded. Yet a multiethnic environment does not automatically increase interethnic tolerance. It still depends on the nature and quality of our individual interactions with ethnic others. I know this from my own personal experiences and from what authors like Gordon Allport (1979) have written. Let me know what you think about all this.

Bye for now.
  Mei-ying

Hi, Qiang:

Thank you for your letter and for sharing your wife's experience in the Netherlands. I can imagine the challenges she faces in trying to break through the cultural boundaries between Dutch and Chinese cultures. Your experience as Chinese Dutch, and as a tourist and resident in more than thirty countries, will be very helpful to her. My first year in the United States was miserable in terms of crossing the cultural borders that were necessary for me to be happy in Seattle.

The first unpleasant experience was finding a place to live. The rental procedure was complicated, troublesome, and tedious. It gave me the impression that the United States was not a friendly country and that Americans were preoccupied with trying to protect themselves. First, we looked at bulletin boards everywhere and newspaper advertisements. Then we called for information and made appointments to take a look at the property. When we looked at the house, we had to fill out an application form with our credit card numbers and references so that the landlord or agency could check our credit. Then we waited for a few days for the landlord's or agency's response, to know if we were accepted. This system forces people to waste time running around the whole city to look at many houses before they hear from the landlord or agency just in case they are turned down.

I always rented in Taiwan, and the landlords made their decision immediately when I looked at their place. When I made an appointment over the telephone, they checked on my occupation and a little bit about my background. They trusted what I showed and told. In the United States, there seems to be no mutual trust between acquaintances, especially when money is involved. This annoyed me. You rented in Taipei. Did you even hear any story that the landlord checked the potential tenant's credit or references?

Another thing I find a bit off-putting in the United States is that the doors of every house are shut tight all the time. I hardly see any door open. Once when I opened the door of my first apartment for some fresh air, my flatmate told me not to do it again because it might attract burglars or robbers. It also wastes heat in the winter. This was quite striking to me. In my culture, shutting the main doors of the house implies that someone in the household has died. That was why my mom prohibited closing the main door in the daytime. Consequently, I open doors and windows wide to demonstrate that everything is fine in the house.

I also observed something that was considered bizarre by even my American friends. The father of my European American housemate came from California for a visit. The father slept on the couch in the living room, while my housemate slept in his king-size bed. My housemate was a nice guy, and he seemed to get along well with his father too. So how could he let his father sleep on the uncomfortable couch while he slept in the comfortable bed? Is it possible that his father insisted on sleeping on the couch to show his love for his son?

This odd behavior made me think about two friends in their mid-seventies. They refused to move to the East Coast to be close to their daughters, so the daughters could take care of them more easily. They preferred the West Coast. Moreover, they didn't want to have meals with their daughters every weekend. Qiang, this is really different from Chinese customs. Typically, Chinese parents try to convince their children to live close to them or visit them on the weekends. You get together with your mom and siblings every weekend, don't you? Apparently, parent-child relationships differ a lot by ethnic and cultural group. This is something I need to remember when I am teaching ethnically diverse students in my classroom.

Sometimes I wish the cashiers in the stores in the United States would not greet me with, "How are you doing today?" What is the function of that greeting? Does it make the atmosphere friendlier? Yes, in a superficial way. So are Americans hypocritical? I recall Brian, our European Canadian friend, complaining that Chinese Taiwanese are hypocritical. This is how I feel about some of the cultural contentions. Can what we once thought was "weird" or "strange" ethnic behaviors be "normal" once we understand them? What makes the difference, and how do these various reactions affect our interactions with ethnic others?

Traveling in a country is definitely different from living in a country. You and I have met people from five continents who are either decent people or jerks. Those decent people like you and Chris G. shared your experiences and understandings of different cultures and societies with me. We were honest and open with each other. I believe what I heard from you about your cultures. Our American friends didn't seem to comment on the United States too much, which made me think that the United States was wonderful, as the governmental propaganda suggested. But since I began living in this country, I have witnessed both beautiful and ugly dimensions of its culture. I have seen incredible technological advancements and modern conveniences, and they exist side by side with flagrant violations of human rights, racial discrimination, and social, political, and economic injustices, especially for ethnic groups that are not part of the majority.

Remember when you, Mr. Yellow, and I watched *The Joy Luck Club* in Taipei in 1994? After the movie, you both were very surprised that I liked it. I had actually read the novel twice and was touched by the story of the female protagonists. I was puzzled why you guys didn't like it. After studying and living in the United States, I now realize that Wayne Wang, the director, actually reinforced some stereotypes of Chinese Americans in the movie, especially the passivity and brutality of Chinese men. It is a castration of Chinese men, isn't it? Living in the United States inspires me to think and reflect critically on what I believe. I now have some different reactions to *The Joy Luck Club* in terms of interethnic relations and stereotypes. Maybe we should look at this movie again through these different lenses and talk about my new visions. What do you think? Some of the explanations that Spring (1992), Tobin (2000), and Cortés (2000) offer about how mass media create and disseminate images of different ethnic groups should help us in our analyses. Spring calls this image making *ideological management*.

Do you remember when you asked Paul, my African American housemate, if he liked to play basketball? Mr. Yellow was a little annoyed by your question, and I was shocked at his reaction. Mr. Yellow explained that you were imposing a stereotype on Paul. He asked, "Why should African Americans be good at or be interested in basketball?" I think that I understand his standpoint now. Two years ago, he and I talked about Asian Americans' being called "model minorities." Being a Chinese American, he expressed that it was just a way to prevent Asian Americans from articulating themselves, especially politically. He is a political science major and wants to be a social activist. This stereotype makes him uncomfortable. He told me that these myths are used by members of the U.S. mainstream culture to manipulate and marginalize other people.

After studying multicultural education for five years and interacting with people from different ethnic groups, I believe that we need to reevaluate our perceptions of the United States. Part of this rethinking should be a more thorough analysis of prejudices and discrimination against groups of color, by whom, in what ways, and to what effects.

Tell me more about you and your wife's situation in the Netherlands and how she is progressing as a cultural border crosser. Please express my regards to her.

Take care,
 Mei-ying

Dear Anthony:

How are you doing? You probably are still enjoying the sunshine in Berkeley while it is getting gloomy in Seattle. In your last letter, you asked me if I have observed any problems resulting from intercultural communications. Yes, there are a lot. I will provide some examples.

Can you believe that I traveled in China with Helena, our German friend from Hamburg? We met in Thailand when I taught Mandarin there. But then she disappeared after the trip. When I saw her in Hamburg a year later, she explained that she wanted to forget Asia because she felt that the Taiwanese and Chinese conspired to cheat her. She didn't want to contact anyone she had met in Taiwan. This surprised and puzzled me. I assume she had unpleasant experiences in China that stemmed from the barriers of culture, language, and socioeconomic status. I recognized that she felt uncomfortable when Chinese peeked in her purse when she took out money. I think the people were just curious about what White people were doing. They had no bad intentions. Without communicating with me, she assumed that I conspired with the Chinese. Maybe she thought this because I too have

Chinese ancestry. This completely shocked me. Chinese in the interior don't see many White foreigners. Certainly, they are curious about them when the rare opportunity occurs to explore. You and Helena were curious to learn about Chinese philosophy and literature, weren't you?

Communication is really important, especially among people from different ethnic groups and cultures. I recall how Peter from Denmark, with the heavy mustache and beard, disliked Taiwanese. He misunderstood children on buses and claimed they regarded him as a "lion" and laughed at him. How did he know the children perceived him as an animal? His Chinese wasn't good enough to understand children's conversation yet. How could he simply presume children were laughing at him? Could this come from his own insecurity about his differences from the Taiwanese? It also could be that outsiders in his country were regarded as aliens and were ridiculed.

This reminds me of a scene I saw in a street market in Chinatown in New York City in March 2000. It shows that people from different cultures have different communication styles. Unfortunately, most of us grow up believing that our own interpretations of certain signals are the only ones. Here is the story. I stood and observed this amazing market for about thirty minutes. Most of the shoppers were of Asian ancestry. Suddenly, I saw a Chinese female elder drop a coin into the pile of vegetables while she was trying to put the money into the hand of the European American vendor. She laughed a little bit at herself (I would have done so too) and tried to pick up the coin from the vegetable pile. The vendor was extremely irritated by her laughter. He responded with "hmmm" in a sarcastic tone and threw the food at the elderly woman.

I was shocked by his reaction. I don't know if this is a typical American reaction or his personal insensitivity. I believe the old woman was laughing at her own error of dropping the coin, not ridiculing the vendor's missing it. I often have been asked why I laughed when I was laughing at my own mistakes or stupidity. I have sometimes seen this kind of situation in Taiwan. Both the customer and the shopkeeper usually smiled at each other and did not feel offended at all. I believe the vendor's irritation stemmed from cultural misunderstandings similar to those underlying Helena's reactions in China. Cultural signals can be very annoying when people don't understand their meanings.

I also have observed a big difference in gift giving between Taiwan and the United States. A universal phenomenon might be that people give gifts on occasions to share happiness, celebrations, and accomplishments. But bridal and baby showers are new concepts to me. There are no such things in Taiwan. In general, it is taboo to ask friends and relatives to buy what you want and get them in your preferred shops (this is called bridal and baby shower registration in the United States). In Taiwan, we feel bad about asking people to buy things for our own needs; that is why we sometimes get unnecessary goods and some people complain. These practices and related reactions might reflect the reserved side of Taiwanese culture and the straightforward side of the American. These values and practices may become part of Taiwanese traditions soon. Who knows? Culture is dynamic. It is true that differences create gaps, yet through interactions and communication, people from various ethnic backgrounds can cross cultural borders. Educating ourselves to be receptive to cultural differences without any preconceived biases can make our lives easier and more beautiful. And we don't have to deny our own cultural and ethnic identities in order to appreciate those of others (Bennett, 1999).

My dear African American friend, I know that you were discriminated against in Taiwan because of the shallowness and ignorance of some Taiwanese people. They don't believe that African Americans can be erudite and gentle, but they privilege European Americans no matter who they are. They also mistakenly assume that only Whites speak Standard English, no matter where they are from. More sadly, some Taiwanese people even believe that African Americans are violent, as the media frequently suggest. My father actually believed so until I told him years ago that my adviser was an African American woman, and many of my African American classmates helped me through some difficulties, especially during my first year in Seattle.

But some people are not as flexible as my father, even though they are much younger and more educated. Quite a few of my Asian and Asian American friends have been in the United States for years but are still brainwashed by the media and myths. They still misperceive most African Americans as welfare abusers or drug users. Even worse, they discriminate against people with dark skin color. A friend told me, "I would be scared to death if a Black person approached me." I wish these friends could learn that African Americans are inviting and intelligent.

I think African Americans are a lot like Chinese Taiwanese in that they are family oriented and appreciate community strength. When I read *Black Children: Their Roots, Culture, and Learning Styles,* by Janice E. Hale-Benson (1986), I could see my folks in the book—understanding, family oriented, and communal. Another aspect I appreciate very much is that African Americans are expressive and honest; they *ze shan gu zhi* (choose the good and stick to it). Compared to them, Chinese are *shi shiwu zhe wei yiingxiong* (tend to know how to ride the tides of their times). As a Chinese American friend revealed, "I would not have participated in the civil rights movements. African Americans did it. Because of them, the minority people started to enjoy a little bit of equity in the States. And I could have the right to buy my house in this White neighborhood." Still, she carried racial misconceptions and strongly opposed her children marrying African Americans, even though she has not had any direct contact or interactions with them.

I am glad that I have opportunities to make friends with African Americans. Knowing you and other African American friends makes me feel secure even in places that are supposed to be harsh living environments, such as Harlem, New York. There, I stayed with a friend's sister, Susan (a German American), who lives on 105th Street. I walked home alone at night. I shopped at a local market around 9:00 P.M. and walked home safely around 10:00 P.M. Before I left for New York, some friends had warned me not to walk around Harlem because it is dangerous. A Taiwanese friend told me that his wife turned down a fellowship offered by Columbia University, a very prestigious institution, because it is located in a Black neighborhood. This kind of phobia about African Americans seems pervasive. Susan, my friend's sister, explained that this fear actually is used to promote a group's or a person's status by not mingling with the "low-class" people. She and her husband enjoyed their stay in Harlem, and I enjoyed mine too. She loves soul food, and I loved the street drumming and gospel broadcasts on Sunday mornings. It was an enlightening and enriching experience that I had never had anywhere else. I learned a lot. I can only imagine how much more I could have learned had I stayed longer or lived there in the 1920s at the height of the African American cultural development period called the Harlem Renaissance.

I bet you are glad to be hearing my story about African Americans. As you said to me, "Mei-ying, you are weird, but I mean in a good sense." After reading through this letter, you probably feel even more so now—maybe even that I am an arrogant woman, and definitely an "unexpected" one. Oh well, that's me! Hope to hear from you soon.

Love,
    Mei-ying

Dear Ben and Diana:

My "Taiwanese sister and brother" [this is my way of showing them my feelings of close friendship], how are you doing? I am writing this letter to you to express my appreciation and share my observations about living in Seattle with you. Before I met you two, the beauty of Seattle didn't really attract me. Your honesty and sincerity let me know that I can establish true friendships with European Americans.

First of all, I want to say that your "eccentricities" broaden my scope about Americans. Diana probably argues she is still Italian. I bet you will just say "American" since it does not necessarily mean a lot to you because you are who you are. As a matter of fact, this is why I appreciate you. Despite that fact, I still see many traces in you and me of the essential values we were taught in our own countries and cultures. They still influence us a lot. For instance, this past summer, Diana, you complained to Ben that American culture is too individualistic and focused on personal interests. Diana and I have the same idea that individual Italians and Taiwanese have to accommodate the interests of the family most of the time. It's hard for us to go against the will of our parents and promote our own interests. Ben, you usually follow your own will and are seldom interfered with by parents or elders. Well, human beings are socially constructed animals, right? It is fine for Ben not to obey the will of his elders, but Diana and I were shaped to respect (even obey) parents.

I particularly appreciate your honesty and how you allow individuals to keep their ideas without hurting their feelings. Just this past spring, Diana, you, and Pat supported an initiative for increasing the salary of teachers. One of your friends refused to support the cause (I have no clue why. Do you?). To my surprise, you were very calm and only said, "Everyone has a right to his or her own choice." These political differences didn't hurt your friendship at all. So fascinating! Your friend would be condemned by some for not supporting friends if he were in Taiwan or China. American culture seems to make clear dis tinctions among feelings, reasons, and regulations. Chinese and Taiwanese are still debating which should be the priority.

The following example helped me understand the difference between American and Chinese mind-sets. Maybe it will help you too. A friend from China introduced his European American friend to a lot of business opportunities. He didn't expect anything in return, but he felt a little strange that this friend charged him as a regular customer when he asked for help. I was quite surprised by this action because Chinese would be happy to return the favor for those who have helped them.

I am not making any generalizations from these two cases. Yet they do make me wonder if Americans deal with business and friendship very differently from the Chinese. Sometimes I wonder if this is because the idea of reincarnation has been ingrained in my society even though Chinese are multitheists. Giving back is a way to clear up debts; it is the Buddhist idea of receiving blessings in the next life for good deeds.

Remember, Ben, when you stopped me from giving your son any suggestions while he was talking to Steve about college? You told me to let him handle things himself and learn about what he needs. In Chinese culture, parents would have led the discussion and collected information for their children. I was struck by the freedom you gave your son and noted, "Wow, this is so different from Chinese values and behaviors." You treated your sixteen-year-old son as an adult and let him take charge of his own business. It was similar to your wanting him to be social and independent at Maureen's wedding. In China and Taiwan, high school and even college students are still regarded as children, and they don't have much opportunity to express themselves to adults. Maybe this is why Taiwanese children are more reserved than American children. These are interesting contrasts, but they have nothing to do with one cultural style's being superior to the other.

You and your friends have exposed me to some other cultural practices in the United States that I might not have experienced otherwise, such as attending a wedding. I was surprised that there were no children at Maureen's wedding. More surprising, I didn't see Jean and her husband at the wedding. Diana, you told me that American culture expects a couple to show up together at this kind of event. I asked you why they didn't bring their children along. Your answer was that the parents of the bride were hosting a cruise party on Lake Union and it wouldn't be suitable for children (there was wine and dancing).

This is quite different from what would happen in my culture. First of all, Taiwanese don't expect a couple to appear together at the wedding (of course they would love to, if possible) due to constraints of schedule or other business. Second, parents are expected to take children, including babies, along to the wedding party. My father reminded our relatives and friends to "bring your children along" when he gave out invitations to my siblings' weddings. The Chinese wedding banquet is always boisterous, and the host family is happy about this. What I want to point out is that there are different methods for handling the same issue in different cultures. Isn't it exciting to observe such phenomena? There is no one absolutely correct way of doing things. It depends on the cultural values, sociopolitical and economic situations, time, and place. Nothing is static, and very little, if anything, is universal. Changes are beginning to happen in some of the Taiwanese traditions. For example, some members of the younger generation are now celebrating their birthdays (this was not done in the past).

I know you two have traveled in Asia and Europe. I wonder if you even noticed that the philosophy of body contact is different among Asians, Americans, and Europeans. I was quite embarrassed in my first year in the United States about some of the practices I observed related to this. For instance, hugging is a way to show friendliness in the United States, especially among close friends and family members. I have never seen hugging as a ritual of friendliness in Asian countries. People might bow, wave, or put the palms of their hands together, but hug, never. I also observed at your parties that couples sometimes sit on each other's laps, pat each other, or hold hands to demonstrate affection. In Taiwan and some other Asian countries, putting food in mutual dishes is affectionate enough.

When I taught in Taiwan, I often heard teachers ask their students loudly, "Why are you staring at me? You made a mistake, and I am trying to help you out. Am I doing the wrong thing?" One can see Taiwanese students lowering their heads to avoid eye contact with teachers, to express their respect, or to silently admit their mistake. By contrast, my European Canadian friend asked his son to look at him when they were negotiating because avoiding another's eyes means ignoring him or her in Canadian and American culture. This is probably the reason that my American colleagues always put down their work when they talk to me. They also stop working while friends are visiting. To me, this is an unnecessary restriction. This is why I told you to continue working when I visited you at your house.

These things can cause major discomfort among friends, business colleagues, and students and teachers if we do not know and respect different cultural practices. I have learned so much about the cultural values and practices of different ethnic groups from my personal interactions. Reading books by authors such as Shade (1989), Hollins, King, and Hayman (1994), Banks and Banks (1995), Pang and Cheng (1998), and Gay (2000) has helped a lot too.

Ben and Diana, thank you again for including me in your friendship network and contributing to my education about ethnically diverse peoples.

Mei-ying

Dear Paula:

You are Chinese in your heart if we need to categorize people according to ethnic identity. It doesn't matter whether you speak any Chinese language well or not. Yes, language is well connected to culture and affects a person's thoughts, but many factors determine who a person is. I could see your struggle in your sharing and gestures, especially when the Chinese woman selling the breakfast food blamed you for not making yourself clear. You felt bad about not being able to speak Mandarin more fluently and clearly. Paula, remember that you didn't have an opportunity to make a choice about where you wanted to grow up or what language you wanted to learn. You would have spoken Chinese as beautifully as your husband does if you had grown up in China or Taiwan.

As you pointed out, many Chinese immigrant parents just wanted their children to carry out the "American/Canadian Dream" and were not aware of their children's personal identity or psychological struggles. Your father was open-minded to his friends, but he never tried to understand the needs of his children. Your mother lived in Chinese ethnic enclaves and didn't have enough knowledge to be conscious of the dynamics of the greater society. Under the ideology of the melting pot, many minority parents and children believed that being proficient in English was the only way to be successful and possibly "pass" into mainstream culture. Didn't you hear the story told by Dr. Chinn that his first-grade teacher in Canada hit him on the head when he spoke Toisanese at school? He carried a stigma and confusion about his life until he went to college and found out it was a kind of hegemony to deny minority people the right to speak their native languages.

It is unfair to marginalize people with Chinese heritage who grew up in non-Chinese countries because they do not speak any Chinese language. Their environment does not usually nurture Chinese language development. A college-age friend told me that her Chinese teacher from China ridiculed her by asking, "You are Chinese. Why don't you speak Chinese?" Most Taiwanese or Chinese have no idea about the difficulties that overseas Chinese have to struggle with for equity, maintenance of their first languages, and achievements. They think that all ethnic Chinese should be able to speak Chinese wherever they live. Many things may seem trivial to those who haven't gone through these kinds of hard times! To those who have undergone these difficulties, every event or detail is significant and has an impact on who they are and want to be. A Chinese saying that reflects this phenomenon is, "It is like drinking the water, only those who drink know the cold and hot" (*Ru ren yin shui leng nuan zi zhi*).

I don't know if you are aware that many Chinese in the United States are offended by Americans who do not recognize the diversity within their ethnic group. We talked about modern Chinese history and the tensions between Taiwan and China at your place in Singapore. You understand why Taiwanese Americans reject being labeled as Chinese and why they proudly call themselves and their descendants Taiwanese. I was amazed by their affection for Taiwan and the intensity of their resistance to being identified as Chinese. Sometimes they are more Taiwanese than Taiwanese in Taiwan!

But some other people don't dare to claim their ethnicity. This is especially common among interracial children. For instance, some descendants of Dutch and Taiwanese did not reveal their backgrounds until recently. They were afraid that they might be discriminated against when people found out that they were not "pure" Taiwanese. Contemporary interracial children of Chinese or Taiwanese and Europeans are perceived as beautiful. I have had quite a number of European American and Chinese American students in my Chinese classes. They appear to be happy with whom they are because of the advantages of being bicultural and bilingual. This pride doesn't necessarily pervade the community of interracial children with African American heritage, especially when mixed with European American. They may be marginalized by both communities. Probably this is why a friend in her mid-forties initiated a monthly gathering for interracial children to share happiness and bitterness. Several authors (Root, 1992; Bernal and Knight, 1993; Sheets and Hollins, 1999; Ponterotto, 2001) have helped me to understand that ethnic identity development and affiliation are critical and complicated aspects of people's lives.

Sometimes ethnic identity is manipulated to boost the social status of individuals from certain groups. This happens more for some groups than others. For example, in the United States, its seems to be a statement of pride for European Americans to claim some Native American heritage in their ancestry (regardless of how small the percentage). But it is not as desirable for them to acknowledge any African American heritage. I have been mistaken as Thai, Filipino, Native Taiwanese, Native American, Vietnamese, and assimilated Native Taiwanese (Pingpuzu). People apologize when they realize they made a mistake because Taiwanese (Minnan) have a higher status than the others. As a matter of fact, I am happy that so many others find my physical appearance attractive. Isn't it good? I enjoy the advantage when I travel in different places, such as bargaining for goods and services and for friendship. I don't think many people will apologize if they mistake a person as a member from a more favorable group.

Paula, I know you are interested in educating teachers. What is your opinion about how their training should deal with these issues? How will you present the topic of ethnic identity in the curriculum you design for high school students?

Take care,
  Mei-ying

Hi, Hong:

I am happy that I met Reiko, a Japanese woman as critical as you are, with whom I can share some politically and culturally sensitive issues. It is like you and I discuss the tensions between Mainland China and Taiwan without patriotic prosecution.

We opened up our in-depth discussion at the Floating Lantern Festival. We were both rather shocked when a student presented a poem about the bombing of Nagasaki and Hiroshima by asking why the American government bombed Japan without justice. My Chinese friend and I asked each other, "Isn't it a well-known fact that the Americans bombed Nagasaki and Hiroshima because the Japanese

government and the soldiers brutalized Asians during the war, including Chinese, Southeast Asians, and Koreans, and also attacked Pearl
Harbor to expand their territory?" Does the student have this knowledge? Could there be any ceremonies that commemorate both the
victims of the American bombing and the victims of Japanese massacre?" After the event, I talked to a Chinese American friend who had
fought against the Japanese. He thought it was fortunate that the
United States had bombed Japan. Otherwise, the war would have continued, and even more people would have died.

Let's look at how this issue has been handled in Japan from different angles. A Japanese friend told me that there was only one sentence
about the Nanjing massacre in her history book. Luckily, her teacher
had different resources about what Japan did during World War II and
provided students with these perspectives. What is "reality" or "truth"
is always dependent on who manages the resources and who holds
power. Constructing blind patriotism is a way of controlling certain
groups while giving power to others.

It is good to love our own country. However, it should be critical
love, not blind love. No person or government is perfect. Blind patriotism is not good for individuals or the government. James Banks
(1997a), one of the leading multicultural education scholars in the
United States, writes about this a lot. He suggests that in preparing
ethnically diverse students for democratic citizenship, they should be
taught skills for understanding, critiquing, and transforming society,
not just simply adapting to it. This is necessary because our countries
and cultures frequently do not live up to their ideals of freedom,
equality, and justice in the treatment of ethnic, racial, and cultural
minority groups.

When I talked to Reiko about the possibility of the Japanese government's apologizing for the Nanjing massacre, she responded that
it was not likely to happen. But Prime Minister Murayama, the first
from the Socialist party to hold this office, did apologize for the mis-
ery that Japan caused during World War II. The reason is similar to
the Chinese government's not wanting to expose the truth about being
invaded by Japan and the catastrophe that resulted because it would
make China seem weak to the rest of the world.

What I want to point out here is the histories of events. We educators should help students analyze historical and contemporary ethnic
issues, events, and experiences from many different angles and perspectives. The purpose of presenting varying viewpoints is to provide

multiple interpretations and determine what we can learn from history. Historical catastrophes should not be used to impose stereotypes on individuals or groups. Older Chinese and Southeast Asians who saw the brutality of the Japanese invasion in their countries still bear hatred against Japanese. They don't buy Japanese goods, and they prohibit their children from socializing with Japanese. It is unfair to compel the descendants to pay for the misdeeds of or seek revenge for the ancestors. To me, there are different layers and perspectives from which to analyze historical events. These need to be revealed publicly to prevent similar mistakes from happening in the future.

Because you have a Ph.D. in history, you probably have different thoughts and perspectives about these issues. Please let me know.

Mei-ying

PRINCIPLES FOR PRACTICE

Five key principles embedded in the stories of my "hanging out with ethnic others" are important for becoming multicultural in general.

Personal contact probably is one of the best ways to understand the diversity of the human world and recognize individual differences within ethnic groups. Within the arena of cultural diversity, reading and traveling can increase understanding of different cultures and ethnic groups, and decrease stereotypes. This may be able to counteract the human tendency to categorize phenomena in order to reduce their burden and make life easier. The first principle speaks to this tendency: *it is crucial to have personal interactions with ethnic others.*

The second principle is that *establishing relationships with ethnic others can help individuals recognize the differences and similarities among cultures, resolve some ingrained stereotypes, and develop a more holistic picture about ethnic others.* Through the exchange of ideas and experiences with members from different ethnic groups, an individual will be able to tease out the nuances of different cultures. It is also important to be aware that unverified cultural observations may create additional stereotypes, which are usually proclaimed as truth. This situation is even more dangerous than the misperceptions without contact because these claims appear to have more credibility. Personal interactions and communications are thus critical for clarifying cross-cultural or interethnic differences.

The major benefit for me in hanging around many ethnic others is that I have learned much about the cultures and histories of different ethnic groups and countries. The most enlightening experiences come from gaining the perspectives of individuals from different ethnic groups and countries on controversial topics, such as Reiko's comments on the Nanjing massacre in China. The third principle is thus that *when teachers understand the histories, cultures, and experiences of different ethnic groups, they become more open-minded and capable of listening to different voices.* The self-liberation will have a positive impact on their ability to teach multicultural perspectives, experiences, and realities to students.

Through interactions with individuals from different professional, social, religious, educational, and cultural backgrounds, we can learn a wealth of multicultural knowledge, perspectives, and skills. The fourth principle is that *balancing learning in school with immersion in different social contexts and personal relationships is tremendously beneficial for self-enlightenment and skill development for multicultural living.* In addition, we have to be conscious of the fact that some students who do not learn well at school are good social learners. Others may prefer to learn in ways that are not valued and used routinely in school. This is often true for students from collectively oriented cultures, such as Native Americans, Latinos, African Americans, and Asian-origin ethnic groups. It is critical for educators to immerse themselves in informal learning situations and thereby reevaluate what they learned in their formal education. Experiences talk. When we have similar social, personal, and cultural experiences as our students, we are better able to help them accomplish academic goals.

Ethnic celebrations signify respect for and meanings of critical stages in life, rites of passages such as birth, adulthood, wedding, and death, and other important accomplishments. The final principle is that *ethnic celebrations provide contexts and opportunities for us to see nuances of culture that are not possible elsewhere. Access to these celebrations offers unique learning experiences about cultural differences.* For this reason, both teachers and students will find ethnic celebrations enriching in their preparation for and practice of multicultural education. A word of caution is needed here: some careful prior cultural knowledge and subsequent debriefing should accompany these experiences. When we recognize the dynamics of culture in and the motivations behind ethnic celebrations, we will be more capable of teaching students about ethnic others.

JOINING THE JOURNEY

The journey toward becoming a multicultural educator can be challenging. It took me almost two decades to share my journey through writing. You do not have to wait this long or journey alone. If you wonder where to begin, here are three suggestions that derive from my personal story:

• Tell your own personal stories through letters about your interactions with ethnically diverse individuals and groups. These stories can be of two types. In one, you and your students can tell your friends about the prejudices, stereotypes, and discriminations you have encountered, including when, on what occasions, by whom, and how they felt. Before telling the stories, there should be an agreement about whether they can be retold to anyone else. You, or some of your students, may not be willing to reveal them publicly. It is important to build up mutual trust among students and between students and teachers before exposing their life experiences. It also is a good idea to have a class discussion about different stereotypes and how to eliminate them. Another form of writing your own stories about experiences with ethnic others may include whom you interacted with, what insights occurred, what advice you have for those who have not had multiethnic experiences, and techniques relating to and establishing friendships with ethnic others. Have your students do parallel activities. Then discuss these experiences, and generate some dos and don'ts for maintaining good relationships with ethnic others.

• Have a conversation about active engagement with ethnically different peoples and experiences. The questions I set out in this chapter are intended to initiate dialogue about different ethnic groups and the interrelationship between dominant and nondominant groups. You can use them to develop your thinking and perspectives on multiethnic issues—for instance, thinking and talking about what multicultural knowledge is transmitted to students by school curricula and the impact it has, how it compares with lived experiences, and how this knowledge might be improved. This dialogue provides opportunities for you and your students to reflect on multicultural learnings acquired from informal settings and social relationships and how they can enhance knowledge gained in educational institutions. Active engagement with these questions and reflections on their experiences may improve decision making about multicultural issues and how to teach to avoid negative outcomes for students.

• Do your own multicultural knowledge construction through personal exposures, interviewing individuals, observing ethnic behaviors in natural cultural settings, and participating in ethnic events. These ways of knowing may have more credibility than books because they are firsthand and recent. Even so, interviews can be problematic if credibility and trust between interviewer and interviewees and the cultural contexts have not been well established. These are especially crucial in interethnic group interactions. Despite these concerns, experiencing ethnic others personally is far more beneficial than written accounts. In preparing to engage in these activities, consider some issues you want to learn about from having personal interactions with members of a given ethnic group, specify the interviews and interactions you want to have, determine the contexts that may generate the most accurate and authentic knowledge, decide how you will determine the credibility of what you learn, consider what obstacles you may encounter and how you will overcome these, and be aware of how your interviewing and interacting strategies may have to be modified as you engage with different ethnic groups.

References

Allport, G. *The Nature of Prejudice.* Reading, Mass.: Addison-Wesley, 1979.

Banks, J. A. *Educating Citizens in a Multicultural Society.* New York: Teachers College Press, 1997a.

Banks, J. A. *Teaching Strategies for Ethnic Studies.* (6th ed.) Needham Heights, Mass.: Allyn & Bacon, 1997b.

Banks, J. A., and Banks, C.A.M. (eds.). *Handbook of Research on Multicultural Education.* Old Tappan, N.J.: Macmillan, 1995.

Bennett, C. I. *Comprehensive Multicultural Education: Theory and Practice.* (4th ed.) Needham Heights, Mass.: Allyn & Bacon, 1999.

Bernal, M. E., and Knight, G. P. (eds.). *Ethnic Identity: Formation and Transmission Among Hispanics and Other Minorities.* Albany: State University of New York Press, 1993.

Cortés, C. E. *The Children Are Watching: How the Media Teach About Diversity.* New York: Teachers College Press, 2000.

Gay, G. *Culturally Responsive Teaching: Theory, Research, and Practice.* New York: Teachers College Press, 2000.

Hale-Benson, J. E. *Black Children: Their Roots, Culture, and Learning Styles.* Baltimore, Md.: Johns Hopkins University Press, 1986.

Hollins, E. R., King, J. E., and Hayman, W. C. (eds.). *Teaching Diverse Populations: Formulating a Knowledge Base.* Albany: State University of New York Press, 1994.

Pang, V. O., and Cheng, L.-R. L. (eds.). *Struggling to Be Heard: The Unmet Needs of Asian Pacific American Children.* Albany: State University of New York Press, 1998.

Ponterotto, J. G. (ed.). *Handbook of Multicultural Counseling.* (2nd ed.) Thousand Oaks, Calif.: Sage, 2001.

Root, M. (ed.). *Racially Mixed People in America.* Thousand Oaks, Calif.: Sage. 1992.

Shade, B. J. (ed.). *Culture, Style, and the Educative Process.* Springfield, Ill.: Thomas, 1989.

Sheets, R. H., and Hollins, E. R. (eds.) *Racial and Ethnic Identity in School Practices: Aspects of Human Development.* Mahwah, N.J.: Erlbaum, 1999.

Spring, J. *Images of American Life: A History of Ideological Management in Schools, Movies, Radio, and Television.* Albany: State University of New York Press, 1992.

Tobin, J. *"Good Guys Don't Wear Hats": Children's Talk About the Media.* New York: Teachers College Press, 2000.

CHAPTER ELEVEN

Footsteps in the Dancing Zone

Mary Stone Hanley

T he play that follows relates some of the critical incidents and individuals who have played important parts in my process of becoming a multicultural person and educator. As you will see, the personal is preeminent and began long before the professional. This may not be true for everyone, but it is a resounding fact for me. As is most often the case with scripting stage performances, metaphorical images and messages are prominent in my story. Embedded within them are ideas and events that make me think, believe, and act as I do about understanding, respecting, embracing, and promoting ethnic and cultural diversity in my life and teaching.

At the overt, tangible level, the play revolves around three characters. The central figure is the conduit for conveying my journey in becoming multicultural. She tells the stories to two younger characters, who symbolize students. They are the audience to her experiences. The telling of the stories is more important than the role of the characters on stage. Their content represents a much larger host of individuals, incidents, and events that are part of the main character's multicultural development. A group of dancers provides background action and transitional bridges for the events within the stories. Their presence suggests that although the specific aspects of our multicultural development may appear to be distinct and separated in time and place, they are, in fact, interconnected. Together they are a synergy of influences that shapes our engagement with ethnic and cultural diversity. Becoming multicultural is indeed a dramatic transformative process, in the best sense of what constitutes drama.

Characters

GRANA: the main subject and narrator of the drama that unfolds; the storyteller, teacher, author, sage

MARTIN and KARLA: the audience for GRANA's storytelling; youth in need of teaching

DANCERS

Setting

The stage is dark and empty. Lights up as DANCERS bring in a rocking chair and a small table, placing them stage left in a pool of light. They also bring in a pile of books, a photo album, and a table lamp, placing them on the table. GRANA enters stage right carrying a big hat. MARTIN carries in a small trunk and places it downstage from the chair. KARLA enters and rummages through the trunk. GRANA tries on the hat, takes it off, then rummages through the trunk for different clothes. MARTIN takes a book out of the trunk and looks at it. KARLA picks up a scarf and waves it in the air. Music begins; she starts to dance. Throughout the play, film footage and still photographs appear on the walls up center, left and right stage. A music trio—stand-up bass, piano, and drums/percussion—play live music and sound effects.

KARLA: Who you gonna be?

GRANA: Grana.

MARTIN: You were Grana last time.

GRANA: Of course, but it's my story, and I get to tell it like I want.

KARLA: Who told you that? Nobody tells her story by herself.

GRANA: Well, you can be my trusty sidekicks, Martin and Karla.

KARLA: Miss Thang got to have two sidekicks; everybody else got one.

GRANA: It's my story! I can tell it like I want!

MARTIN: I don't want to be no sidekick. How come I got to be some old sidekick?

GRANA: [*Balls up fist*] 'Cause I said so!!

MARTIN: Okay, okay. My bad. Didn't mean nothing! I'll be whatever.

[*GRANA and MARTIN watch KARLA while she dances with the Dancers.*]

MARTIN: Karla, girl, you sure can dance!

KARLA: What you say? C'mon, dance with me.

MARTIN: Naw, I'm ashamed to say, I ain't got the gift.

KARLA: Boy, if you can walk you can dance.

[*Slow fade-in of visual images of DANCERS—African, African American, Native American, Latino*]

GRANA: What you say!

[*KARLA gathers MARTIN in her scarf and starts to dance with him as DANCERS continue.*]

KARLA: All dance is, is wonder in motion.

[*KARLA dances close to MARTIN.*]

KARLA: Wonder what you know . . .

[*GRANA joins the dance.*]

GRANA: What you feel when I move, like this?

MARTIN: Wonder how you move like that!!

KARLA: Aw, what's the story, Morning Glory!?

GRANA: I take a step.

KARLA: We step together.

MARTIN: What you say!

GRANA: People got a hunger for rhythm in a cosmic appetite! If you can walk, my brother, you better dance!

KARLA: Rhythm is sustenance and story, and life is a dance.

GRANA: Loving is a dance.

MARTIN: Learning, you dance.

GRANA: What you say!

[*The dance gets faster and faster with scarves of various colors.*]

MARTIN: Love! Life! Knowing! Rhythm!

[*They create designs with the scarves as they dance; slow fade-in of multi-cultural visual art on the screens.*]

KARLA: Story!

GRANA: I got a story . . .

KARLA: I know that's right!

GRANA: It's an old story, but I'll pick it up where I begin.

MARTIN: C'mon with it, then! Show me your moves!

KARLA: What's the steps?

GRANA: Once upon a time, I believed every word—Black kid growing up among mostly Black folk. Grown folks, busy trying to feed the kids and pay the rent, working and praying from day to night for good times. Kids running through the neighborhood, innocent as the rain, putting life together and taking it apart, certain that this right here, right now, and right whatever they thought, or wanted, or needed was the most significant something in the world.

[*GRANA and KARLA put ribbons in their hair; MARTIN puts on a cowboy hat. They become ten years old and chase each other. Images of Black children from the 1950s appear in the background.*]

MARTIN: You're it.

GRANA: Am not. You're it.

MARTIN: I said it first. My game.

GRANA: Look in my eye, what do you see? Little Black dude tryin' to hypnotize me.

MARTIN: Who you callin' black?

GRANA: You. Yeah, you black and ugly, all them nappy kinks. Looking like a Brillo pad. Now, I got good hair.

MARTIN: Shut up!

GRANA: [*taunting*] You don't like it, don't take it. Here's my collar, come and shake it. Shake it rough, shake it tough, shake it 'til you get enough!

KARLA: Stop it, you two. We gonna be late for school. And the crossing guard is looking. If she reports, you Miss Washington gonna shake both you with her paddle! C'mon!

[*They rush to center stage. KARLA stops suddenly; the others bump into her. The three of them stand still and look out at the audience. They put their hands over their hearts. Lights slowly cross-fade until they are standing in a pool of light.*]

GRANA, MARTIN, and KARLA: I pledge allegiance to the flag of the United States of America . . .

[*Images of the civil rights and antiwar movements appear.* KARLA *and* MARTIN *continue to mouth the words of the Pledge of Allegiance, but as an undertone. Jimi Hendrixs's "Star Spangled Banner" plays.*]

GRANA: [*increasingly bewildered and appalled*] And to the republic for which it stands. I pledge allegiance to the flag . . .

[*Image of Emmett Till appears.*]

MARTIN: Bam!!

GRANA: and to the republic . . . One nation . . .

[*Image of Martin Luther King Jr., dead on the balcony, appears.*]

KARLA: Bam!!

GRANA: For which it stands . . . I pledge allegiance . . . one nation . . . I pledge allegiance . . . under God . . .

MARTIN: Bam!

[*Image of Malcolm X in casket appears.*]

GRANA: I pledge . . . under God . . . I pledge . . .

[*Images of ghetto and prison riots appear.*]

KARLA: Bam!

MARTIN: Bam!

GRANA: Fannie Lou Hamer.

KARLA: Bam!

GRANA: Little Bobby Hutton.

KARLA: Bam!

GRANA: Joanne Little.

MARTIN: Bam!

GRANA: Medgar Evers.

KARLA: Bam!

GRANA: Fred Hampton.

MARTIN: Bam!

GRANA: Lumumba!

MARTIN: That happened in the fifties.

GRANA: Yeah, I know. I learned about it in the sixties.

KARLA: But Lumumba wasn't in the United States.

GRANA: Wasn't no borders to the horror.

MARTIN and KARLA: Bam!

GRANA: Allende!

MARTIN: Bam!

GRANA: My Lai.

KARLA: Bam!

GRANA: Even the Kennedys.

MARTIN, KARLA, and GRANA: Bam!

GRANA: The questions bugged me like flies on garbage day.

MARTIN: America! We are the best.

GRANA: Am I a we?

KARLA: Might makes right.

GRANA: Men have the might, and White must be right. They the only ones in the books.

MARTIN: What books?

GRANA: The ones they give me. Must be true.

KARLA: One nation, under God, indivisible

GRANA: Invisible? You mean like when me and daddy stand at the counter in the department store and they wait on everybody before us? Or when my mama can't buy a chair on credit unless my daddy signs for it?

KARLA: She have a job?

GRANA: Shoot, yeah. My mama worked almost all her life! Got her first paycheck when she was eight years old. She worked in the kitchen and yard of this lady she called Miss Anne.

MARTIN: And to the republic for which it stands . . .

GRANA: But you know, when they was at home, my mama didn't take much stuff. Like the time Uncle Tommy call himself beating up on Aunt Serrelia.

KARLA: What happened?

GRANA: Mama and Aunt Thelma, Aunt Louise, and Cousin Sharon Rose, and Cousin Martha Mae went over to Uncle Tommy to "talk" to him. They took a baseball bat just in case he wouldn't listen.

MARTIN: Did he?

KARLA: What you think?

GRANA: A deep sleep in hot, sticky, white nights where black must be evil and poor 'cause the heroes was always white and rich, and men. But I stretched, and yawned, and pulled back the covers, 'cause I heard my mind say, "Get up, Girl! Time to get up now, and handle your business."

KARLA: They say curiosity killed the cat.

MARTIN: Get on up, Girl, while the republic still stands.

KARLA: Satisfaction brought her back, but it sure gave her the blues.

MARTIN: You show me your agency, I'll show you mine. C'mon, Grana.

[*MARTIN and DANCERS pull on GRANA.*]

GRANA: I'm up, I'm up! About my business . . . [*suddenly terrified*]. Oh my God! [*crowd noises*] Who is that?

MARTIN: What?

KARLA: Where?

[*Fade in images of an antiwar demonstration*]

GRANA: They asked me if I wanted to read a poem, that's all! The speaker didn't show up! Now they want me to say something! I didn't come to make no speech. I just came with a poem. I can read a poem. I don't know what to say. I think I'm gonna throw up. There must be ten thousand people looking at me! How did I get to this? I just now woke up!

[*Reads*] "Harriet Tubman didn't take no stuff. Didn't come to be no slave, wasn't gonna stay one either. Wasn't gonna stay one either."

Don't make me say anything else, please! I don't know what else to say. What do I know? I'm not a White activist. I'm Black, I'm a woman, I'm broke, and I don't know what to . . . [*addresses the crowd timidly*] . . . I will not be a slave to war. The work of Harriet Tubman is still going on and that's my job, not this war. [*Crowd cheers and applause*]

MARTIN and KARLA: Hell no we won't go! Ain't no Vietnamese ever called me nigger!

GRANA: [*encouraged*] That's right. The war for justice is at home, right here, not in Vietnam. Thank you.

[*Crowd noises, applause, images of demonstrations*]

GRANA: I did it! I didn't sound too stupid, did I?

MARTIN and KARLA: You were great.

GRANA: I was?

KARLA: Yeah.

GRANA: I was?

MARTIN: For real, Grana, you were.

GRANA: Well, with the taste of possibility in my mouth, I stepped off to see the world.

[*Music. Dance. GRANA puts a feather in her hair and looks around. Images of the Puyallup Indian resistance camp on the Duwamish River.*]

GRANA: This is a reservation? Where are all the tepees? And what's with all the guns and rifles? The cowboys coming? [laughs] What's going on here? I don't understand. Okay. Okay. I'll go with you. Cross the tracks to cross the river, make a barricade, don't seem too hard to do. [*GRANA, MARTIN, and KARLA mime pulling bushes.*]

KARLA: If we can get this road blocked, the pigs won't be able to take us by surprise.

GRANA: Pigs?

KARLA: Oh, oh, somebody's coming.

GRANA: Who?

MARTIN: Can't tell. Can't see nothing but headlights.

KARLA: Oh, shit. Run! Get back to camp.

GRANA: We can't!

KARLA: Why not?

GRANA: 'Cause there's a train crossing on the tracks.

MARTIN: So what?

GRANA: But it's moving!

KARLA: So what!

MARTIN: You only got two choices: staying with whoever that is or jumping on that train! Jump!!

[*Sounds of train passing, lights flashing*]

GRANA: I . . . [looks from one side to the other] I . . . don't understand. How did I get myself into this? Who are these people? What do pigs and salmon have to do with me? Oh, my God, jump!

MARTIN, KARLA, and GRANA: Bam!

[*Sound of train, flashing lights, images of the attack of the federal agents on the Puyallup Indian camp*]

GRANA: Two days after I left, the cavalry charged, and blood flowed into the river. They say that the salmon were particularly bitter that year.

MARTIN: Bam!

GRANA: I had so many questions, I stumbled on my curiosity in search of an answer. So I put on my combat boots and found a path into the unknown. I was looking for teachers, somebody who could take me to the corner of what I know and what's new, somebody who could help me connect my tenuous questions to solid flesh.

KARLA: [*looks at a scrapbook*] Who is this?

GRANA: Who?

[*MARTIN carries the photo album to GRANA. He shows her picture. KARLA crosses to GRANA and looks. GRANA laughs.*]

GRANA: That's me.

MARTIN: Unh-unh.

GRANA: Yes, it is.

KARLA: It is?

GRANA: Yep.

KARLA: Grana, look at all that hair!

GRANA: Yeah, a lot of us thought the revolution was about hair.

MARTIN: Was it?

GRANA: It was a part of the Representation Wars.

KARLA: You better recognize!

MARTIN: [*pointing to a picture*] Dang, Grana! Did you know Angela Davis?

GRANA: Not really. I met her a couple of times, though. She was one of my teachers.

KARLA: She was? Who else?

GRANA: Lots more—mostly Sisters of the Triple Jeopardies.

[*Images of women of color activists talking, reading, studying together, demonstrating, caring for children, working with me*]

MARTIN: The triple who?

GRANA: Jeopardies—race, class, and gender, the Three Sisters who carried our deepest joys and greatest sorrows. Definitely a love-hate relationship . . .

[*The Dancers stand together as a chorus. A drum beats.*]

KARLA: What did they say?

MARTIN: What did they do?

GRANA: The Sisters taught me to live inside myself so I could find and name my position in the world. They taught me that the answers were inside my own questions, and my questions came from my own story. So to understand my questions, to find the answers, I had to understand myself. The dance is forever unfolding.

[*They dance. A* DANCER *gives* GRANA *a book. Grana tries to give it back.*]

GRANA: I won't understand this. I know I won't. Books this thick, I never understand them; I'm not smart enough. I wasn't in the gifted program.

[*The* DANCERS *will not allow her to give the book back. They push the chair behind her and make her sit down.* GRANA *struggles to get up. The* DANCERS *make her sit down; they open the book for her.* KARLA *and* MARTIN *gather around.* GRANA *reads.*]

GRANA: "The history of all hitherto existing society is the history of class struggles. Freeman and slave, patrician and plebeian, lord and serf, guildmaster and journeyman. In a word, oppressor and oppressed, stood in constant opposition to one another, carried on an uninterrupted, now hidden, now open fight, a fight that each time ended either in a revolutionary re-constitution of society at large, or in the common ruin of the contending classes." Marx, 1847. Aha! Pigs, and salmon!

[*The Dancers give Grana another book. She reads where they point.*]

GRANA: "Imperialism is a specific historical stage of capitalism. The economic partition of the world by the international cartels has begun. There are already over one hundred such international cartels, which command the entire world market and divide it 'amicably' among themselves—until war re-divides it." Lenin, 1916.

MARTIN: Vietnam?

GRANA: And Lumumba, Allende, and before that, and before that. The jigsaw pieces of my own experience take shape into something much, much larger than me and much older. I am in my place in line.

[*The drumming grows.* GRANA, KARLA, *and* MARTIN *dance with the* DANCERS. *Images of women by themselves, with other women, and with children and men, living, demonstrating, studying, and working continue.*]

GRANA: First I gathered slogans, because they sounded like a song that I could sing.

MARTIN and KARLA: *El pueblo unido, jamas seran vencido!* The people united will never be defeated! *El pueblo unido, jamas seran vencido!* The people united will never be defeated!

GRANA: And then I collected stories that made me feel strong. "O kinsmen, we must meet the common foe / and though far outnumbered, let us show us brave / Like men we'll face the murderous, cowardly pack, / Pressed to the wall, dying, but fighting back!" Claude McKay, 1927.

[*Images of young Black people talking to older Black people.*]

KARLA: From the elders.

[*GRANA reads from another book.*]

GRANA: "Not to know what one's race has done in former times is to continue always a child." Carter G. Woodson, 1933. [*from another book*] "Radical is a label that is always applied to people who are endeavoring to get freedom. Jesus Christ was the greatest radical the world ever saw," Marcus Garvey, 1925.

KARLA, MARTIN: "We shall not, we shall not be moved / Just like a tree that's planted by the water / We shall not be moved." [*continue humming*]

GRANA: "Let woman's claim be as broad in the concrete as in the abstract. We take our stand on the solidarity of humanity, the oneness of life, and the unnaturalness and injustice of all special favoritisms, whether of sex, race, country, or condition." [*stage voice*] Anna Julia Cooper, 1892.

KARLA: From sisters and brothers, and brothers and sisters, from here, there, all over, I found strength in love.

GRANA: "It was like sewing ruffles on a fence of nails. The will to make life beautiful was so strong." Zora Neale Hurston, 1937. "A revolutionary is guided by great feelings of love." Che Guevara, 1960.

[*Images of the young people of all races and from the Venceremos Brigade in Cuba. Grana picks up another book and reads from it.*]

GRANA: "A deepened consciousness of their situation leads men to apprehend . . ."

MARTIN: Men?

KARLA: We're on a roll, let's not get sidetracked. Go on, Grana.

MARTIN: Sidetracked, hmph! If I'd said that, I'd be laying flat out on the floor by now.

KARLA: Go on, Grana.

GRANA: [*sitting down, she reads aloud*] "A deepened consciousness of their situation leads men to apprehend that situation as an historical reality susceptible of transformation. Resignation gives way to the drive for transformation and inquiry, over which men feel themselves to be in control. Any situation in which some men prevent others from engaging in the process of inquiry is one of violence. . . . To alienate men from their own decision-making is to change them into objects." Paulo Freire, 1973. I see . . .

KARLA: [*joins Grana*] Objectification . . . Life in the thingdom.

MARTIN: [*joins Grana*] And domination. I pledga malegiance through the flag of the nunited states of America. We were just supposed to say it, what does it mean?

GRANA: [*looking at another book*] And I found stories that made me angry. There is so much power in anger. [*Reads*] "Since the earliest days of this nation's history, students attending its schools have achieved competence in the four, not three R's—Reading, Riting, Rithmetic, and Racism." Malcolm X.

[*Drumming crescendos. Images of war, racism, sexism, destruction, imprisonment, hunger, poverty, state-sanctioned murder.*]

GRANA: "Surely it is patriarchal condescension that leads black folks, particularly sexist black men, to assume that black females are incapable of embracing revolutionary feminism in ways that would embrace rather than diminish black liberation. . . . The labeling of black women who engage feminist thinking as race traitors is meant to prevent us from embracing feminist politics as surely as white power-feminism acts to exclude our voices and silence our critiques. In this case, both groups are acting to protect and maintain the privileges, however relative, that they receive in the existing social structure." bell hooks, 1995.

KARLA: What you say!

GRANA: Satisfaction in the air, and I can't sit still.

MARTIN: If you can walk, you can dance.

KARLA: Dance with me; y'all dance with me some more.

MARTIN: Get away child, my feets is too tired. I ain't walking, and I ain't dancing.

GRANA: You don't dance, you don't live. [*Drags him up, and they dance with* KARLA.] "It's a struggle to balance love and rage in a constant rhythm. [*She falters, then continues.* MARTIN *is concerned and rushes to support her.*] "When I liberate others, I liberate myself." Fannie Lou Hamer.

MARTIN: Venceremos!

KARLA: We have to!

[GRANA *doubles over in pain.* MARTIN *and* KARLA *help her to continue dancing.*]

GRANA: It was a new day, the birth of a New World because we knew who we were.

MARTIN: And we was bad!

GRANA: We couldn't imagine anybody's nerve trying to be anything else.

[*Drumming crescendos.* GRANA *doubles over in pain again. She falls to her knees.* KARLA *kneels behind her and holds her. They pant and moan in unison with the drums and the dance chorus.*]

GRANA: Oh, my God, get out the way! Something's coming!

[*Drumming crescendos. Kneeling in front of* GRANA, MARTIN *spreads her legs wide. With awe and reverence, he pulls a long, red scarf from between* GRANA's *legs. He and the* DANCERS *dance with the red fabric. Drumming suddenly stops.* MARTIN *rolls the scarf and gives it to* GRANA. *She cradles it in her arms. She and* KARLA *rock and hum.* MARTIN *kneels behind Karla and rocks with them. All hum together.*]

GRANA: Now I know. On this journey, it's not only the infinite but the particular that gives me reason for being.

KARLA: And dance.

GRANA: These particular eyes. These particular fingers, and ten toes, this particular smile, and particular heart full of questions and stories to tell.

[*They get up, walk to the rocking chair.* GRANA *sits in the rocking chair, rocking and humming.* KARLA *sits in front, her head on* GRANA's *knee.* MARTIN *stands behind the chair and rocks it gently.*]

GRANA: I wonder who would teach him the pledge that will tell him his story.

MARTIN: I pledge allegiance to the one and the many . . .

KARLA: For which it stands . . .

MARTIN: Indivisible, and visible . . .

KARLA: With liberty for all.

MARTIN: And justice for all, not necessarily in that order.

KARLA: Amen.

GRANA: *Jamas seran vencido.*

KARLA and MARTIN: Amen.

MARTIN: We have to teach him—them the stories that we've heard.

KARLA: Subject and verb.

GRANA: And dances we have done, so when they find their place in line, they will know how to ask about the next steps.

MARTIN: But . . .

KARLA: Now what? You always got somebody's but. Martin got a big old butt. I say, Martin got a big old butt.

MARTIN: Shut up! It runs in the family. Like I was saying, what about the ones who gonna look right in his eyes and lie, try to shame him—distort the story, tell them that they are insignificant objects of their own history?

KARLA: Oh, you're right, Martin. They will bend his mind, his back, and his knees until he is lost in the miasma of the masters' message.

MARTIN: What you just said.

KARLA: And they'll forget how much we love to learn, and to tell stories and hear them.

GRANA: All that dancing and all them stories, and that's all you got is hopelessness? C'mere. Let me tell you a story. [*KARLA and MARTIN gather at Grana's feet. DANCERS dance the story. Lights slowly shift colors as GRANA tells the story.*]

Once upon a time, there was a Woman, not too old, not too young; she was just right. She was pretty special, like all of us, because when she was a child, she walked through the end of the rainbow. And forever after, she lived in the world of color and loved the colors of life—the blue-blacks of twilight, sunrise fuchsias, the raging reds, the variegated spring greens. All reminded her of the magnificence of life in all its shades and nuances. When she rubbed the mud brown earth in her hands and held it to her own dark face, she felt the roots of her heart grow deep among the beauty that she found in the world.

But she was alone in the rainbow world, and what is such joy if there is no one to share it with? She had heard that that there were whole worlds where folks ignored the wealth that color brings because they had no eyes to see with, no ears to hear, no knowledge to build with, or no hearts to feel. Warm, colorless tears tumbled from her rich chocolate eyes whenever she thought of a life chained to such pallid ignorance. So the Woman found a multicolored box, and she asked the winter clouds for a little of their deep black grays for her collection.

"Okay, they rumbled. "But first, a story . . ." And they told her about their journey from the sea, to the sky, and back again—an excellent tale full of winds, and sun, and transformations. Then she attended the autumn fashion show put on by the trees, where the wind told jokes and tickled the trees so that they laughed in their leaves until they shook to the ground. The Woman collected the color of the leaves and the color of the jokes and put them in her box. In the Spring, she got some yellow from the daffodils, who told her about the black darkness of warm earth and their surprise when, as newborns, they first saw the orange of the sun.

The Woman sat for years by the sea to collect all of its many grays, and greens, and browns, and blues as the ocean bellowed its stories of pirate ships, coral colonies, and lost civilizations. She collected a shade of sad blue from the gray-haired old man who had long ago lost his heart to the pretty young girl named Rusty, with the carrot-colored hair. The Woman collected all these stories and more as she wandered in her rainbow world. Each color had a story to tell that broadened the palette of her imagination and the appetite of her commitment to share her wealth.

One day when the box vibrated with the rich rhythms of a babble of stories talking together, the Woman decided it was time to share the tales and colors with the worlds that knew no color and heard only one story. She set out on the red clay road until she came to a small cabin. She knocked at the door, once, twice, then three times. Finally, a small, timid voice cringed between the cracks of the little wooden door.

"Who is it?" whispered Small and Timid.

"It's me," said the Woman. "I've come from the rainbow."

"I know who you are. What do you want?"

"Come out and see what I have brought you. I have wonderful . . ."

"Oh, no. I can't come out. Go away, please go away! I'm afraid."

"Don't be afraid. I've brought the most absolutely wonderful stories to share with you . . ."

"I don't want to hear. Go away!"

"Why are you so afraid?"

"You will take what I have, and you will hurt me. I know you will. Go away! GO AWAY!" Then timidly, "Please."

So the Woman sadly took her box, so as not to further frighten Small and Timid, and reluctantly walked down the red clay road. Her spirits brightened when she came to another house, this one larger than the first. She knocked at the door, once, twice, then three times. Finally, a snarling voice slithered from between the cracks of the wooden door.

"Who is it?" growled Snarling.

"It's me," said the Woman. "I've come from the rainbow."

"I don't know where that is, and I don't care. Just get away from my door!"

The door was hot with hostility, but the Woman who found stories in the most unimaginable places persisted.

"Oh, please come out," implored the Woman, "and see what wonderful colors I have brought you."

"Go away! I don't need anything you've got!"

"How do you know if you've never seen them, never heard them? Come out and see. Listen to them." And she held the box close to the door.

"I'm not listening, and I'm not looking."

"Don't be afraid. You'll see. You'll love these colors and their tales."

"I'm not afraid! Who said I was afraid? I've lived here all my life. Long as I keep this door closed, I can control everything I need. Now, go away before I get mad!"

"But," pleaded the Woman . . .

"GO AWAY!"

So the Woman sadly took her box, so as not to further anger Snarling, and reluctantly walked down the red clay road. But her spirits brightened when she came to another house, this one larger than the first two. She knocked at the door, once, twice, then three times. Finally, a listless voice slid from between the cracks of the wooden door.

"Who is it?" sighed Listless.

"It's me," said the Woman. "I've come from the rainbow."

"So? Do you think I care? Go away."

"Oh, please come out," said the Woman, "and see what wonderful hues and stories I have brought you."

Listless pouted petulantly. "Why should I listen to you? Nobody listens to me. Now go away."

The woman was immediately intrigued. "Do you have a story? I love stories. I'll listen."

"No, you won't. They all say that, just so I'll come out. Then they never listen. They talk and talk, and never listen."

"Oh, no, no. I'll listen. Promise."

"Fool me once, shame on you. Fool me twice, you know who's the fool. Besides, I'm not interested in anything else, just myself. Now go away before you bore me to tears."

"But . . . !" pleaded the Woman.

"GO AWAY!"

So the Woman sadly took her box, so as not to further bore Listless, and reluctantly walked down the red clay road. The sapphire sadness in her heart felt heavy, and her soul felt lonely. She sat down beside the road, laid her ear on her box, and listened to the exquisite cacophony of life that it held. She wept when the death of an old friend sang its purple song, and giggled with the young muddy brook with brunette tones, clearly enthralled by rubbing against the speckled gray rocks in its bed. The Woman listened with excitement to the games played by the red-orange, the orange-reds, the golds, and pinks of sunrise. She was awed by the fury of their competition and the harmony of their stories. She looked back down the road at the houses closed and silent in the dreary landscape next to the red clay road, and she wished them a rainbow in spite of themselves. So she opened her box, and the first to syncopate its way into the world was a silky blue-black jazz note that wrapped itself around the Woman and tapped her toes and swayed her hips. It told her of dark, smoky-gray jazz clubs and the sultry twilight blues of doo-wop corners. The Woman shut her eyes and pulsed with the story as the note beat about the drum. She was so entranced that she did not notice the young boy who watched her from across the red clay road.

"Hello," he said. The Woman opened her eyes, surprised to hear a voice.

"Hello," she answered. The boy was pale and looked undernourished, but his eyes shone with curiosity.

"Whatcha doin'?" he wondered.

"Listening," she replied. "To stories, feeling their colors."

"Oh, does it hurt?" he asked. "You looked like you were in pain."

"No, that was passion. Please come listen with me. Share this with me."

The boy took a tentative step, but stopped in the middle of the road when he looked back at the three houses that looked like cardboard cutouts in the milky air. In each house, the curtains stirred ever so slightly.

Terror glazed the boy's eyes. "Maybe, I shouldn't . . . "

Before the Woman could answer, the blue note bebopped itself over to the boy, wrapped its rhythms around the boy's shoulders, and held him in the ecstasy of a gospel singer. The boy moaned with pleasure, and color rushed to his face, kissing scarlet red on his lips, and finding the summer skies in his eyes.

"Oh," he stammered, "Oh. I didn't know. I didn't know."

The Woman crossed to him. "Beautiful, isn't it?"

"Oh, yes, is there more? More?" His cheeks showed their kinship with the pink rose.

"Oh, so much more. Let me show you."

And the Woman called for the greens of deep summer forests, homes to the midnight black birds who remembered the deep redbrowns of the first Iroquois long houses. She coaxed forth the red of an emperor so royal that his feet never touched the ground, and the red earth that North Carolina wept as it described the flavor of the blood-red sweat in the footprints of the Cherokee on their Trail of Salty Tears. The boy and the Woman marveled at the raw red energy of steelworkers and the smooth pink silks of a ballet dancer. The boy blossomed among the trees and the stories. He nourished his curiosity at the feet of the wise ocean who joined the party.

One day, when the boy was strong and his mind was full with the foods of many stories, he said, "Can I bring somebody to our celebration? I want to share what I've felt with everybody I know!"

"Of course," said the Woman. The trees shook with agreement, and the ocean roared in concert. The boy skipped down the red clay road and returned with Timid and Small, wearing a big black hat and sunglasses that hid her face. She cowered behind the boy. He brought

Snarling, who wore earmuffs and grimaced as he crossed his arms across his chest, except when he slapped at the ocean breezes. Listless was there as well. His chin rested on his chest, and he snored softly. There were others the boy brought too, many others from farther down the road.

"These are my parents and my teachers," said the boy. "I want them to hear and to know what I have felt. Tell them the tones and stories you told me." So all the colors and stories started in at once to spread their joys and sorrows.

Snarling tried not to be impressed, but he took off his earmuffs and opened his arms to dance with the pretty young girl with the carrot-colored hair. They laughed at the brook, who had turned into a much louder blue-green adolescent stream. Timid and Small felt comfortable with the blackbirds, and the trees told her their most polite jokes. She still blushed purple, but removed her hat so she could see the lights and shadows of their emerald leaves. Listless could hardly sleep through the blue note's rock 'n' roll, especially the heavy metal. So he woke up and proved to be quite a spunky fellow who liked to dance.

"I have a story," shouted Snarling above the pulsating pink pandemonium of excitement that the sea horse said sounded like an expressionist painting. They all stopped to listen, anticipating the bliss of a new perspective. Snarling told a tale of long winter-white wars, blue Danube waltzes, foxtrots, and fiery red rockets for walks on the moon. After the applause, Listless stopped dancing long enough to tell his story of green Irish jigs around pewter pots of potatoes that mysteriously disappeared. Just as wondrous, they reappeared in a New World, where he sadly lost his song in a pot that melted everything to a mashed gray soup, except on every March 17 when they poured green food coloring into the stew. Being partial to green, the forest trees thought it was an exceptional story and whispered in their leaves that Listless reminded them of the young saplings in spring.

Small and Timid had been so intoxicated by the black songs of the red birds and the red songs of the black birds that she took off her sunglasses and offered a story that began with the pinks of mauve women demurely tying knots in their cross-stitching and ends in an explosion of womanish defiance that ties knots in all the shades of power that went before. By the end of her story, Small and Timid had taken off her pastel clothes and her pink girdle, and was dancing deeply flushed and naked on Snarling's back. The clamor of the party was so much that people and stories and colors of the rainbow heard the laughter from far away and all around, and they came to dance their tales too. And unless the bottom has dropped out of the Woman's multicolored box, I'm sure they are still partying there today.

KARLA: That was a great story. But what's it mean?

GRANA: What do you think it means?

MARTIN: It means that Small and Timid had issues!

KARLA: Oh, you!

MARTIN: It means that people who live in fear, ignorance, and alienation miss all the jammin' throw downs! Uptight, and outta sight. [*laughs*] I like that blue note part. That's was tight.

KARLA: What?

MARTIN: That the arts are sometimes the easiest bridge for people to cross over to each other.

KARLA: Yeah. True dat. A song may win more than the lecture. [*pause*] The story's about how a child will lead us, too, hunh, Grana?

GRANA: Oh yes, children are a door open to wonder. But grown folks can learn too, when they don't feel threatened. I've worked with families, and especially teachers, who find the shame and guilt in their pasts too heavy to bear or expose. They refuse to listen to anyone else's story, so they won't have to examine their own. When I show them how their own stories have been distorted or untold, when they learn for the first time about their own histories in the unfolding of justice and liberation, they are appalled at how little they know about themselves, and begin to wonder about what else they don't know. Then I share this with them so that they know they are a part of something, rather than outside. [*reading from a book*] "Pluralist societies are made up of subgroups that differ from each other on various grounds: social class, ethnicity, race, culture, gender. A number of terms have been used to refer to such societies. The most common description is multicultural, which implies the existence of many [multi-] cultures." Brian Bullivant, 1993.

KARLA: *El pueblo unido,* hunh?

MARTIN: Sometimes united, and sometimes not, but always together.

GRANA: All the more reason for us to listen to each other. I explain how it begins with the children. [*reads from another book*] "Multicultural education incorporates the idea that all students—regardless of their gender, and social class and their ethnic, racial, or cultural characteristics—should have an equal opportunity to learn in school,"

James Banks, 2001. [*another book*] "And this redefinition of educational equality means affirming that problems or shortcomings in learning are located not so much in shortcomings in ethnic minority students as in inequalities in the schools they attend. It also means refocusing schools toward being more responsive to human variability, spending less time manipulating ethnic students to make them comply to institutional structures, and instituting programs and processes that empower students through access to high-quality knowledge and experiences." Geneva Gay, 2001.

MARTIN: Wow, don't sound like no school I ever went to. That's deep.

GRANA: It gets deeper. I open the question of multicultural education as a part of the pigs and salmon debates. [*reading*] "Education that is Multicultural and Social Reconstructionist teaches directly about political and economic oppression and discrimination, and prepares young people to use social action skills." Christine Sleeter, 1996. Then we have at it, like in the story I told you. We read, collect, and tell stories; we listen, and we dance together. We ask questions and collect data. We feel each other out and wrestle with the issues until we have all moved in a process of transformation.

MARTIN: So multicultural education is about change?

GRANA: Of the children, their families, teachers, systems, and anyone and anything else involved in learning—in and out of school.

KARLA: I guess that includes just about everybody.

GRANA: Everybody.

MARTIN: Because knowledge walks in and out of the school doors?

GRANA: Martin, boy, you are as brilliant as the sun in a Georgia summer.

KARLA: What about me?

GRANA: And you, you are as bright and as deep as my love for all of life, its dances and many dancers.

KARLA: For real?

GRANA: Oh yes, for real. So I guess I best be up and about my business.

KARLA: Grana?

GRANA: Same as before, asking and telling stories.

MARTIN: Teach!

GRANA: Asking and telling stories.

[*GRANA kisses them both, picks up some books, wraps the red shawl around her, and then exits. KARLA and MARTIN look through the pile of books.*]

KARLA: Read me one of her books.

MARTIN: Here's one.

KARLA: What's it called?

MARTIN: [*Footsteps.*] By Jesus Christ, Karl Marx, Harriet Tubman, John Dewey, Lev Vygotsky, Alice Walker, Aretha Franklin, Martin Luther King, Paulo Freire, James Banks, Geneva Gay, a lots of other folks, and . . .

KARLA: Who?

MARTIN: Mary Stone Hanley, and [*pause*] . . .

KARLA: What? What?

MARTIN: All the children.

[*The Dancers gather around.*]

KARLA: Next time, I get to tell the story!

MARTIN: What you think, I'm gonna be your sidekick? I have done the last sidekick thing.

KARLA: You always want to be the one in front! Read the book!

MARTIN: Okay! Once upon a time . . .

[*Lights fade to black. Music fade.*]

THE END

PRINCIPLES FOR PRACTICE

A number of key principles of multicultural education are embedded in this chapter. Those that follow can be used to help frame the development of program and practices for multicultural teacher preparation and classroom instruction with students.

The first of these principles is the *importance of ethnic groups' and individuals' telling their own stories.* Students and teachers need to learn accurate information about the cultures, histories, and experiences of ethnic groups. The sources for this information should be varied and multidimensional in that they offer different perspectives on issues and ideas under analysis. Crucial among them is knowledge about ethnic diversity derived from personal and insider vantage points. These provide a level of depth, insight, feeling, and nuance that cannot be achieved from information about ethnic groups produced by scholars who are not members of the groups they write about. Self-authored presentations about the lives and experiences of ethnic groups and individuals are not the only sources of valuable information for multicultural education, but they are imperative. Without them, the kind of quality needed in the study of ethnic and cultural diversity will not be achieved.

Another important principle to include in multicultural education teaching and learning is that *critical incidents and events have lasting influences on our understanding, competence, and sense of place in ethnic and cultural diversity.* Sometimes these are general occurrences that have significance for great numbers of people, such as the removal of eastern Native Americans to the West in the Trail of Tears, the civil rights movement, and the various waves of immigration to the United States. But in many instances, these critical incidents are personal, which means that a transformative incident for one individual may be uneventful for another. Therefore, multicultural teaching and learning has to honor the perspectives and experiences of diverse ethnic groups and individuals, as well as use innovative techniques to identify, unveil, and validate them.

Like any other kind of learning, a principle of multicultural education is that *students have to be psychoemotionally receptive toward learning about ethnic and cultural diversity for it to be most beneficial.* This does not always mean being positive and approving about the content taught, nor do these receptive dispositions occur automatically at some particular points in time. Rather, students can be groomed for and taught to be receptive to multicultural education. The important point here is that we should not assume that because we think something is important, our students will also. If we do not provide historical and contextual information for the multicultural content we teach and variety in the ways we teach it, we may miss the vital relevance link in teaching and learning, and thereby limit our effectiveness.

Action is central to multicultural education. It is not enough merely to discuss and analyze issues related to ethnic and cultural diversity, to have good intentions. Nor is it sufficient to operate in isolation; in fact, the most critical concerns, such as equity, justice, and academic excellence for ethnically diverse students, require that individuals pool their talents, resources, and efforts. Therefore, another important principle for practice derived from the multicultural journey described in this chapter is that *community, collaboration, and communication among ethnically diverse people are essential for effective sociopolitical activism.*

A recurrent challenge for teachers of multicultural education is determining what to teach and verifying the validity of these choices. Many of us don't know where to start in working through these dilemmas. This chapter suggests a principle that is helpful in resolving them: *precedents and progenitors are important anchors and guides in both personal and professional multicultural teaching and learning.* Many of these precedents and progenitors are identified in this and the other chapters in this book.

A challenge in multicultural education related to selecting content is teaching it to students in the most effective ways. Many innovative teaching techniques are available, but they may not be appropriate for use with content about ethnic groups. If they are not compatible with the cultural nuances of various ethnic groups, then these instructional techniques are more problematic than helpful. The best guide for multicultural teaching is to *convey the lives and experiences of different ethnic groups in their own authentic cultural voices.* Part of this authentication is to provide contextual cultural content and help students visualize issues and situations that they may not have experienced personally. To this end, story making and storytelling are powerful teaching tools for capturing and conveying the essence of ethnic and cultural diversity.

Multicultural education requires that we teach students about positive and negative dimensions of ethnic and cultural diversity. One of the most problematic negatives that we must deal with is racism. There is a lot of confusion around this issue. For many, it evokes only historical atrocities such as slavery, lynching, the Holocaust, and the internment of Japanese Americans. This is true, but racism is more than that. It occurs in very subtle and sophisticated form as well and is not restricted to high-profile events. Consequently, an important principle for multicultural education practice is that *cultural hegemony and racism are embedded in the daily routines of schools and society, as well as in horrific acts of ethnic and racial oppression.*

Another important principle for practice is that *multicultural teaching and learning are transformative processes, both personally and professionally.* It can be seen in the movement from ethnic impotence to ethnic disaffiliation to ethnic reconstruction and multicultural activism; from a trusting, unquestionable faith in what is taught to criticism and interrogation of the master narratives and looking for the absent and the silenced; shifting worldviews and realities from the presumed universality of provincially lived experiences to understanding the bigger uncaring world and recognition of other ethnic people's realities; and from feeling you are alone and your ethnic group's issues are unique to realizing they are part of a collective struggle that has a long historical lineage and a broad band of involvement that encompasses other ethnic groups as well.

Because change is essential to transformation, multicultural education cannot be achieved without it. Little of this needed change will occur under safe and gentle circumstances or by merely tinkering with the status quo. Promoting social justice and educational equality for ethnic groups that have been brutalized by racism (as is one of the major goals of multicultural education) involves a certain amount of conflict and adversity. Power and privilege will need to be redistributed, and these are not accomplished without some anguish. Nor are these kinds of changes necessarily popular. Nevertheless, the results are worth the potential trauma. Therefore, a final principle for practice that can be extrapolated from this chapter is that *risk taking is a necessary part of multicultural education; fear and timidity are its greatest inhibitors.*

JOINING THE JOURNEY

I hope that reading this chapter has stimulated you to recall some major events in your own life that helped to initiate or facilitate your multicultural development. If that is not the case, here are some suggested activities that might get you started or help to accelerate your process of becoming a multicultural person and educator:

• Review your knowledge of African American communication styles. Geneva Smitherman (1977) and Thomas Kochman (1981) will be helpful here. Then locate examples of different African American cultural communication nuances and techniques used in this chapter. Translate them for members of other ethnic groups, students, teachers, and communities who may not understand what they mean. Extend this activity to a larger scale by examining other ethnic groups' communication styles as well. Develop a dictionary of ethnic terminology used daily in schools and classrooms. Identify words, phrases, and nonverbal nuances that different ethnic groups use, define them, and provide a specific behavioral or expressive example of each one. Collect the entries for the dictionary by listening to and observing ethnically diverse students in classrooms and informal school settings, such as the playground, cafeteria, and hallways, and on buses. It is best to complete this last task by working in collaboration with three or four colleagues.

Field-test the draft of your dictionary with students from each of the ethnic groups represented. Ask them to give you feedback about the accuracy, currency, and comprehensiveness of the content. Use their feedback to revise your draft. When all the refinements are completed, make copies of the dictionary, and give them to colleagues. Encourage them to use the dictionary, let you know how it benefited them, and add their own contributions derived from their observations and interactions with ethnically diverse people. Update the dictionary periodically to include new and shared observations and to delete obsolete ones.

• Make a list of the statements, symbolisms, and metaphors that were most memorable to you from the play in this chapter. Ask your colleagues or students to do so too. Then form groups of three to five members to share these lists and discuss the meanings of them, as well as how they affected your engagement with the content of the play. After you have deciphered the symbolisms and metaphors, read the play again. Were your interactions with the content different because of this new understanding? If so, explain how. Use these learning experiences as training in understanding what and how metaphoric language is used by yourself, your ethnically diverse students, and multicultural scholars. See if you can discern any differences in the kinds, frequency, ways, places, and purposes of metaphoric usages across ethnic groups. You might capstone these learning experiences by creating a document entitled, "What They Mean When They Say _____." Share this document with others. Based on these understandings, write a short statement about the function of metaphors in multicultural education. Or write a statement in metaphoric voice about an issue, principle, or practice of central concern to multicultural education, or about your own personal process of becoming multicultural.

• If you are not familiar with the significant individuals and critical events introduced in the play, find out about them. Use a variety of methods to collect your information, including library and Internet searches, interviews with those familiar with the individuals and events or even the individuals themselves, and mass media (television, videos, films). Answer questions such as: What did the individual or event do? What prompted the actions? What were the effects of the actions? When did these events occur? What are the implications of your findings for teaching and promoting multicultural education? This project can be done alone or in small groups. After you have completed it, critically reflect on how you were affected by the learning experience; refer to the knowledge gained, feelings and other emotional reactions, and your sense of confidence and competence. Do reciprocal sharing of these reflections with one or two other people who were involved in the learning project.

• Identify at least five obstacles or resistances that you have encountered in your own efforts to become and be multicultural. These should be actions and attitudes that you have experienced personally and professionally. Remember that some of the most powerful resistance to multicultural education is subtle and can appear as subterfuge or under the guise of something else. It may be of your own making or from other individuals and institutions. As you identify these five resistances, focus on subtleties. Then develop some specific pedagogical strategies for overcoming them. In crafting your strategies, remember that multicultural education deals simultaneously with knowing, thinking, feeling, valuing, and doing about issues of ethnic and cultural diversity. Therefore, your proposed pedagogical responses should attend to each of these dimensions of engagement. After you have completed your "resisting resistance" pedagogical strategies, compare them to theoretical criteria for high-quality antiracist, equitable, activist, and social justice multicultural education to determine the goodness of fit among them.

• Be creative in embodying or signifying your understanding of the process that is involved in becoming multicultural educators. You might want to begin with my story. Using a variety of art supplies and techniques (for example, collage-making materials, paints, photographs, video cameras, and writing tools) and working with a small group of peers, create a three-dimensional or visual artistic representation of my journey toward becoming a multicultural educator. The results can be a dance, a dramatized poem or song, a multimedia model, or a mixed media painting. Share your product with others who were involved in this activity, such as members of your teacher education classes or your in-service staff development training. Discuss the similarities and differences of the creations across groups.

Now do the same thing for your own process of becoming multicultural. Decide which creative medium or genre fits best for symbolizing your development, and explain why. Compare these creations, decisions, and explanations across study groups.

References

Banks, J. A. "Multicultural Education: Characteristics and Goals." In J. A. Banks and C.A.M. Banks (eds.), *Multicultural Education: Issues and Perspectives*. (4th ed.) Needham Heights, Mass.: Allyn & Bacon, 2001.

Bullivant, B. "Culture: Its Nature and Meaning for Educators." In J. A. Banks and C.A.M. Banks (eds.), *Multicultural Education: Issues and Perspectives*. (2nd ed.) Needham Heights, Mass.: Allyn & Bacon, 1993.

Freire, P. *Pedagogy of the Oppressed*. New York: Seabury Press, 1973.

Gay, G. "Educational Equality for Students of Color." In J. A. Banks and C.A.M. Banks (eds.), *Multicultural Education: Issues and Perspectives*. (4th ed.) Needham Heights, Mass.: Allyn & Bacon, 2001.

hooks, b. *Killing Rage*. New York: Holt, 1995.

Kochman, T. *Black and White Styles in Conflict*. Chicago: University of Chicago Press, 1981.

Lenin, V. *Marx, Engels, Lenin: On Historical Materialism*. New York: International Publishers, 1972. (Originally published 1916.)

McKay, C. "If We Must Die." In H. L. Gates Jr. and N. Y. McKay (eds.), *The Norton Anthology of African American Literature*. New York: Norton, 1997.

Sleeter, C. E. *Multicultural Education as Social Activism*. Albany: State University of New York Press, 1996.

Smitherman, G. *Talkin' and Testifyin': The Language of Black America*. Boston: Houghton Mifflin, 1977.

Woodson, C. *The Mis-Education of the Negro*. Washington, D.C.: Africa World Press, 1990. (Originally published 1933.)

CHAPTER TWELVE

From Color Blindness to Cultural Vision

Laura Kay Neuwirth

As I began my first year of teaching, I had some strong feelings about how I wanted to create a positive classroom climate for my students. Growing up, I had experienced much personal negativism in school. It was a hard place for me to be; I never felt comfortable or as if I fit in. I can remember faking illness as early as first grade to avoid going to school. I was put down by my classmates, and even some teachers, on a daily basis, treatment that caused me to retreat socially and intellectually from the school environment. Yet I loved school. I enjoyed learning and being challenged. It was not until late in high school that I began to feel accepted in the school I attended.

My love of learning and intense desire to prevent other children from enduring experiences similar to mine led me to choose teaching as a profession. I chose special education as an area of concentration because I believe that this population, more so than others, experiences negativism from the school system. They are challenged and treated unfairly, both socially and academically, more often than the general school population. My desire to level the playing field for these students made me focus heavily on equality for all in my personal viewpoints and professional preparation and action. It led me to pursue graduate studies in the area of multicultural education and to strengthen my efforts to become a better multicultural teacher and person. Although my journey is tied closely to my graduate studies, an advanced degree is not a requirement. I actually began the process of becoming multicultural before I decided to continue my education. Significant things happened during my graduate studies to accelerate and sharpen the process.

SHIFTING CULTURAL CONTENT KNOWLEDGE AND CONSCIOUSNESS

My views of teaching multicultural education have changed significantly since I began learning more about the histories, cultures, contributions, and lifestyles of different ethnic groups. I have always been interested in challenging the norms set by schools and, to some degree, society. I wanted to present materials in a way that students had not seen before. From the time I started teaching, I tried to use materials that I thought were multicultural in content, even though I adopted a color-blind philosophy for interacting with students. I tried to interact with students without paying any attention to their race and ethnicity.

I now understand and accept the meaning of statements made by Horace Kallen (Marrow, 1971) many years ago about the futility and disadvantages of trying to ignore race and ethnicity in education. He (like I) recognized the good intention behind the idea of color blindness, which is to achieve equal treatment of diverse people by being indifferent to differences and conducting business as if they didn't exist. But because differences do exist, color blindness requires that we pretend not to see them. If we acknowledge their existence, then we "must deny that there is anything to recognize; . . . so far as the difference is a difference of color, [we] must be *color-blind*" [emphasis in original] (Marrow, 1971, pp. 51–52). Using, as a point of departure, President Andrew Johnson's declaration that color blindness was necessary for the emancipation of African Americans to be a fact instead of merely a proclamation, Kallen explains further that

> if the operative condition be what Mr. Johnson's language took it for, emancipation will always be a proclamation, never a fact. To embody proclamation in fact calls for awareness of race, seeing of color; for

accepting, respecting, appreciating and working with them *as* they are *where* they are. For morally, color is a fact, a global fact; color is *the* fact, the vital decisive fact, the actually and potentially creative fact, and today's Great Divide for any future mankind may propose for themselves. Refusing to see this, to recognize it as it is for what it is but deepens the predicament into which the hope of alienating the un-alienable sinks alike the aggressors and resisters among Americans. . . . It would found a moral and cultural necessity by analogy with a phys-iological defect and a psychological lack [Marrow, 1971, pp. 52–53].

Janet Schofield (1997) added another point that resonated strongly with what I came to understand about trying to be a color-blind teacher: "Even though the color blind perspective is very appealing, and it is consistent with the long-standing American emphasis on the importance of the individual, it also leads very easily to misrepresen-tation of reality in ways that are likely to encourage discrimination against minority group members" (p. 20). These explanations helped me to understand that I cannot be an ethical and effective teacher if I ignore the race and ethnicity of my students. Understanding and ac-cepting this reality was an important turnabout in my multicultural development.

Many teachers lack the knowledge and techniques they need to im-plement effective multicultural education in classrooms—in Kallen's word, to engage fully in the struggles to resist "alienating the unalien-able" (Marrow, 1971, p. 53). The more knowledge and techniques I gain to do this, the more furious I am that I did not obtain them ear-lier. How can teachers inform their students about this vital multi-cultural knowledge if they do not possess it themselves? If I had had it when I entered the classroom, I would have done things very dif-ferently, and my students probably would have performed much bet-ter academically.

Good intentions are not enough; sometimes they can even be dan-gerous. Let me illustrate how good intentions can lead to miscon-ceptions. I thought it was important for me to teach about Native Americans while we studied early U.S. history. While in college, I was exposed (for the first time) to information that challenged the notion that Native peoples were a homogeneous group that willingly stepped aside as Europeans moved West. It horrified me that I was not taught this viewpoint of history until so late in my student career. I created a new "Native American Unit" for my students to keep them from being in a similar situation.

The unit focused on the Penobscots of the Northeast, the Makahs of the Northwest, the Creeks of the Southeast, the Hopi of the Southwest, and the Lakotas of the Central Plains. It stressed the variety of the geographical areas of the United States that these peoples inhabited. We watched videos that explained the many gifts Native people have contributed to the United States and used other media that explained names, images, and implements found in society now (for example, Redman Tobacco; Winnebago recreational vehicles; Cherokee Jeeps; the Indians, Braves, and Chiefs mascots) were forms of exploitation. We created bead designs, totem poles, and prayer bundles.

At the time, I thought I was doing some radically improved teaching compared to some of my colleagues. But as I have continued my studies in multicultural education and American Indian studies, many flaws in this unit have become apparent. The first error that stands out is my sources of information. I used books that gave so-called objective accounts of these groups but were written by scholars who were not intimately knowledgeable about the subject. The instructional materials emphasized the past, with no analysis of Native Americans in the present or possibilities for the future. I should have used materials that were written by people from within the various Native American groups or by others who had firsthand knowledge about both historical and contemporary issues. Furthermore, I could have chosen a group of Native Americans from my own geographical area to make the information more meaningful to the students and involve local community resources, such as guest speakers, in our learning.

I have made another discovery about my earlier teaching efforts that I now see is inconsistent with multicultural education. In my lessons, I taught culturally diverse concepts and practices in isolation and did not integrate them into subsequent lessons. For example, during my first year of teaching, I became aware of Kwanzaa, a winter holiday celebrating African American history, community, pride, and traditions. Well over half of my students were African American at the time, so I felt this would be an important issue to study. We read books about the holiday and made *zwadi* (gifts), *mekekas* (mats), and posters and discussed the seven principles of Kwanzaa. Each day of the holiday celebrates one of the principles, which serve as personal guides to action throughout the year.

I also have come to realize that there is a vast difference between looking at race, ethnicity, and gender throughout the curriculum and merely supplementing existing instructional materials on special occasions, such as Cinco de Mayo, Brotherhood Week, and Black History Month. All other ethnic groups should be included throughout all units of instruction in all subjects. When I think about multiculturalizing my teaching, I imagine including ethnic and cultural diversity in such units as rhetoric in speech communication; place, space, and location in geography; problem solving and citizenship in social studies; career awareness in business education; comprehension in reading; family relationships in home economics; and wellness in health. These will help illustrate that diverse ethnic groups are part of the U.S. past, present, and future; that they have a distinct viewpoint on events in this country; and that they are part of the full range of human experiences. Relegating Native Americans to the wars on the western frontiers without any mention of the continuing struggles for civil rights, social justice, and human dignity in contemporary society is simply unfair. Nor is it fair to treat other ethnic groups in a similar restrictive fashion.

EMBRACING MULTIPLE VOICES

The more perspectives and experiences students are exposed to, the stronger is their ability to understand alternative interpretations of situations and events and to relate to people different from themselves. This is a crucial step in accepting and celebrating ethnic and cultural diversity. It enriches those who are being studied and those who are learning.

Teachers must use the voices and expressions of different ethnicities, races, and genders when discussing nearly all topics in order to have well-educated students. In graduate school, I took classes on Chicana and Native American histories, cultures, and contemporary social issues. I was exposed to Asian American, African American, and European American issues in my multicultural program as well. As I synthesized this information, I began to see new patterns and complexities. When I reexamined certain periods in history or critical issues in society, I no longer saw a flat, static, or monolithic picture. Rather, I heard the dynamic and multiple voices and perspectives of these diverse groups. Historical and contemporary events became more vibrant and alive, as these ethnic stories fit together to make an enlightening, exciting, and engaging composite whole. Persecution of the Puritans, slavery, the Trail of Tears, the Japanese internment, the red scare of the 1920s, and the civil rights movement of the 1960s converged around issues of equality, oppression, discrimination, and powerlessness, making each of them far more illuminating than when studied separately.

Through these personal experiences and increasing knowledge base, I am beginning to realize that simply adding isolated ethnic content to existing curricula will not accomplish my goal of teaching in a multicultural manner. This approach fails to reveal fully the complex cultures, lives, and experiences of ethnic groups and rarely challenges the main text being supplemented. However good the intentions and information are, they still keep these groups at the periphery of mainstream classroom curriculum and instruction.

Another shift I am making in becoming multicultural is distinguishing between generalizations and stereotypes about ethnic groups in instructional materials. I have become conscious of who writes the material I read and select authors from a variety of ethnic backgrounds because who the author is affects how that person has presented information. This is true as well for who teaches students. Teachers are authors of instructional action. Being aware of how authorship influences knowledge and teaching behaviors is a vital step in finding representative voices to speak for the ethnic groups being studied and selecting more authentic instructional strategies. In-group authors decrease the chance that stereotypes will be presented in the material used to teach children. Individuals who are members of the ethnic, cultural, or gender groups they are writing or speaking about are generally more informed about and in tune with the views and feelings of the group, and therefore are less likely to misrepresent the group. In future teaching, I will identify the ethnic background and cultural perspectives of the authors, teach students how to critique instructional materials and assess their ethnic accuracy, and use a variety of ethnically diverse teaching resources.

FACTS ARE NOT ENOUGH

Simply passing on facts about ethnic and cultural differences is not enough. I used to teach about school segregation as a form of discrimination during a unit on government and law. I was attempting to provide information that was not in the standard curriculum and include ethnic groups that had been left out. I provided information about *Brown* v. *Board of Education* and examined Jim Crow laws. We looked at only one group, though, African Americans, rather than the large spectrum of discrimination that many ethnically diverse groups have encountered. Students must develop a thorough understanding of causes, expressions, and effects of ethnically and racially related problems in schools and society. Isolated facts go only so far in accomplishing this. Analyses of them should address feelings, values, beliefs, ethics, and actions as well.

I am beginning to grapple with how to provide students with more in-depth and comprehensive learning experiences about cultural diversity and social injustice. I now have a very different understanding about teaching immigration. I used to explain how many people came to the United States from all over the world and how their settlements spread westward. What I was really teaching was the dispersal of people from England and western, southern, and northern Europe. I now know that people came from eastern, western, southern, and northern portions of the world. There were many people who were living in Mexico until the United States acquired land in the Southwest, and all of a sudden they found themselves living in a different country. Hundreds of indigenous groups were living from coast to coast in what is now the United States who were there long before the first European settlers arrived. Each group of immigrants, and each group of Natives, experienced the realities of immigration in very different ways. Sometimes thinking about how to visualize and legitimize all of these experiences feels overwhelming to me. But I am striving to gain more knowledge for and confidence in teaching experiences like these with a multicultural focus.

THE IMPERATIVE OF SOCIAL ACTION

It is not enough for students to acquire knowledge about ethnically and culturally diverse issues; they need opportunities to act on the information. I believe that schools have the responsibility to empower students to do this. Social injustices imposed on ethnically diverse groups should not be discussed and then dropped. They need to be analyzed and acted on. Service-learning is one way for students to practice social action.

I had a little exposure to service-learning during my third year of teaching. I observed a group of middle school students studying ecology in science, and as part of their study, they cleaned up, did repairs, and planted flowers in a local park. After studying World War II in history, a group of students visited war veterans in a nursing home to find out more about the experience of war firsthand. A third group weatherproofed low-income housing after studying energy costs in math. The goal of these service-learning projects was to connect content being studied to student-led community action. Reflecting back on these experiences challenges me to think about how I will make my multicultural teaching more action oriented.

Teaching social action is a vital part of educating others, children and adults, about important issues related to ethnic and cultural diversity. Many structural factors in our country, states, and communities limit people's upward mobility, education, and even their personal safety. This is especially true for people whose ethnic, racial, and cultural backgrounds differ from those of mainstream European Americans. Examples are all the racially based hate crimes that occur, such as those monitored by the Southern Poverty Law Center in Montgomery, Alabama. As I began teaching, I was aware of some racial issues that make it difficult for some people to gain employment or secure housing in certain neighborhoods. Living in Memphis, Tennessee, as a child, I heard of the police being called if an African American was seen in the neighborhood after 5:00 P.M. because all the gardeners and maids should have left by then. The assumption was that the person did not belong there and was looking for trouble. Acts of racial discrimination do not seem to have diminished much from the time I was a child. Racial profiling is just one compelling indication of this.

My own surface understanding of racial and ethnic issues transferred into the lessons I taught. My class, for example, discussed racial slurs and redlining of neighborhoods. But never did I point out or even notice the segregation happening right in front of me in Columbia and then Kansas City, Missouri, where I taught. Never did I dig deeper to find out why this was happening. I certainly never considered teaching my students to rise up and speak out against the deep-rooted structural problems that maintain these racist behaviors. I did not do these things because I did not want to, or out of fear, or simply because I did not know how. I was unaware and was not pushing myself to become more knowledgeable. My lack of knowledge and confidence caused a great disservice to my students by not teaching them how to take action for social justice. A critical part of my becoming multicultural is recognizing the flaws in my prior teaching beliefs and behaviors, admitting these mistakes, and being deliberate about correcting them.

DEVELOPING CRITICAL CONSCIOUSNESS AND TRANSFORMATIVE ACTION

During my study of multicultural education, I have learned about patriarchy, structural racism, colonialism, and related concepts that are part of the very foundations of the United States. As a person of privilege because of my membership in the majority ethnic group, I have to be especially conscious of how these tools of domination operate. Otherwise, I may inadvertently perpetuate them even as I claim to be opposing them. In my journey toward being a multicultural educator, I am coming to appreciate the depth of this challenge and the need to be diligent in meeting it.

One reasonable place to practice critical consciousness about cultural hegemony and other acts of domination is the analysis of textbooks. We see textbooks, the most frequently used source of content for teaching (Keith, 1991), as containing vital knowledge necessary to becoming successful citizens across cultural, racial, and ethnic boundaries. But too many of them are not providing fair treatment of the richness of ethnic and cultural diversity. After doing a project focusing on this issue, I discovered several themes throughout several textbooks for various subjects and produced by different publishers. People of color were underrepresented in the narrative text and the illustrations. When they were included, they were mostly performing manual or menial tasks or were from other countries. This seemed to be a deliberate tactic to avoid focusing on race within the United States. When issues such as racism and oppression were discussed, the information used to illustrate them was taken from countries in Africa, Eastern Europe, and the Middle East. Rarely were these issues looked at within the United States or in contemporary contexts. White women were often presented as people who helped men achieve notable success or achieved success themselves through the aid of men. Across the board, the vignettes of White women and people of color were token, distorted, or nonexistent.

These new visions of how I feel teaching should look fit in with the idea of transformative education and action. This is another main theme in my becoming a multicultural educator: pushing the boundaries of what is considered valid and essential information for students to learn. Transformative education uses the viewpoints and stories of people from various racial, ethnic, social, and cultural backgrounds. It is a comprehensive way of analyzing issues. Teacher education, student textbooks, the canon, and the societal and media curricula are all vital to educational transformation. So is how teachers have perceived students. My own transformation began when I abandoned the notion that I could look at ethnically diverse students in my classrooms and see no difference—that color blindness in the classroom was desirable. For me, becoming multicultural involves learning how to acknowledge the racial, ethnic, and cultural diversity of students and using this knowledge to help me teach them better.

Teacher education is the place to begin multicultural transformation. Future teachers should be educated on issues surrounding cultural diversity, racism, social action, and multicultural education. An important piece of knowledge that will be useful to teachers is the specific learning styles of different ethnic and cultural groups. When I learned that many Native, Latino, African, and Asian American children tend to work well in cooperative groups, I began to consider what this means for teaching styles. In fact, in elementary classrooms, students already do a lot of work together. In middle and high schools, though, teachers use more individual learning assignments.

John Goodlad's book *A Place Called School* (1984) confirmed my general beliefs. But I was still left with the challenge of how to imagine revising approaches to teaching. Were cooperative learning arrangements enough? What if the students do not like group learning? Will some students lose out on learning in groups? Will some students not do their fair share of the assignments? Is there more that needs to be included in matching teaching to ethnic group learning styles? Work by Shade (1989), Banks and Banks (1995), Hollins, King, and Hayman (1994), and Gay (2000) helped me find answers to these questions. All children should be given a chance to engage in a variety of learning styles and experiences. If teachers have accurate cultural information about many different cultural and ethnic groups, they will be more successful at helping diverse students achieve. To my immense frustration, this kind of information was missing from my teacher education program, and its absence led to my not serving students in the best way I could. My classroom was racially and culturally mixed in my first year of teaching. Information about cultural trends in learning and the cultures and experiences of various ethnic groups would have helped me be much more successful with my students.

Teachers who are looking for materials to implement must question the validity of the canon with respect to its inclusion of ethnic and cultural diversity. Canonical texts tend to be exclusively by Europeans or European Americans, and predominantly men, for example, Shakespeare, Twain, Chaucer, and J. D. Salinger. This is clearly a limited idea of good literature. Yet many authors of color have written wonderful works that illustrate their perspectives of life and living and issues of universal concern to humanity. Replacing some of the canonical texts with work by these authors would lead to multiple viewpoints of our society rather than viewing it from only a limited perspective.

For example, *Mean Spirit* by Linda Hogan (1990), which takes place in Oklahoma in the 1920s, provides a view of this historical period from the perspective of Native people living in the region. The book is about the rich supply of oil that was found on the land of the Osages and how the Native people were coerced, tricked, or forced off their land so that the U.S. government could gain control of this resource. Although the book is fiction, it relates actual events that are a shocking part of our country's history. Yet the only novel I was exposed to about the 1920s was *The Great Gatsby* by F. Scott Fitzgerald (1995), which reinforced the view of the 1920s as an era of great prosperity, good times, freedom, and self-indulgence. This may have been the experience of some members of some ethnic groups, but it is not an adequate description of the total life experiences of all ethnic groups, most certainly not Native Americans.

It is not fair to present one group's experiences to students and let them assume that they apply to everyone. When the canon is broadened, students will come to understand the perspectives of many groups and acquire more accurate portrayals of historical, social, political, and cultural realities. This is paramount for creating informed citizens who will engage in civic action that leads to educational equality and social justice for everyone.

Another example of how vital multicultural information is omitted from mainstream school curriculum and texts is the way that U.S. history books deal with the enslavement of Africans. They give the impression that slaves were merely pawns in and reactors to a vicious system. But Lerone Bennett Jr. in *The Shaping of Black America* (1975) shows the ingenuity and creativity of people of African descent as resistors and actors in forging a culture of their own. Books by Ronald Takaki, such as *From Different Shores* (1987) and *A Different Mirror* (1993), also offer insightful challenges to conventional historical interpretations. Takaki turns the Eurocentric historical perspective inside out, reveals how racism has always divided U.S. society, and shows how ethnic groups have made worthy contributions to life in spite of these obstacles. Transformative education does not call for the exclusion of the European Americans from literature, history, or any other discipline, but rather the equal inclusion of multiple ethnic groups' perspectives, experiences, and contributions. In this way, students will acquire a richer and more accurate education about U.S. culture and humanity.

Popular culture and media offer their own ethnic and cultural diversity curricula that we all learn from. This education too needs to be transformed. From the advertisements that show us what is beautiful to the media that select what important events and people we view, we are inundated with images and information about ethnic groups that we must decipher. Carlos Cortés's analyses of these media curricula (1995, 2000) provide a rich pool of data to use in discussing how ethnic images are systematically created and the purpose they serve. What people are seen as good? What people are bad? Who is successful? What groups continue to fail? The most important questions for teachers, and the rest of us, to consider are, Who is in charge of these images, and Whom do they benefit? Transformation needs to occur because there are very few groups in control and even fewer benefiting positively from the information that is presented on a consistent basis. Yet media are powerful perpetrators of situations that obstruct the multicultural agenda. This realization of how much teaching about diversity occurs through television, newspapers, and cinemas, as well as the need for school teaching to deal directly with these, has led to a big transformation in my own multicultural becoming.

The problem of the control of information is prevalent in every facet of our society. For example, when East St. Louis and the inner city are shown in my local media, only the rampant crime and poverty are presented. By focusing only on these, the rest of St. Louis can feel that the problems are removed from their lives and are the complete fault of the people involved. The media usually do not explain why the violence in this area happens or how oppression affects people's lives. I have often heard comments such as, "Why don't they just move? They could get a minority scholarship and go to college for free if they wanted. Some of those kids get to go to the best county schools. Why don't they use the education wisely that the taxpayers are spending their money on?"

The fact that the students in this area attend substandard schools (both physically and academically) and are taught by overworked, underpaid, and often undertrained teachers is seldom, if ever, discussed. The students who do win scholarships are woefully underprepared for the academic rigor they face in college. Even if the scholarship pays the entire tuition, housing and transportation costs can prove to be a daunting challenge.

The media do not reveal that the students who attend school in the suburban communities face many hardships. Elementary school children are on the bus as early as 6:00 A.M. for the ride from the city that can take up to ninety minutes. They arrive sleepy at schools that often resent having to serve them, not a situation conducive to learning. Because the media neglect this kind of information, the rest of St. Louis can go on pretending it is not happening or remain truly ignorant of the facts. If I were not becoming multicultural, I too would probably be much like other citizens in my community and accept without questioning what the media present.

A questioning spirit is a product of my becoming a multicultural educator. In my personal and social life, as well as my role as an educator, I am on the alert for how issues of ethnic and cultural diversity are presented, confronted, elevated, or ignored. This questioning spirit can be disconcerting, yet I welcome how it forces me to think about making things better. It causes me to grow and to keep renewing my commitment to act in a way that promotes social justice in education.

After I began to understand the structural problems of racism that are pervasive in the United States, I looked at the media's portrayal of desegregation in St. Louis with new eyes. I became critically conscious of how the media manipulate information and how susceptible people are to these distorted images and messages. I became increasingly perturbed by what I saw going on. The need to be critical thinkers about the information presented to us about issues concerning ethnic and cultural content, and to take deliberate action to resist distortions, became even more imperative to me. My hope is that the new perspective I am developing will help me to teach students similar skills. The educative process should question the material that is supplied in the texts, engage students in social action learning, and critically examine the structural ethnic, racial, and gender biases prominent in U.S. society. Being an effective multicultural educator means that I need to lead the way for my students to follow in doing these things.

JOURNEYING ONWARD

I was taught that we live in a meritocracy; a person becomes successful and upwardly mobile by hard work alone. I was incredibly naive to believe this, but I was not alone. Many others also accept this myth as truth. Now I know that if there were not discriminatory practices and meritocracy truly existed, we would see the same percentage of European American women and people of color in positions of power as in the general population. It was a striking revelation to me how problems in the microstructure reflect the macrostructure. This is a concept that will be well integrated into my future multicultural personal and professional actions.

What to do with this kind of information and general knowledge has been utmost in my mind since learning about it. One of the most important corrections to be made is to get the information out. Teacher education programs need to be educating students about broad multicultural issues, as well as cultural content about specific ethnic groups. The wonderful title of a book by Gary Howard, *We Can't Teach What We Don't Know* (1999), sums up the reason that multicultural education should be a vital component in every teacher education program in the United States. Many teachers see no issues with the materials they are using. Others (like me) see problems but are not quite sure what to do about them. I would like to have been taught knowledge and skills to be proactive within my classroom, school, and community with regard to multicultural education.

In my process of becoming multicultural, I have found enormous benefits to using a multicultural education paradigm in the classroom. Having to view an event, issue, or problem from several different ethnic viewpoints, synthesize that information, and then act on what I have learned requires infinitely more critical thinking and analytic skills than the standard drill and practice with the textbook. I have also found that multicultural education increases the chance to create a lifelong love of learning within students. It engages students in active learning, sparks dialogue, and deepens thought and reflection. Multicultural education gives all students a chance to see themselves reflected in instructional methods and materials. Many viewpoints can be presented and taught as true and valid. These constitute the essence of quality learning for me.

Now that I am beginning to understand the issues at hand better, I am questioning how to most effectively bring about the changes I feel are so necessary. Should I return to the middle school special education classroom where I taught before going to graduate school? Should I go to another school in a different ethnic community or a different state or even a different grade level? I am even questioning if K–12 classroom teaching is the setting where I can bring about the most effective change in the structure as a whole. My question now is: Where can I come in contact with the most people while still creating effective changes in attitudes, beliefs, and behaviors about multicultural issues and experiences? I do not yet have the answer.

There are many things that I will be changing about my teaching once I decide in what role I will reenter the educational system. I am continuing to process the information I have received and trying to find ways that I can effectively pass it on to my students as well as colleagues. I originally chose the field of special education because I felt it would present me with challenges that would help me continue to grow as an educator. I now have new reasons to push myself to continue to grow thanks to my involvement in multicultural education, an area of personal and professional development to which I am strongly committed.

The multicultural education knowledge, values, beliefs, and skills I now possess are just a start in a life-long process. I want to find out how to help students and teachers join the journey to reveal the truths of the issues surrounding multicultural education and how to make effective changes based on these truths. Although I expect the journey to be challenging, I am not discouraged, because I already have some insights into how exciting and rewarding it can be.

PRINCIPLES FOR PRACTICE

Four general principles for multicultural education practice embedded in my personal developments in this area can be used to design training experiences for prospective and in-service teachers.

The first principle is that *developing a critical consciousness about cultural diversity in multicultural curricular materials is imperative in the process of becoming multicultural.* This means critically analyzing instructional materials, evaluating the validity of their multicultural content, and making sure that they include multiple viewpoints representing different cultural and ethnic groups. Never assume that a book, film, newspaper, or professional journal is multicultural in content just because it is so labeled. Develop a critical eye for distinguishing materials that are about nonmainstream groups but have been written in a way that presents them from a mainstream European American vantage point. It is also important that educators become conscious of presenting multiple views of any issue in order to bring clarity and depth to the situation.

That *multicultural education should focus on key themes, events, issues, and concepts rather than isolated facts about different ethnic groups* is the second principle. This allows educators to look at particular issues across time, cultures, and ethnic groups. It also allows students to see that all issues have multiple facets and are experienced very differently by each group involved. Key themes that are central to multicultural education are discrimination, White privilege, patriarchy, oppression, power, social justice, and transformation. Multicultural educators can take one of these issues and look at how it has been manifested in different ethnic groups at a particular time. Thorough examination of a specific issue brings knowledge and events alive for both students and educators.

The third principle for multicultural educators is that *it is important to examine where you have come from, where you are, and where you are going.* When I reflect back on my teaching career, I can see mistakes I have made. It is only by this self-reflection that I can determine how to change my behavior in the future. Multicultural educators should examine lesson content, teaching behaviors, and attitudes when engaging in this self-reflection. All of these elements affect the quality of multicultural education. Personal and professional multicultural actions, attitudes, values, and knowledge should be examined. Personal experience informs all other aspects of life. You cannot teach multiculturalism in the classroom if you are not living it outside the classroom. Because of this, self-reflection in regard to personal life should be practiced as often as reflecting on professional life.

Without multicultural content knowledge, it is very difficult to choose valid materials, reflect on the effectiveness of one's teaching, and determine how to present all the different viewpoints necessary when discussing particular ethnic issues. This fourth principle is one of the most important elements of becoming multicultural. It involves finding content for students and teachers and becoming well versed about multicultural education issues, scholarship, and instructional strategies. Among the many books that present information about ethnic and cultural diversity in the United States and human stories that educators missed in their own studies are Berkhofer's *The White Man's*

Indian (1978), Horsman's *Race and Manifest Destiny: The Origins of American Racial Anglo-Saxonism* (1981), Garcia's *Chicana Feminist Thought: The Basic Historical Writings* (1997), and Takaki's *Double Victory: A Multicultural History of America in World War II* (2000). Becoming well read in multicultural nonfiction and fiction will give you a solid foundation on which to base lessons. It is helpful to read books on specific ethnic groups and how they dealt with particular issues over time, such as the one by Garcia (1997) about Chicana issues. It is also useful to read books like the one written by Takaki (2000) that employ many different ethnic perspectives in analyzing a single event (in this book, World War II). Both types of resources are important for building a solid fund of knowledge for multicultural teaching and learning.

JOINING THE JOURNEY

I hope you have already started your own multicultural journey and are making the kind of progress that you are seeing demonstrated by the authors of this book. But if you need some help on how to get started, here are some suggestions for consideration:

• Determine the multicultural quality and effectiveness of curricula and instructional materials. One of the easiest things to check is who wrote the material. Using instructional materials written by ingroup members lessens the amount of misinformation and stereotypes present.

• Find instructional materials that represent a wide spectrum of cultures and ethnicities. Make sure women are also included, and not just European American women, as is often the case. Some questions to ask when examining curriculum materials for their multicultural appropriateness are: Who wrote or created them? Who is the intended audience? How did the author get the information? Whom does the information benefit? What is the relation of the author to the ethnic, cultural, or social group being discussed? Are these materials sanctioned and accepted by the ethnic group they are about? Here are some more specific analytical strategies:

> Examine the illustrations for identifying the race, ethnicity, socioeconomic status, ability level, and gender of the people shown. Is the race of the people illustrated clearly discernible, or are there only White and ambiguous "brown" people?

Examine the Contents page on particular topics to see if different viewpoints are given and to see if people of color are discussed in special features as well as in the main text.

Determine if females and males from different ethnic and racial groups are used as the main characters in narratives and illustrations, if people of color are depicted in their own distinctive cultural backgrounds, and if stories show people of various ethnic groups and races interacting with each other within and across group boundaries.

Assess the supplemental activities in the textbooks and decide if they adequately represent the cultures of many different ethnic groups and provide a variety of exercises (art, movement, social action, singing, and other acts of expression).

• Consider how to use some of the parts of the text that are not up to par to elicit critical thinking skills in students. Have the students examine the materials, and discuss omissions and problem areas. Share the results of your analyses with other educators who use the same materials. Together, suggest some strategies for how to improve the quality of the multicultural content. By creating a community of people invested in improving the content presented to students, all parties will benefit.

• Over a period of one month, keep a journal about all the things you have done, personally and professionally, in becoming multicultural. Examples are attending cultural events and seminars; planning and teaching lessons that include content about ethnically diverse groups; reading books and articles; having conversations to gain insights into and knowledge about ethnic and cultural diversity; and considering other media, such as ethnically specific newspapers, movies, and magazines, that you have used personally in your classroom with students. Videotape your class on several occasions to see how you interact with ethnically diverse students while teaching. At the end of the self-observation period, critically reflect on your journal entries by making note of the following:

The number of activities you did to promote personal and professional growth and how you distributed your time and effort among them

The races and ethnic groups included in your social, personal, and professional activities, by what means, and how frequently

If the materials and events you read, observed, and interacted with in and out of the classroom included fiction, nonfiction (past and present), leaders, and common folk

The social actions you took part in personally and what you did to help your students combat racism and promote social justice for ethnically diverse groups

How you felt about your multicultural performance in the classroom, such as teaching social justice, and engaging ethnically diverse students in critical thinking and transformative activities

After noting these reflections in your journal entries, make a list of your successes and areas that need to be improved. This assessment is important so that you do not continue practices that are not positive in becoming multicultural.

• Develop your own personal multicultural improvement contract. To do this, identify specific areas that you want to improve, strategies for how you plan to accomplish the improvements, a time line for making the changes, indicators that will be used as evidence of your progress, and some accountability consequences for failing to meet the terms of the contract. Monitor this contract carefully to ensure that you live up to its terms. Whether you have been on the journey to becoming multicultural for one or twenty years, it is important to strive for continuous improvement. Setting specific improvement goals for yourself and your students at regular intervals is an effective way to monitor progress. You might also have your students develop similar contracts for themselves.

• Get into the habit of engaging in self-reflection about what you are doing to promote ethnic and cultural diversity in your personal and professional lives. Some questions you can use to do quick assessments of your position along the multicultural journey are: What is the level of my multicultural content knowledge in relation to the subjects I teach? How do I employ social action in my classroom and in my life outside school? What beliefs, attitudes, and behaviors do I have that hinder or help my multicultural journey? How do I feel about my multicultural beliefs, knowledge, and actions? What can I do to be a multicultural example to my colleagues, students, family, and friends? In what ways are my lessons and personal learning transformative? By answering these questions, you should become conscious of the patterns or trends in your multicultural beliefs and behaviors. It will then be easier to see what needs to be improved and how to make the changes. In planning change, make your goals specific, significant, doable, and personally meaningful to you.

References

Banks, J. A., and Banks, C.A.M. (eds.). *Handbook of Research on Multicultural Education.* Old Tappan, N.J.: Macmillan, 1995.

Bennett Jr., L. *The Shaping of Black America.* Chicago: Johnson Publishing Company, 1975.

Berkhofer, R. F. *The White Man's Indian.* New York: Vintage Books, 1978.

Cortés, C. E. "Knowledge Construction and Popular Culture: The Media as Multicultural Educator." In J. A. Banks and C.A.M. Banks (eds.), *Handbook of Research on Multicultural Education.* Old Tappan, N.J.: Macmillan, 1995.

Cortés, C. E. *Our Children Are Watching: How Media Teach About Diversity.* New York: Teachers College Press, 2000.

Fitzgerald, F. S. *The Great Gatsby.* New York: Simon & Schuster, 1995.

Garcia, A. M. *Chicana Feminist Thought: The Basic Historical Writings.* New York: Routledge, 1997.

Gay, G. *Culturally Responsive Teaching: Theory, Research, & Practice.* New York: Teachers College Press, 2000.

Goodlad, J. I. *A Place Called School: Prospects for the Future.* New York: McGraw-Hill, 1984.

Hogan, L. *Mean Spirit.* New York: Ballantine Books, 1990.

Hollins, E. R., King, J. E., and Hayman, W. C. (eds.). *Teaching Diverse Populations: Formulating a Knowledge Base.* Albany: State University of New York Press, 1994.

Horsman, R. *Race and Manifest Destiny: The Origins of American Racial Anglo-Saxonism.* Cambridge, Mass.: Harvard University Press, 1981.

Howard, G. R. *We Can't Teach What We Don't Know: White Teachers, Multiracial Schools.* New York: Teachers College Press, 1999.

Keith, S. "The Determinants of Textbook Content." In P. G. Altbach, G. P. Kelly, H. G. Petrie, and L. Weis (eds.), *Textbooks in American Society.* Albany: State University of New York Press, 1991.

Marrow, A. J. (ed.). *What I Believe and Why—Maybe: Essays for the Modern World by Horace M. Kallen.* New York: Horizon Press, 1971.

Schofield, J. W. "School Desegregation Forty Years After *Brown* v. *Board of Education:* Looking Forward and Looking Backward." In D. Johnson (ed.), *Minorities and Girls in School: Effects on Achievement and Performance.* Thousand Oaks, Calif.: Sage, 1997.

Shade, B. J. (ed.). *Culture, Style, and the Educative Process.* Springfield, Ill.: Thomas, 1989.

Takaki, R. (ed.). *From Different Shores: Perspectives on Race and Ethnicity in America.* New York: Oxford University Press, 1987.

Takaki, R. *A Different Mirror: A History of Multicultural America.* New York: Little, Brown, 1993.

Takaki, R. *Double Victory: A Multicultural History of America in World War II.* New York: Little, Brown, 2000.

CHAPTER THIRTEEN

Navigating Marginality
Searching for My Own Truth

Yukari Takimoto Amos

M oving into the social context of the United States from Japan has given me abundant opportunities to think about my own and others' ethnicity and culture in ways that I never imagined in my home country. I have experienced culture shock and marginality in the United States and in this sense have been discovering and recovering myself every day since my arrival. In this chapter, I share some of these experiences of cultural shock and marginality and claim them as a fundamental part of my growth and development as a multicultural educator and person.

When an individual moves into an unfamiliar cultural matrix, it is not uncommon for some collisions of lifestyles, values, and beliefs, or culture shock, to occur. These tensions can shock a person into awareness about his or her own perceptions and recognition that one creates his or her own life world (Pinar, Reynolds, Slattery, and Taubman, 1995). According to Adler (1975), culture shock can be a fruitful learning process that brings understanding of different cultures and deepens knowledge of self. It also "provides an individual with an opportunity to deeply reflect on one's taken-for-granted, commonsensical view of things" (McEwen, 1980). In other words, culture shock is part of becoming culturally conscious of self and others. Nevertheless, being in the midst of a different cultural system can be a disconcerting and decentering experience. Some of the same situations underlying cultural shock can produce marginality, or being invisible and relegated to the periphery of a mainstream system. These processes of self-discovery, self-consciousness, and coping with marginality are major features of my development as a multicultural person and educator.

MY HOME CENTER

I was born and raised in Japan and educated there to the beginning of graduate school. Japanese culture, language, and identity are the core of my being.

I am aware that there are people called *Zainichi* (Korean Japanese), *Ainus,* and *Burakumins* (outcast groups) in Japan and that they are treated differently from the ethnic Japanese. Yet I did not seriously consider the social problems they face because I am part of the majority ethnic group. It never occurred to me that their social dilemmas were my problems. As Ayabe (1993) admits, "It is difficult for Japanese people to understand the problems of ethnicity and identity because they live in an ethnically homogeneous society and do not experience the oppression and exploitation by other ethnic groups" (p. 110). Japan is not entirely homogeneous; 3 to 4 percent of the population belong to minority groups (Siddle, 1996). Yet the Japanese majority ethnic group acts as if Japan is a society where only they reside. They oppress, exploit, and exclude other ethnic groups living in the country, consciously or not. It is extremely difficult to realize how privileged persons of Japanese ethnicity are in Japan because all aspects in Japanese society exist for our benefit and we take them for granted. Being a part of the ethnic, cultural, political, and economic majority created a kind of cultural blindness for me.

This realization was one of the first times I recall being conscious of marginality. Although I knew cognitively that some people existed on the margins of Japanese society, I didn't think too deeply about what this meant or who these people were. I certainly didn't feel much emotional discomfort about their circumstances. I had not experienced them personally, since I was part of the ruling majority. I marginalized the minority groups in my own country by making them invisible and insignificant in mind, values, beliefs, and behaviors. Later, this "blindness," "objectified knowing," and "invisibility of the other" changed radically for me, partly by my personal experiences with being marginalized.

Although I was not very conscious of my privileged social status as a member of the majority ethnic group, I deeply understood on a personal level the subordinate social and political status of women in Japan. Women are marginalized in my culture by having no power or authority. It is curiously ironic that I could be so aware of one kind of oppressive discrimination (gender) but not another (ethnicity). I think that a major reason for these perceptual differences was my personal positionality. Knowledge of these realities helped me to understand more quickly the major concepts and principles of multicultural education.

I remember my grandmother's reaction when I was about to enter a college that required me to leave my rural home village and move to a city. She asked, "Why do you want to go to a four-year college? That's for men. It's not good for a girl to get higher education. Why do you want to go to a big city, far away from us? Big cities are dangerous for girls." If she were still alive, I wonder what she would think of me now, with a doctoral degree completed in a foreign country? Would she still lament my stepping beyond the accepted boundaries of Japanese femaleness? Would she think that there is something wrong with me? Might she even be a little proud of me? On a broader scale, what do my grandmother's (and my traditional culture's) expectations mean for my becoming a multicultural person and educator? Is it necessary to confront, challenge, and change socialization? Do we have to cross boundaries, chart new terrain, and explore different ways, places, and spaces of being? Probably.

I worked as a salesperson for a financial company immediately after completing my undergraduate degree with a major in Russian language. No matter how hard I worked or how far I surpassed my male colleagues in selling stocks and bonds, I knew that I would not be promoted. The career tracks for men and women are very different in Japan than in the United States. Women are supposed to help men in their work, not compete with them for promotion. After I left my native country, I began to wonder about and explore parallels between the economic and gender marginality in Japan and gender and racial discrimination in the United States. I now regularly speculate about whether my personal experiences and perceptions are generalizable to broader groups within my own and other countries, a good habit for all multicultural educators to develop and teach to students.

One by one, my female friends got married after college and quit working to become traditional housewives. When I turned twenty-five years old and was still single, people told me, "You are too old for marriage. Men don't like women older than twenty-five years old." And so I experienced another brand of marginality in my own culture. In Japan, marriage opportunities become increasingly limited for females after the age of twenty-five. Thus, it seems that progress in one domain is sometimes accomplished at the expense of others, especially when a person's progress challenges the status quo. Another way of saying this is that successfully navigating one type of marginality is no guarantee that others will not occur. In the process of getting an education, I overcame the marginality associated with illiteracy, only to be marginalized again because I was "too educated for a Japanese female," and "too old" to be a desirable marriage partner. I realized that I would have to prepare myself to cope with recurring and varying kinds of marginality. Becoming a multicultural person is helping me do this for myself and preparing me to teach students to do the same.

After I moved to the United States, I became free of the constraints imposed on women in Japan. But at the same time, I began (or perhaps was forced) to think about things I had never given a second thought to in Japan. The more privilege I had at home, the less I thought about my existence as a racial and ethnic being. My changing status from majority to minority in the United States helped me to understand better the importance of sociocultural context and personal privilege in teaching and learning about cultural diversity.

CROSSING BORDERS FROM WEST TO EAST

In September 1996, I flew from Osaka, Japan, to Seattle, Washington. Leaving my parents, friends, and boyfriend behind, I swore on the plane that I would study as hard as possible and return to Japan in two years for good. As the plane approached Seattle, the pilot announced cheerfully, "Welcome to the United States! Welcome to the Emerald City, where it rains nine months a year!" That this message was spoken in English initiated for me processes of border crossing and navigating marginality that made the gender, job, and age discrimination I had experienced in Japan pale by comparison. There I was, still en route, and the pilot was speaking in a language and making cultural references that I didn't understand. What was this Emerald City? Wasn't my destination Seattle? The geographical borders I was crossing were profound enough, but they were minor compared to the cultural, linguistic, and social borders I would have to cross in the United States.

On the first day at my American university, my boyfriend faxed me a charming and encouraging message from Japan: "Good morning! Good luck today! Just smile a lot and everything will go well. You are a star!" *I will be a star,* I told myself, and I believed this would happen in due time.

In my first classes, I smiled a lot—not because I wanted to or found a lot to smile about, but because smiling was the only thing I could do. I did not know what was going on at all because I could not understand what the instructors and students were talking about in English. How many students from other ethnic, cultural, and linguistic backgrounds find themselves in situations similar to, or even worse than, mine? What happens to their sense of self and their academic achievement? I understand now and can answer these questions, but I didn't then. I didn't know enough to wonder about the educational fate of others. I was too consumed with my own dilemmas.

International students who study in the United States are required to take the Test of English as Foreign Language (TOEFL) and earn an appropriate score for university admission. My TOEFL score was very high, and I had confidence in my ability to speak English. But when I found myself in the midst of native English-speaking students and being taught by native English-speaking professors, my confidence soon shattered. I smiled to hide the fact that I did not understand most of what went on in the classroom. I could not participate in classroom discussion because I had no idea what issue was on the table. I sometimes wonder how my classmates and professors interpreted my smiling.

That was my first major culture shock—a border that I did not cross, a margin I crashed into instead of navigating. As those first few weeks in the United States passed by, things got worse. At supermarkets, I repeatedly said phrases like, "What? What did you say? Pardon? Say it again" to cashiers who tried to tell me the prices of my purchases. I acquired a habit of using a debit card instead of paying in cash so I did not have to talk to the cashier. I also remained dead silent in all the classes I attended. This self-protective survival strategy confirmed the stereotype of "quiet Asians." I took extreme measures to avoid confronting the situation when I really had to speak English. E-mail became a very good friend of mine immediately.

It is not that I did not want to speak English, but I did not want to humiliate myself in public by speaking English with an accent. People made faces at my English, and they still do. Whenever they hear me speaking English, they say, "You are not American. Where are you from?" My initial response (inside my head) was, "I know my English does not sound native, but could you please forgive me for that? I am not a native speaker. Are you expecting everybody in the world to be a native speaker of English? Can you speak Japanese as well as I do? Of course, you can't. But I promise you that I won't laugh at you or make faces even if your Japanese sounds awful." The process of forming those thoughts was a critical beginning in creating a foundation for me to cross the border and leave the margins of linguistic silence. I had begun to realize that all of my limited English proficiency skills were not of my own making. Some of these rested with the attitudes and expectations others had toward me.

My fear of being categorized as other surpassed the fear of linguistic humiliation. It did not take long for me to realize how much people in the United States make distinctions according to language skills. Those who cannot speak English in a grammatically correct way are not considered very intelligent. Those who speak a language other than English are outsiders, and this means they cannot be fully integrated into mainstream society. They are alien, suspect, outside the borders of normalcy, even exotic, and never just another person.

Listening to myself pose questions and explanations, I began to realize that I was shifting my view of my linguistic dilemma. It was not a one-sided issue, nor was it only negative or a disadvantage. Some positive values, some worth, and some strength can be found in the marginality of otherness and linguistic diversity.

Is this marginality of the other something that happens only in the United States? Isn't Japan the same? Don't the Japanese regard people who do not speak Japanese as other and treat them accordingly? Didn't I, as a member of the Japanese ethnic majority, consider minority groups in my country to be not quite as good as me? My mind raced trying to solve this complicated problem of being an insider in Japan, with the privilege of categorizing others, but an outsider in the United States, vulnerable to the same categorization. Was I simultaneously the marginalizer and the marginalized? What were the geographical and cultural journeys I was making by coming from Japan to the United States doing to my mind? Was I in the process of sorting out yet another navigational routine, this time within my intellect? I wondered if others were dealing with similar challenging dilemmas.

RETURNING TO MY ROOTS

About six months after arriving in the United States, I returned home to Japan for a visit, filled with the anticipation of being back where I could speak Japanese all the time and did not have to worry about being humiliated in public. It was marvelous to be surrounded by familiar faces, feelings, sights, sounds, and cultural rhythms. I could move through daily living with the ease that comes from being in tune with everything. I visited a class at the university where my friends studied and was excited by the fact that I could understand what was going on without any difficulty. People in Japan would not doubt my intellectual ability by the way I talked. For a little while, the cacophony of voices inside my head stopped. I could relax and just be myself. This was a welcome relief and a happy change of pace.

Although it was comforting being home among the culturally familiar, I felt somewhat as if I was standing on the sidelines of my own being, observing what was going on. I looked more critically at the people and things going on around me and noticed incidents and behaviors I had not before. There were times, though, when I began to feel less troubled even as I continued to question the changes occurring in my personal and professional life. I felt again the comforts and security of being home. Although diminished, my feeling that something was different didn't stop entirely. Why did the feeling of being somewhat out of sync (another kind of marginality) with my own culture stop? Maybe it has to do with having intimate connections with significant others even in the midst of our own cultures. These relationships are valuable in general and especially so for navigating marginality within our own and other cultures.

BACK TO THE BORDERLANDS

I returned to Seattle at the end of my visit home still unable to clearly identify the "something different" I had felt in Japan. When I cleared immigration and customs and called for an airport shuttle van, that feeling of "something" fell on me again. This time I succeeded in naming it: it was the gaze—the looks directed toward me from men and women of various ethnic groups in the United States. I am always being watched and put into someone's spotlight.

The gaze seems to be saying, "You will never fit in the United States. Go back where you came from." Giving a name to this difference in how people respond to my public presence in Japan and in the United States was both rewarding and challenging. It answered one question while prompting many others. I suspect this kind of intellectual activity is a common feature of the process of crossing cultural borders and coping with marginality.

I pondered the gaze while looking at myself in the mirror in my bedroom. I wondered about it while watching television and while chatting with my Japanese friends and American classmates. Finally, I concluded that the reason people watch me is my race and ethnicity. My race and ethnicity matter in the United States. In Japan, my race and ethnicity are not cause for notice because I am a member of the majority group. In the United States, I look authentically Asian, and people look at me as Asian, with the stereotypical and restrictive connotations that came with the image. I cannot enjoy the privilege of just living as an individual. I have to deal with my Asianness, my Japaneseness. Learning how to cope with the gaze and its spotlight on my minority status is a major form of navigating marginality, which is a critical element in my becoming multicultural. Part of its challenge is not allowing myself to claim responsibility for causing the gaze. Developing knowledge of self, an inner strength, a strong self-concept, and a good understanding of how minority groups are treated in various majority settings are helping me avoid doing this.

It was around this time that I came across Edward Said's *Orientalism* (1979), which helped me to understand my experience in the United States and expanded my knowledge about what it means to be Asian in Western countries. It thus became a tool for improving my ability to navigate marginality. According to Said (1979), Orientalism freezes Asians into positions of observational objects and outsiders by Westerners or European-origin people, but it never allows the opposite. There exists, however, a distinct separation of Asian men and Asian women. Asian women become sexual objects, while Asian men's sexuality is identified with femininity.

I have encountered many incidents that remind me of this ethnic profiling of Asian woman. For example, wherever I go, men (especially

European Americans) say things like, "You have beautiful long straight black hair. You have a traditional Japanese face." Thank you for praising my hair and face, but please consider my character and capabilities as an individual too. One of my American male friends once said to me, "I like Asian women, but especially Japanese. They are very nice, kind, polite, cute, and obedient. I want to marry a Japanese woman." Does he believe that every Japanese woman is kind, cute, and obedient? Another American male friend shocked me when he said, "I love Asian women. They are small and submissive. That is what is nice about Asian women. But, Yukari, you are not like traditional Japanese women. I thought every Japanese girl is trained to be obedient to men. You are not. You challenge me, a man." Ironically, these individuals saw no problems with their attitudes and behaviors. They thought they were giving me high praise, but perceiving and treating me as a stereotypical sexual being is another effective way to marginalize me. It is a practice that I must resist for my own sake, as well as for Asian women in general. I am a complex human being whose essence cannot be reduced to my sexuality even if it were accurately portrayed, yet sexuality is a critical part of the identity of Japanese women.

Navigating marginality can give an appearance of vacillation, ambiguity, and uncertainty. The more you know about issues of ethnic and cultural diversity and how they are used to advantage some and disadvantage others, the more you realize you need to know more. Also, what you thought you once knew has to be continually renegotiated in view of new knowledge. Within the context of the major themes of my process of becoming multicultural, this means that in the act of crossing one border or navigating a particular margin, I encounter still others that have to be crossed. Sometimes in making the subsequent crossings, I have to revisit and rethink my actions on earlier ones. These changing positions and understandings are part of what multicultural scholars mean by knowledge construction. It is, along with multiple perspectives and comparative analyses, an important skill that I am cultivating .

Sometimes marginalized people appear to be participating in their own marginalization when in fact they are not. They are simply navigating the margins with the resources at their disposal. For example, enslaved African Americans gave the impression that they were passively accepting their enslavement while they were actually engaged in subversive resistance. Japanese Americans cultivated normalcy in the internment camps during World War II by doing regular everyday things like playing baseball, falling in love, and getting married. These people were overcoming the obstacles and oppressions imposed on them. This is the essence of navigating marginality.

IN THE MAINSTREAM—MAYBE

On the plane for a return trip to Japan in 1997, I was reflecting on the linguistic, racial, ethnic, cultural, and gender differences I had encountered in the United States and the tremendous impact they had on me. I had learned that I cannot be the same person in the United States that I am in Japan. I assume a different persona in each country, and the one I wear in the United States is stressful most of the time. Am I living a schizophrenic life, simply "style-shifting" to meet the demands of crossing cultural borders and coping with marginality, or traversing my shifting majority and minority status? I am inclined to accept the latter possibilities. I don't think I can be a good multicultural person and educator if I operate the same way in different cultural, social, and national settings. Nor can I use a single set of understandings and skills to resist marginalizing and being marginalized. So as I develop my multicultural education competencies, I want to improve, not diminish, my abilities to engage differently with diverse ethnic groups, cultures, communities, and countries.

During this contemplative stage, I struggled with the legal and practical meanings of citizenship, another issue I had not seriously considered in Japan. I was staying in the United States on a special student visa, so my legal status mattered. Simple definitions of citizenship taught in social studies classes, such as "right or obligation of people living in a country," didn't apply adequately to my situation. I was living in the United States but certainly did not have full rights and responsibilities. I was a citizen of Japan but was not currently living there and thus could not exercise the rights and responsibilities that Japanese citizens have. If the more surface meanings of citizenship were becoming diffused in relation to me, what about the deeper one, such as the right of human dignity, freedom of thought, and representation protected by the laws of the country in which I was a guest? Were they too losing their clarity? I haven't answered these questions with certainty yet, but they began a process of thinking that is continuing. They are connected in my mind to the multicultural education issues of who is an American, what it means to be American, and having diversity within unity and unity within diversity.

Like most of the other international students who study in the United States, I struggle with money matters. Education for us is enormously expensive. We pay nonresident tuition and must take a full load of classes to satisfy our legal status. Thus, I found myself having to navigate financial marginality along with the gender, cultural, and geographical marginality. What does this have to do with becoming a multicultural educator? Three real connections come readily to mind. First, dealing with my financial problems consumed valuable time, energy, and attention that I could have otherwise devoted to my academic studies. Second, I did not have the money to access most of the cultural events by and about different ethnic groups presented on campus and in the larger community. This meant that I missed some valuable knowledge and experiences that were not provided in textbooks and classroom instruction. Third, my limited finances placed me in a situation where I could better empathize with students I may teach who have similar economic constraints. Educators frequently analyze teaching issues and make instructional decisions that reflect their own comfortable middle-class realities, which are not meaningful to poor students. Underachieving children of poverty across ethnic groups of color are the most marginalized in schools and need the most multicultural education interventions. I think my relative poverty will help me to better understand their situations, empathize with them, and prepare teachers to work with them.

Although my financial situation is challenging, what bothers me even more are the racial prejudices and stereotypes that exist. I encounter racial slurs and discrimination based on my racial and ethnic identity. Am I a member of a minority group? Can I ever be a Japanese American instead of a Japanese in America? What is the difference between the two? How will the margins I have to navigate change depending on how I am identified ethnically and culturally? I ask myself the same questions about other ethnic groups. How is marginality different for Chinese Americans, Filipino Americans, Mexican Americans, Navajos, Jamaican Americans, or immigrants from different African and Middle Eastern nations? I wonder if people in other countries do the similar things to immigrants as I experienced in the United States. There are some international students in schools in most countries who may confront issues and tensions of social, cultural, and institutional fit as well. These realities and how to deal with them are important parts of my becoming a multicultural educator and person.

I was contemplating all of these issues as I was on my way home to Japan for a summer break. I had imagined that my mind would be filled with the anticipation of the joy of being home, yet I was still living and processing my U.S. experiences. Why didn't I leave them behind when I boarded the plane? Why was I taking them with me? Is this what happens when you have to navigate marginality—that it's always with you wherever you are?

Being home allowed my cultural center to rise to the forefront once again. It was good to just be myself without wondering if my presence was notable. I could get lost in the crowd and relax. It was refreshing and renewing to reclaim what Bowers and Flinders (1991) call the "taken-for-granted," that is, things you think, feel, and do without any deliberate consciousness. I felt in complete sync with the dynamics of my home cultural contexts—as long as I didn't allow issues of gender inequity and my marital status to surface. During this short visit home, I focused more on being culturally renewed. For some brief moments, I could be totally Japanese again. Unfortunately, those moments didn't last for long. The demands of navigating marginality began to resurface the closer the time approached for me to return to the United States.

THE BORDERLANDS AND MARGINALITY PREVAIL

In the United States, my race and ethnicity matter. I look Asian, and people consider me Asian. As a member of a minority group, I know that abandoning my Asianness in any way is nonsense. My Asianness, particularly my Japaneseness, will always be a part of me. I am beginning to realize that this is not the case with Whiteness. Whether Whites can really abandon their ethnicity is not the real issue. Rather, the claim of doing so is itself a proof of privilege. MacCannell (1989) and Haymes (1995) describe it as a tendency of Whites to refer to themselves as cultureless and bestow on themselves a quality of personal detachment, objectivity, and omnipotence. I believe that abandoning Whiteness is as impossible to attain as it is for me to abandon my Japaneseness. Whites should understand their privileged status in the United States and all over the world, as well as how it is used to marginalize other ethnic groups. It is here that we see a serious problem. The cultural, political, ideological, and economic influences of Whites are tremendous everywhere, but they hardly recognize this deep hegemony.

Whose marginality is this? Can majority groups as well as minorities be marginalized? I think so, especially when it comes to being knowledgeable (or not) about ethnic and cultural diversity. Ignorance, and all its consequences, are the causes of some of the worst kinds of marginalization. I am trying to learn as much as I can about different ethnic and cultural groups to resist the margins of ignorance. This is why I consider making sense of Whiteness and other race-specific issues important aspects of my becoming a multicultural educator. I want to understand thoroughly Cornel West's (1993) declaration that race matters. This should be high on the agenda of all students and teachers of multicultural education.

There is another reason that I point to privilege among Whites in the United States: it derives from the power of the language they speak, that is, the power of English. English is a major international language. Almost 90 percent of academic literature is written in English. Wherever they go overseas, English speakers encounter far fewer problems in communicating. In Japan, Americans can earn a tremendous amount of money, regardless of their instructional qualifications, by teaching English simply because they speak English. Many of these teachers do not try to speak Japanese when communicating with local Japanese outside school. Whenever I see this type of American, I feel angry. I want to say to them, "Hey, I speak your country's language in your country. You should at least try to speak my country's language in my country."

For my master's thesis, I interviewed many Japanese students living in the Seattle area. I asked them to name their friends and their nationalities if they knew them. They made comments such as, "Natalie is American. Charlotte is American. Jennie is Black." In their minds, African Americans are only partially American. Being an American is one privilege and being White another. I am trying to make better sense of this distinction, and why it occurs. Teasing out differences among ethnic groups is a part of being multicultural, but I need to be careful to avoid creating new stereotypes and prejudices in the process. Examining the motivations and bases for how people categorize others provides helpful check points.

Whenever my European American friends mention to me, "I envy you. You speak a foreign language. You know two different cultures," I wonder if they are sincere. At the same time, some of their peers are making fun of how I speak English and closing cultural doors in my face. Do these individuals want to speak another language or know other cultures? I think probably they do not because they can survive by speaking only English. What my acquaintances see as a benefit is another kind of marginality for me. I speak English not because I want to but because the situation forces me to do so for survival. Having to think, talk, write, learn, and live in two languages and cultures is often a demanding challenge. Why do I, and many other individuals of color, have to deal with it, while most European Americans do not? Where is the equality here? These differential requirements reek with marginality for some and privilege for others.

White hegemony is worldwide. Steven Haymes (1995) asserts that "mainstream white culture plays a pivotal role in the formation of our cultural identities and therefore how we see ourselves in relationship to others. Its influence is not only in terms of how we think but also in how we construct our fears, pleasures, desires, and dreams" (p. 105). While living in Singapore, I often heard the parents of my students (especially mothers) say, "We want American or European friends, not Singaporean or Malay friends. They are dark and dirty." Of course, when they said "American," they meant Whites, not any of the peoples of color. I could clearly see their superiority feelings toward other Asian people and their inferiority complex regarding Americans and Europeans with white skin color. Some Japanese also aspire to white skin color. It is not just an aspiration for an affluent Western lifestyle. If affluence were the reason, why do Japanese living in Singapore, for example, not aspire to be like affluent Chinese? These issues and their devastating consequences cannot be avoided in genuine multicultural teaching, learning, and living.

CAUGHT IN THE MIDDLE

Going back and forth between Seattle and Osaka, I find myself wanting to be in the United States but still wanting to be Japanese. Seeing myself as Japanese has been brought to the center of my consciousness from the time I lived in Singapore, and it was reinforced after I came to the United States. These foreign cultures have pushed me to realize how profoundly I am Japanese, mentally, physically, culturally, and, most important, consciously. As a person whose country has had a powerful economic impact in today's capitalist world, I sometimes feel privileged simply because I am Japanese. I demonstrate this attitude, perhaps even in an arrogant way, to others. Becoming multicultural has helped me begin to critique my ethnicity and nationality instead of simply taking them for granted. Finding myself in a context where my status shifted from being a majority person (as I am in Japan) to a minority (in the United States) helped to launch this reflective process. As I continue to think about marginality, how it comes to be, and how to counteract it, I look at these issues from many different vantage points. I remind myself that marginality has different manifestations and must be attacked in many different ways by many different people. I am trying to learn how to elicit the assistance of European Americans and help them learn the appropriate skills as I develop my own multicultural education competencies.

Speculating about Whites' deconstructing their illusions of cultural, racial, and ethnic superiority is a significant thinking process for me. Prior to my involvement in multicultural education, I had never given this any thought. Yet issues of whiteness are unavoidably a part of multicultural education. This realization results from a curious kind of marginality navigation for me. It involves trying to look at issues from other people's perspectives. You don't know if your analyses are truly other people's realities or your own perceptions. This possibility requires that I think critically about my own thinking and actions so that I don't do what I am proposing for others not to do: for me to avoid becoming hegemonic as I argue for the destruction of White hegemony and not to marginalize as I fight against marginalization. As I engage in these processes, I am doing what Henry Giroux (1993) describes as "critical questioning of the omissions and tensions that exist between the master narratives and hegemonic discourses that make up the official curriculum and the self-representation of subordinated groups as they appear in 'forgotten' or erased histories, texts, memories, experiences, and community narratives" (p. 35).

Some intellectual dissonance and deconstruction of status quo standards, beliefs, and practices are necessary for implementing the changes that multicultural education mandates. We as teachers have to model for students how to be skeptical and critical about conventional educational practices and programs, how to recognize power relationships within and among majority and minority groups in societies and schools, and how to acquire the knowledge, courage, and skills to confront ethnic, social, cultural, and racial injustices in school and society (Giroux, 1993; Banks and Banks, 1995). These actions won't make us popular with many of our personal and professional peers, but they are morally imperative. We must do them if we are to be good multicultural educators.

No one European American, Japanese, Japanese American, African American, Latino American, or Native American can change the world alone. But each of us can do a lot in our own classrooms and personal spheres of living. Concerning Japanese education, as long as the majority of Japanese do not recognize themselves as having similar privileges of Whiteness, multicultural education in Japan will be just a dream supported by the efforts of minorities. How can I, as a future educator, raise the collective consciousness of Japanese about inequities among ethnic and cultural groups? The educational systems of the United States and Japan are so different that I cannot just transfer what I learn in the United States to Japan. Race and ethnicity are still taboo topics in Japan. We rarely talk about such issues in private, much less in schools. But I cannot overemphasize the importance of critically analyzing our ways of thinking, believing, and behaving as Japanese people. How very ironic to find that I must criticize my Japaneseness as well as Japanese education while in the process of criticizing American education in the context of multicultural education.

STILL AT THE MARGINS

After six years, I'm still in the United States and still having to navigate experiences and perspectives that marginalize me in both the United States and at home in Japan. Maybe this is the fate of anyone who challenges old notions about diversity and is an advocate for multicultural education.

My boyfriend became disillusioned with my decision to continue my education in the United States and ended the relationship. My professor at the Japanese university gave up on me and said, "Don't ever come back to Japan. Stay in America until you die. You are much too Americanized. We need women who look and act Japanese." Did I do something wrong by obtaining an education in another country? Should I have returned to Japan and its conventional conceptions of Japaneseness, as several people suggested? Other people recommend that I find a job in the United States after I complete my degree rather than return to Japan, where the academic job market is much tighter, especially for women. Isn't this what I dreamed of? Didn't I want to do research and teaching at an American university? Why am I not so excited about remaining in the United States? What's wrong (or right) with me? What has made me change? Have I been in too many margins for too long?

I am tired of living in the margins in the United States. I am tired of dealing with the stereotypes and negative expectations my ethnicity and race provoke. I get exhausted and disgusted whenever I encounter racial remarks from individuals who think they are not racist. I am tired of my English being laughed at because of my accent. Maybe I should just learn to endure these slurs, discriminations, and stereotypes. Maybe I am just hoping to escape to a place where I can be whomever I want to be. Maybe I'm just disconcerted by all of the energy and effort it takes to navigate the margins of ethnic and cultural diversity, the struggles it takes to promote multicultural education. Would I be truly happy in conventional settings and their traditional marginalizing practices? I think not.

My personal dilemmas here are similar to those of Asian and Pacific Islander Americans, groups that are examined by Valerie Pang and Li-Rong Cheng and their associates in *Struggling to Be Heard: The Unmet Needs of Asian Pacific American Children* (1998). What choice is there but to continue onward with my multicultural journey. Although it is disconcerting at times, it offers a more desirable future than the past I am leaving behind. I want and intend to be involved in creating schools and societies where multicultural people like me are normative. Exactly how I will always do so is not yet entirely clear.

The 1996 faxed message from my former boyfriend still is hanging on a clipboard in my bedroom: "You'll be a star!" Maybe I will be someday, wherever I end up living, teaching, and learning multiculturally.

PRINCIPLES FOR PRACTICE

Although the life events related in this chapter are particular to my own process of becoming a multicultural person and educator, the underlying messages of them are not. They can be used to help others plan for and make sense of their own multicultural ambiguities and eventual transformations. Here are some for you to consider.

The first principle is that *language is an important aspect of culture.* It can inhibit or facilitate multicultural interactions because of the ways it is used to establish boundaries of race, ethnicity, and privilege. Even when negative words and intentions are not present, the careless or unconscious use of language can be detrimental to interethnic group relations. We need to understand both verbal and nonverbal aspects of language and how they can affect communication among ethnically and culturally different students. As we prepare for and act as multicultural educators, we need to be very conscious of language behaviors and the messages they convey.

Living and learning in multicultural contexts are dynamic processes. Engaging in them requires that we play different roles. Sometimes we are agents of change; other times we need to be the targets of change. Stated differently, there are very few, if any, of us involved in the multicultural education movement who are always as positive and constructive as we need to be. Our growth processes are not yet complete. We should be mindful of this as we think about our obligations as multicultural educators. Part of this is to learn as we expect our students to learn. It also is important for us to remember the principle that *individuals can be both marginalizer and marginalized simultaneously and privileged in some ways while disadvantaged in others.*

Another closely related principle is that *marginalization is not absolute, monolithic, or universal. There are multiple kinds, causes, and manifestations of marginalization.* Individuals and groups who are forced to exist at the margins of society in some situations may not occupy this position in others. For example, individuals may be marginalized in mainstream society but at the center of their own ethnic and cultural communities. As multicultural educators, we need to understand the multiplicity of the marginality that many ethnically diverse people cope with daily.

Marginalization is usually imposed on a person or group by someone else, and the victimized do not necessarily accept the imposition without some kind of counterresistance. This is an important principle to teach because many people assume that marginality, powerlessness, and helplessness are synonymous. A lot of coping devices are developed to deal with marginalization. They involve critical consciousness and analysis of marginalizing processes, and separating one's own self-worth from being marginalized and counteracting the negative effects of marginalization. These needs and actions are closely related to, but not identical with, developing skills to combat racism. Both are fundamental components of multicultural education.

Being at the margins does not mean automatic powerlessness. Although this may be the intentions of the marginalizers, the margins can be places where power is cultivated. Many revolutionary challenges to the mainstream have been launched by people relegated to the edges of society and opportunities. Classic examples are grassroots egalitarian movements throughout history, such as the civil rights and women's movements of the 1960s and 1970s. Insider viewpoints from the margins can offer perspectives on sociopolitical, civic, and quality-of-life issues that are not possible from the mainstream center. Because many social changes are initiated and conducted by individuals and groups who are not part of societal mainstreams, a key multicultural education principle is that *there are power and agency in and from the margins.*

Members of ethnic groups of color usually are conscious of how majority groups in power see them. Many indicators of this exist in both schools and societies, in formal policies and informal practices. They also are aware of some of the common ways they are marginalized in and by mainstream society, but may not have a depth of knowledge about the facts and effects of ethnic group–specific marginality and counteracting strategies. This is content that should be taught in school with a *focus on multiple perspectives, comparative analyses, and collective activism within and across ethnic groups to fight all forms of marginalization, injustice, and oppression.*

We as teachers need to understand the principle that *many different variables affect how culture and ethnicity are manifested in expressive behaviors.* However, they do not nullify the existence and importance of culture and ethnicity in our personal lives, our societies, and our teaching and learning. I discussed at length four of these mitigating variables: gender, language, race, and immigration. The first three are dealt with rather extensively in the multicultural education scholarship, but immigration is just beginning to be analyzed and needs to receive much more attention for many reasons. First, there is an immigration contingency within most ethnic clusters. Second, issues of significance in multicultural education have different meanings, manifestations, and effects for immigrants than U.S.-born members of the same ethnic groups. Third, the length of residency of immigrants in the United States (and other countries), the circumstances of their arrival, and how they are received by the host mainstream culture are important differences within differences that should be addressed in multicultural education.

A final multicultural education principle for practice that can be extracted from this chapter is that *a clarified ethnic identity is a source of psychological strength that can be a launch for improving academic, social, civic, and personal performance.* Students who have positive self-concepts about their social, cultural, and ethnic identities tend to perform better in school than those who are confused about or reject them. But positive ethnic identities are not necessarily automatic, nor do they always occur. They are learned and therefore can (and should) be taught.

JOINING THE JOURNEY

I hope this chapter has affirmed some of what you are already doing and encouraged you to do more in your own journey toward becoming a multicultural educator. Other people's stories can activate our own. If you need some additional ideas to stimulate your multicultural education knowing, thinking, feeling, and doing, here are a few suggestions:

• Recall times when you have encountered or witnessed cultural collisions in trying to relate to or teach people from ethnic groups other than your own. In these recollections, describe the collisions in detail, and group them into categories of various cultural components (for example, traditional values, beliefs, and communication styles), how you felt about these situations, and how they were resolved. Judge the quality of the resolutions according to standards of good multicultural education. Use your self-reflections as a basis for developing some guidelines for recognizing and reviewing cultural collisions. Then use these to interview some of your colleagues, or observe in pluralistic classrooms to determine what collisions occur between ethnically diverse students and teachers and how they are resolved. Determine what effects these collisions have on the comfort, confidence, and competence of students and teachers. Compare the results with your own personal experiences.

• Write a letter to a friend, relative, or colleague describing personal and professional situations in which you have been marginalized within your own ethnic group and in relation to others. Explain what you did in response to being victimized. Then add some instances of when you marginalized others. Tell how you became conscious of your actions and what you are doing (or planning to do) to change them. Conclude your letter with what you learned from these experiences for teaching multicultural education.

• Respond to me by explaining the extent to which you think my experiences with being marginalized because of race, gender, language, ethnicity, and culture are uniquely my own or commonly shared by many women across different groups of color. Find out if your conclusions are supported by evidence. To do this, read at least one autobiography, biography, fiction, media account (newspaper or magazine articles), research study, or statistical report, or examine a visual art sample on women in ethnic groups different from mine (Japanese). Examine these documents for information about the kinds of marginalization presented in this chapter, as perpetrated by the dominant power group and by one's own ethnic group. Compare the results of these analyses across ethnic groups and with your earlier speculations about the uniqueness or commonality of my marginality. You also can have your students do similar analyses in small groups. This will allow you to create broader databases and more comprehensive intragroup and intergroup comparisons of marginalization.

• Develop a list of do's and don'ts for navigating marginality. Include in your list intellectual, emotional, and action strategies. Try presenting your list in a variety of expressive modalities, such as poetry, advertisements, songs, slogans, and codes of ethics. Share your creations with members of different ethnic groups of color, and ask them to give you constructive feedback on your suggestions. Also develop some activities for how you can teach these navigational strategies to your students.

References

Adler, P. S. "The Transitional Experience: An Alternative View of Culture Shock." *Journal of Humanistic Psychology,* 1975, *15*(4), 12–23.

Ayabe, T. *Gendai sekai to esunisiti* [Modern world and ethnicity]. Tokyo: Kobundo, 1993.

Banks, J. A., and Banks, C.A.M. (eds.). *Handbook of Research on Multicultural Education.* Old Tappan, N.J.: Macmillan, 1995.

Bowers, C. A., and Flinders, D. J. *Culturally Responsive Teaching and Supervision: A Handbook for Staff Development.* New York: Teachers College Press, 1991.

Giroux, H. A. *Border Crossings: Cultural Workers and the Politics of Education.* New York: Routledge, 1993.

Haymes, S. P. "White Culture and the Politics of Racial Difference: Implications for Multiculturalism." In C. E. Sleeter and P. L. McLaren (eds.), *Multicultural Education, Critical Pedagogy, and the Politics of Difference.* Albany: State University of New York Press, 1995.

MacCannell, D. *The Tourist: A Theory of the Leisure Class.* New York: Schocken Books, 1989.

McEwen, N. "Phenomenology and the Curriculum: The Case of Secondary-School Geography." *Journal of Curriculum Studies,* 1980, *12,* 323–340.

Pang, V. O., and Cheng, L.-R. L. (eds.). *Struggling to Be Heard: The Unmet Needs of Asian Pacific American Children.* New York: State University of New York Press, 1998.

Pinar, W. F., Reynolds, W. M., Slattery, P., and Taubman, P. M. *Understanding Curriculum: An Introduction to the Study of Historical and Contemporary Curriculum Discourses.* New York: Peter Lang, 1995.

Said, E. W. *Orientalism.* New York: Vintage Books, 1979.

Siddle, R. *Race, Resistance, and the Ainu of Japan.* New York: Routledge, 1996.

West, C. *Race Matters.* Boston: Beacon Press, 1993.

CHAPTER FOURTEEN

Teaching Them
Through Who They Are

Terri L. Hackett

My becoming a multicultural educator is centered in the students and school settings where I taught. I didn't start my career with much formal preparation in teaching ethnically diverse students, but I nevertheless thought I was well prepared to teach reading and language arts. I received my undergraduate degree from a prestigious historically Black college and my master's from a large, predominantly White institution. I did not have any courses in multicultural education or culturally responsive teaching during my pre-service preparation. I didn't think this was a handicap to me since I had a strong desire to teach African American students. I was confident that I would be a good teacher because I knew my subject matter and methods for teaching it. Furthermore, I was sure I could motivate my students to value learning by sharing my own good fortune about how I overcame some struggles to succeed in college. Now I know better. I would have been in a much better position as I started my teaching career if I had had some formal preparation in multicultural education.

I still have that confidence about being a good teacher after several years teaching middle school, but it is now grounded in knowledge and experiences very different from what I had as a beginning teacher. I acquired them from being immersed in teaching ethnically diverse students. I was unaware that many of the things I learned to know and do in this process were components of multicultural education. They just made sense to me as the right things to do. A big part of my becoming multicultural is learning to name and conceptually frame my personal and professional beliefs, values, and behaviors about interacting with ethnically diverse people and finding a community of professionals who have values and commitments about teaching similar to my own. These discoveries are very empowering to me.

Some of Christine Bennett's ideas (1979) helped me to frame and name my processes of becoming multicultural. She explores the importance of teaching ethnically diverse students through their own cultural and experiential frames of reference—what she calls "teaching others as they would be taught" (p. 268). This is imperative for students from different ethnic groups to perform well in schools. But it can't be done if we "don't understand their language, when we misinterpret their behavior, when our 'tried and true' methods of diagnosing and motivating don't work," when "schools remain monocultural despite the fact that we live in a polycultural society" (p. 268). I soon realized that I would have to incorporate the cultures and experiences of my students into my teaching if I was to teach them well. This meant including ethnic content into the subjects I teach, using teaching techniques that reflect cultural diversity, and relating differently to ethnically diverse students.

ARRIVING ON THE PLAYING FIELD

My first full-time teaching assignment was sixth-grade language arts and reading at an urban middle school that had a reputation of being a "bad" school. It was known for fights, gangs, and the dubious distinction of having the most suspensions in the entire district. It was one of two open concept schools in the city, which meant that there were no windows or doors in the classrooms, just partitions that separated them. Most of the students were on free or reduced lunch and included mostly African Americans. Other ethnic groups in attendance were Vietnamese, Cambodians, other Asian Americans, Samoans, and a few European Americans. Most of the White students at the school were bused in for Spectrum, a gifted and talented program, and were separated from everyone else. The first year I taught at this school I had two Europeans Americans in a class of twenty-eight and two or three students from other ethnic groups; the rest were African Americans.

According to some standards, the students at my school were considered at risk: because they were poor, of color, and underachieving. They were a hard bunch; they had seen far too much harshness in a very short amount of time. They looked, and sometimes acted, like short adults, even though they were only eleven and twelve years old. They also seemed as if they would beat up anyone for any reason. These descriptions were more a source of curiosity instead of threat or intimidation for me. I certainly wasn't fearful of these "short adults." After all, I had a few years of experience and adulthood on them.

I didn't think much about these problems as I entered my classroom. I was more concerned about how my students and I were going to relate to each other. From the mistakes I made during my student teaching in Oklahoma, I had learned some important lessons about teaching: do not make assignments and tests too hard for the students, do not be reluctant to ask others for help, and remember that I was the one who set the tone for my classes. Whether my classroom would have order or chaos, learning success or failure, harmony or hostility depended largely on how I set things up with respect to what I wanted from students, and these expectations had to deal with social, personal, and moral behaviors, as well as academic achievement. Multicultural scholars, such as Gay (2000), Ladson-Billings (1995), Foster (1997), and Lee (2001), agree about using holistic approaches in teaching students of color, especially African Americans. I wasn't sure what my students were going to be like, but I was anxious to find out. I was on a mission; I wanted to help my students, and I was ready to move ahead with my plans.

I was excited but a little nervous about teaching in my home town, where people knew me and my family. I wondered what kind of effects, if any, this would have on my interactions with students. Yet I was the new kid on the block, and so were they (as sixth graders in a middle school). We needed to check each other out and see where we stood before we could proceed with our educational agenda. They challenged and tested my strengths and weaknesses as a teacher, as well as the credibility of my ethnicity. Some of my students needed to know "how Black I was," and some wanted to determine if I was "too Black." Others wanted to know if I would show favoritism to the African American students. These are not unusual occurrences for new teachers in ethnically and culturally pluralistic classrooms. Sometimes students run these "tests" to determine if teachers of color are going to be any different from the mainstream European Americans they are accustomed to. Other times they question the right of European Americans to be involved in multicultural education or to teach ethnic-specific curricula, such as African American history or Chicano literature. Still others simply want to see how vulnerable new teachers are, and "newness" is not always limited to youth. It can be having a teacher of color for the first time. Dealing with these tests is a routine part of becoming and being a multicultural educator.

I learned early that if I wanted my students to cooperate with me, I needed to demand that they do so and teach them how. Sometimes students don't know how to do what we want them to do, and this lack of ability is not limited to academic skills. For example, some immigrant students are not familiar with the U.S. style of schooling that emphasizes critical thinking, problem solving, and prolific classroom discourse. Some are being introduced to formal schooling for the first time in their lives, even though they are well beyond the age for starting school in the United States.

My attempts at getting students to like me while I was student teaching had been a colossal failure; they had walked all over me. Now I was teaching for real, in my own classroom, and I had to get us off on solid grounding. The question was how to transmit my expectations to the students and express my authority as teacher while respecting their human dignity. I wanted to send a signal to them that I would care about and for them, but in a no-nonsense way. I wasn't going to be a pushover, and they were going to have to be serious about their studies. I remembered some suggestions from my teacher education programs about being firm with students from the outset, especially if they are poor and children of color. I needed to let students know what I demanded of them, but I knew I couldn't just be a control freak and expect everything always to go my way. I couldn't be a door mat either.

I slowly figured out that I had to be firm yet fair with the students for them to respect me in my classroom. I learned that if I showed them I was on their side and no one could mess with them without hearing from me, they would give me the best they could. I learned this by trial and error. I started doing things to show my students that they belonged to me. I proved to them I could be trusted. Accomplishing this was not easy. Over time, so many students of color have developed a deep distrust of teachers and alienation from school because of promises made to them that are broken over and over again. Once my students understood that I was true to my word—that I could be trusted—I became a confidante for them. They told me things that would normally get them in trouble with other teachers. For example, they would tell me about pending fights; who was involved, where, and when; or who stole something from someone else. I held what they told me in confidence as long as no one got hurt, and I made this caveat clear to them. I also let them know that if I had to break up a fight and in the process I was damaged in any way (such as breaking a nail or running my hosiery), they were going to have to "pay me some dues" as well as the penalty imposed on them by the school principal.

These promises were not enough incentive to keep them from fighting, but I didn't abandon them simply because they exhibited social behaviors I didn't like. I was there when they fought, and I screamed at them for being wrong because they knew "Miss Terri Johnson's" kids were not supposed to fight. I was in their corner when it was time to face the consequences with the principal and their parents. I went to the principal's office with them, explained that they knew what they did was wrong, and tried to get them lighter punishment if they were willing to work with me. I called parents first and talked to them before I made the students explain their actions to them. I let the parents know their children were special and could do the work if they had the support. Unfortunately, many times this support was not readily given, so I had to keep pushing from my side. I also was there with my students when they did positive things and made accomplishments, whether academic, personal, or social. I was as adamant about celebrating their success as I was about chastising their behavioral shortcomings. I knew all the latest slang, songs, gossip, and television shows, and I was not above using them to connect with the students. As a result, they thought I was "cool" even if I did "scream too much" and was "so mean."

In establishing these relationships, I told my students, "I'm going to work for you, but you are going to have to work with me." This seemed a reasonable bargain to make so that there would be some reciprocity of accountability between us. I knew very early on that we would have to work together if I expected to get any teaching accomplished. I thought I would make more progress in what I wanted to do in teaching them by eliciting their assistance instead of becoming their adversary. This sharing of rights and responsibilities with my students is a fundamental element of my process of becoming a multicultural educator. It evokes Dorothy Heathcote's ideas that "as an excellent teacher, I must be able to bring power to my students and to draw on their power. This negotiation, this exchange of power is a realignment of relating" (1985, p. 21). It also has elements of the inclination among many African American teachers to treat their students like their own children (Lee, 2001). Just as most of us won't give or throw away our own children just because they aren't perfect, I felt the same way about my students. They were mine; it was my responsibility to teach them, and they were obligated not to fail without trying. That was not an option to me.

Some people might take issue with my style of relating to students and argue that I was insensitive and uncaring. The reverse is true: I cared too deeply to allow them to do things I found objectionable without letting them know that these behaviors were unacceptable. They needed to know that someone cared enough about them to set limits and teach them how to operate within these limitations. I cared deeply about their minds, bodies, and souls. So I took it upon myself to do as John Dewey (1902), Arthur Wells Foshay (1975), Gloria Ladson-Billings (1995), and others have advised: to teach the whole child by developing their intellectual, social, moral, personal, and cultural skills simultaneously. It wasn't always easy, but I persevered because this is so important to me as a teacher. For instance, my ethnically diverse students had to know how to respect each other if we were to have a congenial classroom climate, build good working relationships, help each other learn reading and language arts, and manage their classroom behaviors. I wanted them to know that their lives and learning were interconnected both in and out of the classroom. In this sense, I was trying to develop some of the attributes of an excellent teacher that Heathcote (1985) describes. These include distinguishing between relating to things and people and giving priority to the latter, recognizing the potential of students and what they are in the process of becoming, meeting children where they are, and seeing the world through students rather than seeing students through the world.

MY KIDS "DON'T GO THERE"

I established some bottom lines and nonnegotiable points about their behaviors. I told them if they did what they were supposed to do and worked with me, everything would be fine because I was going to work for them. Each year, in a rather traditional fashion, I started with a battery of rules for classroom behavior: be respectful; complete all your work; don't talk when someone else is talking; don't get on my nerves by chewing gum, eating candy, tapping on the desk, or sleeping; no fighting; no "he say, she say"; and no talking back to the teacher in disrespectful ways. These may sound harsh and inflexible, but I delivered them with loving care. I like to think that my demands of students and the structures I imposed on their classroom functions are more akin to how many African American teachers operate rather than their being purely idiosyncratic or merely controlling. According to Michele Foster (1995),

> the model description of excellent African American teachers, found in the scholarly as well as the more popular literature, is of concerned adults who command respect, are respectful of pupils, and who, though caring, require all students to meet high academic and behavioral standards. . . . This style of teaching closely resembles the authoritative parenting style, which integrates acceptance and involvement, firm control, and psychological autonomy [p. 576].

My students and I knew that if some classroom rules were broken (as they would be!) without deliberate intent and under extenuating circumstances, they would have many opportunities to redeem themselves. Together, we would find a way to right the wrong and make everything okay.

Sometimes this meant they had to suffer the consequences of their actions. Other times we had to concede that a particular rule needed to be suspended temporarily because of unanticipated personal situations that made it extremely difficult for students to abide by it. The students knew the consequences for breaking a rule could be a stare, a word of warning, detention, a call home, a private consultation, a class sanction, or the last action, which they didn't even want to know what it was (and was never actually named). They always asked what "the last one was," but I would never tell them. I couldn't because I didn't know in any abstract and absolute way; it had to be specific to the person, situation, and context. The few times I had to "go there," I came up with a "last one consequence" that was befitting the occasion. Something about the fear of the unknown is very helpful in preventing kids from stepping over that last line of tolerance. In most instances when rules were broken, I used more corrective than punitive strategies. These became opportunities for students to think through the issues of contention, analyze options, own responsibility, and renew their efforts to improve their individual and collective performance. I checked my own behaviors along with theirs.

My kids seemed to crave the academic structures and routines we established. They could count on spelling on Monday, corrections on Tuesday, English on Wednesday, writing on Thursday, and a test on Friday. They could count on reading each day and doing different kinds of book reports to keep the reading interesting. It was not often that anyone stepped far out of these boundaries. I am not saying I was a super teacher. I made plenty of mistakes along the way. Sometimes I was too hard on a student who was really trying, or I wrongfully accused someone of a misdeed. I didn't always listen to both sides of a story, was not as patient as I needed to be, and made more than my fair share of students upset with me. My salvation was that students knew I was working for them and with them—that a flaw or error committed one day (by either them or me) was not going to haunt us forever. One day we might get on each others' nerves, but the next we would be the best of friends and smooth working partners. We didn't have time to dwell on past events, and vendettas were not happening in my class.

In the end, students remembered that I said, "You gotta always try and be your best," and they tried to live up to this expectation. We had enough mutual respect for each other that we kept working to establish better relationships. One of the things that helped a lot was my apologizing to students when I was wrong or misjudged them. I told them, and wanted them to understand, that "we are humans and we will make mistakes, but we must always maintain dignity and respect for ourselves and each other. It's more important in how you handle yourself in working through your mistakes than in trying to be perfect or flawless." I was pleased to see how quickly they followed my example in learning to apologize to each other. It made a world of difference in our academic and social interactions.

My students knew I did not play about certain things and knew when I meant business. We could laugh and play at the appropriate time, but when it was time to learn, we all had to be serious. They knew that I was there for them and would help them solve their problems or find someone who could. I was more than their teacher; I was their advocate and their protector. I told my students that if anyone messed with them (another student, a high school student, a teacher, anyone else) to let me know and I would put a stop to it. I was going to make certain that my students knew that I would not let them be treated unfairly or disrespectfully. Nor were they going to treat others this way in my presence. We were building a community for living and learning together, and the students had to understand that they were responsible for and to each other. There were many times when I had to deliver on these promises by putting a stop to many things, such as letting another teacher know that she could not talk negatively about my students without my letting her know that I found her behavior objectionable.

Not all of my students trusted my commitment to them. This was aggravating at times but not surprising. So many of them had not had much genuine trust from the adults in their lives. Some responded by trying me out on little things, coming to me with some gossip and telling me about bigger things such as fights to see how I would react. I reminded them of our "no gossiping" rule and stopped the fights without revealing how I learned about them. Or I would make the students involved in the conflicts talk through the tensions. I tried to keep them out of the detention room as much as possible, if for no other reason than that this removed them from my immediate supervision and influence. These were my kids, and I wanted us to learn how to solve our own problems without involving other school personnel. But sometimes the issues were too serious to avoid these involvements.

As my reputation for being "mean but fair" spread throughout the school, other teachers' kids wanted to spend time with me too. Students would say, "Miss Terri Johnson is cool. Go to her; she'll help you." Soon students from other classrooms were coming to me. I helped all I could, and the ranks of "my kids" expanded beyond my official enrollment lists. To help these children, I had to think of novel strategies and always be mindful of who the students were and the nature of their particular needs. Some students tried to trip me up on this by making comments like, "You didn't do me [or he or she] like that. Why you ain't treatin' everybody the same?" I responded by simply saying, "Well, you ain't . . ." and reminding them that when they were the ones who needed particular help, they would be treated special too. At the time, these were instinctual and commonsense reactions on my part. Now I realize I was acting on the principle of multicultural education that ethnically and culturally different students must be treated differently (even within the context of common standards of performance) if they are to have equal educational opportunities. I am indebted to authors like Gay (1994, 2000), Shade (1989), Hollins and Oliver (1999), and Banks and Banks (1995) for helping me make these connections.

It was funny to me how amazed students were that I knew what was going on before anything really happened. I told them, "I know everything; you can't get over on me." Although surprised, they were pleased that they were important enough for me to keep informed about what was going on in their lives, both in school beyond my class and outside school. I didn't think there was anything unusual about this. After all, isn't this what all teachers do? I was taught that good teachers who really care about their students will do anything for them. You can't do this if you don't know what is going on in their lives. It involves more than knowing how kids are performing in the subjects you teach, such as their fears, friendship networks, what's going on in their communities, and what they spend time doing when not in school. Some of my colleagues had trouble with these ideas. They tried to deal with only the students' academic needs or were doubtful about how far they should go in knowing about other aspects of students' lives before invading their privacy. Some of them were even hesitant because the students were from ethnic groups other than their own. This made no difference to me. I spent more time with and knew more about African Americans for the simple fact that they were the largest population in the school and surrounding community. But I stayed informed about my Vietnamese, Samoan, and Cambodian students as well. They were all my kids, and I had to know them to teach and protect them.

My students knew that I would "call them out" in a minute, that is, embarrass them in a somewhat playful way and use innuendo to get the point across but not enough to harm them emotionally. Some of my favorable techniques of doing this were to say, "What part of 'sit down' don't you understand?" or "If I have to come over there, it's not going to be nothin' nice," or "I am going to lose my job today if you don't stop acting like you don't have any sense." I had to have a strong rapport with my kids for this to work, and they had to understand that while I was there to teach language arts and reading, I was also going to teach them how to be good citizens and respectful human beings. These commitments are similar to Christine Bennett's statements about the purpose of multicultural teaching. She says it goes beyond developing the highest academic potential of all students to include "social justice . . . feelings of compassion, fair-minded critical thinking, and a spirit of social responsibility and participation" (1999, p. 37).

TEACHING THROUGH LIVING

Many of my students came from backgrounds where someone in their family was incarcerated, their caregiver lived off the welfare system, or they themselves were gang members or knew someone who was. Many friends and family members had died violently. They had little or no concept of what being a good citizen meant. They lived in a world of instant gratification and they were used to getting things NOW. Many considered going to college out of the question or a waste of time. Preparing now for something that would pay off in the future was laughable to them. I could have been discouraged by these circumstances and given up, but I didn't. I wanted to teach my students that they could transcend their current conditions and make a better life for themselves. I knew that simply preaching this to them wasn't the answer, so I decided to work with what I had.

These students were street smart and very knowledgeable about popular culture. I decided to use what they knew or what was of immediate relevance to them to teach the skills I wanted them to know. Therefore, many of my English lessons incorporated real-life experiences, such as filling out job applications, how to interview for a job, how to ask a parent if they could go on a date, how to act on a date, and what to do if they were arrested. We talked a lot about how getting in a gang was the quickest way to die and how a good education could lead to a better and longer life. Our analyses of the consequences of becoming a street pharmacist (translation: drug dealer) were many and varied. In the process of these explorations, we practiced standard reading and language arts skills such as comprehension, descriptive and persuasive writing, critical thinking, prediction, problem solving, and hypothesizing, along with social action and moral and civic responsibilities.

My kids' lives were inundated with television and video games, so I used the things they were familiar with to teach them the unfamiliar. To make the effort work, I had to suspend my value judgments about whether students should be watching what they were and deal with the fact that it was happening. And I had to watch the programs and videos myself so that I would know what was going on. Otherwise, I couldn't teach my students through them. This style of teaching students through who they are and what they already know is what Moll and Greenberg (1990) refer to as using students' social and cultural funds of knowledge to support school learning; some educators call it scaffolding, and multiculturalists such as Au (1993), Gay (2000), Hollins and Oliver (1999), and Ladson-Billings (1995) describe it as culturally relevant or responsive teaching. It also is in the same vein as the work that Carol Lee (1993, 1995, 2001) is doing in teaching and studying the effects of using a specific cultural communication style common among many African Americans, known as "signifying," and samples of ethnic literature to teach Black students skills of literary interpretation of canonical texts.

The students and I watched their favorite soap opera, *The Young and the Restless,* to practice and demonstrate mastery of fundamental language arts skills. They counted how many times different characters used pronouns, nouns, adjectives, verbs, and conjunctions. We talked about the feasibility and cohesion of the storylines and the adequacy of character development. We rewrote scenes, changed actions, and recast the roles to accommodate diverse ethnic and cultural perspectives. The students wrote the lyrics to their favorite songs and practiced learning the parts of speech from them. We created our own songs to reinforce these learnings. I was using community-based, cultural, and personal knowledge in somewhat the same way and in the same spirit (but on a much smaller scale) as the Rough Rock School did for Navajo children (McCarty, 2002).

My students and I wrote our autobiographies as well (the project lasted the entire grading period) to tell our own life stories in our unusual ways. One technique was to start the telling with words that described us through our names—for example, for my name, Terri, I used *T*–terrific, *E*–exciting, *R*–rambunctious, *R*–rarin' to go, *I*–indisputably intelligent. Then the students wrote a page about their birth and early childhood by interviewing their parents. Next, they drew pictures describing the highs and lows in their lives. After that, they wrote about their dreams and aspirations. At first, the students were unsure what was going on, but once we worked together and shared our stories, they really got into it. In the end, we put it all together and wrote a book. In addition to incorporating different content, using different sources of information, the project provided opportunities for the students to practice various forms of expression, such as poetry, pictorial, interviews, descriptive essay, reflections, and interactive dialogues. They also had to practice their language arts and literature mechanics (such as grammar, paragraph development, and sequencing ideas) in the process.

I asked the students what they wanted out of life. No matter how outrageous their aspirations, we tried to figure out how to accomplish these goals. I encouraged them to imagine unusual futures so that they would be more challenged in their explorations of these possibilities. As the students talked on their own about how they were going to do this and that, they became more interested and involved in what they were doing. The research, writing, and presentation of these projects allowed the students to practice a lot of reading and language arts skills without their realizing it.

Many times my classroom was organized confusion, but it was fun, and the students were always learning something. It appeared more chaotic to those on the outside looking in than to us who were living the experiences. Some of my colleagues and the parents of my students second-guessed my choice of teaching methods because they were not by the book. They didn't seem to realize that my "book" was the students themselves. Just because some of my teaching methods were unconventional didn't mean they were ineffective. If my students were unconventional, my method would have to be unconventional as well for them to learn to the best of their ability.

As I become more involved in multicultural education, I realize that this "suspicion of the unusual" can be a major hindrance in teaching ethnically diverse students. Undoubtedly, some of my colleagues will continue to question the validity of my selections of new content and novel teaching methods and assume that they are not serious enough. I will nevertheless continue to press on with these efforts. I cannot allow myself to concede to the pressures of tradition or status quo assumptions because they are detrimental to my students and others like them.

I taught my students inside and outside the classroom and quickly learned that my outside teaching was immensely helpful to what I did inside the classroom. As a teacher, I was very involved in schoolwide affairs. I chose to do so because I wanted to be available to students, get to know them, and demonstrate to them that my support did not end at the classroom door. I was the activities coordinator, the Associated Student Body adviser, and the dance mother, and I never missed a basketball game. I reminded those ball players who thought they would be the next Michael Jordan that it probably wouldn't happen, but I cheered them on nevertheless and encouraged them to play their best. I sold pickles and candy for the dance team, then danced and took pictures at the actual events. I ate lunch in the cafeteria with the students so my kids could see me and I could see them.

These informal settings provided opportunities for me to see if classroom teachings about respect for self and others, citizenship, and making good decisions were being applied, and if not, to reinforce them. I also was able to see some other dimensions of my students: who their out-of-school friends were, how they related to parents and other adults from the community, and what kind of nonschool knowledge and skills they possessed. This was valuable information to know for its own sake and for making my classroom teaching more relevant to students. My being all over the school and community also allowed my students to see me in contexts and roles other than as formal classroom teacher and for them to know me better—or at least to realize that I was a multidimensional human being. It helped us to establish better rapport with each other and higher levels of trust. I felt it was my responsibility to participate in all aspects of the students' lives. Being a teacher involves more than what goes on in the classroom; it means being a visible presence in the school and the community. I have never had much respect for teachers who worked from 7:15 A.M. until 2:45 P.M. and felt that they should get paid for any extra work. My payment was the joy of the students' faces and their gratitude that I was there cheering them on and sharing in their joys of success and pains of defeat, or simply being there with them, wherever that happened to be. This may have been an after-school movie, a grade-level campout, or just socializing in the hallways for a little while at the end of the school day before everyone left to go home.

Extending my availability to and teaching of students beyond the walls of the classroom fits well with those principles of multicultural education identified as culturally relevant teaching for ethnically diverse students. Based on her research in elementary classrooms, Gloria Ladson-Billings (1994) concludes that culturally responsive teaching develops "fluid and humanely equitable" teacher-student relationships, cultivates relationships "beyond the boundaries of the classroom," demonstrates connectedness with each student, and "honors the students' sense of humanity and dignity. Their complete personhood is never doubted. Self-worth and self-concept are promoted in a very basic way, by acknowledging the individual's worthiness to be a part of a supportive and loving group" (pp. 61, 62, 76).

I also see myself in the descriptions of effective African American teachers generated by Michele Foster (1995, 1997) and Tyrone Howard (1998). Among these are having a strong cultural identity and affiliation with the African American community; feeling responsible for educating the whole child by teaching values, skills, and knowledge for school success and participation in society; linking classroom teaching to out-of-school personal experiences and community situations; including communication styles and cultural features familiar to students in instructional content, structures, and methods; and demanding that students work together to help each other learn to the best of their individual and collective abilities.

WAS MY BEST GOOD ENOUGH?

I wish I could say that all of my students were very cooperative, eager to learn, and successful in school. That was not the case. Their resistance to my efforts challenged me to keep trying to find ways to get through to them. However much we may hope this won't happen, there are always some students from ethnic groups who are reluctant learners. They are the ultimate test of our teaching commitment, creativity, resilience, and effectiveness. Understanding this, I went after those of my kids who seemed determined not to do right. I was determined not to fail them or allow them to fail me.

At one end of the spectrum of my frustration were a few "do-nothing" students who didn't seem to care about learning at all. They frustrated me so because I could see their potential, but they refused to put it to good use. These students had good attendance, yet never participated in classroom discussions and learning activities. Their homework was late, if done at all, and they interfered with others as they were trying to do their work. I could see in the little work they did that they were capable, but it was almost as if they wanted to do poorly. No matter how much I yelled, threatened, cajoled, pleaded, or called their parents, they were steadfast in failing. I really worked my imagination and energy to try to find some content and methods that would interest them. I talked with each one privately to find out what the problems were and gave them alternatives to the work we were doing. I offered individual tutoring during lunch and after school. I even tried bribing them (a desperate move for me because it was so far afield from my value beliefs about acceptable motivation for learning) by telling them that if they did their schoolwork, I would do something for them that they wanted, such as let them leave five minutes early for lunch or eat a piece of candy—anything. I threatened to flunk them and told them that if this happened, they would have to repeat the sixth grade with me. Surely they wouldn't want to suffer a second year with me always on their case. I tried to shame these students into learning by telling them that they would be driving before they finished middle school since they were going to be there so long. I pretended to cry when everything else failed. On occasion, these maneuvers worked, but most of the time they didn't.

As I reflect back on these encounters, I am reminded of a story that Marva Collins tells about a "reluctant learner" at her Westside Preparatory School in Chicago (Collins and Tamarkin, 1982). When six-year-old Erika arrived at the school, she was out of control; she exhibited some infantile behaviors and others that suggested mental retardation or emotional disturbance. She appeared to be unable to do the simplest academic tasks and cared little about them. Erika roamed aimlessly at will around the class, disturbing or entertaining other students and acting as if she was crazy. Marva refused to ignore or exclude her; she kept insisting that this student could and would learn. At times, she cradled the little girl in her arms like a baby to demonstrate "loving touch" and to constrain her behavioral wildness. After many efforts and little results, Marva lost her patience one day and spoke very harshly to the student, insisting that she would stop her foolishness and get her work done NOW. Surprisingly, the child did as she was told and performed quite skillfully. Collins interpreted the radical change in behavior in this way:

> Erika had been listening all along! All the time she had been acting up, all the time she had been tearing her papers and chewing her books, seeming not to pay attention, she had been listening and learning.... Erika seemed convinced that there was something wrong with her, that no one would accept her. Through her actions she issued a challenge: "Are you going to believe in me and accept me no matter what I do" [pp. 106–107].

I wonder if my kids who resisted learning were living out the roles and expectations that have been imposed on them about who they are and what they can (or can't) do by other teachers, community members, and even parents. Maybe their apparent uncaring demeanor meant something else entirely.

Unlike some teachers who take steps to get these kinds of students out of their classrooms, I refuse to make this concession. It would have been an even bigger defeat for me. Regardless of how unengaged and exasperating they were, these students were still my kids, and it was my responsibility to teach them. If I had sent them to the principal, counselor, or detention room, I would have felt as if I was foisting my responsibilities off onto someone else. How could I do that while simultaneously telling students to be good citizens, take care of their business, and live up to their responsibilities? I also thought I could do more for them (however little that was) if they remained in the classroom. At least they were where teaching was happening, and maybe they would learn something in spite of themselves.

These students taught me more about what role modeling really means in practice than I have ever learned from a textbook. Theory gives the impression that the model is the epitome of success and smooth sailing all the time. Virtually no attention is given to the process of becoming to get into the positions that role models hold. In working with my "do-nothing kids," I modeled perseverance and resilience in struggling to fulfill commitments and achieve goals. True, they still didn't do as much as I wanted them to do, but I think they learned a lot about not giving up on something you believe in, because I wouldn't give up on them. These students also taught me to be more tentative about my interpretations of the motivations behind their behaviors. There were many things in their ethnic, cultural, and experiential backgrounds that I understood, and probably even more that I did not. I resolved to continue learning more about them and multiple possibilities about why they did what they did, how I can teach them better, and not be so quick to make judgments or arrive at final conclusions.

At the other end of the spectrum were the "know-it-all" students. They were constantly trying to monopolize the spotlight and let everyone know that they were superstars. They needed so much love and attention that it was exhausting. They handed their papers in on time or even early, and wanted me to give them immediate feedback, regardless of whatever else the rest of the class and I might be doing. They were insistent about redoing work that received less than a perfect grade, and they always wanted to be the leaders of their cooperative learning groups. In one sense, their academic aggressiveness was positive because they performed very well in their studies. But these students weren't the most pleasant and desirable community members. They were snitches, relished in pointing out the flaws in others (including me), and wouldn't help others who needed it.

I loved these scholars, but I was concerned about their human relations abilities, their sense of morality, and their commitment to giving back to their communities, important elements of the good citizenship lessons I was trying to teach along with reading and language arts skills. I had to work hard to adapt my teaching to accommodate their needs, while not sacrificing the needs of other students. I wanted to do right by all of my students, and I didn't want to inadvertently perpetuate the caste structures among them that existed outside school. I didn't want my "know-it-all" kids to be intolerable snobs, or my "do-nothing" ones to be perceived as slobs and human derelicts. I felt obligated to teach all my students that everyone deserves respect and needs to work together, regardless of their individual intellectual abilities, racial identities, or economic means. The biggest challenges I faced with my "know-it-all" kids were for them to learn these lessons for themselves and to stop other students from reciprocating in kind with meanness and disrespect.

In between these two extremes were many students who, despite dysfunctional family lives, were diligent and successful in their efforts to be good students. I call them my "KOP" (keep on pushing) kids. They stayed focused on learning tasks, got their homework done, and came to tutoring faithfully (whether because of a need for help with assignments or to delay going home). They even helped others who were having more difficulty learning. They were very proud of their accomplishment, and I was even prouder. These students cried the hardest at graduation. I suspect these reactions were prompted as much by the joy of their achievements as the realization that they would have to leave a place where they found support, validation, accomplishment, and caring. High school meant starting all over again. They got what I wanted to happen in my teaching: skills of personal pride, morality, good citizenship, and a sense of community along with some basic language arts and reading skills.

It was obvious to me that the "KOP" kids would work hard to succeed and make themselves and others very proud. They were already exhibiting these work habits in my class and around school. I was tremendously proud of them, and I had to go the extra steps to support, encourage, and assist them in their efforts. There were many times when I didn't want to stay after school to tutor someone, go to a student function, listen to yet another heart-wrenching story at lunchtime, or go on a rescue mission for one of my kids. But they were trying hard to be successful according to my standards, and I had to try equally as hard (if not harder) not to fail them.

Not long ago, I saw a former student of mine. She is twenty years old now, and I did not recognize her at first, but she remembered me. She came up to me and asked if I were "Miss Terri Johnson," and I said yes. She told me how she was doing and introduced me to her child and boyfriend. She told her boyfriend she would never forget how strict I was and how grateful she was to have had me as a teacher. I was a little surprised by her comments, but they made me feel good. To me, one of the indications of being a good teacher is having a positive impact on students that persists long after they leave school. This student had had some problems with me in class (she called it hate!) and was not shy about telling anyone who would listen. Eight or nine years later, she was expressing gratitude for my stubborn refusal to allow her and others to run wild or do nothing in my classes. Something I said or did made an impression on her to the point that she went on to be the success she feels she is. The impression I tried to make on my students paid off with this one.

As a teacher, you are never quite sure what is going to work with which student. This is why it is so important to have your own anchors in teaching, but to use a wide variety of techniques that are responsive to the experiences and points of reference to a lot of kids. It is even more important when the students come from different ethnic, racial, language, and cultural backgrounds.

Many of my former students I taught are still in my life. One called recently and said she wants to be a teacher and needed some advice on how to go about changing her major. Another student works at the airport and recognizes me right away as I passed through security. I am glad that my former students think enough of me to still come to me. It shows me that they really believed me when I told them they belonged to me forever. Good teaching (and bad, too) stays with students forever; this is why I take my charge to teach very seriously. "My kids" are growing and changing and doing pretty well. They keep me informed about the ones working, going to college, in the NBA and NFL, and, unfortunately, on drugs or in jail. So far I have buried one. That is an experience I hope never to repeat.

GOING AGAINST THE ODDS

My students taught me that actual teaching is much different from and far more complex than descriptions in the best books. None of them were ideal students, and most tried my patience, tested my commitment to teaching, and challenged my creativity frequently. I learned that I had to work hard and smart to do even an adequate job of teaching them. But they were my kids, and I had to do what was needed to provide them with real chances to develop their minds and become decent human beings. Teachers do have to make a personal investment in students. I cared so much about all my students, but especially the African American ones. With them, it was like looking in a mirror and seeing myself. As a student, there were times when I was bad, lazy, and just took up space. I had teachers who would not tolerate that kind of behavior, and I benefited from their care. I wanted to be like them; I wanted my students to benefit from my care. I tried to open doors to knowledge and hoped they would walk through and never look back.

There are chilling statistics about students of color not succeeding in school and about other risk factors in their lives. But statistics don't tell the whole story. They don't convey the joy of students who beat the odds against dire circumstances, how much success can be achieved by students who are barely passing tests and other assessment measures, or how those who have high grade point averages and test scores can be immoral and uncaring human beings. Nor do statistics tell about the determination of students who keep trying to do better, or others who could do much better if they had someone who believed in them unequivocally to give them a genuine helping hand. These are things you learn as you live with students and as you design your instruction so that you are teaching them through who they are. You see promise where others see only problems. I was determined to focus my efforts on cultivating the students' potential. Of course, I had to deal with many problems along the way. I wanted to save each one of my kids by teaching them to recognize their own values, knowledge, strengths, and skills.

I knew that the streets with the drugs, gangs, sex, and hard living were just outside the door and very enticing. I wanted my kids to be exposed to some alternatives—to know that high school, college, and good jobs also were right outside the door, well within their reach, and provided better pleasures with fewer devastating consequences.

My students had few fanciful illusions in their lives. Many of their homes and communities were plagued with chaotic and harsh living conditions. Their dogs had names like King, Roc, and Big Dog, and were rottweilers, German shepherds, and pit bulls—dogs that would kill, not just run, frolic, and fetch. Their worlds and experiences were radically different from the books they read. In order for them even to consider that school was relevant to them, they had to see how it connected to their lives. I had to establish these connections by knowing their experiences and using them as filters of meaningfulness in my teaching. This meant that sometimes my teaching had a somewhat raw edge to it and included some of the roughness of life that was uncomfortable to some of my colleagues. I needed to be imaginative, bold, entertaining, and tough. The educational experience I offered my students had to be real. In this sense, their needs are no different from those of any other learner. We learn better when new knowledge is filtered through our existing frames of reference. The problem is that many teachers won't incorporate the life experiences of ethnically and culturally diverse students in their teaching, especially if the students are poor, of color, and live in urban centers.

Much of what I do in teaching and the way I do it are driven by the African American cultural principle of reaching back and giving back. It's good to know that my beliefs and behaviors are situated in multicultural education as well. Our foundations for being teachers are much stronger where there is a union of our personal and professional selves. I was given much attention, love, care, high expectations, support, and a good education by my teachers, and I want to give back in kind. The only way I can repay them is to pass these things on to my students.

I didn't have an African American teacher until I was in the sixth grade. She was young and full of energy and made each of us feel special. She taught us right from wrong, expected us to be good citizens, and to go far in life. We wanted to please her, so we did whatever she said. We criticized students who did not cooperate and were puzzled that they misbehaved in such a wonderful teacher's class. In the seventh and eighth grades, I had an African American male teacher who also made us feel special and worked with each of us as if we were his own. He taught math, and I have never tried so hard to succeed in my life. By the time I graduated from the eighth grade, I knew I wanted to teach. I wanted to do what Jeanette Jones and Wayne Melonson were doing: teaching students to be proud of their ethnic identity and cultural heritage, believe in themselves, work hard, and care for others. They made me feel as if teaching was the greatest job in the world, and it is. They used real-life examples and played games with us too. Both of them were fun loving, but there was never any question as to who was in charge of the classroom. They set high expectations and refused to allow us not to live up to them. They came to our games and cheerleading tryouts, got to know our parents, and hugged us all the time (that was before you could be dismissed, and worse, for such a simple gesture).

These two teachers brought to the quality of my education the added dimension of being ethnic role models as cultural beings and professional educators. I realize that effective teachers don't have to be members of the same ethnic groups as their students. But it doesn't hurt at all to have teachers of color working with students of color. This has made a difference in my own education career, from sixth grade through my graduate studies. I want to do the same for my students who are African Americans and from other groups of color as well. Consequently, being a multifaceted personal and professional role model and mentor is a critical part of multicultural education preparation and practice.

PRINCIPLES FOR PRACTICE

I hope you have been thinking, living vicariously, and reflecting about your own teaching as you have been reading my story. A good way for this chapter to contribute is by revealing some of the general principles for multicultural practice embedded within it that you can use to guide your own and your students' development.

The first principle is to *know your ethnically diverse students*. This is not a new idea. It is one of the first things we learn in our professional development experiences. Yet too often, it is not applied to students who are ethnically, culturally, and racially different. Knowledge about them is still too sparse and sporadic in preservice and in-service education programs. But if you don't know your students, you can't teach them as well as they should be taught. Knowing your students should include understanding their cultural heritages, background experiences, and school achievement strengths and weaknesses.

The second principle is to *become critically conscious of your own values and beliefs about teaching ethnically diverse students*. Sometimes teachers have notions about teaching these students that are destructive, even if well intended. For example, some may have lower academic expectations for them because they "have such hard lives and come from such academically impoverished backgrounds." Others might assume that students of color should only be taught mainstream content through mainstream techniques since "they have to function in mainstream society if they are to be successful." There is nothing wrong with teaching diverse students skills for functioning in mainstream culture, but not at the expense of their own cultures. Nor should teachers have lower academic expectations for them simply because some students of color may be hard to teach. We need to believe that they are capable of high achievement, hold them accountable for it, and help them live up to these expectations.

That teachers must be advocates for ethnically diverse students is the third principle. This does not mean always liking or accepting what these students do or refusing to chastise them when necessary. Advocating for students involves speaking for them when they can't speak for themselves, defending and ensuring their right to speak for themselves when they can, and teaching them when and how to speak. It also means celebrating their victories and supporting them through their failures and disappointments. Therefore, there is a strong element of personal autonomy and self-determination for diverse groups in multicultural education.

The fourth principle is that *multicultural education is a holistic enterprise*. It extends beyond academic learning to include social, moral, civic, personal, and cultural development; understanding self and others; and relating and working with others within and across ethnic boundaries in multiple settings. This comprehensive approach to teaching and learning is necessary for two important reasons: children learn better when their education is integrated and attend to their composite being at the same time, and dealing with critical ethnic and cultural issues in schools and society requires knowledge, values clarification, reflection, and action.

JOINING THE JOURNEY

By now, I hope you have many ideas about what you can do to join us and others in the process of becoming multicultural educators. Remember that a critical part of this process is working on your own personal development as (if not before) you develop professional skills. If you are still in need of some ideas of how to get started, here are some suggestions:

• Do an inventory of your multicultural attitudes, values, and behaviors. You may already be doing a lot that resonates with multicultural education but may not be aware of it. (That was the case with me.) Start by reviewing this chapter (and others in the book) to make sure that you can identify multicultural attributes. Group these by attitudes, values, and behaviors (for example, "using examples from the lived experiences of different ethnic groups to teaching various subject matter concepts, principles, and skills"). Once you feel confident about being able to connect multicultural actions with ideas in other people's stories, apply the process to your own teaching. Look reflectively at your instructional behaviors to locate examples of culturally responsive teaching, and specify these by different ethnic groups. If you teach or live in monoracial or monoethnic situations, imagine what you could do to modify some of your teaching behaviors to make them more inclusive of ethnic and cultural diversity not represented in your local environment.

• Make a contract with yourself for improving your multicultural knowledge and skills. Think about areas of your current competencies where you see voids in understanding cultural diversity. Identify four or five of these and two or three strategies for how you will correct them within a specified period of time. For example, you might say, "I know nothing about the non-English language spoken by the students in my class [or school building, district, or community]. Over the next six weeks, I am going to learn and teach my students how to say hello and good-bye in five of these languages. By the end of this study period, we will be able to say these from memory and will use them routinely in greetings, with possibly one day of the week set aside for a specific language (for example, Monday for Chinese, Wednesday for Arabic, and so on). Include in your contract what you will do if the terms are fulfilled and if they are not.

• Conduct an interview with a group of ethnically diverse students from your local school, or ask a panel of them to visit with one of your teacher education classes or staff development sessions. Make sure that the group is multiethnic and from different levels of schooling (elementary, middle, and high school). Ask them to speak on the topic of "What's Wrong with Teachers," where they explain, from their own personal experiences and perspectives, what teachers say and do that are problematic in working with ethnically diverse students. Ask the panel to make some suggestions for what should be done in the selection, preparation, and retention of teachers to correct these problems. Use what you learned from the students to make some recommendations in a selected aspect of teacher preparation to make it more responsive to ethnic and cultural diversity.

• Choose one or two aspects of learning about teaching students through who they are, and add your personal stories about similar insights and techniques you have gained from your own multicultural teaching and personal growth. Ask three or four friends or colleagues to do the same thing. Compile these contributions into the beginnings of a primer on culturally responsive teaching strategies. If you are already teaching, try out some of these strategies with your students, and refine them based on the feedback you receive. Add to this collection as you continue your journey toward becoming a multicultural person and educator.

References

Au, K. H. *Literacy Instruction in Multicultural Settings.* New York: Harcourt Brace, 1993.

Banks, J. A., and Banks, C.A.M. (eds.). *Handbook of Research on Multicultural Education.* Old Tappan, N.J.: Macmillan, 1995.

Bennett, C. "Teaching Students as They Would Be Taught: Importance of Cultural Perspective." *Educational Leadership,* 1979, *36,* 259–268.

Bennett, C. I. *Comprehensive Multicultural Education: Theory and Practice.* (4th ed.) Needham Heights, Mass.: Allyn & Bacon, 1999.

Collins, M., and Tamarkin, C. *Marva Collins' Way.* Los Angeles: Jeremy P. Tarcher, 1982.

Dewey, J. *The Child and the Curriculum.* Chicago: University of Chicago Press, 1902.

Foshay, A. W. *Essays on Curriculum: Selected Papers.* New York: A. W. Foshay Fund, Columbia University, 1975.

Foster, M. "African American Teachers and Culturally Relevant Pedagogy." In J. A. Banks and C.A.M. Banks (eds.), *Handbook of Research on Multicultural Education.* Old Tappan, N.J.: Macmillan, 1995.

Foster, M. *Black Teachers on Teaching.* New York: New Press, 1997.

Gay, G. *At the Essence of Learning: Multicultural Education.* West Lafayette, Ind.: Kappa Delta Pi, 1994.

Gay, G. *Culturally Responsive Teaching: Theory, Research, & Practice.* New York: Teachers College Press, 2000.

Heathcote, D. "Excellence in Teaching." In L. Johnson and C. O'Neill (eds.), *Dorothy Heathcote: Collected Writings on Education and Drama.* London: Hutchinson, 1985.

Hollins, E. R., and Oliver, E. I. (eds.). *Pathways to Success in School: Culturally Responsive Teaching.* Mahwah, N.J.: Erlbaum, 1999.

Howard, T. C. "Pedagogical Practices and Ideological Constructions of Effective Teachers of African American Students." Unpublished doctoral dissertation, University of Washington, Seattle, 1998.

Ladson-Billings, G. *The Dreamkeepers: Successful Teachers of African American Children.* San Francisco: Jossey-Bass, 1994.

Ladson-Billings, G. "Toward a Theory of Culturally Relevant Pedagogy." *American Educational Research Journal*, 1995, *32* (3), 465–491.

Lee, C. D. *Signifying as a Scaffold for Literary Interpretation: The Pedagogical Implications of an African American Discourse Genre.* Urbana, Ill.: National Council of Teachers of English, 1993.

Lee, C. D. "Signifying as a Scaffold for Literary Interpretation." *Journal of Black Psychology*, 1995, *21*, 357–381.

Lee, C. D. "Is October Brown Chinese? A Cultural Modeling Activity System for Underachieving Students." *American Educational Research Journal*, 2001, *38*, 97–141.

McCarty, T. L. *A Place to Be Navajo: Rough Rock and the Struggle for Self-Determination in Indigenous Schooling.* Mahwah, N.J.: Erlbaum, 2002.

Moll, L., and Greenberg, J. B. "Creating Zones of Possibility: Combining Social Contexts for Instruction." In L. Moll (ed.), *Vygotsky and Education: Instructional Implications and Applications of Sociohistorical Psychology.* Cambridge: Cambridge University Press, 1990.

Shade, B. J. (ed.). *Culture, Style, and the Educative Process.* Springfield, Ill.: Thomas, 1989.

Index

CPSIA information can be obtained
at www.ICGtesting.com
Printed in the USA
BVOW06*2054070817
491415BV00010B/55/P